OUTLAWS
STILL AT LARGE!

A Saga of Roots Country Music Since the 1970s

by

NEIL ALEXANDER HAMILTON

From a silent guitar arises the mighty Phoenix of Outlaw, with fiery determination to again make roots country the spirit of who we are.

BE SURE TO BUY

OUTLAWS STILL AT LARGE!
THE MUSIC

AND ENJOY MANY OF THE SONGS DISCUSSED IN THIS BOOK

AVAILABLE AS A DOWNLOAD AT AMAZON.COM

Also at Itunes and other sites, and as a CD at Outlaw venues

CREDITS

Book cover design and "The Outlaw Backline" sketch by Efren Flores

Contact: efrenfloressifuentes@gmail.com

Historical Outlaw sketches (Chapters 4, 5, 7, and 8) by Kenneth Marr

Contact: kenneth_marr3916@yahoo.com

Historical sketch of Billy Joe Shaver (Chapter 6) by Jackson Taylor

Photograph of Dallas Moore standing with guitar by Jenna Danielle Moore Photography

Contact: jennadmoore@yahoo.com

Photographs of Bert David Newton by Suzie S. Newton

Contact: suziesprinklenewton@gmail.com

Photograph of Joey Allcorn sitting on railroad tracks with his guitar by Sammie Saxson Photography, Columbus, GA

Photograph of Hellbound Glory on the road with Kid Rock by Hellbound Glory

All other photographs copyrighted by the author

In Loving Memory of
My Mom
And to my wife, Lesli,
For her Love and her Heart

CONTENTS

FOREWORD

Time. It's always going. It never stops. It works *just* like that. You never get one moment ever again, so take everything out of it you possibly can. The good, the bad, the heavier it is the more it's worth. That feeling you get when your heart drops from finding out your girlfriend has been sleeping with somebody else. The feeling you get when you hear a loved one has been in an accident and you hear their voice for the first time after it and you know they're okay. *Those* moments are the ones you remember for the rest of your life. It's almost like an electrical shock in a positive way or a negative way, the moving needle of life, where the larger the shock, the higher that needle jumps, the more expansive and beautiful the mountain and valleys in the landscape of your life get painted on your canvas, created by the twists and turns of your life. These are the motions, deviations, and explosions that make us who we are.

This sounds so dramatic to begin a book about a bunch of hell raising, beer drinking, groupie chasing, hillbilly vagabonds, but to me it is *time* itself that seems to be the one element that ties this and almost everything in this book all together.

I met Neil Hamilton when a mutual friend and artist, Joey Allcorn, told me that he had a friend who was writing a book about the history of renegade country music and where it stands in this pre-apocalyptic nihilist day in age. Neil and I arranged to meet at a show of mine, and we sat together for quite a while and just, well, spent *time* together. He clearly knew what he was talking about and the questions he wanted answered. Neil had spent a lot of *time* with country music young and old, classic or fresh. He'd already spent *time* with some of my favorite bands of my generation and the generation below me, getting inside their minds to create profiles for what he'd assembled as the new breed. I found this to be extremely cool.

I'm not trying to hammer in the word "time" so much into this piece, but I really can't say what I want to say without time being such a big factor. And this is really my point. Neil spent much *time* working on his appreciation of music—listening to hours and hours of music, absorbing music, becoming obsessed with music. Every one of those songs that he listened to reveals the *times* in folks' lives that they love, or hate, miss, or await. Every one of those songs took hours of bleeding upon the page to compose and to become those three minute masterpieces that changed Neil's life.

But see, now, later, after much *time*, and many songs have passed in Neil's life, Neil has decided, upon his own will and his passion for writing and music, to devote *time* to understanding, organizing, and painting a portrait in words about the history of this music that he was and is so dedicated to. This gift of *time* is the single thing that keeps music as a whole alive.

My mother (Jessi Colter) and my father (Waylon Jennings), joined by Willie Nelson and Tompall Glaser, were part of a movement of musicians that changed the course of country music forever in 1976 with the release of the album *Wanted!: The Outlaws*. The record served as a "Outlaw Country Sampler Platter," as a way for these artists to combine their fan bases and get as wide of an audience as possible, but also a way to introduce country music fans to the new breed of cooler, realer and dirtier country.

Willie, Tompall, Jessi, and Waylon thus made up the first wave of Outlaws. Though Tompall never had nearly as successful of a career as the other three, I firmly believe it was his sound and, more importantly, his influence and business sense that made up a big part of his piece of that powerful 1-2-3-4 punch. But we've all heard about that generation. Neil knows it as good as anyone. They changed everything and the next thing you knew, every act was trying to have that sound. It wasn't the way they dressed, it wasn't the way they sang, it was the *freedom*. Surprisingly to Music Row, *Wanted!: The Outlaws* became the first platinum country music record in history. They had to open more plants because they couldn't make them as fast as the demand required them to be shipped. Country for the first *time* had to keep up with Rock n' Roll and Pop.

But it wasn't long that after that, as with everything, that the Music Row suits figured out a way to imitate the sound; they slowly made the sound uncool, and then they introduced a new kind of pop sound that people bit into because they were lost in the Johnny Not Cashes of the world, and the cool kids had left the party a long time ago. This is where good art loses its way, and fans are often left to hang on to their old favorites and just pray something new comes along. And it's never going to come the same way.

We saw that with Elvis, we saw that with the Beatles, we saw that with Waylon & Willie, and we saw that with Nirvana. And all of them ushered in the next generation of music and dethroned the pop rehash mess that had come from the perversion of the revolution of the preceding age. *Time* keeps on moving. Each one of these *times* changed the world and gave a home to a younger generation that felt separated from and oppressed by the previous generation. It's the wheel of *time*. And with each moment comes another change.

Fast forward to now. We are looking at an entirely different world than in Elvis' *time*, the Beatles' *time*, Waylon & Willie's *time*, or Nirvana's *time*. This is *our time*. We live in a world where Napster has destroyed the commerce of musical art. MTV doesn't show videos, so big budget videos don't get made. You can make your own album and video for free and put it in a technological stratosphere where anyone from anywhere in the world can buy it from you in a minute. The days of going from garage band or local singer or songwriter, to private-jet, 10 million record selling superstars overnight are over. The music business is the Wild West, and it's brutal out there. These are *desperate times* folks.

But the people that you will find in this book, the people that Neil Hamilton chose to include and write about, are people who have chosen to spend *their time* playing music for the love of keeping it alive and for the love of wanting to express what they have spent so much *time* absorbing, learning from, admiring and ultimately giving their lives to. I've met and spent good *time* with most of the people in this book, and each one truly cares about music. And they make it by waiting for those giant vibrations of the life needles to carve the mountains in their story so they can tell the world about it.

I truly believe that this is the *hardest time* there's every been for the commerce of art and good music, but I also believe it is the *best time* for passionate, beautiful, driven, creative, risk-taking music and art. We *know* we aren't going to be the next Elvis. We *know* we aren't going to be the next Waylon & Willie. But we also know who we are. We are us. Plain and simple. And all we need is just enough love, inspiration, and gasoline to keep us playing that music. Making that art.

And this is why Neil's *time* is so valuable to me. Besides his *insanely* neurotic attention to detail, or his *relentless* obsession with perfection, Neil is someone who cares *very* deeply for music and art. He cares so deeply that he's willing to spend as much *time* as he finds necessary to do this right, to do it true, and do justice to the thing he loves and protects with such grace and dignity. He is, like us, a warrior. And that *time* spent is as important as all the *time* each one of those folks in the audience devoted to the concert they paid for with the money they made by spending *time* working a job that week.

You see what I'm getting at? It's a self-sustaining wheel of *time.* Whether it's the song written about the *time*, or the *time* it took to write the song, or the *time* spent listening to the song, or the *time* spent practicing the guitar. *Time* is the most valuable thing in the world and every moment only happens once. These artists inside are serious. They are dangerous. And they will remind you that you must be yourself, no matter the odds. You must play the music you want to play, no matter the crowd that comes to see it. You must believe in yourself, and you must choose to spend every precious moment of your *time* being who you want to be, doing what you want to do, and sharing that.

I, personally, need people like Neil in the world, because they are telling our story. Neil is paying attention, he is connecting the dots from a much different *time* to a newer generation of artists. Neil is traveling deep into the heart of darkness and drawing the best map that he can so that the next traveler can know the terrain and explore further. He is an important cog in the machine of the era of music and art that we are in. His *time* will produce more *time,* and this is where we win over the machine.

My last point in this foreword (it seems way more like a thesis to me, but hey, Neil was dumb enough to ask me to write it. Ha.) is a much simpler but more quantum ideal. It's the fact that all of us in this book, if we haven't met yet, will probably meet soon, as this book has tied us together. But to all of the artists in this book, as well as all of the artists or fans or groupies or gallery owners or managers or roadies or whoever's out there keeping the fire alive: I appreciate what you are doing, because you're inspiring a lot of other folks, including myself, and keeping us going in that big wheel of *time*. Know what I'm sayin'? Don't let your lights burn out no matter how hard it gets, because there's always someone watching *you*.

I covered a Harry Nilsson work on my last album called "Flying Saucer Song," and I'm not trying to promote my own work by any means, but I want the reader to see how *strongly* Mr. Nilsson's work has inspired me. Not only did I sing the song on one of my albums, but I got the entire piece tattooed on my back. It's really only one chorus, but it's the one phrase that I really believe sums up the point and power of inspiration and why perseverance is so necessary. They were also the lyrics that Harry wanted to be remembered by.

Late last night, in search of light, I watched a ball of fire streak across the midnight sky. I watched it glow & grow, then shrink and sink into the silhouette of morning, and as I watched it die –you know what I said to myself, I said 'Hey! I got a lot in common with that light!' You see, I am alive with the fire of my life, that streaks across my span of time, and is seen by those who lift their eyes in search of light, to help them through the long, dark night.

In closing, carry on, keep on keepin' on, rock the fuck out, keep hope alive, drugs are for quitters, and mamas don't let your babies grow up to be cowboys. Now enjoy *Outlaws Still At Large!*, Neil Hamilton's in-depth look into the landscape of the current scene of independent, renegade country music and the road that leads there.

–Shooter Jennings

INTRODUCTION

Writing a history of Outlaw country music can take several different forms: it can be a narrative or an analysis, or it can even tell a personal story. I have striven to include all three elements. Quite frankly, however, this book has gone in a different direction than in the one I first intended it to go. I never thought that my pursuit of these Outlaws would cause me to change *as a person*, especially to the point of considering the personal to be important enough to serve as an undercurrent to my main focus. But "the hunt" has indeed changed me, and as a result, I have written this book at two levels. Most of my observations are meant to show the link between the Outlaws of the 1970s and those of today within the context of changes in society as a whole and, more extensively, within the music industry. I wanted to emphasize the current scene, and I believe I have done so. Yet I have also written this book at another level, the one of how my experience with the Outlaws transformed me. I am hoping this approach provides not only a more interesting account but also a more fulfilling one.

If the reader finds in this book a hint of the formatting found in Willie Nelson's path-breaking album *Red Headed Stranger* (1975), I can only say that I have purposely used that work as a model and in my own modest way have arranged the material herein according to how Willie structured his album. This is particularly true for section V. I did this not to take away from the originality of what I have written but to stand as a tribute to what Willie Nelson did and to what his album means as a continuing spiritual and musical influence on today's Outlaws and their fans.

Influence, however, should never be taken as a synonym for replication. One point I have learned from the Outlaws is that their music is not the music of their ancestors. While traditional roots country serves as a basis for what they do, this is not their father's music. The Outlaws are sincere, creative, and original. If I were to begin my "hunt" for them again, I would not find them as they were two years ago or even a few months ago. It's what separates them from the Nashville mainstream. Leave Music Row for a few months and come back and you don't have to worry about being hit in the face with originality, for you will find the same hackneyed themes pandering to the same highest bidders.

In the land where Outlaws are still at large, to paraphrase a line from the movie *The Big Lebowski,* "The spirit abides."

LINER NOTES

Thanks . . .

To Joey Allcorn. What a tremendous asset to this project and to roots country music. Joey got me in touch with Shooter Jennings, took me around Nashville, introduced me to numerous studio musicians from the 1960s, gave me advice about Hank Williams and Jimmie Rodgers, and throughout acted selflessly on behalf of Outlaw music. To Jackson Taylor, for encouraging me to begin this book. To Wayne Mills, for helping me make contact with Bert David Newton and Blackberry Smoke. To Dallas Moore, for getting me together with Jody Payne and lifting my spirits when the workload sometimes dragged me down. To Shooter Jennings, for his excitement about the project and his writing of the foreword. To Bret Heim, a consummate classical musician, a friend, and a research librarian who provided me with invaluable musical advice. To Mark Brink, for transcribing several interviews, contacting artists, and accompanying me to honky-tonks in the pursuit of historical truth, Outlaw music, and a decent beer. To John Fagot, for allowing me to pick his brain, loaded with information from his many years as a record promoter, and for telling me early on that I had something good going on. To Aunt Ida (Aunt Cider), for her much-needed encouragement, words of wisdom, and faith in what I can do. To Matt Moore, for his work in putting together the website for this book. To Efren Flores, for creating the cover to this book. He's a young graphic designer with considerable talent and great prospects. To Kenneth Marr for his historical sketches. To Brain Debruler for mastering the CD at Sol records. To my wonderful wife, Lesli (my Lela), for maintaining the faith she has in me and for loving me—without her I would never and could never have done this. To my mom, for letting me hold onto her coat as I did those many years ago. And to all the artists, producers, and executives for their time, patience, and overall contributions. They allowed me to enter their world to pursue a dream and to come out the better for it.

PRELUDE

It Was the Time of the Hunter: When the Story Began

The War Bama Club near the town of Silas, a settlement of fewer than five hundred people, sits along a two-lane country road that winds and curves and then drops down from the hills of west-central Alabama into a river valley. Pine trees form a backdrop, and a gravel parking lot fronts a whitewashed, bunker-like concrete building that is the club. Outside, a portable sign reads DAVID ALLAN COE with an arrow pointing to the entrance.

Possums, raccoons, and deer populate the surrounding woods that stretch for miles, a haven for hunters who each fall turn out well equipped and in high spirits for the kill. The trees hide the scattered houses and provide a canopy for anyone who might want to grow cannabis, cook meth, or distill alcohol. In such a rural setting, where miles can separate one house from another, it seemed impossible to say how the club would find enough customers to stay in business.

But on this night, people turned out in droves. By the time I arrived, the club was already filled with a raucous crowd. They wanted to get drunk and see Coe, the old man of the original Outlaw country music movement created some forty years ago, in the 1970s. Coe long had the reputation of being a roughneck, an ex-con who would fast kick you in the teeth if you looked at him wrong. That, however, was back-in-the-day Coe; this was seventy-one-year-old Coe.

The club carried its bunker look into its interior: it had a vast concrete floor with a long bar on one side, a few tables and chairs scattered about, and a stage jammed into its far end. By now the crowd was beginning to press forward, waiting for Coe to appear. The Dallas Moore Band, though, played first. They represented the new Outlaw country, or at least the kind influenced by Southern rock. Moore strode onto the stage wearing a skullcap and displaying braids and piercings. His face was scruffy, and he wore torn jeans, scuffed boots, and a shirt whose short sleeves revealed an assortment of tattoos. He looked menacing and intimidating. In his song "Outlaw Country," he brandished the images of Outlaw past and present when he sang about having listened to the eight-track version of *Honky Tonk Heroes*—a classic recording, first released in the 1970s by Outlaw artist Waylon Jennings—and having "laughed at the danger with Cash and Coe and Shaver," along with the "redheaded stranger," Willie Nelson. And he referred to the present when he added that he had cut his own teeth in the honky-tonks.

The audience grooved to the band, and Dallas was clearly enjoying playing to a full house. His set lasted about an hour. He and his fellow musicians then tore down their equipment while the crowd drank more and got louder. Coe's drummer, his steel guitarist, and his son and rhythm guitarist, Tyler Coe, came onstage and set up their instruments. They did a quick sound check. Then they left.

Before long, they returned. The crowd now scented David Allan Coe, who oozed redneck to the point that his fans were in a frenzy. Then he appeared. Over the short distance from the side door to the stage, he hobbled as he held tightly to a cane. He wore a denim shirt, vest, and jeans, and his hair draped down to his butt. He was grossly overweight, and the pressure on his knees seemed unbearable. If this was what twenty years in prison, odd and often crude behavior, and hunkered-down nights in honky-tonks brought, it was not a pretty picture.

Coe sat down on a stool, strapped on his guitar, and peered through rose-tinted glasses beyond the stage lights. By now the crowd was chanting, "David Allan Coe! David Allan Coe!" He launched into his set and, several songs later, played one of his hits, "The Ride." His voice cut through his age and showed he still had it. Suddenly, before he could get fully cranked up, a beer bottle flew from the crowd and hit him on his forehead. This was a chicken-wire crowd without the wire.

The experience was hardly a new one for tough-guy Coe. He finished his song, told the crowd thank you, and then left the stage. Two security men descended on the culprit. It was a weird moment: a backwoods bottle-thrower dressed in pink overalls—probably created by an incompetent mix of clothes in a washer— smashes a singer beloved by his fellow rednecks. As the security men yanked the assailant from the building, the club owner diverted the crowd's attention by blaring recorded music from the speakers. Some in the bar started dancing, and fueled by more alcohol, most everyone soon forgot the assault.

If a love for Coe runs rampant in the backwoods, so too does suspicion about anyone who has risen above the meager standing that validates Silas as a town of convenience stores, auto repair shops, and greasy-spoon restaurants. While an Outlaw legend such as Coe can be seen as slapping a hand across the face of upright "privileged" America, he can also be seen as a man who has made it, and in doing so has become too "uppity" and has forgotten where he came from. One man reflected this view when he told me—as he relieved himself of many beers in the men's room and missed the urinal several times—that he thought Coe hadn't gotten hit at all; instead, the Outlaw had just wanted to grab his money and run, bandit style.

Meanwhile, Coe was led to his limo and rushed to a distant hospital, and the calamitous night continued. As the car sped along the country roads, shadowed under a full moon by the forests on both sides, a deer jumped into its path. Car and animal collided, and the deer's blood splattered across the windshield. Coe waited while the shaken driver checked the vehicle and contemplated the carcass—one less target for the hunters that fall. Coe arrived at the hospital, was treated and released, and later claimed that because of the attack he'd been forced to shave his head so he could have it stitched.

I exited the club with my clothes and hair saturated with cigarette smoke and my nerves jangled by what had happened. It was a good time to breathe in the night air and think about where I was.

At that point, I was into Outlaw country, but only of the old school, the Waylon Jennings, Willie Nelson, David Allan Coe era. I had especially listened to a lot of Coe earlier in my life. I had recently returned to his music and saw in his lyrics, in his determination to live his way, and in his determination to forge ahead something that again appealed to me.

My revived attraction had brought me together with a few of my students at Spring Hill College (a liberal arts school in Mobile, Alabama), where I teach American history. Because these students, young and fascinated by the early Outlaws who they romanticized, also identified with Coe, we began an underground group on campus, a takeoff on Greek fraternities whose name, Delta Alpha Chi, when converted into the acronym DAC made reference to Coe's full name. The students even invented a secret handshake and began shouting to each other on campus, "What about David Allan Coe?" This was in reference to a Coe DVD, a recording of a show he had done at

Billy Bob's ("the world's largest honky-tonk") in Fort Worth, Texas. Initiation into Delta Alpha Chi required either attending a Coe concert or watching the Coe DVD. In the recording Coe raps about how he has been neglected by mainstream Nashville and implores his fans to contact the Country Music Association (CMA) to ask them, "What about David Allan Coe?"

We were so dedicated to Coe's music that we traveled to his concerts in Alabama and Florida and as far distant as Vinton, Louisiana, on the Texas border, a journey of six hours each way. Every trip was an adventure and a rolling party and brought more students into the group, and before long our discipleship numbered thirty.

At the time I knew little about modern Outlaw. But I knew that I disliked the Nashville pop music scene. What was passing for country music seemed filled with *American Idol* winners and losers chasing a commercial crown intended to complete their outfits of pressed jeans and Cavender's shirts. They were making a mockery of Hank Williams and Waylon and Willie and all that had made country, well, country—a type of music that certainly had some features in common with pop but which was nevertheless distinct in form.

To hear one more Nashville pop song about pickup trucks bouncing along dirt roads threatened to send me into complete despair. Nashville pop isn't where Hank Williams died in the backseat of a car, still young and carrying so much more potential. It's where teenage girls and jaded women find their dreams fulfilled by the ruggedly handsome jeans-clad men who roam the lyrics and melodies found in the modern record studios—studios dominated by groups of "experts" intent on making sure the music they produce will generate big money.

But here I was at the War Bama Club near Silas, where I was listening to Dallas Moore, who had come back out onstage, thus completing a cycle from new Outlaw to old and back to new. That deep, graveled voice took me back to the 1970s Outlaws who sang from the heart, not for the wallet, who saw their work as an art, not a commodity. In that sense it had an intimacy with the music of Mississippi native Jimmie Rodgers and the Virginia-born Carter Family, both of whom, in 1927, traveled through the Appalachian Mountains to record in Bristol, Tennessee, the songs that ran through their blood like a river coursing through the American countryside.

Seeing Moore in Silas made me contemplate the connection between the present and the 1970s and what had happened to cause Outlaw to wane in the 1980s and pop country to captivate a larger audience. And I wondered what was causing Outlaw to surge again.

So I started digging, entering the world of YouTube and iTunes, downloading the works of artists who fell under the heading of I Never Thought Music Like This Even Existed. I was getting into Moore and a whole bunch of musicians who might rightly be considered alternative country (Alt-country) rather than Outlaw: Dave Alvin, Alejandro Escovedo, James McMurtry, and so on. At that stage, though, I didn't really know the difference between Outlaw and alt, and I'm not sure that I do even now. But the music sounded different to me, it sounded fresh, it sounded unlike anything emerging from the Nashville pop grinder.

One of the Outlaw artists I began listening to was Jackson Taylor. I started with his *Dark Days* CD (2007). The guitar-driven songs, the heavy bass drumbeat, the often masterful lyrics captured me. The lay-it-out-there stories. "Goodbye Morphine," for crying out loud. What the fuck was going on here? "Outlaws Ain't Wanted Anymore" was a theme I could embrace, the rebelliousness and the sense of having been kicked in the ass for being so rebellious. I had always wanted to be a rebel but had seldom acted on it. I was a closet rebel.

Moreover, there was a certain mystique about this Outlaw music. And a certain mystique about the artist too. Who in the world was Jackson Taylor?

I downloaded more Jackson Taylor songs. I didn't know what other artists had influenced him. I thought—incorrectly, as it turned out—perhaps Coe. But I was digging his stuff no matter where it came from. I went to my computer and looked up Jackson's tour schedule: Kansas, Missouri, Oklahoma, and Colorado. The closest show to my home was in Houston, Texas. I talked to my wife, Lesli, about it. I wanted to see him live, I told her; I wanted to get closer to what this was all about. Her sister lived in Houston. We could make the long drive for the show and stay overnight with her. Lesli was not a fan of Outlaw, but she wanted to encourage me, so on to Houston we went.

During the trip I thought about how cool it would be to have an Outlaw band, to be onstage, getting a crowd excited about your music. But, hell, I was way too old for that, and even if I weren't, I played no musical instruments. Some people claimed I had a decent voice, but I had no songwriting gift. So it was all fantasy.

That fantasy, though, flowed from a deep wound inflicted by the passing of my mom some fourteen months earlier. I felt so hurt that I was still struggling mightily with depression. Thinking about being in a band was a way to visualize some of my hurt. "Too old for that" was another way of saying I had missed out on something and wished I could change my life more but didn't know how to do it.

Fourteen months might seem a long time for the pain to be running so strong, but the unusual relationship I had with my mom accounted for most of it—the love and the dependency that had bound us together for many years. (She passed away at ninety-five.) My own sensitivity accounted for the rest. Joey Allcorn, an Outlaw country musician and friend of mine, would later tell me that two things most affect the human spirit: love and death. Even though I loved my mom—and still love her—she had died. The two, love and death, usually separate entities, had come crashing down on me in one big, hulking, ugly, disorienting avalanche.

I had been working hard to lessen the hurt. When my mom first passed, I turned to music to ease it. Yes, at first to David Allan Coe. Why Coe? Because I knew his music from years before. Because of his *Rides Again* record—the songs on it, with their free-spirited attack on convention, but also the old vinyl LP cover showing a badass Coe riding his Harley in an air of fuck-you defiance.

Then I moved on musically to Dallas Moore and Jackson Taylor, frequently listening to Jackson because his music was heavily autobiographical. He had gone through so much shit, and I felt that I was going through so much shit; a different type, for sure—in fact, way different—but shit nonetheless.

With Moore and Taylor, I could listen, close my eyes, and imagine that I was one of them, creative and talented enough to do what they were doing and bold enough to say, "Here is how I lived, here is how I live today, take it or leave it." Their music was helping me change, helping to transform me and move me in directions I had never thought possible when my mom was alive.

When Lesli and I arrived in Houston, we went to her sister's house and then to the honky-tonk where Jackson Taylor would be appearing, the Hardy Street Tavern. As we awaited him, we ordered drinks. The place filled with several hundred people, which strained the air conditioning. When the opening act finished, two metal walls behind the stage were rolled up, opening the room to the fresh breath of night air. Jackson Taylor and his band, the Sinners, took the stage. My eyes focused on his signature white cowboy hat, his guitar, and the nearly full sleeve of tattoos on both of his arms.

As Jackson started to play, the sound system acted up. The next several minutes were frustrating, as he was forced to interrupt his show to implore the engineer to fix the mess. Mostly, Jackson kept his cool, but you could tell that it bugged him. He was committed to doing a good show, not just presenting any old crap. The sound system, however, continued to malfunction, and Jackson was forced to accept his losses, lick his wounds, and continue. He was, above all, determined. As he neared the end of his set, he asked the crowd to make requests and so went into unexpected parts of his catalog. He never showed any fatigue; in fact, he became more energetic as he played what the crowd asked for.

I was taken aback by the Sinners as Jackson spread down into a punk-rock stance and drove his guitar sound into the walls, the floor, the ceiling, and as his drummer, Brandon Burke, pounded hard and heavy, with the bass drum dominant. From their first song, the Sinners had the crowd with them. Jackson was much more than a musician; he was a craftsman who took pride in his art. Moreover, *he was his music*.

When the show ended around midnight, Lesli and I went over to the bar. Then in walked Jackson Taylor. He was gracious, he was charming; he signed autographs, spoke with his fans, and posed for photographs with them.

I hesitated, afraid he might reject me. Then I approached him. I told him my name. "Would you mind if my wife took a picture of us together?" I asked. "Sure," he said, "no problem." The picture was taken, and there my relationship with Jackson Taylor likely would have ended (other than through his music) and no hunt for Outlaws would have occurred. Except…

Except Lesli mentioned to him that I taught American history at Spring Hill College and had written several books. "Really!" Jackson said. "Man, I love to read that stuff. Have you read *Undaunted Courage* by Stephen Ambrose?"

I had. He surprised me. An Outlaw country musician reading an acclaimed, serious history book?

"Man, we need to have a drink and talk," Jackson said.

I was amazed that Jackson would want to hang with me. I was the professor; he was the musician. I was the wounded one unsure of myself after my mom's death; he was the cool one who had been wounded by life but *seemed* to have it all together.

In its own way, our get-together was as surreal as the Coe concert had been at the War Bama Club—Jackson and I discussing the book, which narrates the Lewis and Clark Expedition of the early 1800s, while doing shots, Jackson interrupted by groupies while the rest of his Sinners laughed and drank and cut up. Toward the end of the night, Jackson suggested that we exchange phone numbers, and we did.

Later, as Lesli and I drove through Louisiana on our way back to Alabama—at about the point the wetlands become a fatiguing site— my cell phone rang. It was Jackson. "I've got an idea for you," he said. "Why don't you write a book on the history of Outlaw country music? Nobody has done it."

I was surprised that he even remembered me. "I don't know," I said. "I've been away from writing for a year, and I don't think that I want to get back into it. Got too many other things I want to do."

"I've got a couple of contacts I can get you started with."

"Let me think about it." I wanted to discuss it with Lesli. But I already could feel some of my stagnant writing juices percolating.

And I loved the music. I loved what these guys were trying to do, how their songs came from their hearts. *This is amazing*, I thought. I had just been dreaming about becoming an Outlaw musician. That was, again, fantasy and could be nothing more. But the "next best" had developed: writing about these guys, getting into their lives as an outsider, seeing what they were all about.

I wanted to taste rebellion; I wanted to breathe it and immerse myself in it. These Outlaws were proclaiming that they would live their way, and if others didn't like it—well, tough. They were Outlaws musically—they would create their art as they wanted to, not as Nashville wanted them to. They weren't killing people, robbing banks, or grabbing a government bailout.

In short, their lives revolved around a commitment to the way they expressed themselves through their art, which was connected to their daily experiences. Of course, they sometimes questioned themselves, but we all make commitments and deal with questions. For them, commitment was choice, and it was also something done because inside, deep inside, an inner resolve made selling out impossible.

Commitment. For years I had committed myself to my mom, as she had committed herself to me. We were partners in life, and no matter what other relationships I had, the commitment prevailed above all. No matter what developed for me professionally—as a teacher or writer—no matter what developed in that vast perplexing entity called the outside world, we were partners committed to each other's welfare. We slogged on, but we did so through a partnership based on love.

Our attachment was made all the stronger because as a child I hardly knew my father. He was an alcoholic and left my mom, my brother, and me when I was about seven years old. She never remarried, and when my brother got married when I was twelve, it left me and my mother to face the world. We never had much money. She worked hard, but her pay as a secretary was paltry, so we clung to the lower end of the middle class and, for a time, lived in a low-rent trailer park.

She sacrificed much for me, but so did I for her. As I write this, my sacrifice sounds much more noble than it was, for commitment comes not only through those conscious choices but also through that inner drive that tells a person this is what must be done.

For my part, the sacrifice was in giving up huge chunks of my individuality, containing my personal independence and expression in committing myself to my mom. In her later years, in the years shortly before I returned to Outlaw music and began this book, her health declined. As she became increasingly immobile and confined to home, I became her primary—really, her only—caregiver. Then she suffered a severe heart attack, and as she went from intensive care to rehab to a nursing home, my caregiving load got heavier, my burden grew, my nerves frayed.

> *Well, it's broke and shattered,*
> *Everything that mattered.*
> *But I've done the best that I,*
> *I could have done.*
> *So please let me up,*
> *'Cause I've had enough.*
> "Broken"
> Jackson Taylor
> From *Let the Bad Times Roll*

With my mom's passing, I sank into complete despair, beset by suicidal thoughts. I thought I should have and could have done more. Moreover, a feeling of tremendous loss—a lost partner, a lost love; it was my mom, for crying out loud—was intensified by thinking about what I had given up when I had committed myself to her. My personal growth had been limited, any rebelliousness contained, any fantasies made to remain fantasies. I had been a good son. I had been a good teacher. I had been a good writer. But my self-expression had been stunted.

So I began a search for self and for meaning. Some people would look at me and say I had weirded out. Here was a guy who for years had short hair and typically wore button-down shirts now growing his hair long, getting tattoos carved into his arms, and adding piercings to his ears. But I was shouting that I was alive. I was becoming more than a closet rebel. I wasn't robbing banks, killing people, or grabbing a government bailout. But I was rebelling against my previous containment and the life it had brought. I was doing something many people would like to do: I was starting over.

Outlaw music became a part of my change. At first the old stuff, the David Allan Coe. It freed me by telling me I could be free.

I deepened my faith in God. This began with spiritual direction. It grew more intense through meditation. Then it became a part of my everyday life. I became committed to my faith, not as a crusader waving the Bible in front of others but as a pilgrim trying to become a better person as revealed in the gospels' teachings—a difficult endeavor indeed, but one I hope will allow me to more effectively help others.

The new me even got married in the most unusual of circumstances. Lesli and I had taught at Spring Hill College for years. But even though it's a small school, we had barely made eye contact. In fact, I don't remember ever having talked to her, and she saw so little of me on campus that she doubted I even existed. In my commitment to my mom, I had practically no time for college events, and she had no opportunity to get to know me.

Never in my wildest imagination did I think I would ever get married, let alone to a woman with such a big heart. She didn't try to shape me according to an image in her mind. Instead, she supported me as I ventured onto untrodden ground, and she encouraged my self-expression. So I marched down the wedding aisle with leather jacket, cowboy boots, and braided hair—in an Episcopal church, of all things. If anyone thought that I looked odd or ridiculous, all I can say is that I felt liberated and loved.

Then came the new Outlaws: Jackson Taylor and Dallas Moore and Joey Allcorn and Wayne Mills and Whitey Morgan and... Their music entered my life, as did their commitment to be themselves and be honest in their art.

My change was painful, daunting, and rewarding. My story remains incomplete and with an unwritten ending. But Outlaw country helped me better appreciate the music of life and helped me grow in my self-expression and in my relationships with others.

It might seem strange that songs that include frequent references to drinking and carousing can be personally and spiritually uplifting. Yet it's not the songs alone but the lives of the artists behind them, and the *spirit* at work in the making of the music, that provided for me a reason to go on.

As I started to write this book, I began to think that, at the least, Outlaw music, and the story about the artists involved in it, would serve for others as a diversion from the frustrations of everyday life. Beyond that, maybe, just maybe, Outlaw music could be transformative, much as it was for me. If the music didn't work that way, I thought, then maybe the story of my change would give hope to others for a better life through whatever means would best transform them. In this way the lives of the artists, and the story of the creation of Outlaw country and its impact, could become a tattoo to stand as a commitment to growth and honesty in the art of life.

About two weeks after having met Jackson Taylor, I journeyed back to Silas for another Outlaw show. Dallas Moore was again playing there, and I wanted to revisit the music that had awakened me to new Outlaw and begun to raise questions in my mind. I arrived early. Dallas was going through the sound check with his band. I took the opportunity to introduce myself and tell him about the book I was thinking about writing. He was eager to be a part of the project. "Sure," he said, "I would love to be interviewed. Let's talk about it after the show."

Another Outlaw artist, Wayne Mills, would later tell me, "When I first met Dallas Moore, I got scared as shit. I took one look at him with his long hair and scruffy appearance and thought I had better stay away from that guy. But then he said something to me, and when Dallas Moore says something, you want to become his friend."

Dallas came up to me when the show ended. Wayne was right about Dallas's warmth, and I hoped that at some point down the road I would indeed become his friend. Dallas again told me he wanted to do an interview. But I wasn't prepared for it, so we agreed to wait.

He said that he would be playing in a month at the Flora-Bama, a popular beer joint on the Gulf Coast near the Florida/Alabama border, and that we could meet at the band house he would be staying at.

A few days later, I spoke with Lesli about the book. I said that if I did it, the workload would be heavy and the time involved extensive. I pointed out that I didn't even have a publisher and that I would need to put out money for travel, a better camera, and a laptop computer.

"You shouldn't begin the project expecting to make money," she said. "If that's your main motivation, then don't do it. You should do it because you like the music and want to have fun putting the book together."

"I do like the music," I said. "And I couldn't do this unless the effort was coming from my heart." That sounded sanctimonious, but it was true. "These Outlaws," I continued, "I really want more people to know about what they are trying to do. But if the fun ends and it becomes all work, I'll give it up."

A couple of days later, Jackson Taylor gave me some advice about how the book could be formatted. It felt great to hear from him; it made me realize that he was really into the project, and his excitement eased my doubts about getting started.

I began sketching an outline and put together a list of current Outlaw artists. Of course, there were the obvious ones: Taylor, Moore, and Texas musician Dale Watson. But I really was at a loss beyond that, partly because I couldn't separate Outlaw from alt-country, and so my list lacked precision.

I sent it to Jackson. As I suspected he would, he rejected most of the additional names that I proposed. But his response made me more thoughtful about the differences between Outlaw and alt. Those differences would never be clearly delineated, and as the project continued, I would learn how impossible it is to get even the Outlaw artists to agree on what defines Outlaw music. It was clear that if I were going to deal in absolutes, I would get nowhere.

I then asked Jackson about an interview. I noticed that his schedule was going to take him back to Houston in a couple of weeks, to a honky-tonk called the Firehouse Saloon. He said, sure, we could meet up before the show.

So I went there with camera and voice recorder in hand. The honky-tonk was decorated with worn-looking wood and worn-out metal antiques. On the wall next to the stage, and on the railing in front, previous performers had signed their names. Shortly before midnight Jackson Taylor and the Sinners appeared with their punk-driven sound. The honky-tonk crowd shouted, sang, and danced. One blond young lady, slim, dressed in jeans and a tight, white blouse, jumped onto the stage and gyrated next to Jackson, waving her arms above her head and clapping her hands. He loved it and played on.

When the show ended, Jackson left the stage, removed his hat, and used his forearm to wipe the sweat from his brow. He was, at that moment, a tired but satisfied man. He waded into the crowd and, like I had seen him do the first time, signed autographs and posed for pictures. I already had in my head my own picture of what I wanted to do. I had made my choice, my commitment.

I was on the hunt for Outlaws.

I'm just a story looking for a happy ending,
A faded rainbow searching for a pot of gold,
An old fable looking for a new beginning....
        "Better Life"
        Jackson Taylor
        From *Let the Bad Times Roll*

Section I

BREAKING OUT:

A Red-Blooded Outlaw

STRIPES

When I took to the road to hunt for today's Outlaws—camera, laptop, and recorder in hand—my first stop was to see Jackson Taylor, the artist I had met previously in Houston. Although I had read some about the 1970s Outlaws to prepare for this book, I decided to forego any in-depth research of that period until I had interviewed Jackson. I wanted everything to be raw, fresh, and forthright before delving into the past. I wanted to earn my stripes in the honky-tonks.

I decided to make Jackson the first chapter in this book, in part because he's the artist who gave me the idea for the project, in part because he was the first Outlaw I interviewed in a hunt that would take me some eighteen thousand miles down the road, and in part because his experiences are truly absorbing. But there's more. He had earned *his stripes* in the honky-tonks, and his music—and Jackson as a person—is raw, fresh, and forthright. It's what makes him a red-blooded Outlaw.

Jackson Taylor, Firehouse Saloon, Houston, TX (2011)

CHAPTER 1

JACKSON TAYLOR

Modern Day Joad

Boys and girls, get your knives and forks ready for the main course.
All the way from Austin, Texas.
You all give it up for the bad boys of country music,
the Jackson Taylor Band.
INTRODUCTION BY THE ANNOUNCER,
LIVE LOCKED & LOADED AT LONGHORNS SALOON *(2006)*

The background to the stage at the Wichita Ballroom was vivid blue—similar to the Kansas sky on a sunny day—and adorned with the word WICHITA in large silver letters. It was the most colorful part of a building whose worn appearance conveyed drabness. From stage left, his stout body dwarfed by the sign, entered Jackson Taylor wearing a white cowboy hat, a black leather vest over a black T-shirt, and blue jeans. He limped and winced from pain as he climbed several steps. He grabbed his guitar and sat down in a padded chair next to his lead guitarist, Austin "Slate" Garrett, who was similarly seated. Behind them was Jackson's drummer, Brandon Burke. This was Jackson's band, the Sinners, recently stripped down from five pieces to just three. They no longer had a steel or bass guitar.

Jackson would later ask me what I thought about the three-piece. I told him that I thought he needed a bass. Thinking back on it, I have changed my mind. For this group, with all of its focus and energy, the steel and bass were clearly optional.

Jackson gave a signal, and the Sinners tore into their show, releasing a pummeling sound that surged through the building and declared Jackson Taylor's allegiance to rockabilly icon Elvis Presley, '70s Outlaw country pioneer Billy Joe Shaver, and punk rock band Social Distortion. Beat, beat, beat on the bass drum, and with a searing backbeat—Brandon showed no hesitation. Relentless, unforgiving—there was not to be any swishing brushes across snares or cymbals. He had all the frenetic fervor of a punk hard-rock drummer. Jackson and Slate drove their guitars into the music, and if Jackson, because of his injury, could not get into his customary punk-like stance, he could still strum and thrash.

Brandon later told me: "If we sound good to ourselves, we'll go out there and put out one hundred and ten percent. There's no manufactured energy there; it's kind of the three of us really do love what we're doing now. We've gotten nothing but positive feedback since we've switched over to this new setup. People are begging us to come play, in places in Texas and stuff where they never even cared about us before."

The Wichita Ballroom could hold a thousand people. This night, however, there was but two hundred, and the building's distant, curved ceiling and vast openness—it used to be a warehouse—made the crowd seem smaller. (Jackson later told me that the turnout came from poor promotion, that the Sinners typically attracted crowds of six or seven hundred in Wichita.) I had never, ever seen a dance floor as big as the one in this ballroom. The legendary barren plains of Kansas, I thought, must have been created when the trees were felled to make this floor's wooden planks.

Jackson's physical pain came from a fractured thighbone. He was on painkillers and drinking whiskey offered him by his fans. The additives ignited his musical fire, and alcohol ignited two fans who, midway through Jackson's set, brawled on the dance floor until security stopped them.

But it was nothing like the old days, when some in Jackson's crowds would clamber onto the stage and fight each other and the band there, leaving pools of blood on the floor. Jackson himself would sometimes wade into the audience and start fighting. The Sinners got such a reputation for being dangerous that numerous venues refused to book them. Those time are gone, Jackson told me, and to a certain extent he regrets them, for while they gave the Sinners a reputation for being dangerous, there are bars and honky-tonks that to this day want nothing to do with the band.

That night, back in Wichita, Jackson played for about ninety minutes. He had been preceded onstage by Whitey Morgan and Billy Joe Shaver, so it was 1 a.m. by the time Jackson finished. Then the house lights came on, and he reacted by ordering them to be lowered. "I know the official show is over," he said. "But I want to play some more."

For a tight knot of dedicated, alcohol-saturated fans, Jackson launched into a half hour of acoustic work. A drunken Whitey Morgan joined him. Slate had left the stage, and Brandon was sprawled out on his back, next to his drum set, a grin on his face and a cup of whiskey in his hand.

Jackson had dealt with a faulty sound system all night long. Now he encountered a balky guitar whose battery pack failed, causing him to fling his musical instrument aside for another. He was frustrated and still in pain but determined. The songs would be played; the art mattered most.

Question: Getting back to that show in Wichita [on January 14, 2012], you seem to have had a number of obstacles. You had the [leg], you had some sound problems, and you had problems with your guitar. But you kept going, and when the official show ended, you did an acoustic set. What made you do all of that?

Jackson: That's our payoff, bud. We like to play. That's what we traveled across the country to do, was play. I don't charge anybody for playing a show; I charge them for traveling. One of our problems that I've got to quit doing is that I always play too long. I come back and I play too long. You know, it's like Elvis [Presley] said: you've got to leave them wanting more.

❧❦❧

The show had been billed as part of a Honky-Tonk Heroes tour. In this instance, honky-tonk really meant Outlaw. It was meant to bring together the Outlaw music of the past with that of the present. Billy Joe Shaver had helped start the original movement when he provided Waylon Jennings with a sheaf of songs that became the *Honky Tonk Heroes* album, which was released in 1973. Whitey Morgan and Jackson Taylor were the new Outlaws, dissimilar in many of their musical influences but similar in their commitment to keeping heartfelt music alive.

Jackson had previously declared his Outlaw credentials with, among other efforts, a CD titled *Outlaw,* (2005) and his song "Outlaws

Ain't Wanted Anymore" from *Dark Days* (2007). That CD, as with the rest of Jackson's work, said that he was going to do *his* music *his* way.

Question: On *Dark Days* you include a song, "Outlaws Ain't Wanted Anymore." You tell of going to Nashville, tell of being rejected there.

Jackson: I wasn't rejected. Nashville was very, very good to me. I got good writing deals. I enjoyed Nashville. I made a lot of friends in Nashville. It just wasn't what I wanted to do.

Question: But you talk about some fat man on Music Row.

Jackson: The song is about the fat guys on Music Row that run everything. They wanted me to be kind of what a Jason Aldean is. [Jason is a popular mainstream country singer.] You know what I mean, they wanted me to be a puppet. But they didn't hold what my vision was, so that's what I mean by they didn't get it.

> *Outlaws ain't wanted 'round here,*
> *Your whiskey-drinking deep thinking*
> *Ain't selling this year.*
> *So tear down the posters,*
> *Get back the rewards,*
> *Outlaws ain't wanted anymore.*
> "Outlaws Ain't Wanted Anymore"
> From *Dark Days*

Jackson: But country music is supposed to be honest music. I've had songwriters tell me: "Jackson you shouldn't be so honest about your stuff in your music about what's going on." You don't write a song like "Goodbye Morphine"[if you're going] to try to get laid or fucking have a hit record.

I actually wrote that as a letter. When I quit heroin, I got off that shit, I wrote a letter. It was like breaking up with a lover, a long-time girlfriend. I actually sat down and wrote a letter, as if I was writing to somebody else.

> *Just like all those good and bad times,*
> *Our time's come and gone.*
> *I think it's time I stand on my own....*
> *So good-bye and so long, morphine.*
> "Goodbye Morphine"
> From *Dark Days*

Jackson holds nothing back in singing about his experiences with and addiction to drugs. He has pretty much run through a gamut of them and gone down the rabbit hole more than once. At times it was a tough struggle for him. He says in "Mother's Prayers" that "the tracks are there to follow when whiskey wasn't enough/Hell, my soul ain't worth the trouble because even Jesus has given up."

Most of Jackson's songs indeed read like letters—ones that speak to events in his life. Some, in fact, read like diary entries, they are so bluntly stark and personal and confessional. In the case of his ballads, often mournful and tender, he crafts like a Van Gogh, using vibrant, swirling brushstrokes and, sometimes like a pointillist, leaving the listener to take his colors and blend them. Outlaw in his sincerity, artistic in his soul, Jackson lays it all out there. Billy Joe Shaver and Kris Kristofferson come to mind as predecessors with similar talents. Maybe Outlaw artist Jamey Johnson from today. Jamey, though, is more of a smoky honky-tonk balladeer. Jackson is more in your face, rat-a-tat-tat, and here's the shit that I've gone through. (It's much how he talks, too; his words come at you Tommy-gun style.)

Within the diversity of the Outlaw country movement a common theme, a common thread, emerges: mainstream Nashville has lost its connections to country roots and, moreover, lacks commitment to any form of music that doesn't make a lot of money. If Nashville has any roots at all, they're shallow ones, resting atop the green folds of pop music.

Question: If you were to define the word "Outlaw," how would you define it?

Jackson: A certain amount of actual tangible danger to it. To me the definitive Outlaw album was Waylon Jennings's *Honky Tonk Heroes*. I think Outlaw country is—has got to be—a little sparse, you know what I mean? A little more sparse. I think the production needs to be a little more of a band production and not a singer production with canned music,…and I think it's got to be…. I wish I could articulate this better…

❧❧

What he has trouble articulating in words, however, comes across strongly in his songs—both the feel and the lyrics—as he gyrates within his works and among them from one musical form to another. He is creative and original—and these days "original" doesn't get an airing from the Nashville establishment. It's also evident both in his music and in his statements that he defies being labeled.

Question: You have said that you don't call yourself Outlaw. But one of your CDs is titled *Outlaw*. So do you want to be known as Outlaw or not?

Jackson: I didn't choose that. That was with the man at whoever the company was, because we did look at the tons of stuff written about us that year, and they all said "Outlaw." As a matter of fact, now that it's resorted back to me, I don't sell that one anymore; that one's on the discontinued list.

Question: Why, you don't like it?

Jackson: I didn't like it being called *Outlaw*.

Question: So you don't want to be known as that?

Jackson: I don't want to be fucking known as anything. Like I said, there is nothing remotely Outlaw about my songs, about a lot of my songs. I think that our band, more than any other band in the last twenty-five years, has stayed into that Outlaw country mold. But we're still..., you can't call "Bare Feet on the Dash" Outlaw. There is nothing Outlaw about that. There is nothing Outlaw about "Better Life" or, you know, a bunch of our stuff.

Perhaps his contradictory comments—he doesn't want to be labeled Outlaw, but his band has stayed in the Outlaw country mold—come in part from how he feels about his standing in the wake of the 1970s Outlaws. "Anything that comes and gets declared as Outlaw country," he says, "is like trying to be a '70s punk band. [Those bands] that were formed at that time were really those bands. Everything that came after that, whether it was good or not, subsequently copied that, which makes it disingenuous just by the point. Even as to the point of calling ourselves an Outlaw country band. You know, Outlaw country to me was a few artists in the mid-'70s that did something that came natural to them. There was nothing contrived about it. They didn't plan out to do it. It just happened."

In other words, the original Outlaws were the real Outlaws because they didn't have anyone to copy. Today's Outlaws have other Outlaws to look back at.

While this is true, it can be argued that today's Outlaws operate in a different environment with its own unique challenges, so that while they can borrow from the past (and who doesn't?), they can, and do, cover a lot of ground never before trod. Indeed, today's Outlaw movement embraces a greater variety of forms and styles than existed in the

1970s, some of which have been influenced by musical developments that had just begun to appear, or had not yet appeared, in the era of Willie Nelson and Waylon Jennings.

Jackson is a far cry from contrived. He's dedicated to his music, sincere with it, willing to take it wherever it might go, money changers be damned; they will not be allowed to defile his musical temple. He might be uncomfortable with the label, but he is Outlaw.

As with the original Outlaws, why should Jackson give a shit about what anyone thinks? Crank it out, and let it fly and settle into the minds of listeners or the dustbin of irrelevance.

Question: In "Country Song," you slam Nashville pretty good.

Jackson: Yeah, yeah, because I think what is coming out of there is horrible. I understand that Nashville has got to change with the times, but they have completely and totally turned their back on what country music is. Country music…is a real definable genre. It's not pop. Country music has a culture to it, it has a history to it, it has a lineage to it, and they have just completely and totally pissed all over it. I find it offensive. Jason Aldean offends me. Colt Ford offends me. Rascal Flatts offends me.

> *This ain't no country song*
> *About your fucking pickup trucks or your grandpappy's farm.*
> *This ain't no Nashville scene,*
> *I ain't no spiky-haired, half-assed, pop-star wannabe….*
> *No, your labels don't mean shit to me*
> *And neither does the Grand Ole Opry.*
> "Country Song"
> From *Aces 'N Eights*

Question: [Outlaw artist] Shooter Jennings recently said that there are a lot of Outlaw posers out there. Do you agree with him?

Jackson: Oh yeah. I mean, we're all posers at some point. We're not out there robbing banks. Literally, we don't call ourselves Outlaw country. I just call ourselves a honky-tonk band. Yeah, anybody that uses the word Outlaw in their songs is, you know, I'm trying to think about how to explain it....

Look at Jason Aldean, look at all that group of guys there, man— they come across like they are trying to be hard. You know, their songs mention Johnny Cash, some of them mention Merle Haggard, but they sound more like Poison [a 1980s hair band] than anything else. And so I find it very posing; you can't have a country hip-hop and then wear a cowboy hat and try to come across like you're someone authentic.

Nashville is a one-hundred-percent total machine, it's a money-making machine. It's got nothing to do with art, it's got nothing to do with expression. Those guys could be selling fucking plastic rings, they could be selling cocaine, they could be selling shower curtains— it doesn't really matter. It's just that they happen to be in the business of selling really, really bad music.

Jackson's conviction comes out in his video for "Country Song." In it, he wears dark eye makeup and glares at the camera while Brandon Burke plays the drums as angrily as if he were calling up Armageddon to slay the harlots of Nashville.

In the pantheon of musical influences, Jackson pays homage to Outlaw artists from the 1970s. His dad loved Willie Nelson, and when Jackson was twelve, the elder Taylor took his son on a trip from Yakima, Washington, to the Nelson birthplace in Abbott, Texas. Brandon claims that Willie ranks among the Big Three of country performers the Sinners listen to while on the road, with Waylon Jennings and Johnny Cash the other two. Within each they find a simplicity, a music devoid of orchestrated polish and rooted in the country of Hank Williams, Texas-swing master Bob Wills, and, even further back, of country founding father Jimmie Rodgers.

But Waylon Jennings also means Billy Joe Shaver. The writer who provided all but one of the songs for Waylon's pioneering *Honky Tonk Heroes* LP has provided inspiration for Jackson. Actually, it's as if Shaver courses through Jackson's blood. "I was brought up with [Billy Joe] so much as a kid," Jackson says, "that he's just part of my DNA. Billy Joe's just there because my dad listened to him all the time. So his writing, his chord progressions, are just part of my makeup."

I once asked Jackson if there was anybody of more recent origins in country he could look up to. He didn't hesitate: Dwight Yoakam. "I have a fucking man crush on him," he said. "He more than any other person outside of maybe Elvis [Presley] is responsible for what I do. I fucking love Dwight Yoakam. I've been in love with that guy since 1986. I don't care what he releases, I go out and get it."

Jackson, though, has another idol, and as he mentions above, it's 1950s rock 'n' roller Elvis Presley. Elvis. There he is, in youthful glory, his face tatted large and brilliant on Jackson's right arm. Elvis. Striding into the studio and laying it down without contrivances. Letting heart and honesty and simplicity propel the art. And juking it out.

> *Hold it, fellas, that don't move me.*
> *Let's get real, real gone for a change.*
> Elvis Presley, "Milkcow Blues Boogie"

Question: You said in talking about influences on you and on your music that Elvis is a big [one]. But I think in a sense, you know, there were different Elvises: there was the Sun Records Elvis, there was the RCA Records Elvis. I'm wondering which Elvis—

Jackson: I love all the Elvises. But the one that set my life, completely has dominated my life, is the Sun Elvis, the eighteen- to twenty-one-year-old Elvis. That's the Elvis Presley who completely and utterly cast me into whoever I am, more than any other single thing in the world. More than my family, more than my kid, more than anything. That Elvis Presley that walked into Sun Records; that guy that cut "That's All Right Mama" and "Blue Moon of Kentucky" in July of '54, that's the Elvis....

Not just Elvis. You know, those Johnny Cash recordings from right around the same time. Those two guys together, more than anybody else, set into motion whatever I am.

❧❧

That eighteen-year-old Elvis had come from poverty—Jackson Taylor's background. Elvis came blazing onto the music scene and ultimately "revolutionized it." He had a limited musical background yet danced the blues and country and gospel. "He didn't steal shit from anybody," Jackson says. He used his natural talent. Jackson observes: "To me, Elvis is...the greatest single singer who ever lived. Elvis was the pinnacle of as cool as a man could fucking be."

Talking to Jackson, though, sometimes involves an immersion in unqualified statements to which he later adds additional layers. Ultimately the layers get jumbled up, and it becomes less a layered cake than a marbled one, filled with the complexities that mark artistic influences, everyday life, and Jackson's own efforts to make sense of it all. Jackson's statements about Elvis and Cash and so on are supported by his music and, well, his tats. But so too is another layer in the marble cake when he talks about punk.

In his book *Punk: Young, Loud, and Snotty* (2004), Steven Wells writes that "punk was a musical revolution. Before punk, rock music was dominated by longhaired, self-indulgent millionaires. Bands composed of incredibly skilled musicians bored audiences rigid with tedious concept albums and wanky guitar solos. Punk blew all that away."

Wells's statement could be reworked for a person drawn to country: "Outlaw is (or was, if we go back to the 1970s) a musical revolution. Before Outlaw, country music was dominated by self-indulgent millionaires. Bands composed of incredibly skilled musicians played rigidly formulaic songs filled with condescending lyrics. Outlaw blew all that away."

When punk emerged in the 1970s, however, it did so as a protest against social conditions. In England, it was largely a pillaring of an economically depressed and highly stratified society. In the United States, it excoriated the nation's stagnant economic conditions. But whereas in England punk was more working class, in America it was more middle class and often took the form of an attack on the shallowness of mainstream society.

For Jackson, punk was important because it stripped rock of its pretensions. Outlaw *is* important because of the way it strips Nashville pop of its pretensions through an alternative form of country.

Jackson was married to his third wife (they have since divorced) in a Social Distortion jacket. This sartorial choice for a crucial life passage reflects how deeply punk has influenced him. And quite likely Mike Ness, Social Distortion's lead singer, ranks at the top of Jackson's list of punk artists. Ness grew up in Southern California as an angry young man, and he aimed his anger at the materialistic selfishness and bland conformity found in the middle class. In one song, "Mommy's Little Monster," released in 1982, a rebellious, petulant Ness sings about himself with shocking honesty: "Mommy's little monster shoots Methedrine/Mommy's little monster had sex at fifteen." Ness once said in an interview, "As a songwriter, I am a reactionary. Everything I write about is in reaction to the life around me."

The Ness-type lyrics, the attitude, the alienation—Jackson brings these to country. Moreover, the connection to Ness is buttressed by Ness's own love for country music. His 1999 album *Cheating at Solitaire,* a solo work, includes a cover of a Johnny Cash song. But Ness displayed a country influence well before that. (In a curious twist, Jackson "countrified" a Ness punk song, "Ball and Chain," in 2009 that Ness had made more honky-tonk ten years earlier. Thus where Ness had made punk more country, Jackson made country more punk.)

Question: Is the [punk] influence [for you] more thematic, [either] politically or in terms of alienation, or is it more melodic?

Jackson: I like the music.... *Never Mind the Bollocks*, that first Sex Pistols album, is one of the greatest albums ever, the only Sex Pistols album. I like the energy of it. My big love for punk, I think, you see—remember I grew up on Elvis a lot too—but the punk music from '75, '77, that's music that was very much like rockabilly from the '50s that I grew up so much with. These guys would go in and rock out a record to put it out. They weren't worried that everything was perfect; they went in and did it on their own.

The Sinners have followed the punk, even the hip-hop. We've followed that format, man. When we make our records, we make the records we want to make. We do our own T-shirts. We don't give a fuck about what anybody thinks. We don't talk to record companies. We don't fucking talk to T-shirt companies. We do what we do. We take it down the road, and what comes of it comes of it, you know what I mean? That whole idea of punk, of doing it yourself—you know, fuck you—of fucking the establishment above you—and they did it themselves. Most of the politics, I don't agree with.

In a video for "Boys in the Band," Jackson points to a word on the T-shirt he's wearing: Turbonegro. It's the name of a Norwegian punk band. (Interestingly, the song is one of Jackson's more traditional country ones, reminiscent of a 1970s style.) Turbonegro has said that their form of punk defies all previous punk labels. Jackson's form of country defies all previous country labels. Turbonegro attacks political correctness. Jackson doesn't so much attack political correctness as vent with no concern for it. "Fuck the World" is the title of a Turbonegro single released in 2003. Jackson states the same, with a bull's-eye on Nashville.

Question: I was reading a statement by a punk musician that said punk rock, at least originally, was of the attitude of learn three chords and you can do it. Basically, anybody could do it. Where does that leave you, where does that leave music, if anybody can do it?

Jackson: Well, I know four chords.

Jackson's childhood was so outside mainstream America, how else could he feel except alienated? As alienated, he believes, as an unemployed Brit. "When I heard the Clash's *London Calling*," he told me, "[it] could have been talking to me too."

Cast out. Jackson went with his dad from one migrant labor camp to another. "My first music that I found on my own, that talked to me as a poor kid, as a kid that didn't fit in with anybody else, who completely and totally felt alienated," he says, "was the Ramones, the Sex Pistols, the Dead Boys, [and] Fear." That music helped save him in his youth and has since shaped his songwriting.

Jackson once told me that if it weren't for his music, he would have gone to prison or slit his wrists. Maybe, I wondered, he just might have done—in a state of depression and self-loathing—as Van Gogh purportedly did and chopped off his ear.

Jackson says: "Even my family, my mom [was a] fucking junkie, my sisters are all prostitutes. Dad was a fucking lovable loser, fucking drunk that pulled me around from fucking labor camp to labor camp. I grew up with no resemblance at all of family, stability, that people I saw around me grew up with."

That experience has prevented him from understanding family functions that many people take for granted. He says: "You know, my wife's family comes over for Thanksgiving, and I'm sitting there watching them all go through this ritual bullshit. It's so much stress on their lives to do it, and I'm like 'Why the fuck do they do it?' I don't relate to it, I never had it."

The nature of his childhood means, he insists, that he doesn't really have any peers. "I don't know anyone who grew up like me," Jackson observes. "I have no one who grew up the way that I grew up. Guys who grew up like me are almost all dead. When I read a book about Waylon or Johnny Cash or Billy Joe Shaver…, that's why me and Billy Joe Shaver hit it off so big. He saw in me [that] I was brought up like he was."

Waylon Jennings and Johnny Cash and Willie Nelson grew up dirt poor, shoeless, picking cotton, Jackson says, before adding: "I grew up picking cherries, apples, and pears and strawberries. I think I grew up even poorer than those guys did…. My song "Whiskey," that's a real song…, it's not something I make up, it's not me making up stories…. My songs are therapy, one hundred percent therapy. It's me dealing with my issues, not me making up stories for people.

> *I left my blood in the alley, my guts on the floor,*
> *Laid up with regrets and some hundred-dollar whore.*
> *Hey, whiskey, hey, what you doing to me?*
> "Whiskey"
> From *Live Locked & Loaded at*
> *Longhorns Saloon*

Jackson's song "Modern Day Joad" draws a connection between his own upbringing as a migrant worker and the Joad family in John Steinbeck's novel *The Grapes of Wrath* (1939). Well read, Jackson likes to delve into history books and serious novels while on the road. That he would draw from *The Grapes of Wrath* because of this fact, and because of his background and creativity, should surprise no one.

At one point in the novel, after the Joad family has lost their farmland in Oklahoma and taken to the road in a broken-down truck for California, Ma Joad turns to her eldest son, Tom, and says to him: "That would be nice work…, pickin' peaches. Even if they wouldn't let you eat none, you could maybe snatch a little ratty one sometimes. And it'd be nice under the trees, workin' in the shade. I'm scared of stuff so nice. I ain't got faith. I'm scared somepin ain't so nice about it."

Jackson told me about the connection between the book and his song: "Well, what it means is, [the Joads] took off trying to find a better life. The difference is, to me, those Okies had found it. I'm still kind of out there looking for it." In that sense he remains the migrant kid looking for the peach to eat. And an artist who distrusts the shade, the comfort it represents. As he once told me, comfort, in fact, could get in the way of his music. Seeking justification for his life or not, he says that "extreme poverty and alienation is an artist's greatest gift. It's success and acceptance that will kill him."

I'm a seed of the dustbowl, born of dirt and weeds.
I have lived the hard times, they'll never leave me.
I'll always be that haunted kid out there in the streets
With nothing in this world but some out-of-reach dreams.
"Modern Day Joad"
From *The Whiskey Sessions*

If he were a seed of a dustbowl, the kid must have wondered if he were a bad seed, or at least a defective seed, fated to struggle for survival in a modern America more in tune with its cities than with the rural poor. In kicking around for cherries, peaches, and apples, he went from Washington to Montana to California. "You'd see the same families wherever you were at," he says, "because they'd be doing the same fucking thing you were doing." Some of them became his friends, but he was one of few Anglos among a largely Mexican workforce, and this intensified his sense of isolation. Even though he learned Spanish and spoke it fluently until he was eleven or twelve and so could develop friendships with some of the Hispanics around him, the closeness of the Mexican families made him feel more rejected, for he traveled around those labor camps only with his dad.

His mom entered his life fitfully. In his music Jackson portrays her as derelict, both in her morals and in her responsibility toward him. "Jezebel" he calls her in "Wicked, Wicked Me," and the pain and the anguish merge when he sings "Mother's Prayers," a song about his drug addiction. How he could have used his mother's prayers—but they weren't there for him, not as a child and not as a young man.

When Jackson says that punk was the first big musical influence that *he found on his own,* it stands rightly as a qualifying statement.

His formative years in those labor camps in the 1970s saturated him with Mexican music. He says: "We'd go out into the fields, we'd go out from around four in the morning until six o'clock at night, and that's all you heard, Mexican music." It's easy to imagine Jackson as a boy, exhausted from the long day of work, lying awake at night in a labor shack listening to those sounds so close and, across a cultural divide, so far.

Even beyond the farms, it touched him: in the warehouses, for example. "That's all Mexican, too," he says. In particular, it was mariachi music that, he says, had a "Waylon [Jennings] bass line." Mexican and seventies Outlaw thus had a common feature.

Jackson says he had Anglo friends, but their families were racked by crime. He was always around crime, always around badness. He points out that in his childhood he considered kids on welfare to be the wealthy ones. His mom, who died young but was married nine times, and his sisters lived on food stamps. They lived better than he did. There was a difference being poor in those fields—being working poor—and collecting welfare. The pecking order had sifted him to the bottom.

Besides being a musician, Jackson loves to paint. When he casually mentioned this to me, I asked him to let me see some of his portraits. One he chose to show me was Charles Bukowski. The naturally fiery-eyed Bukowski, who appears even more fiery-eyed in Jackson's work, was known for his prolific writing—poems, short stories, and novels—and a life—part image, part real—completely free with little concern for social restrictions. His childhood was largely loveless—his mother and father brought him up, but abused him—and this led to Bukowski, much like Jackson in his childhood, feeling like a misfit. Bukowski withdrew—in school to his artwork and later in life to his writing.

Jackson also showed me his portrait of Friedrich Nietzsche, the German individual-*über-alles* philosopher, the Nietzsche who said that happiness comes from the pursuit of the will, from overcoming obstacles. Maybe from overcoming the migrant labor camps, the malfunctioning guitars, and the bad sound systems. "I am well disposed to those moralities," Nietzsche said, "which goad me to do something and do it again, from morning till evening, and then to dream of it at night, and to think of nothing except doing this well, as well as I alone can do it."

Jackson's Nietzsche looks at once contemplative and determined, his steely-eyed gaze set against an urban background colored with browns, blacks, and blood reds. The sky emits no light, only a darkness, as if factory smoke had gripped a city and was refusing to let it see any beauty, a city that had been overcome by the power of the human will to create and destroy.

And Jackson-of-the-Sinners showed me a portrait he recently did of Billy Joe Shaver (different from that which appears in this book), a thoughtful-looking Billy Joe, one who has command of his maturity and of his art. One whose music defines his stature, one who feeds off his music, as does Jackson.

"I am living better than I have ever lived," Jackson once told me as he stood by the window in his hotel room, running his hand through his dark blond hair and looking at the streets below. The better life he now has was built on the catharsis he talked about, on a stream of autobiographical songs.

Question: You got [knifed] in an Austin parking lot [as you say in your song "Wicked, Wicked Me"]. Is that true?

Jackson: I still have the scars. I cut him up too. The only thing that I've ever put into my songs that are fictional is in "Maria" and in "Shallow Grave." I know what I wanted to do. In "Maria," I did everything in that song except for kill them: I broke in and pissed on them while they were in their bed. So I did shoot through the covers, I just shot them with my cock and not my gun.

As evident from "Modern Day Joad," "Maria," Shallow Grave," and on and on, Jackson's songwriting breathes honest and blunt—exactly the way he speaks: "Country music is supposed to be real music by real people," he says. "I love Loretta Lynn; there's nothing phony in her at all. When she sings, man, that's what she sounds like, dude, that's what her accent is like. The girl who sings for Sugarland, she sits there and her accent is so overdone—just completely, totally bullshit and disingenuous."

Regarding the origins of his creativity, Jackson says that songs come to him "pretty much formed." Unlike some other musicians, "I don't really sit down with the guitar and write." A song can come to him most anywhere: on the road, at a bar, while at home.

Brandon Burke confirmed this with me. "As much as I see [Jackson], it just comes," he says. "He doesn't have to work at it. He's not one of those guys that sits around for hours on end with a guitar, banging out chords. He just kind of sits around and all of a sudden.... I've seen him write a song in the van. We'd be sitting there, and I'll see him; he starts staring down at the floor and bobbing his head. Then he'll say, 'Check this out. Okay, we're playing it tonight.'"

For Jackson, the intensity of songwriting becomes psychosomatic and materializes in a physical disability. "I'm the only person I know like this," he says. "And I've asked a lot of other people, and they've looked at me like I'm crazy. If a song comes to me—and this started when I was very young—if a song comes to me, if I don't go and record it and get it out, if I don't go and get it out, as closely as I can in my head, I get sores on my head. I get sores on my body. I get big, bleeding, painful sores. And I get so irritated and so agitated that I get sick."

Songwriting and his life in a band have taken a toll on his personal relationships. "It has pretty much cost me everything I ever loved to care about in life," he says. "But it's something I can't quit doing."

Question: Like what? What has it cost you, specifically?

Jackson: Families, not seeing my kids, not having any type of security whatsoever. I just lost my wife and my son. I was gone all the time. So when you're gone all the time, weeds get in your garden. A man's got to be home to keep the weeds out of his garden. If he's not, then shit happens.

His commitment has taken its toll, but he can't quit, he must go on. He can't quit his songwriting. He can't quit playing. He can't quit touring. Jackson once said to me that if he could get an eight-to-five job, he would. He would like to be working at something secure and come home to a wife and children. But he can't. His commitment keeps pulling him back; his inner self tells him what he must do.

If songwriting and the road have taken a toll on his marriages and his children, however, so too has his childhood, the one where he grew to be alienated, where he felt left out in those picking fields. It has created a man who protects many of his inner feelings, and a man who struggles to love. That's part of Jackson's complexity. He can be forthright and honest in his songs, and even in his interviews, at one moment and defensive at another. Friendly and gracious at one moment and pushing people away at another. Beautiful in expressing love lyrically but struggling to come to grips with the actual emotion. He refers to such characteristics in his song "Easy Loving Stranger," where he says that he's "too easy to touch, but too hard to hold."

To hold Jackson would be to hold a man with a big chip on his shoulder. So big that it propels his anger; his emotions form a strong-box that often begs to fly open. To hold Jackson, as he again says in "Easy Loving Stranger," would take someone "strong enough to hold and let go."

Jackson self-medicates through his music, a dosage that might prove to be insufficient. "I'm pretty miserable," he once told me. Jackson Taylor needs love; the hope is that he finds it, but the fear is that when he does, he will fail to comprehend it, cast it aside, and again reaffirm his alienation.

Without a doubt, life on the road presents a challenge to the Sinners: it's a grueling endeavor of more than two hundred shows a year. They travel in Texas, Oklahoma, Kansas, the Midwest, along the West Coast, and in Europe. They ride mile after mile in a van stuffed with their personal belongings—their disagreements, camaraderie, joys, and frustrations also packed together—while pulling a trailer that contains their guitars, drums, amps, and the customary merchandise to sell—T-shirts, stickers, and CDs.

The Sinners' *Boys in the Band* video concludes with the band members (at the time, there were five) gathered in a tour bus, where they play their musical instruments as young, well-endowed chicks with glistening lips hug a stripper pole. Jackson actually toured in this bus for a while, and it truly became a Gomorrah on wheels.

But the bus has since been abandoned. In fact, while the Sinners reduced to a trio to get to a more "stripped-down sound," they also went into that mode to cut their expenses.

Rip-offs and con artists stalk the road. While some come in the form of managers or promoters, many are club owners. As do many bands, the Sinners equate club owners to used-car salesmen in the level of trust-worthiness, and might sometimes wish for them to become roadkill.

Question: I know that you posted recently on Facebook that you weren't paid, and then the owner came [up with the money] the next day. But you were pretty pissed off initially about that, and I was wondering how often...

Jackson: He was a dick, man. You know, here's the thing. He knows that I'm in a knee brace, that I can hardly walk. He's out there trying to push me because we didn't play for four hours when our contract was ninety minutes.

Jackson doesn't strive to be rich or famous. He strives to make a living and to be good. If big money ever did come his way, it would have to come to him on his terms. Some might say that he goes over the top to reassert his position as an outsider and preserve his "artistic integrity."

In one instance, he was playing a show in Fort Worth, Texas, that had drawn a diverse crowd wanting to see what the Sinners and some other bands were all about. When a group of young people near the stage started chanting for him to play a few songs by other artists rather than his own stuff, he got mad and stomped away. In doing so, he angered potential new fans and was ripped by the local media. In one of his songs, "No Show," Jackson laments his bad-boy behavior. "I should have been a no-show," he sings, "just like ol' George Jones."

But while there might be regret, Jackson's anger constantly hovers about, ready to be tapped. Onstage the anger can be seen with his short temper. In his music it appears in the blistering punk and self-declarations. "I'm an angry white man," Jackson admits. "I put out nine records in nine years. My source of anger and discontent is what fuels me. I mean, you've got to have something to rebel against. I guess I am fucking angry a lot; a lot of things piss me off."

Well, I'm still the one, son, all you bitches love to hate
'Cause you know you can't control what I do or what I say.
"No Apologies"
From *The Whiskey Sessions*

Question: So how do you go about getting more fans?

Jackson: If it happens, it happens. I don't pursue that. If I get more successful and we get more fans, it will be a by-product of doing what we do. That's the way it's always been. We don't go looking for it. If something's good enough, it's going to get attention on its own. I truly believe that.

That doesn't mean waiting on the sidelines and holding hands with the status quo. So in 2012 the Sinners cut a CD titled *Bad Juju,* with a sound as raw as that found on the early Sun records done by Elvis Presley and Johnny Cash. "I [wanted] to do some of the songs the way they came to me," Jackson says. "When I go into the studio,... sometimes I listen to other people too much.... You might have a great basic song, and every-one wants to keep adding shit to it. So[I went] back in and [recorded] some new songs, and [stripped] away all the shit that was added to [the others]. There's no steel padding, no fiddle padding; it's vocal, rhythm section, and one accompanying instrument, which is one guitar."

But the CD's rawness comes from more than stripping down; it comes from punking up. Way up. In fact, Jackson goes well beyond replicating early Elvis or Johnny Cash. Like a Jason venturing to reclaim the Golden Fleece of punk, Jackson opens with a scorch-ing hell's-let-loose version of Cash's "Stripes." The entire CD jumps down your throat, burns through your intestines, and reams out your bowels. He covers Elvis's "That's All Right [Mama]," but worships

Presley by punking it and showing that, in doing so, he has the same love for creativity as did the King.

After Jackson left the stage in Wichita, he couldn't let go of the moment:—its music, energy, and excitement. He wanted to extend that, he wanted to extend the present. And maybe too he wanted to find a way to forget about what his trade, born in the picking fields of his youth, was costing him, to forget how his commitment to his music, his life as an Outlaw, had robbed him so much of a family life and a home to go to.

Whitey Morgan had earlier told me that while he was a crazy person, Jackson, whom Whitey loves, was just one plain old crazy motherfucker. With that in mind, I waited for Jackson's next move.

Jackson came up to me. I had earlier tried to get him to sit down for an interview before his show, and because that didn't happen, he now proposed we do it at a post-show party with alcohol and drugs. I said I would be happy to party, but privately I knew that the interview was never going to happen in such a setting.

Before long, he walked over to a car being driven by a friend, talked a bit to the driver, and sat down in the front seat. He motioned for me to join them but cautioned that we were about to flirt with danger. *I came along for adventure and to learn more about Jackson,* I thought, *and the interview is shot, so why not go?*

We took off into the night, bound for the south side of town, Wichita's black ghetto. Jackson was searching for drugs. The houses he stopped at were ramshackle dens, where the large black men who sat on the porches packed heat and looked menacingly into the darkened streets. The scene was as devoid of light and promise as Jackson's bleak painting of Nietzsche. At any moment, the situation could have turned horribly bad, but Jackson was living on the edge and not wanting to face the dawn. The "gift" or "curse," as he had conjectured, was propelling him, and would keep propelling him until he got what he wanted.

Question: How do you want to be remembered as an artist?

Jackson: I don't give a fuck. I don't care about that. When I'm dead, I'm dead. You don't have any control over that. Once you start getting into that shit, you start thinking about your legacy, you start making decisions now based on what's going to happen later.

In the '80s people used to make fun of me for listening to Johnny Cash. They made fun of me listening to Johnny Cash in the '90s. Now those same people have Johnny Cash T-shirts. Who would have known that every single person alive would own a Ramones T-shirt? Everyone's playing Ramones guitars in car commercials. I can guarantee you in 1985, even in the '90s, no one knew that Johnny Cash was going to become the huge American icon that he is. Think about it. Go back to 1997; who the fuck was listening to Johnny Cash? How many Johnny Cash T-shirts did you ever see in 1988?

If I were to think about that right now, I would like to be remembered as a man who loved his kids intensely, and a guy that, you know, I never sold out. I never sold out, and I never bought in.

Question: And you never bought in?

Jackson: Yes.

Never sold out and never bought in.

The next afternoon, the Sinners loaded their van and trailer with the gear of the road. It was a clear and unusually mild and bright January day for Kansas, with the rays from the sun marking relief from the drabness of early winter. Jackson was still in pain from his leg injury but nevertheless smiled. The wandering life meant another town, another show, another chance to immerse himself in his music, his art. Another chance to commit himself to what he believed in, to make a choice and go with it—as we all do, not just every year or every month but every day.

Jackson got into the van and winced as he squeezed his leg into the passenger space. The journey was obviously going to be painful.

So the Sinners ride, Slate and Brandon captured by Jackson's gravitational pull, the two orbiting him as planets do the sun, whose intense energy surges and ebbs, bringing the solar system warmth and light, making life possible—but always simmering and sometimes exploding with self-destruction.

Question: In the live version of your ballad "Broken," you sing: "There ain't no lucky stars up there shining on me. There ain't no over the rainbow for old Jackson Lee. It don't exist. There ain't no pot of gold for the broken like me." Do you feel that way?

Jackson: Oh yeah, sometimes. Sometimes I wanna go to the top of a building and beat my chest and say the world's mine. There's never one emotion that owns you all the time. I am a person of extreme highs and extreme lows. One day I want to cut my fucking throat, the next day I want to cut somebody else's throat, the next day I want to give the world a hug and kiss somebody on the cheek.

"Broken" was written about,... I think you get to a point..., people need that love, maybe from their mom, their family. They need that somewhat of a connect which I never had. So I've always had a hard time connecting with women on more than a physical level, you know. The only people I've really been able to [connect to] is my sons. I have an unconditional love for my children, and it always seems to get taken from me. I've lost three sons now to divorce. So there's that issue.

Question: Where are your sons?

Jackson: Two are in Washington state, and one is in Denver, Colorado.

❧ ❧

Jackson—who never had that "somewhat of a connect" with his mom or family—often posts on Facebook photos of his youngest son, who lives in Denver and with whom he feels particularly close. He's nicknamed the Lil' General, and he looks much like his dad. As I gazed at one of the photos, Jackson's words about his music echoed in my mind: "It's pretty much cost me everything I ever loved to care about in life." But it's one of the loves in his life, a love he can caress (should he want to), along with the Lil' General and his other sons.

For Jackson, his music and his children live in his heart every day. And every day, as an Outlaw, Jackson lives with the choice he has made, to follow his muse and his songs, and to travel the highways and roads that take him away from Denver to places like the warehouse venue in Wichita and into the land of smoky roadhouses and honky-tonks that lie beyond.

> *Now that I've got three little boys of my own,*
> *Lord, I hope they don't go down the same roads that I've gone.*
> "Modern Day Joad"
> From *The Whiskey Sessions*

CODA

Music and prose have many points in common, not the least of which is that they comprise snapshots of a person's life. Go back through any old photos we may have of ourselves and we might likely say: "Boy, have I changed." To write a contemporary profile of someone, then, is to catch them as they move in front of a lens, and while their essence may remain the same when they leave the scene, they will continue to develop (and that can be either in black and white or a color mosaic). I say this as a preface to a phone conversation that I had with Jackson shortly before this book went to press. Here's how it went:

Me: I really appreciate all of your help with this book, Jack. I just wanted to check how you're doing man.

Jackson: Great, great—better than ever.

Me: Is there anything new?

Jackson: Well, yeah, yeah, something I'm really proud of. My oldest son, Jack, he's going to work for me. He's a tattoo artist. He's going to be my road manager.

Me: That's cool, Jack, that's really cool. I'm happy for you.

Jackson: I'm a changed person. I'm not like I was when you spoke to me for the book the first time. That's over a year ago. I'm more settled. I had just gone through a divorce. I was miserable. I was in a bad spot.

Me: Yeah, man, so was I.

Jackson: We were both pretty fucked up. It's like when I used to do all that wild stuff onstage when I was younger. I don't do that shit anymore. My sons have never seen me drunk or cursing. I'm healthier, my shows are under control more. I mean, you still get me....

Me: And you're back to the four piece?

Jackson: Yeah, well, we're always changing.

Me: Who you got now?

Jackson: Brandon is still on drums, but there's Dan Johnson on steel and Rance Cox on guitar. I'm playing bass. Don and Rance are great additions—they've brought a lot to the band.

Jackson was excited about Rance. Here's a guy who came in to play with the Sinners when their back was against the wall. As Jackson tells it, around the time his band was returning from Europe, his lead guitarist stole a guitar and amp so he could sell them for money. Once again, Jackson had to rise to the occasion, and this time it meant quickly finding another guitarist. Onto the scene came Rance, and in an unusual way: Jackson discovered him on YouTube, where he was playing Sinners songs. He then invited him for a tryout, and from there it all fell together.

Me: I did as you suggested and I got a Kindle. My wife got it for me for Christmas. So far, I really like it.

Jackson: Yeah, bud, I thought you would. It takes a little getting used to, especially for us old-school guys who like books.

Me: How's your new girlfriend, Jack? How's that going?

Jackson: OK. Well, I mean, we aren't seeing as much of each other. She's got different interests. She wants something different from what I want.

As we were ending our conversation, Jackson told me he was getting ready to go out on another tour. For the first time, though, his son Jack would be with him, traveling the same roads to the honky-tonks that beckoned.

Jackson Taylor, Firehouse Saloon, Houston, TX (2011)

SECTION II

THE BACKLINE

PLUGGING INTO THE BACKLINE

Musicians call the main system into which they connect their instruments the "backline." It provides the electrical support for what they do. The past is the backline for today's Outlaws. The main system they plug into is the pulsating roots of country music, and those roots extend from the era of Jimmie Rodgers and the Carter Family in the 1920s to the first wave of Outlaws in the 1970s. If you don't plug into this backline, you ain't Outlaw.

CHAPTER 2

WALKING THE NASHVILLE LINE

Confluence: a flowing together of two or more streams. This dictionary definition might lead us to conclude that the word applies only to water. But it can also be applied to social developments, such as the birth of modern country music when in 1927 a record executive, Ralph Peer, came to Bristol, Tennessee, to record local musicians. The merging of Peer with the artists and the music that had existed for decades in the region shows how human developments can resemble natural ones. First one force, then another, twists and turns, molding and shaping the social terrain much as one element—soil, for example—and then another—rainfall—surges and recedes to contour the rivers essential to life.

In August of that year, Jimmie Rodgers, riding in a jalopy on rutted, dusty, and sometimes muddy roads, left Asheville, North Carolina, with fellow members of the band called the Tenneva Ramblers and rattled down the mountains past moonshine stills to arrive in Bristol. With his guitar in hand and his already rich background in country music, Rodgers was anxious to share his songs with others.

He had been born in Pine Springs, Mississippi, in 1897. While still a child, he roamed the streets of the nearby town of Meridian, a regional rail and trade center that bustled with cotton gins, lumber mills, and streetcars. Jimmie loved to sneak into the pool halls, watch the silent cowboy movies, and sit under the large canvas tents to see the vaudeville acts put on by traveling theater companies. The shows were typically melodramatic and dealt with work, love, and sex. Rodgers would later infuse his songs with these themes as shaped by his own experiences and would carry with him into his performances the enthusiasm he first felt for show business when he was still that excited, mischievous kid.

Writing in *Jimmie Rodgers: The Life and Times of America's Blue Yodeler* (University of Illinois Press, 1979), Nolan Porterfield says that the young man "apparently decided, very early and very definitely, that he wanted to be An Entertainer—one of those rare and select people who are called, almost as if by divine right or intervention...[to] dazzle, delight, and ennoble [others], and with all the confidence and determination that later characterized the whole course of his struggle against impossible odds, he made up his mind and headed straight for the mark."

By age twelve Rodgers was singing in amateur contests and learning how to play the mandolin, banjo, and guitar. While still in his teens, he worked on the railroads—the same ones that carried others to their destinations—first as a laborer hauling water for the gangs under his dad's supervision and later as a flagman, baggage master, and brakeman. In those jobs he learned the blues from African American workers and from the hoboes who snuck onto the freight cars.

The poor working conditions, however, weakened his already frail body and made him susceptible to tuberculosis, which soon took hold. But while TB invaded Rodgers's lungs, music captured his heart.

It was while he was in Asheville and performing on the local radio station that he learned about Ralph Peer, who had just arrived in Bristol. Peer carried with him portable recording equipment, only recently made available by changes in technology.

The Bristol Sessions, as they later became known, lasted from late July into early August, during which time Peer recorded nineteen artists and seventy-six songs. He even tracked down Blind Alfred Reed, an amateur performer and songwriter from West Virginia known for his railroad ballad "The Wreck of the Virginian." The *Bristol News-Bulletin* portrayed the sessions as attracting "notables of this mountain country" who were doing "their best stunts" for the microphone "turned into records, and spread at home and abroad." The sessions have since been hailed by musicologists as a treasure trove of Appalachian songs—pure, unadulterated, and straight from the heart, with no effort to write or perform them just so they would sell.

> *I go back to Jimmie Rodgers, and then on beyond that. From my mom, a lot of the Appalachian music she plays is the stuff that came over on the boat. There's old songs from the old country...[on which] she's playing on a dulcimer, an autoharp, and a lot of songs that ended up becoming Appalachian.*
> —Dallas Moore*

Of course, material concerns existed. The type of music Peer recorded already had a potential audience as urbanites, many of them having been uprooted from their rural homes, longed for the sounds

---

*All italicized quotations in this chapter and in chapter 3 are from the interviews I conducted in 2011 and 2012 with Outlaw country artists

of a fading, preindustrial America, and Victor Records expected to make money from this nostalgic desire. Rodgers hoped to make money too, but he was determined to present an honest rendition of the songs he knew and loved. When released on Victor Records, two songs that Rodgers sang solo, "The Soldier's Sweetheart" and "Sleep, Baby, Sleep," sold only moderately well, but on "Sleep, Baby, Sleep" Rodgers displays the trademark yodeling he would use on many of his recordings, which also became known for his use of complex harmonies.

At about the same time that Jimmie Rodgers was arriving in Bristol, so too was the Carter Family. The trio, who hailed from Virginia, consisted of Alvin Pleasant Delaney Carter—called A. P.— his wife Sara, and Sara's cousin, Maybelle. As with the other Carters, Maybelle brought with her a strong attachment to Appalachian music. Her grandson, John Carter Cash, later said that she "had a great sense of roots, and of the importance of the work ethic."

Maybelle also brought with her a distinctive way of playing the guitar, later dubbed the Carter Scratch. With this technique, she used her thumb to strum the bass and middle strings for the melody while she picked at the remaining strings for the rhythm. She had learned to do this from an African American guitar player, Lesley Riddle, but the method was around even before his day as Southern slaves used it to play the banjo (an instrument brought over from Africa).

Riddle, in fact, often traveled with A. P. Carter to collect mountain songs. Carter made it his job to remember the lyrics, while Riddle remembered the melodies. There can be little doubt that Riddle also played songs for the Carters that were rooted in African culture and that these, in turn, helped shape their music.

People don't realize that back in the turn of the century, and in the '20s and '30s and even up through the '50s, poor white folks and poor black folks, that's one thing they always shared was music and musical folklore.

—J. B. Beverley

The black influences on Rodgers, and those on the Carter Family, make it all the more clear how much country or hillbilly music owed to a diversity of sources. One historian, Art Menius, emphasizes that no clear line divided blues, folk, and country, so that "rural musicians drew upon a common well."

As with Jimmie Rodgers, the Carter Family presented Ralph Peer with invaluable roots music for his recording sessions in Bristol. Yet the technology required a compromise, for the old records, the 78s, were severely limited in what they could hold. Consequently, to create "The Storms Are on the Ocean," Peer and the Carters took a lengthy, traditional ballad of Scottish origin and converted it into a three-minute song, with several verses and a chorus. This type of structure became the format for most popular music.

Have you ever heard the words to "Wildwood Flower"? It's like beautiful. And those people came out of the hills, and they drove to Bristol to record. They didn't know what it was going to be like. They didn't think about recording. They just went up there and played their songs.

—Jody Payne

After the Bristol Sessions, Jimmie Rodgers got together again with Peer, this time at the Victor site in Camden, New Jersey. The recording session resulted in four songs, the most notable of which was "Blue Yodel No. 1," better known as "T for Texas." The record sold about half a million copies and made Rodgers a star. He now toured more often and was billed as the Singing Brakeman and the Blue Yodeler. Based on his success and work at the Bristol Sessions, he later became known as the Father of Country Music.

"T for Texas" stands in stark contrast to the songs recorded by the Carter Family. The Carters used close harmony and delved into themes about home and spirituality—no sneaking into the pool halls for them.

"T for Texas" sends a chill through the listener's bones. As Rodgers sings and yodels his way through the song, the T becomes T for Thelma, the woman who "made a wreck of me" by cheating on him. So what's he going to do about Thelma? Pine for her return? No, he's going to get a gun—a long pistol, at that—and shoot at her "to watch her jump and fall." Then he's going to buy a shotgun—with a great, long, shiny barrel—and blow the brains out of the guy who stole Thelma from him. There we have it: violence, revenge, and sexual allusions permeate the song.

Much like the later legendary Hank Williams, Jimmie Rodgers sped meteor-like across the country music sky, his career cut short by an early death. In 1933 the scrawny kid from Mississippi went to New York to record again for Ralph Peer. By then Rodgers had become so weakened from the TB in his body that a cot had to be set up for him so he could rest between songs. Yet he insisted that he stand in front of the mike as if he were "normal," even for his last tune, "Years Ago."

The next day Rodgers felt better and went with two friends to Coney Island, where they had hot dogs and beer and relaxed along the beach. That night he hemorrhaged—as he had before—but this time he slipped into a coma and drowned in his own blood.

Rodgers was dead at the age of thirty-three. To send his body home, a special baggage car was added to a train of the Southern line, and his casket, covered in lilies, was placed inside of it on a raised platform. The train, which left from Washington, blew its whistle during the journey—a long, wailing cry —and much as he had made his way down the hills to record for Ralph Peer, thousands of people now made their way through the overgrown fields of the South to see Jimmie's body pass by. Jimmie Rodgers had done his work, and country music had been gifted with an incredible talent whose own heart touched the hearts of America.

With Rodgers and the Carter Family, the country genre showed not only its common roots but also its diverse personality. Culturally, influences from Europe and Africa, from white and black America, from the past and present, from unique experiences, and from natural or learned artistic talent flowed together. Once we add technology and Peer's business acumen, along with that of Victor Records, a powerful confluence was underway, birthing and shaping modern country music.

Other developments also helped to create the genre. For example, in 1925 WSM radio in Nashville began its *National Barn Dance*, which offered vaudeville acts, polka music, and cowboy songs. The show morphed into the *Grand Ole Opry* in 1927 (the same year as the Bristol Sessions) to become one of the leading showcases for country acts.

Then there were the honky-tonks. These roadside bars and dance joints attracted the working crowd and earned a reputation for crude and even violent behavior. Respectable society looked down on them as unsavory, while some musicians called them "skull orchards" for the unseemly activities, such as fistfights, that took place. When Al Dexter recorded "Pistol Packin' Mama," which became a hit for him in 1943, he said the lyrics were inspired by an actual scene he had witnessed of a gun-toting woman in an east Texas honky-tonk.

At first, honky-tonk music was almost all about drinking. That, of course, remains a big part of it, but over time the honky-tonk artists developed more complex themes of guilt and conflict. And they changed instrumentally too when in the early 1940s Ernest Tubb amped up the sound in "Walking the Floor over You" by using an electric lead guitar.

And then came Hank Williams. Born Hiram Williams in Mount Olive, Alabama, in 1923, Williams carried with him the musical influences that went back to his childhood in Georgiana, Alabama. There he became friends with a black man, Rufus Payne, who stood on the street corners and played his guitar for nickels and dimes. Williams, who was only eleven years old, marveled at Payne's grasp of the blues and gospel and loved to watch as Payne, all raw energy and good times, laughed loudly and stomped his feet while singing. Williams already knew some basic guitar chords, but from Payne he learned blues notes. The odd pair, the older black man and the skinny white kid, became inseparable music companions, and the blues became an inseparable part of Hank Williams's music.

As a country artist, Williams sang about love and love lost, about the sometimes fickle and trying nature of relationships, and about deceit and cheating—themes so universal that his songs reached beyond the honky-tonks and into pop music. His lyrics were simple and poetic, and together with his voice and guitar, they cut deep into a person's soul.

In 1948 Williams began appearing on the *Louisiana Hayride*, a new radio show broadcast from Shreveport. When he performed "Lovesick Blues," an "oldie" written around the time he was born, so many listeners kept requesting it that he decided to release it as a record. With the song a hit in 1949, the *Grand Ole Opry* made him a member.

More hits quickly followed, and after Williams's self-written "Long Gone Lonesome Blues" reached the charts in 1950, he decided to play the music that *he* had composed. With the talented steel guitarist

Don Helms added to his band, and with a desire to capitalize on record sales, Williams toured extensively in 1950 and 1951.

Williams struggled with alcohol throughout his career. A binge drinker, he would disappear for days and sometimes weeks on end before resurfacing. After a failed spinal operation in December 1951, he became addicted to prescription painkillers—potentially lethal for anyone when combined with alcohol, but especially for Williams, who had been diagnosed with a weak heart.

In 1952 the *Opry* fired Williams for having missed tour dates (a result of his alcohol abuse). He then returned to the *Louisiana Hayride* and played in small honky-tonks.

At the end of December 1952, Williams left Montgomery to perform in Charleston, West Virginia, and Canton, Ohio. He had hired a college student, Charles Carr, to drive him in his Cadillac to the venues. When they reached Tennessee, an ice storm forced the cancellation of the show in Charleston. At a hotel in Knoxville, Carr called a doctor to tend to Williams, who was feeling ill from the combination of alcohol and chloral hydrate (a sedative and antianxiety drug) that he had consumed on the trip. The doctor administered two shots of vitamin B_{12}, with a quarter gram of morphine.

When Carr and Williams checked out of the hotel, Williams had to be carried to his Cadillac. Early in the morning of January 1, 1953, Carr stopped at a gas station near Oak Hill, West Virginia. Williams had been sleeping in the back seat, and when Carr checked on him, he discovered that the singer was dead.

Mystery still surrounds the passing of Hank Williams. Carr has said that Williams had nothing to drink the night he died, but the police found empty beer bottles on the back floor of his Cadillac. Most likely, Williams had passed away from the cumulative effects of alcohol and chloral hydrate that had been working on his weakened heart.

Today most roots country artists count Hank Williams as a major influence in their careers. Historian Colin Escott, who wrote *Hank Williams: The Biography* (Little, Brown and Company, 2004) says about him: "His is the standard by which success is measured in country music on virtually every level, even self-destruction."

> *A song like "Your Cheatin' Heart" is just as relevant in 1953 as it is today because it's just purely about emotion.*
> —Joey Allcorn

One Williams biographer has called him "a proletarian prophet" who touched the everyday person with "his simple heartbreaking lyrics." Listen to "Your Cheatin' Heart," and it steals you away; Hank's voice and guitar cry together. They wrap themselves around emotional scars and make the tears fall down like rain.

The same year that Hank Williams died, Kitty Wells released "Paying for That Back Street Affair," which brought a woman's perspective to honky-tonk. In it she sings about unfaithful husbands who desert their wives and children.

By the mid-1950s, however, honky-tonk music had peaked. Rockabilly had appeared and combined the steaminess of the blues with a fast-paced urban sensuality. One observer said that it "vindicated the music that many country artists were already playing in the honky-tonks." But such vindication came at the price of young people turning away from country.

Elvis Presley was the leading rockabilly artist. In becoming so, this poor boy from Tupelo, Mississippi, dipped into several musical streams. He learned country songs from an uncle who played in the honky-tonks, the blues from black musicians, and gospel from shows put on by quartets. Presley biographer Peter Guralnick says: "There probably was no type of music that he didn't love, but quartet music was the center of his musical universe. Gospel music combined the spiritual force that he felt in all music with a sense of physical release and exultation for which, it seemed, he was casting about."

Country artist Carl Perkins once defined rockabilly as "a country man's song with a black man's rhythm." It was record producer Sam Phillips who saw in Presley that rhythm. In the South, Phillips had listened to African Americans singing while working in the cotton fields and worshipping in their churches. In 1950 he began what ultimately became Sun Studio in Memphis to record their rhythm and blues.

But he also recorded white artists, and in August 1953 Presley showed up at Sun to make a two-sided acetate for about four dollars. Even though he displayed a fresh sound, it took a while for Phillips to invite the young man into the studio. When that finally happened, in July 1954, Presley at first failed to impress Phillips, and the entire recording session seemed doomed to failure. During a break, however, Presley and his band mates started kidding around and launched into a blues number, "That's All Right [Mama]," which had previously been a hit for a black artist, Arthur Crudup. Phillips loved it. He loved the raw energy and the originality. And with Presley he knew that he had something, and someone, unique.

> *The Elvis that set my life, completely has dominated my life, is the Sun Elvis, the eighteen- to twenty-one-year-old Elvis. That's the Elvis Presley who completely and utterly cast me into whoever I am, more than any other single thing in the world.*
> —Jackson Taylor

In the fall of 1955, a newspaper in Virginia reported that Presley had crossed bebop with country and had become "the hottest thing in the hillbilly field." Presley made it clear, though, that the music he was doing originated with Southern blacks. He said: "The colored folks been singing it and playing it just like I'm doing now, man, for more years than I know. They played it like that in the shanties and in their juke joints, and nobody paid it no mind till I goosed it up. I got it from them."

Phillips liked it that Presley ignored the boundaries between genres. The music could be blues or gospel or country—it didn't matter. He would cross lines, he would mix forms, whatever. This was early Elvis, in the Sun studio, unabashed and coming right at you.

Rockabilly was honky-tonk without the twang—the fiddle and the steel guitar had been dumped. As rockabilly lost more of its country attachments, it transformed into rock 'n' roll. Like country, it diversified and ranged from nearly straight-out blues to the white suburban sound packaged by songwriters who worked at the "music factory," in the Brill Building in New York, where they turned out songs quicker than cream could be churned into butter.

Rock soon converged with the increasing number of teenagers— whose ranks would be enlarged by baby boomers reaching their teen years—and the growth of a "youth culture." To them, country seemed too stale and too redneck. Be hip, man, be hip. Under the assault from rock 'n' roll, country record sales plummeted, and by 1961 the number of country radio stations nationwide had dwindled to eighty-one.

The country music industry reacted in 1958 by forming the Country Music Association in Nashville. Under its direction, disc jockeys, broadcasting executives, artists, songwriters, managers, and the like came together to fight the rising tide of rock by engaging in market research and promoting country music at broadcasters' and advertisers' conventions. The group's efforts helped boost the number of country radio stations to more than six hundred by 1970 (and more than two thousand by 2011). In 1961 the CMA created the Country Music Hall of Fame, which in 1967 opened a museum on Nashville's

Music Row. That same year the CMA held its first awards show, also in Nashville, which was broadcast on national television in 1968.

Primarily, though, country regained a bigger following by restyling its music into country pop or Nashville pop, with performers who were smoother vocally and less harsh instrumentally than the honky-tonkers and whose songs were more romantic. To do this, the industry became centered in Nashville, along Music Row, and thus became less splintered and more consolidated. Songs were now geared to what the market researchers indicated would sell, and the reliance on charts, such as the Hot Country Singles in *Billboard* magazine, further homogenized what was being produced.

This development required that Nashville record executives control the artists and keep them in line—keep them tied to the formula for making money. As a result, producers determined which songs an artist could record and which musicians the artist could use in the studio. To go outside of Nashville to make a record was considered treasonous for it meant a loss of studio control and a potential loss of the money being enjoyed by record companies and artists alike.

As a big part of country pop, Chet Atkins, an entertainer-turned-producer at RCA Records; Owen Bradley at Decca Records; Don Law at Columbia Records; and Ken Nelson at Capitol Records created the Nashville sound. Their formula used extensive backup vocals and orchestral strings and placed a polished veneer—a conformist shellac—on every song.

Atkins himself called the style "the sound of money," for it appealed to both country and pop audiences, and in particular urban listeners who found country to be, well, too country. In 1978 *New York Times* critic Al Reinert described Nashville pop as "background music, [with] shallow vocals adrift in vanilla arrangements" and said it was "all strings and no sting."

It's about money. People with the most decide to make even more of it; therefore, they take control.
—Jason Boland

On Music Row a producer might have as many as twenty artists under him, and since each record label was trying to copy and match the success of the others, it assured that the Nashville sound stayed uniform. Even the Nashville recording schedules were standardized. The studios used four three-hour sessions per day. The first began at 10 a.m. and the last at 10 p.m., with one-hour breaks in between. The session musicians were highly talented and knew how to work quickly and professionally with the producers. They included drummer Buddy Harman; guitarists Ray Edenton, Grady Martin, and Hank Garland; bassists Bob Moore and Henry Strzelecki; pianists Floyd Cramer and Hargus "Pig" Robbins; and steel guitarists Pete Drake, Don Davis, and Lloyd Green.

Within this system a country artist might have his song completely reworked by the producer. Through the technique of multitrack tape recordings—which allows the layering of sounds—additional background vocals and instruments, such as those orchestral strings, could be added to a track long after the artist had left the studio. Many an artist, in fact, on comparing what he had originally done with what emerged as the final product, could hardly recognize it as his own.

Of course, there were exceptions to the Nashville sound. Hank Snow was one whose tradition-based country music remained popular through the 1960s. Johnny Cash was another, as his distinct style and determination to pursue it found favor outside the standardized production line. And the Bakersfield sound (discussed in chapter 3), pioneered by Wynne Stewart and Buck Owens, was being created in California.

With the dominance of Nashville pop, some discontented artists grumbled that they were pawns of the studio master and a mere afterthought in the making of music. The conformity that came from the pursuit of bigger profits, they started to claim, had ruined country. Call it country music if you want to, but it really wasn't. The record executives insisted, however, that the artists should challenge nothing, for the bottom line was painted green for everyone to enjoy.

Despite this insistence, by the 1970s a grimy-looking group of creative musicians who chafed at having their considerable art constrained by what was variously called the Nashville sound, the Nashville machine, or the studio system wanted to stage a breakout and replace their prison garb with cowboy hats, jeans, and boots and those orchestral strings with guitars and fiddles—yes, *genuine country instruments*. These were the original Outlaws. They were determined to revive honky-tonk, and to do so, they were ready to cross the Nashville line.

CHAPTER 3

HANDS ON THE WHEEL

Turmoil: a state of great confusion, commotion, or disturbance.
—*ENCARTA DICTIONARY*

Turmoil permeated the 1960s to the point that nearly every day was so supercharged it threatened to tear society apart. The "conflict" in Vietnam polarized America as pro- and antiwar factions attacked each other's principles, morals, and patriotism; the hippies—with their long hair, free-love communes, and drug culture—raised the ire of mainstream society; the black power movement stoked racial tension as whites and African Americans confronted each other across a sometimes violent divide. Where would it all lead?

Nearly everywhere the old order was under assault, and authority—the Man—was being challenged. This was labeled a counterculture: a massive assault on mainstream ideas, values, and practices. To many, the world was spinning hopelessly out of control. It was hard to tell: Who were the deceivers ? Who were the believers ? Who had the hands on the wheel?

Those who embraced Nashville pop generally looked at the counterculture with disgust. The dopers, the freaks, the political radicals were what was wrong with America; they were why the nation was going down the toilet. If only *they* could be flushed, society would be saved. Looking back on this counterculture, journalist John Spong (writing in *Texas Monthly* magazine) says: "Nashville, with its pompadours, whiskey, and quiet reliance on truck-driver amphetamines, had no use for any of it."

Into this heated cauldron, music was bound to be stirred, and it was. While Music Row continued to ply its slickly shined formula, the record executives and producers soon found their style, and the authority behind their style, under assault by artists labeled as Outlaws. This wasn't going to be the same ol' song.

That rebellion in country music, however, would not be until the 1970s, after rock had set the example in the previous decade. Consequently, it is important to consider first what occurred in that genre.

The 1960s began with rock 'n' roll becoming *less* rebellious. More and more songs were being written in those songwriting "factories" in New York. Performers seldom composed what they sang, and the major studios seldom allowed the artists any creative independence.

This began to change with the British invasion, as the Beatles, the Rolling Stones, and other groups played what they wrote and demanded more control over what they recorded. Added to the mix were domestic artists, such as Bob Dylan, whose creativity and astute sense of the music industry made containment nearly impossible. Ironically, while Outlaw musicians are usually more conservative politically than their rock 'n' roll counterparts, and certainly more conservative than were the 1960s protestors, they would owe their emergence to the turmoil wrought by the counterculture.

Even before the Outlaw movement emerged, country was obtaining a greater following from young people. Their interest, however, wasn't in pop country, which they considered to be fake, hokey, and old-fogyish. Rather, they gravitated to an evolving mix of rock with roots country, a combination being created by artists attracted to the honesty found in what had been rejected and buried by the studios on Nashville's Music Row.

Two prominent musicians involved in creating that mix were Gram Parsons and Townes Van Zandt. Coming from a wealthy family, Parsons seemed an unlikely person to embrace "workingman's" country. But when his International Submarine Band recorded *Safe at Home* in 1967, they used country instruments, such as a pedal steel guitar, in songs that expressed countercultural values. The LP also included works written by Johnny Cash and Merle Haggard.

Shortly thereafter the band broke up, and when Parsons briefly joined the Byrds, a folk-rock group, he convinced them to record *Sweetheart of the Rodeo* (1968), a mix of country standards and Parsons originals. The Byrds hired top Nashville musicians for the LP, including banjoist John Hartford and steel guitarist Lloyd Green.

> *There was a year period when all I could listen to was Gram Parsons.... I tried to figure out his whole musical background and what he came from and what he loved and what he listened to. It's a definite love affair—his music.*
> —Caitlin Rose

Parsons left the Byrds in 1968 and formed the Flying Burrito Brothers, whose steel guitarist, Pete Kleinow, added distortion to the group's songs. In the early 1970s, Parsons recorded the album *GP* with country singer Emmylou Harris, followed by a solo effort, *Grievous Angel.* Parsons died in 1973 when he overdosed on alcohol and heroin.

Even though he never had a hit record, he holds a notable place in music history for his passionate effort to fuse rock with country.

Like Parsons, Townes Van Zandt was born into a wealthy family. But he was manic-depressive with schizophrenic tendencies and made the road his home. He began performing in Texas folk clubs in the mid-1960s, where he showed a special attachment to the music of Bob Dylan and Hank Williams. He recorded fifteen albums but remains best known for the songs he wrote that were covered by other artists, especially country musicians. These include "Pancho and Lefty," later a hit record for Willie Nelson and Merle Haggard, and "If I Needed You," recorded by Don Williams and Emmylou Harris. Van Zandt's lyrics have been called rich with poetic imagery. Since his death from a heart attack in 1997, numerous tribute albums have been released by country artists, most notably Steve Earle's 2009 work *Townes.*

Other efforts in the 1960s also brought rock and country together. Most prominently, Bob Dylan made country music more acceptable to young people by recording several albums in Nashville. Dylan said that he did his double LP *Blonde on Blonde* (1966) there because he liked the combination of professionalism and laid-back fun he found on the Music Row scene. In his *John Wesley Harding* (1967), Dylan moved toward a heavier use of country elements, brought to life by such Nashville studio musicians as Charlie McCoy on bass, Kenny Buttrey on drums, and Pete Drake on steel guitar. But Dylan kept the instrumentation sparse and handled all the harmonica, guitar, piano, and vocal parts. "I didn't intentionally come out with some kind of mellow sound," Dylan said in 1971. "I would have liked...more steel guitar, more piano.... I didn't sit down and plan that sound." But there it was, in roots-type glory.

Johnny Cash urged Dylan to record *Nashville Skyline* (1969), on which the two artists sing a Dylan composition, "Girl from the North

Country." Cash provided liner notes for the LP, and his involvement in the project brought Dylan yet more acceptance among country fans.

The coming together of countercultural rock with country roots was a surprising development given the contempt that many young people held in the 1960s for the South, whose racism they equated with barbarism. Case in point, Neil Young and "Southern Man": "I heard screamin'/And bullwhips cracking." Yet historian Zachary Lechner explains: "The 1960s and 1970s freak counterculture frequently embraced rural white southerness as a collection of noble, long-forgotten values perfectly suited to its critique of an impersonal, technocratic 'Amerika.'"

In short, young people saw that to embrace the idyllic part of the rural South (minus its racism), and rural America in general, was to protest the cold, cruel, crime-ridden modern urban society. That's why they were attracted to pop artist John Denver, whose hit records embodied this theme in songs such as "Rocky Mountain High" and "Take Me Home, Country Roads." Take me home, where? To the place *I belong*, namely West Virginia, with its mountains and rivers (something else to ignore: the strip mining) so opposite from the decaying world of machines, war, and hate.

Even though country music was finding its most creative outlet in league with rock, country on its own was not devoid of artistic creativity. In California, Buck Owens rebelled against the Nashville sound with the Bakersfield sound: honky-tonk pure and true. He counted among his musical influences Bob Wills and the legendary Hank Williams but also the rockers Chuck Berry—Owens covered Berry's "Johnny B. Goode" in a show at the London Palladium—and Little Richard.

Owens said: "As a small kid, I was working in the fields. It was hot, and it was miserable.... After everybody worked all day, after you got cleaned up, playing music was what we'd do for enjoyment.... Once I'd been in a honky-tonk, I found that as bad as the honky-tonk might have been, it was cool in the summer and warm in the winter. That's where the music was. I went there to listen and to try to learn, to hear what those people were doing. The majority of songs I do [today] are straight-ahead honky-tonk."

The Bakersfield sound involved a heavy backbeat and a distinct twang from a Fender Telecaster guitar. Owens said that he wanted his music to sound like a freight train, and it shows on songs such as "Act Naturally," with its railroad-track-like click. Fellow country artist Merle Haggard said about Owens: "He wanted to be his own man. He didn't want to be a part of the *Grand Ole Opry* scene."

Merle Haggard has that Bakersfield dust in his lungs too. He specializes in creating the sound that *he* wants—a light-on-the-touch acoustic guitar backed by heavy drums—and sings about people society has forgotten or disparages: criminals, crooks, and drunks. His songs often reflect the time he once spent in juvenile institutions, military schools, and prison. (While incarcerated at San Quentin in 1959, he saw Johnny Cash perform.) He once told a reporter: "I would've been a lifetime criminal if music hadn't saved my ass."

Bob Dylan has said about Haggard: "[He] has always been as deep as deep gets. Totally himself.... Even too big for Mount Rushmore. No superficiality about him whatsoever. He definitely transcends the country genre."

Critics of country music's "reactionary content" point to Haggard's 1969 hit "Okie from Muskogee" as a flag-waving symbol of redneck intolerance. But Haggard, who has never clearly stated his reasons for the song, once condemned the Vietnam War and has written

"Irma Jackson," about interracial romance, "Big City," a criticism of President Ronald Reagan's economic policies, and "America First," which slams President George W. Bush. One academic writer says that Haggard's music combines "chauvinistic patriotism with social and economic liberalism."

Although not as original or creative as Owens or Haggard, country singer George Jones (1931-2013) maintained his individualism through his captivating voice. Almost every country artist has at some point wished they could sing like Jones, with his versatility and distinctive phrasing.

There had always been loose cannonballs rolling around Music Row, artists who didn't fit the Nashville sound but who, because of their talent and popularity, could do most of what they wanted, and Johnny Cash was one of them. "My brother Jack's death, when I was twelve, put a mournful tone in my life—not just in my voice, but in my whole life," Cash said. "I listened to black gospel and what they called hillbilly.... When it came out of me, it was a little more countrified, but the influence was the blues."

Cash had his first hit records in the mid-1950s with "Folsom Prison Blues" and "I Walk the Line." His distinctive bass-baritone voice was complemented by a repetitive rhythmic bass guitar technique called the "walking bass."

Cash was experimental and willing to challenge accepted practices. His "Ring of Fire" (1963), for example, included trumpets—hardly a country instrument. He used blues and rock sounds in his songs and performed in prisons, where he recorded two albums, *Johnny Cash at Folsom Prison* (1968) and *Johnny Cash at San Quentin* (1969).

> *Johnny Cash's music, it's just timeless. It's unconditional. If you're going to pick up a fucking guitar...*
> —Dallas Moore

Cash called it a mistake when Columbia record producers chose which songs he had to record and which musicians he had to use for his LP *John R. Cash* (1974). He later said, "I went through the mid-'70s doing my own thing, staying away from politics on Music Row, making my own albums my own way." He wasn't about to let the mistake be repeated.

During that performance at the San Quentin penitentiary, Cash lost his patience and blurted out: "Put the screws on me, and I'm going to screw right out from under you, is what I'm going to do, you know that? I'm tired of all that shit. I tell you what: the show is being recorded and televised for England. They told me, they said, 'You gotta do this song; you gotta do that song. You know, you gotta stand like this, or act like this.' I just don't get it, man. You know, I'm here to do *what you want me to and what I wanna do.*"

With that statement Cash was making a declaration of independence, and he was doing so in front of a wildly cheering crowd *in prison*. The men with numbers on their shirts most keenly felt what Cash was talking about, and they were roused by his middle-finger salute to authority. While the start of the Outlaw movement can be difficult to pinpoint—maybe Cash was the progenitor, or maybe Buck Owens—Cash was expressing a frustration on the part of country artists amid the model being set by rock musicians, amid the rising rage of protests, and amid the ceaseless questioning within the counterculture.

Country musicians were begging for answers: Why shouldn't the artist have the final say over what he creates? After all, isn't he an artist and not a mere money machine? Why shouldn't country be more diverse with its sound? After all, since rock was already reaching into country and the blues and exhibiting *its* roots, why not country? Why shouldn't the artist be able to record where he wants and with whomever he wants? After all, the last of feudalism in the Western world had come to an end, and the serfs had been freed some one hundred years before in Russia, so why not free the ones on Music Row?

As can be seen, since the 1950s there has existed a tension between Music Row and those who believe that Nashville has lost touch with its country roots. Truth of the matter is that Music Row, more often than not, is Commercial Row, and any creativity linked closely to roots country will have to come from outside those studios. For Music Row, change of this sort comes not from within but from without. The studios have to be pushed to be hillbilly rather than slick.

You say you want a revolution...

Such was the requirement and the situation when Waylon Jennings challenged the Nashville "authorities," the Man. He had achieved modest success as a mainstream performer before he rebelled, but that had come at the price of containing and frustrating his creativity. Now he was about to launch a rebellion from within the heart of the beast, from within Nashville itself.

Jennings's efforts dovetailed so closely with what his friend Willie Nelson was doing in Texas that it's difficult to declare who was "first" in the rebellion; so suffice to say, at different times, and sometimes at the same time, they took hold of the standard and marched with it. In 1972 Austin had become a magnet for creative songwriters and performers. Michael Murphy located there, as did Jerry Jeff Walker. In March, Nelson staged a three-day country music festival near the city, at Dripping Springs, that brought together rednecks and hippies, country artists and folkies. They glared at each other across beer cans and bongs but also jammed and grooved and shared the good times.

As the other counterculture—the 1960s one that had produced so much protest—was winding down—imploding, actually—Jennings, Nelson, rednecks, hippies, country pickers, and folkies were converging—uncomfortably so, given their differences, but still converging. Maybe it wasn't the perfect storm, but it was a darn well powerful one. It was ready to blow, and all anyone could do was wonder who had the hands on the wheel.

SECTION III

BACKLINE PROFILES:
Honky-Tonk Outlaws

THERE AIN'T NO GOD IN NASHVILLE

Appalachian music, rockabilly, the blues, rock 'n' roll, Texas music, Hank Williams, the Bakersfield sound, honky-tonk—all of it formed the musical foundation for Outlaw. Each element, however, affected Outlaw artists differently. Ultimately, Nashville pop was to be assaulted in more than one way.

The historical profiles of the original Outlaws from the 1970s that follow should be read against the backdrop of the musical influences mentioned above and discussed earlier in this book, along with the prevailing social currents. At the same time, each profile needs to stand on its own for revealing the uniqueness of the particular artist in a country music industry that placed a premium on conformity.

Waylon Jennings by Kenneth Marr (2011)

CHAPTER 4

WAYLON JENNINGS

Are You Sure Hank Done It This Way?

*With Waylon it was soul and that voice and that sound, that sound
that he had with Ralph Mooney [the steel guitarist] and himself
going back and forth, and with Richie Albright [the drummer].*
—BERT DAVID NEWTON*

Waylon Jennings said that all he ever wanted from his challenge
to the Nashville system was his own "piece of land." When
the Outlaws expressed their desire for independence, they did so in
terms of the American Dream—that piece of land, that place where
they could live peaceful and free, express a bit of the "fuck you" to
everyone else, and get some respect for who they were. It all was in
keeping with the Old West spirit and what it had meant for years in

---

* Each historical profile begins with a statement from a current Outlaw artist and
concludes with a statement from the artist under discussion.

American culture; "Go west, young man, go west," journalist Horace Greeley had said in those frontier days. For the Outlaws, *artistic freedom was their West and their piece of land.*

Jennings, who was born on a farm near Littlefield, Texas, was as a kid attracted to the music of Hank Williams. "When Hank died," Jennings once recounted, "it was like my world had ended." In his youth Jennings hung around the Dew Drop Inn, an African American bar, where he saw Chuck Berry play, and in 1954, when he first heard Elvis Presley on the radio sing "That's All Right [Mama]" and "Blue Moon of Kentucky," he was captivated. He said: "Maybe it was the flapping of that big doghouse bass, all wood thump, and the slapback echo of the guitars wailin' and flailin' away."

Jennings began his music career as a disc jockey and then as a bass player for rock 'n' roll pioneer Buddy Holly. In 1963 he was signed by A&M Records, but he got an even bigger break when Chet Atkins lured him to RCA. By 1966 Jennings had singles charting into the Top 25. At first, he could hardly contain himself over being produced by Atkins, who was famous for creating stars. "He let me find my way within the framework he set up," Jennings said in reference to the Nashville sound that Atkins had been essential in creating, with its smooth style, background vocals, and lush orchestral strings.

But Jennings felt that he didn't fit the music (and most certainly the music didn't fit him). He kept pushing for changes, such as the use of a different drumbeat, only to be told that his requests went against what the producers wanted. Under the Nashville system, Jennings said, "I'd go in, cut the tracks, come back the next day, and I wouldn't even recognize that it was the same tune." When Atkins left production to return to playing music, Jennings chafed even more as he watched his new producer, Danny Davis, overdub song after song.

"We were proud to be country," Jennings said about his work on Music Row. "But that didn't mean that we had to be trapped by country music's conventions or the way the artists were [being] treated." Seeking change, Jennings looked at what rock musicians were doing and saw that they were getting good money, lots of studio time, and heavy promotion.

With the help of an astute, high-powered lawyer, Neil Reshen (who became his and Willie Nelson's manager), Jennings nabbed a new contract from RCA that boosted his royalties and, importantly, gave him his own production company. This meant he had control over his music: the advertising, the promotion, and the mixing. He even began recording in the studio he wanted, one owned by fellow Outlaw Tompall Glaser, rather than RCA's. Jennings had made his choice, and with it he began propelling a revolution in country music.

With all but one of the songs written by songwriter Billy Joe Shaver, Jennings recorded the album *Honky Tonk Heroes* in 1973. He intentionally gave it a ragged sound and made it as simple as possible. The track "Ain't No God in Mexico" used only three instruments. This was the ultimate kick in the ass to the Nashville sound and akin to how punk rockers would simplify their music in reaction to the elaborate orchestrated rock of the 1970s (represented by such groups as Pink Floyd and Yes).

Shaver later said about the album that "I knew it was good. Waylon was known as a guy who could pick songs as good as Elvis Presley and was a great writer himself. Waylon, with his arrangements, had a lot to do with the way people played, and everybody jumped on it. And Waylon didn't have nothin' to go by, but as people started to copy [him], they had a plowed row to follow."

Additionally, in recording *Honky Tonk Heroes* Jennings used Glaser's studio, Hillbilly Central, which was located in an old house on Nineteenth Avenue South, not on Music Row. Jennings was learning what *he* could do: have artistic control, use his road band in the studio to record, create his own album cover, choose his own booking agent, and pick a manager who was outside the good-old-boy Nashville scene.

Jennings was also freed from the Nashville music schedule. He could come and go as he pleased and be as creative as he wanted. So there he was, writing and singing *his* music and playing *his* guitar—and hanging out with Tompall at the pinball machines in the Bump-Bump Room, slapping those flippers. Things that went bump in the night were fun for Tompall and Waylon but getting ever more scary for Music Row.

To complement his newfound creativity, Jennings grew his hair long, sported a beard (which he had originally grown while sick in the hospital), and wore scruffy shorts and jeans. The sartorial change would declare, just as openly as the music, that Outlaw had arrived. In fact, as Jennings plied his trade, the word "outlaw" emerged to describe what he and other renegade country artists were doing in going their own way. Yes, a new breed was evolving from the Nashville muck: *Homo erectus Outlaw*. (Who first applied the word outlaw to the music remains an ongoing debate, but Jennings was the first to use it in a title, with his release of the album *Ladies Love Outlaws,* and the song of the same name, a year before *Honky Tonk Heroes* came out.)

Jennings specialized in the sound of a Fender Telecaster guitar. He loved a four-on-the-floor (a steady, accented beat in 4/4 time in which the bass drum is hit on every beat in common time) and a heavy bass. "He knew exactly what he wanted," said Floyd Domino, a piano player for Jennings in the 1980s. "Whatever you played, he'd tell you to play it an octave lower. He always wanted the emphasis on the downbeat." It takes only one listen to "You Can Have Her," from Jennings's 1976 *Waylon Live* album, to appreciate Richie Albright as a drummer able to perfect what Jennings wanted.

Jennings brought this style into the honky-tonks six nights a week. He said that it was there that an artist had to convey the music and have it come back appreciated: "If it just goes out and lays in the audience, you haven't reached them."

Certainly, Jennings's music was heavily influenced by the rock 'n' roll that had attracted him as a young man—he was once fired from his job as a radio DJ for playing too much of that "crazy-ass shit"— but as with so many roots country artists, he counted Hank Williams as his musical model. Jennings said that he and his band measured most everything by Hank's experiences; if their bus broke down or they got stranded or they traveled five hundred miles only to find that their gig had been cancelled, they would say that their troubles were like Hank's. "We wanted to be like him, romanticizing his faults, fantasizing ourselves lying in a hotel room sick and going out to sing," Jennings said.

With this in mind, in 1975 Jennings wrote and recorded "Are You Sure Hank Done It This Way." The structure of the song broke new ground for country music since it had no distinct verse and chorus, no fiddle as a middle break, no bridge, only what Jennings called "an endless back-and-forth seesaw between two chords." Moreover, when it was mixed, the guitars were not separated, so they sounded like one big instrument.

The song was also a plaintive cry about life on the road stealing his youth. The grueling schedule made his time on earth seem to move that much faster. This appears in the lyrics when Jennings sings about "speeding my young life away." Yet the song also makes it clear that *Jennings chose this way of life.* Presumably, he could have remained in the mainstream—but *he chose* to be a revolutionary.

The breakthrough album for Jennings, and for the entire Outlaw movement, was *Wanted! The Outlaws.* RCA marketed it in 1976 to take advantage of the increasing popularity of Outlaw music, and it consisted of previously recorded songs by Jennings, Glaser, Jessi Colter, and Willie Nelson.

It was simple and honest music—nothing slick or heavily polished. Music critic Chet Flippo provided the liner notes: "Call them outlaws, call them innovators, call them revolutionaries, call them what you will. They're just some damned fine people who are also some of the most gifted songwriters and singers anywhere." The LP was designated the Country Music Association's Album of the Year for 1976, and Jennings and Nelson were awarded Duo of the Year by the CMA for their hit single from the LP, "Good Hearted Woman."

RCA was ecstatic about the Outlaw emblem. Here was an *image*— and for them image ruled (as it still does on Music Row)—that could be easily identified and easily sold to consumers. Music is, after all, a business as well as an art, a way for the corporation and the musician to make money, and here was the way that the business side could be satisfied for both of them.

Maybe it was loneliness, maybe it was the private Jennings wanting to flee from the public Jennings, maybe it was the pressure to perform, to be in tune with his audience—whatever the reason, he became addicted to cocaine (and wrote openly about it in his autobiography). "I had wanted to play my music in my own way," Jennings said in explaining himself. "I didn't give a shit about the rest of it."

Jennings was making a lot of money—his LP *I've Always Been Crazy* (1978) was the first country album to *ship* gold, and he became more commercial when he wrote the theme song for the hit TV show *The Dukes of Hazzard*—but he was spending all he made—on drugs, on property, and on whatever pleased him—and went broke. He later said he was throwing away $1,500 a day on cocaine alone and that his total debt topped $2.5 million.

As he rearranged his finances to avoid bankruptcy, he also quit doing coke. In his autobiography he credits his wife, the Outlaw singer Jessi Colter, whom he had married in 1969, for having the patience, love, and care to help him kick his addiction. (Jennings had been married three times previously and had several children by those marriages.) During the spring of 1984, Jennings spent his time detoxing by sitting on his front porch at home and watching his five-year-old son, Shooter, play in the yard. (Shooter was born to Jessi and Waylon in 1979 and has since become an Outlaw artist in his own right. His profile appears in this book.)

Even after Waylon Jennings left RCA in 1985 to sign with MCA Records, he maintained control over his work. He continued to tour for the next decade, though he later said that by that time he was burned out on it. In 1995 he left MCA for Epic Records. His sales, however, were already in decline, and *The Eagle,* which had been released in 1990, was his last Top Ten album.

Between 1985 and 1995, Jennings joined Johnny Cash, Willie Nelson, and Kris Kristofferson to form the Highwaymen, a country music super group. (Although, combined, they never reached the artistic heights of their early careers.) They recorded two albums for Columbia Records and one for Liberty. Their Columbia LPs resulted in three chart singles, including the number one "Highwaymen" in 1985.

As the Highwaymen were recording and touring, Jennings underwent heart bypass surgery. By then he had diabetes, and as it worsened, he had surgery again to improve his blood circulation. In 2001 his left foot was amputated. In 2002 he died in his sleep of diabetic complications. Jennings wrote in his autobiography: "Playing the music inside you. That's what a musician is. What I am." He might not have done it exactly Hank's way, but he had taken on the old order, scaled its walls, and planted at its summit the flag of the Outlaw nation, flying free.

> *When I put the black hat on and walked to the stage carrying my Telecaster, I was staking out my own piece of land where the buffalo roam. Don't fuck with me, was what we were saying.*
> —Waylon Jennings

Willie Nelson by Kenneth Marr (2013)

CHAPTER 5

WILLIE NELSON

Red Headed Stranger

Willie made everybody their own star in their own right.
Everybody contributed, everybody added to the whole thing.
—*DALLAS MOORE*

illie Nelson was once asked: "What's the difference between rednecks and hippies?" He responded: "Whiskey makes you feel like fightin', and marijuana makes you feel like listenin' to music." The convergence of these two—or four, more accurately— makes Willie Nelson's role in the birth of 1970s Outlaw music all the more intriguing.

Like his friend and fellow Outlaw artist Waylon Jennings, Willie Nelson was born in Texas. In his case, it was in the town of Abbott, north of Waco, in 1933. As a young man he listened to the *Grand Ole Opry* and was also influenced by the swing music of Bob Wills. Moreover, he says, "I grew up listening to Mexican music, and [guitarist] Django Reinhardt was a hero of mine." He gives credit for his career to his grandfather, who started teaching him guitar when he was five; his grandmother, who was a music teacher; and his older sister, Bobbie, who later played piano in his band and who encouraged his musical efforts.

Nelson was in several bands in the early 1950s while working as a disc jockey and writing music. He later said that he took up songwriting because it beat returning to Abbott to pick cotton and bale hay for fifteen cents a day.

Nelson left Texas for Nashville in 1960 and at first found it to be a dispiriting move. He said: "Sitting around and talking to writers in Nashville is the most depressing thing in the world. There are so many of them." Then he began writing songs for publishing house Pamper Music that became hits for other artists, among them "Hello Walls" (for Faron Young in 1961) and "Crazy" (for Patsy Cline in 1962). Following up on those, Nelson signed with Liberty Records, and for them two of his singles reached the country Top Ten: "Touch Me" and "Willingly." But he would not have another major hit again until 1975, partly because his singing style—staying slightly ahead or behind the beat—was too quirky for many listeners.

Again like Jennings, Nelson signed with Chet Atkins at RCA, a leading producer and the inventor of the Nashville sound (see chapter 2). Atkins used the best session players in the city to elevate the quality of Nelson's recordings. *Country Willie: His Own Song,* released in 1965, was heavily infused with orchestral strings. Nelson's next two albums, *Country Favorites, Willie Nelson Style* and *Make Way for Willie,* sold well, but his next few fared poorly. By that point RCA was having trouble trying to figure out what to do with Nelson, who disliked the Nashville pop formula. Songwriter Kris Kristofferson later observed that Nelson was a poor fit for the Music Row production line because he "loved the soul of country music" more than the money. To corrupt his songs with strings was, to him, blasphemous.

Restless and discontented, Nelson left Nashville to return to Texas, where he had many fans. Those from the conservative redneck part of society liked his respect for Texas roots music and the way he expressed what they felt in their everyday lives; those from the more liberal hippie part liked his free-spirited nature and originality. Both groups liked the rapport he had with his audiences—Nelson put up few barriers and spent considerable time signing autographs and posing for pictures.

Some historians say that Willie "courted" the hippies by growing his hair long and wearing earrings and jeans. To an extent that may be true, but Willie took to that appearance primarily because it fit him. He had always been an iconoclast, so why shouldn't he wear the symbols of the iconoclastic hippies? He says: "People wore bandannas, tennis shoes, and jeans, *and that's the way I grew up.*"

In 1973 Atlantic Records was drawn to Nelson as a songwriter and his popularity in Texas and so decided to take a chance on him. Helping with Nelson's move was Neil Reshen. A lawyer and manager, he had been instrumental in getting a contract at RCA for Jennings that gave to him creative control over his music and more of a financial return. He did the same for Nelson. This being the situation, Atlantic showed more patience for Nelson's penchant to record concept albums than had RCA. Two of those, *Shotgun Willie* (1973) and *Phases and Stages* (1974), sold modestly but received good reviews. (*Phases and Stages* contained the hit single "Bloody Mary Morning.")

At the same time that Waylon Jennings was in Nashville recording his LP *Honky Tonk Heroes* (1973), which became a breakthrough for the Outlaw movement both in its style and popular appeal, Atlantic was facing the same problem with Willie that had been the case with

RCA: what to do with a talented man who didn't fit the Nashville sound and whose record sales were mediocre. Nelson may have been drawing crowds in Texas, but he had yet to find a national audience.

Nelson soon went to another label, Columbia, the home of Johnny Cash and other artists who didn't fit the Nashville mainstream. By then Nelson had added an exceptional guitarist, Jody Payne, to his band. One night in 1975, Nelson called Payne over to his house to listen to some songs he had brought together. He told Payne that he wanted to use them to create another concept album, and that he wanted it to have sparse instrumentation. Thus emerged *Red Headed Stranger*, recorded at a studio in Austin.

When Nelson sent the tapes to Columbia, Rick Blackburn and other executives there were befuddled. They thought it was a demo tape that would have more musical instruments added to it at a later date. "Blackburn thought this was a joke," Payne says. "And Willie said, 'No, we have a contract, and you're supposed to put it out exactly that way.'" Producer Billy Sherrill listened to it and called it a "piece of shit." Another producer, Ron Bledsoe, similarly evaluated it. To them, the songs lacked energy; they were too laid-back. But when Nelson, with the help of Jennings, kept insisting that they release it as he had recorded it, they did. (Perhaps they thought that once it flopped they would be rid of Nelson, or would have at least shown him the errors of his ways.)

To the surprise of the Columbia higher-ups, the album became a hit and was certified gold in 1976. Moreover, "Blue Eyes Crying in the Rain," Nelson's cover of a song from the 1940s, became his first number one single.

The thirty-four-minute-long *Red Headed Stranger* revolves around the story of a man who becomes a fugitive after he kills his wife and her lover. The album received a few harsh reviews, but most were favorable. Music critic Chet Flippo, writing in *Texas Monthly,* said: "The difference between Nelson's *Red Headed Stranger* and any current [country and western] album, and especially what passes for a soundtrack [in] Nashville, is astounding. What Nelson has done is simply unclassifiable; it is the only record I have heard that strikes me as otherworldly. *Red Headed Stranger* conjures up such strange emotions, and [it] works on so many levels that listening to it becomes totally obsessing." *Billboard* described the album as having "particularly fine piano by Bobbie Nelson, and the usual highly stylized Willie Nelson vocals." *Mother Jones* magazine added: "Texans have known for 15 years what *Red Headed Stranger* finally revealed to the world: that Nelson is simply too brilliant a songwriter, interpreter, and singer—just too damn universal—to be defined as merely a country artist."

The record made Nelson an Outlaw with a national audience. In the *New York Times,* music critic John Rockwell wrote that "Willie was the acknowledged leader of country music's 'left wing,' working to cleanse Nashville of stale excesses by bringing it up to the present and its own folkish roots." *Newsweek* called him the King of Country Music, and he appeared on the cover of *Rolling Stone,* the tabloid for the young and hip.

Outlaw music was clearly taking hold. By 1975 several FM radio stations were broadcasting what they called "progressive country," including KAFM in Dallas and KFAT in San Francisco. They frequently played mixes of Nelson, Jennings, the Allman Brothers, and Pure Prairie League.

When RCA released the album *Wanted! The Outlaws* in 1976 to take advantage of the popularity of "the progressives," it enhanced Nelson's prominence as a renegade. The LP consisted of previously-recorded songs by Nelson, Jennings, Jessi Colter, and Tompall Glaser.

It stayed at number one on the country album charts for six consecutive weeks and became the first country LP to sell one million copies. The track "Good Hearted Woman," which Nelson recorded as a duet with Jennings, became a hit single.

The best-selling *Waylon and Willie* (1978)—that included the number one single "Mammas Don't Let Your Babies Grow Up to Be Cowboys" (written by Ed Bruce and his wife Patsy Bruce)—placed Jennings and Nelson closer together in the public mind by making them appear to be "brother Outlaws." The studios accepted the whole Outlaw image because it helped sell records, and Jennings and Nelson were just as willing to accept it and tend to it for the same reason. Yet they didn't create it for that purpose, and as Outlaw became more commercialized and tended to box in their music, they often felt trapped.

Back in 1973 Nelson had begun an annual country music festival in central Texas, near Austin, and he continued to hold the event each year during the Fourth of July. Although the gatherings at times generated controversy—such as in 1975 when the Banditos motorcycle gang showed up and chaos ensued—Nelson thrived on the energy as he embraced the unexpected, a trait evident in his recordings. For example, in 1977 he released an album tribute to country artist Lefty Frizzell, *To Lefty from Willie,* that celebrated honky-tonk roots. Then the following year he changed course and released *Stardust,* a collection of pop standards. That LP sold in the millions.

Nelson was making so much money that he began flying around to gigs on a Learjet. In the late 1970s, he took to acting in motion pictures and received laudable reviews for his work. For the movie *Honeysuckle Rose* (1980), he wrote the hit song "On the Road Again."

His artistic and commercial accomplishments proceeded hand in hand with a tumultuous personal life. He went through a divorce and eventually owed millions of dollars to the Internal Revenue Service. He worked to pay off that debt but clearly had squandered a lot of what he had made.

In the 1980s Nelson recorded "To All the Girls I've Loved Before" with Julio Iglesias. There was no Outlaw in sight—and any Outlaw on hearing it might have run for the hills, as a sweet melody and lush strings took over. But on another level, Nelson was doing his own thing, and maybe that was Outlaw enough. That same decade he toured and recorded with Johnny Cash, Kris Kristofferson, and Waylon Jennings as the Highwaymen. Nelson has also worked on behalf of disaster relief, biofuel development, and animal welfare; has held an annual Farm Aid benefit for struggling farmers; and has been a crusader for the legalization of marijuana. In his book *Roll Me Up and Smoke Me When I Die* (William Morrow, 2012), he says: "I started the TeaPot Party after I got busted for pot in Sierra Blanca, Texas. I thought, 'Hey, there's the Tea Party [which he strongly opposes for advocating measures damaging to workers], so why not a TeaPot Party?' There are now TeaPot Party representatives in every state of the union.... On a few occasions, the TeaPot Party has backed...politicians who believe, as we do, that marijuana should be legalized, taxed, and regulated the same way we do alcohol and tobacco."

As Nelson approaches his eightieth birthday, he continues to record and tour. He has joined Ray Price and Merle Haggard for duets and has also teamed up with Toby Keith and Asleep at the Wheel. He has remained eclectic, ranging from country to pop to folk to the blues. But his Outlaw heyday and the height of his creativity resides back in the 1970s and early 1980s, and he will be most remembered musically for having challenged the Nashville establishment so he could make his own music, one whose artistry has reflected his honest and considerable talent. He showed that there was an alternative to the stale packaging being produced along Music Row and that it was an alternative deserving of a wider audience.

When Willie Nelson first rode into Nashville from Texas in his 1951 Buick, he was the redheaded stranger, for he knew little about the city. Even when he wrote his earliest hit songs, he remained such a person, for Music Row executives, who looked at his ideas as alien and unsalable, ignored the deeper music within him. The rule was clear: don't rock the boat, stay with the Nashville sound, and don't be a troublemaker.

So Willie Nelson returned to Texas, and the rest of the story has been told. For those who have never been exposed to Outlaw music— or, pray tell, who have been so conditioned by Nashville to think that country pop really is country—Willie Nelson will always be the redheaded stranger. But he's no stranger, redheaded or otherwise, to history. Instead, he's the man who, with Waylon Jennings, created Outlaw country when he challenged the Nashville establishment by reaching back to country's roots and insisting they must live.

> *I've been called a troublemaker a time or two. What the hell is a troublemaker? you ask. Well, it's someone who makes trouble; that's what he came to do, and that's what he does, by God. Like it or not, love it or not, he will stir it up. Why? Because it needs stirring up! If someone doesn't do it, it won't get done, and you know you love to stir it up.... I know I do.*
>
> —Willie Nelson

Billy Joe Shaver by Jackson Taylor (2013)

CHAPTER 6

BILLY JOE SHAVER

The Earth Rolls On

*You'd be surprised how many guys hang out with my music who
don't even know who Billy Joe Shaver is, and he's the one who
invented it, he started it. He's the guy who wrote those songs; he's
the catalyst of it all.*

—*JACKSON TAYLOR*

The way Billy Joe Shaver tells it, he got Outlaw artist Waylon
Jennings to record the songs that would appear on the historic
Honky Tonk Heroes LP (1973) only after a confrontation with him
in a studio. Shaver had met Jennings in 1973 at a music festival near
Austin, Texas—the famous Dripping Springs gathering put on by
Willie Nelson—and Jennings had been so impressed by Shaver's
songs that he promised to hook up later with Shaver to record them.

But when Jennings didn't follow through on his promise, Shaver
went to Nashville and spent six months trying to track him down.

Jennings avoided him and refused to speak with him. "I'd call [his office]," Shaver recalled, "and they'd say he was on the other line—I knew damn well he only had one line."

Finally, Shaver gained entry into a studio where Jennings was recording. The room was filled with babes and bikers—the Jennings groupies. When Jennings heard about Shaver being there, he had someone give Shaver a hundred dollar bill as a way to appease him and make him move on. That just angered Shaver even more, however, and steeled him for a showdown.

Shaver waited and waited. Finally, Jennings came out of the studio's control room with two bikers at his side. "What do you want?" he demanded of Shaver. The room grew quiet as Shaver answered: "Waylon, you said you were going to do a whole album of my songs. I've got those songs, and you're going to listen to them—or I'm going to kick your ass right here in front of God and everybody."

The bikers glared at Shaver and looked at Jennings to see what he wanted done. Jennings said he would listen to one of Shaver's songs but that if he didn't like it Shaver would have to get his "ass up and leave." They then went into the studio, whereupon Shaver picked up his guitar and played "Ain't No God in Mexico." Jennings loved it and asked for another song and then another and then another. "I know what I've got to do now," he shouted. He decided to record a batch of Shaver's songs, and thus came about the historic, groundbreaking LP *Honky Tonk Heroes*. "For me, it was a magical night," Shaver says.

Shaver was born in 1939 in Corsicana, Texas, and was raised by his mother in Waco. (As a young man, he would hang out at the bar where she worked, the Green Gables, a site that gained fame when Shaver later referred to it in his song "Honky Tonk Heroes.") After he was kicked out of the Navy for punching an officer and spent six months in prison because of it—turned out the officer hit him first and was in civilian clothes, so Shaver wound up getting an honorable discharge—he held a series of low-pay jobs, including one in the early 1960s at a sawmill where he lost most of the index and middle fingers on his right hand. The accident jolted him into writing songs.

Shaver arrived in Nashville for the first time in 1966 (he left there in disgust and returned on numerous occasions), when the city was brimming with creative young writers, such as Guy Clark and Kris Kristofferson. In fact, Shaver got his first big break when Kristofferson recorded a song of his, "Good Christian Soldier." In his autobiography *Honky Tonk Hero* (University of Texas Press, 2005), Shaver recalls: "That was the heyday of the *Opry*, and the top singers were guys like George Jones, Faron Young, and Webb Pierce, and their records...were heavily produced, with orchestras and strings and shit you'd never find in a honky-tonk."

Shaver recorded his debut album, *Old Five and Dimers Like Me,* in 1973 for the Monument label. His songs displayed his talent for taking a simple phrase and turning it into poetry and his ability to create unique images. Unfortunately, Monument didn't promote the LP, so it sold poorly.

Shaver's music went back to the honky-tonk roots he loved so much in Texas. As a free spirit determined to create what he felt was in his heart—be damned what Music Row wanted—he was at the forefront of the Outlaw movement. *Honky Tonk Heroes* did nothing less than revolutionize the Nashville music scene, and the LP has gone platinum five times over.

Shaver says that Jennings sang those songs as good as anyone ever could but that his relationship with him grew testy when *Rolling Stone* magazine said that the real honky-tonk hero was not Jennings but Shaver. He also claims that Willie Nelson would never have been able to put out *Red Headed Stranger* (1975) without the path having already been broken by *Honky Tonk Heroes.*

Shaver made two albums for Capricorn Records, *When I Get My Wings* (1976) and *Gypsy Boy* (1977), with the first widely praised by reviewers. But he was much more the songwriter than the performer and had little commercial success with anything that he recorded.

As the Outlaw movement waned, so did Shaver's career. At the same time, his personal life was suffering. "I was doing everything I shouldn't," he says. "Drugs, booze, chasing women, you name it…. My body was breaking down, and I felt sick all the time." He made a pilgrimage to an outdoor altar, asked God for forgiveness, and felt saved. As he left the site, he wrote a song, "I'm Just an Old Chunk of Coal." In 1981 it became a hit for John Anderson.

Shaver recorded three albums for Columbia in the 1980s, while his son, Eddie, was working with him. In 1993 they released *Tramp on Your Street* on the Praxis/Zoo label, which showed a spirited rock 'n' roll influence. Few people could play the guitar as well as Eddie Shaver, and it showed. The father and son collaboration ended tragically, however, in 2003, when Eddie died from a heroin overdose after attending a party of drugged-out musicians in a low-rent motel.

Billy Joe Shaver continues to write songs, make records, and tour. He still travels in his white van to the honky-tonks that have defined so much of his life. "I'm out on the road," he says, "because I need what little money I can make. I'm still driving a fifteen-passenger van and pulling a trailer. But Jesus rode up on a jackass, so it ain't no big deal."

Rolling Stone was right: it's no exaggeration to apply the phrase "honky-tonk hero" to Billy Joe Shaver—honky-tonk hero and Outlaw progenitor. And now as his van rolls along those highways, his legend, like the earth itself, rolls with him—on and on and on, leaving a legacy few, if any, country songwriters will ever be able to equal.

> *Throughout my career as a songwriter, I've written songs about me—the good and the bad, the funny and the sad. I've written songs about other people, but I don't sing other people's songs. They're just little poems about my life, and I've never pretended that they were anything more.*
> —Billy Joe Shaver

Johnny Paycheck by Kenneth Marr (2013)

CHAPTER 7

JOHNNY PAYCHECK

The Only Hell My Mama Ever Raised

He's the underdog, and he's the greatest country singer that ever lived and nobody knows it. I've had people from Nashville, old-school pickers, tell me that. Fred Newell, who recorded the steel guitar on our last record—he played with Porter Wagoner and Waylon and Jerry Reed—told me that one night at a bar. I already kind of thought that, but for a guy like that, that's played with those guys, to tell me that Johnny Paycheck is the greatest singer ever,... I don't know, I've got a spot in my heart for that guy. I just hate the fact that nobody knows how great he was.
—WHITEY MORGAN

Torn by the currents that surged through Nashville and the gales that blew through his life, Johnny Paycheck was a troubled musician, driven to self-destruction by his own interpretation of "Outlaw." When most country fans think of Paycheck at all, they think of his number one record, "Take This Job and Shove It." But that record just scratches the surface of the talent that made him a dedicated honky-tonk artist.

Born Donald Eugene Lytle in Greenfield, Ohio, in 1938, Paycheck played the guitar nearly his whole life. "It's my baby," he once said, "I've played it since I was six." He was also a wanderer. He left home while he was in his teens and started playing in honky-tonks as the "Ohio Kid." He then joined the Navy but was court-martialed in 1956 for slugging an officer and, as a result, served two years in a military prison.

He subsequently went to Nashville and obtained a recording contract with Decca Records. Using the stage name Donny Young, he cut four singles, but none of them cracked the charts. When these and two more records for Mercury failed, he decided to play with other bands. From 1962 to 1966, he was the bass player for George Jones, and as the two men traveled together they helped each other develop their vocal styles. "You Better Move On," a duet with Jones, clearly shows the similarity in their voice inflection.

After Paycheck had some success for the Hilltop label, with "A-11" (a honky-tonk song written by Hank Cochran) and "Heartbreak Tennessee," he joined producer Aubrey Mayhew to found Little Darlin' Records and legally changed his name to Johnny Paycheck. His career seemed set in high gear as several of his singles charted, including "The Lovin' Machine," which became his first Top Ten record in 1966. Also that year Tammy Wynette reached the charts with a Paycheck song (cowritten by Fuzzy Owen and Bobby Austin), "Apartment No. 9," and Ray Price did the same with "Touch My Heart." The songs that Paycheck recorded at Little Darlin' featured the steel guitar work of Lloyd Green, one of the great musicians on that instrument, and had a sparse but sharp sound to them, clearly reflecting Paycheck's attraction to rockabilly and straight-out honky-tonk.

At a time when Music Row was wedded to the Nashville sound, with its orchestral strings and overdubs (see chapters 2 and 3), Paycheck was getting down, getting dirty, and getting basic in the studio. With his instrumentation and with his topics, he ventured along musical side streets that Nashville execs were loath to touch as they tried to stick to the bright, clean boulevards of suburbia where big money was being made. How about "(Pardon Me) I've Got Someone to Kill"? Or there's "(Like Me) You'll Recover in Time," which tells of mental collapse. And then there's "The Cave," which paints a haunting picture of a post-nuclear world.

By the time Little Darlin' folded and Paycheck and Mayhew parted ways, Paycheck had already spent nearly everything he made, much of it on booze, and wound up in Los Angeles, where he wandered the streets destitute and alone. Tracked down by an industry executive, Nick Hunter, who liked Paycheck's work, Paycheck was convinced to reduce his drinking and return to performing.

Renowned producer Billy Sherrill then signed him to Epic (where Paycheck had much less control over his work than he had enjoyed at Little Darlin'), and by the end of 1971 the former LA street wanderer had returned to the Top Ten with his cover of a blues number, "She's All I Got." He followed that in 1972 with another success, "Someone to Give My Love To."

Once again, however, his personal troubles took over, as he was arrested and convicted for forging checks and received a suspended sentence. He had also gone back to drinking heavily. He was literally the king of Barstool Mountain, and it was hurting him. At the same time Sherrill marketed him as a crooner of love ballads, and Paycheck kept reaching the charts.

As Outlaw artists such as Waylon Jennings and Willie Nelson gained more fans, Sherrill decided to remake Paycheck to resemble them. (Some observers say that, for his part, Paycheck was desperate for acceptance by Jennings and Nelson.) Of course, Paycheck had already written songs that reflected country's honky-tonk roots, an essential element in Outlaw. And for those who interpreted Outlaw to mean antisocial behavior, Paycheck had plenty of that in his past as well.

Writing for the online magazine *No Depression,* Rich Kienzle points out: "It is no small irony that the Outlaw era of that decade, which finally made Paycheck a household name, was in some ways the most contrived phase of his career. The Outlaw ethos as practiced by Waylon, Willie, and Tompall [Glaser] involved total artistic control of recordings." Paycheck, however, was under Sherrill's direction.

The revamped Paycheck reached the charts with "Slide Off of Your Satin Sheets" and "I'm the Only Hell (My Mama Ever Raised)." Then came "Take This Job and Shove It," written by Outlaw artist David Allan Coe. The song became a megahit because it expressed the frustration so many Americans were feeling in the mid-1970s; the economy and wages had stagnated, and as more and more workers felt abused by their bosses, "take this job and shove it" became a catch phrase and Paycheck became their "spokesperson."

But the success of that record, linked to Paycheck's status as an Outlaw, only reinforced his self-destructive behavior. In fact, combining Paycheck with the Outlaw label was like tossing kerosene onto fire. As more money came in, he consumed more alcohol and drugs, and problems with the Internal Revenue Service forced him into bankruptcy. Then in 1985 he got into a barroom brawl with a man in Hillsboro, Ohio, and shot him in the head. The man lived, but Paycheck was found guilty of felony assault. As he was going through the appeals process, he was signed by Mercury Records and achieved a Top 20 single with "Old Violin," a tender and revealing song for what it says about an aging country artist nearing his end.

Paycheck spent two years in prison and then turned his life around. He embraced sobriety, renounced drugs, and gave antidrug talks to young kids as part of the community service required of his parole. He also refused to give up on his music and thus returned to songwriting, recording, and performing. In 1997 he was made a member of the *Grand Ole Opry*. He died in 2003 after a long illness. So little of his money remained that George Jones stepped in to help cover the cost of Paycheck's funeral.

Paycheck represents one of the more peculiar stories in the Outlaw movement. Socially, he was an outlaw even before the word became attached to country music and led to popular perceptions, or misperceptions, that it meant borderline behavior by unseemly renegades. Musically, he was writing songs as he wanted them before he was recast into the salable Outlaw image by Sherrill, who then gave him *less* freedom.

Johnny Paycheck raised hell for Nashville with his erratic behavior. He raised hell for his friends, who wanted him to control his excesses but felt helpless as he self-destructed. He raised hell with himself as he struggled with the demons inside of him. He was, quite possibly, the only hell his mama ever raised.

> *Money don't mean anything unless your heart feels good.*
> —Johnny Paycheck

David Allan Coe by Kenneth Marr (2013)

CHAPTER **8**

DAVID ALLAN COE

Spotlight

Coe was a ferocious and fearless songwriter. I've always respected that about him. He also has always done it his way.... I don't like everything he's written; I don't agree with everything that's come out of his mouth, but I do respect him because he's true to himself. He comes by all of it honestly.

—*J. B. BEVERLEY*

"**I**'ve sang about things that no country and western singer has ever sang about," said David Allan Coe. That's certainly the truth. Blazing down the highways of Texas on a Harley, Coe shook up Music Row with eccentric behavior that included claims he had once killed a man in prison and had three wives at the same time. Although his behavior often obscured and detracted from his exceptional talent as a songwriter and musician, it might also have fueled his creativity. Whatever the case, he has always been the type of guy who approaches life by slapping people in the face and then standing back to see their reaction. His modus operandi won some friends and made many enemies to the point that today opinions about him as a person range from "I never had any problems with Coe" to "He's a real prick."

At a time when artists such as Waylon Jennings and Willie Nelson were being called outlaws, Coe insisted that he was the only real Outlaw. Their claim to Outlaw status was that they were challenging the Nashville establishment. Coe's claim was that he was not only doing that but had also served twenty years in prison. He was as badass as badass could be. "So the real Outlaw is on the outside," Coe said about himself, "watching all them fuckers pretending to be outlaws. Yeah, it bothers me. It bothers me a lot."

Coe was born in Akron, Ohio, in 1939 into what he has described as a poor, dysfunctional family. He spent most of his teens and twenties in reform schools and prisons, including the Ohio State Penitentiary. Later, in an attempt to embellish his status as the "real" Outlaw, he claimed that this was the place where he had spent time on death row for having killed an inmate who tried to assault him sexually. (Supposedly, Coe hit him with a mop bucket.) A journalistic investigation in the early 1970s found the story to be false.

Coe arrived in Nashville in 1967 and, in an attempt to gain attention from a record company, at one point parked a hearse with his name on it outside the Ryman Auditorium, home of the *Grand Ole Opry*. He was signed to the Plantation label by the company's owner, Shelby Singleton, more so for his musical ability than his prankish ways. At Plantation, Coe recorded *Penitentiary Blues*, which displays his attachment to the music that influenced him so much as a young man, as did rockabilly, early rock 'n' roll, and country roots.

Coe developed the ability to, at one moment, write a tough drinking song, and at the next, a tender love song, such as the one that Tanya

Tucker made into a hit record in 1973, "Would You Lay with Me in a Field of Stone." Its lyrics evoke heartfelt love and the test of that love through the sacrifices a man and a woman might need to make in a relationship, all presented in the man pleading for the woman to be loyal and the woman promising she will.

Also in 1973 Coe signed with Columbia Records and adopted the persona of the Mysterious Rhinestone Cowboy. He appeared onstage in a black, tight-skinned suit replete with rhinestones, wore a huge black cowboy hat, and donned either a black mask or black facial makeup. Was Coe trying to create a sensation? Obviously. But when asked why he was hiding his face, he said that he was trying to say that how he looked meant nothing, that the music meant everything.

The music. When a couple of years later country pop star Glen Campbell scored a hit with a song titled "Like a Rhinestone Cowboy," Coe was forced to change his own appearance—no way would he allow anyone to confuse him with the clean-cut, mainstream, Disney-like Campbell. He never forgave Campbell for the unintended damage to his stage act. "Now I don't even want to use the term anymore," Coe said in the mid-1970s. "I even took it off my bus. It used to say the Rhinestone Cowboy on my bus, but I...painted it out."

With music that combined honky-tonk, the blues, and rock, Coe fit into the Outlaw movement without missing a beat. Columbia, however, struggled with trying to fit him into a category. At times the record label encouraged his Outlaw behavior, such as with the LP *David Allan Coe Rides Again,* which includes song lyrics where he proclaims that he lost his soul in Nashville and the cover of which has him wearing the "colors" of the Outlaw motorcycle gang (of which he remains a member). At other times Billy Sherrill tried to smooth over his image and direct him to more tender tunes that would find a wider audience.

Coe had recording success with "You Never Even Called Me by My Name" (1975). Written by Steve Goodman, the song parodies country music as Coe sings that for a country and western song to be perfect, it has to mention mama, trains, trucks, prison, and getting drunk. Coe's own composition "Longhaired Redneck" (1976) reached the charts, as did his "Willie, Waylon and Me" (also 1976), in which his bragging reaches ultimate heights as he tries to force his way into the Outlaw scene created by Nelson and Jennings and latch onto their fame. "In Texas the talk turned to Outlaws," he sings, "like Willie and Waylon and me."

The song was the leadoff track to his *Rides Again* album, which also includes "If That Ain't Country," in which he calls his oldest sister a "whore" and says he grew up having to "work like a nigger" for his room and board. Coe was right: these were things other country artists would never sing about. It's a humorous song, which also presents a clear image of the conditions Coe faced in his youth. ("My parents didn't want me," he once told a reporter.) He doesn't use the n-word so much as a racial slur but more as a way to compare his life to the downtrodden one that many blacks faced and depict how those "superior" whites thought about blacks and about whites like him: namely, they were trash.

Yet Coe also made some triple-X albums whose pornographic *and* racist-tinged lyrics have haunted him for years. He has never adequately answered why he made them and has presented conflicting stories about them. He says he intended them for bikers and that he regrets having ever recorded them. Yet he offers them for sale at his website and at his shows. Coe says, with some justification, that the lyrics to the "racist" songs are satirical and take a dig, for example, at the Ku Klux Klan. He adamantly denies being a racist. (At one show of his I attended, a woman standing next to me and who knows Coe confirmed this in a backhanded way when she said: "David doesn't hate black people. He hates everybody.")

By the 1980s Coe's career was waning at the same time as the Outlaw movement. Then in 1983 he reached the Top Ten with his cover of "The Ride" and "Mona Lisa Lost Her Smile," a song saturated with lush strings and clearly meant to appeal to the mainstream. (At that time he told *Billboard* magazine that he wanted to become more commercial.) Coe hasn't known exactly what to do with his Mona Lisa any more than he knows what to do with his XXX stuff. He usually avoids playing the song in concert and certainly would never play it for his biker buddies, who might howl with laughter at his retreat from his Outlaw ways.

Coe became a more settled family man in the 1980s when he married Jody Lynn Beaham. (This followed several marriages and divorces and remarriages, relationships so entangled that future genealogists might well find themselves needing to consume hefty supplies of aspirin while trying to figure it all out.) She gave birth to their son, Tyler Mahan, who today plays guitar in Coe's band; their daughters Tanya Montana and Shyanne Sherrill; and another son, Carson David.

Coe's 1999 CD, *Recommended for Airplay,* showed that he was still gifted as a singer and songwriter. While several of the tracks on it could fit seamlessly into the caliber and type of material he was recording decades ago, others show his continuing ability to incorporate new musical influences into his work. In the 2000s Coe has performed with the heavy metal band Pantera, with Hank Williams III, and with Kid Rock. Much slowed by poor health, Coe nevertheless continues a brutal tour schedule of some two hundred dates a year, and his gravelly voice remains impressive, although he has trouble walking and has to sit down while performing.(A serious car accident in spring 2013 sidelined Coe and made it uncertain as to when he would return to the stage)

Coe has produced an incredible catalog of songs—hundreds in all—that range from outrageous to bona fide artistic. As historians look back on his legacy, they will likely debate whether his excesses, particularly when promoting himself as the Mysterious Rhinestone Cowboy and as the only "real" Outlaw, helped him by drawing a clear line in the sand between himself and others or hurt by taking attention away from his music.

Whatever the assessment, if Outlaw means singing from the heart, no matter how it might hit the commercial fan, then Coe fits right in with his fellow rebels. If Outlaw means being true to yourself, then Coe again fits the category. Often manipulative and self-promoting, Coe nevertheless has expressed who *David Allan Coe is*, like it or not, take it or leave it. If that ain't country—and in this case, Outlaw country— well, then, you can, as Coe says in a song, "kiss my ass." "I don't like the word *image*," he once told a reporter. "When a lot of people hear that word, they think it's something we created. But, man, it's just my lifestyle. I just have a lifestyle that I live. I'm a biker. I mean, I'm no fuckin' different than any other fuckin' biker in the world."

In his song "Spotlight," Coe sings that he wishes someone would turn off the glare shining on him so he can be himself. The man in the spotlight is Coe, and it is not Coe. Or maybe it is both at the same time. Figure that one out, he says.

> *I don't think people really listen and really look.... If my face was important, I'd just come up here [onstage] and have a bunch of spotlights shining on it and sit on a fuckin' stool for an hour.*
>
> —David Allan Coe

Many other artists contributed to the creative period of country music that took hold in the 1970s and that challenged the studio control and Nashville sound dominant on Music Row. Space limitations in this book preclude them from being covered by full profiles, but overall, and to varying degrees, they display the creative attachment to roots country, and to the honky-tonk heritage, found in Outlaw music. (Yet additional artists are covered in the historical sketch found in chapter 2.)

As a songwriter, **Kris Kristofferson** showed tremendous originality in comparison to the bland lyrics and melodies Nashville promoted. The son of an air force officer, Kristofferson studied the poet William Blake and Shakespeare at Oxford, became a US Army captain, and served as a helicopter pilot. He was scheduled to teach literature at West Point, but dropped out of the military to become a songwriter.

His works reflect the sense of alienation and the desire for love and freedom that ran through the 1960s counterculture. And despite his cerebral and literary approach, he has always retained a sensibility for country music's roots. Among his most notable songs in the 1970s were "Me and Bobby McGhee," "For the Good Times," "Sunday Morning Coming Down" (a number one hit for Johnny Cash), "Help Me Make It through the Night," and "Why Me." His influence on country and rock artists remains considerable. Referring to Kristofferson's legacy, prominent Nashville record producer Randy Scruggs says: "Kris possibly more than anyone helped to define a new wave of music through his lyrics and his dedication to speaking out."

Jessi Colter, who married Outlaw artist Waylon Jennings in 1969, released her debut LP, *A Country Star Is Born,* in 1970. It was produced by her husband but sold only modestly. Five years later, however, her *I'm Jessi Colter,* recorded for Capitol Records, was certified gold with the help of the track "I'm Not Lisa," which was a hit single.

Later that year another single, "What's Happened to Blue Eyes," reached the Top Ten. Her LP *Jessi* in 1976 also sold well, and her single "It's Morning" climbed into the Top 20. She achieved Outlaw prominence primarily with her appearance on the album *Wanted! The Outlaws* (1976), which also featured Waylon Jennings, Willie Nelson, and Tompall Glaser and became the first country LP to sell more than a million units.

Jerry Jeff Walker, one of the leading artists on the progressive music scene in Austin, Texas, was at first a part of the Greenwich Village folk movement in New York City then joined a rock band and released his album *Mr. Bojangles* in 1968 on Atlantic Records. The title song became a big hit in 1971 for the Nitty Gritty Dirt Band.

Guy Clark, who was sometimes a cowriter with Walker, also inhabited the Austin music scene. His most notable album was *Old No. 1,* released in 1975. Although his work has been widely praised by music critics, most of his commercial success has come through his songs being covered by other artists. These include "L.A. Freeway" (Jerry Jeff Walker), "Heartbroke" (Ricky Skaggs), and "She's Crazy for Leavin'" (Rodney Crowell).

Ray Wylie Hubbard wrote one of the anthems of the new country music, "Up Against the Wall, Redneck Mother," which became a hit for Jerry Jeff Walker in 1973. Hubbard has presented music that mixes country, folk, and the blues, but his style is more often classified as Americana than Outlaw.

Mickey Newbury, who died in 2002, never placed a record in the country Top 50, but he was an influential songwriter whose work ranged from psychedelic pop to dark, moody ballads. His songs often displayed more blues than country, but his "Sweet Memories" was recorded by Dottie West and Don Gibson (as a duo), and several other of his songs were recorded by Roger Miller.

Promoted as a performer by his mother, Audrey, to take advantage of the Hank Williams name and heritage, **Hank Williams Jr.,** the son of the legendary Hank, began appearing onstage in 1957 at age eight. Up until the early 1970s, however, his music was largely a replay of his father's songs. Then he began to offer his own artistry, a combination of honky-tonk and Southern rock influences. In 1975 his LP *Hank Williams Jr. and Friends* clearly showed this trend, and by the late 1970s he emerged as a true Outlaw with such singles as "Family Tradition" and "Whiskey Bent and Hell Bound." In these he presents himself as a heavy-drinking, pot-smoking man who's living on borrowed time.

There followed several more hits that became increasingly Southern rock in character. These include "Dixie on My Mind," "All My Rowdy Friends (Are Coming Over Tonight)," and "Born To Boogie," which was the title cut from his 1988 Album of the Year (as declared by the Country Music Association). In his autobiography, *Living Proof* (Putnam, 1979), Williams reveals a more complex man than appears in his songs, but he once told an interviewer that when it came to his music, what his fans wanted the most was "to rock," and that was what he intended to do.

SECTION IV

THE TRANSITION

CHAPTER 9

THE BRIDGE TO NOW

Maybe it was *Urban Cowboy* that ruined Outlaw. John Travolta, the star of that 1980 movie, widened the appeal for the honky-tonk that had been gaining more popularity in blue-collar and white-collar America, both on assembly lines and in offices. Honky-tonk became a fad, but as it did so it degenerated into a watered-down, mellowed-out version of the edginess and creativity that had come out of the 1970s Outlaw movement.

"Hard hat days and honky-tonk nights" declared the movie poster for *Urban Cowboy.* Travolta played no redheaded stranger riding his horse into the western wilderness. Instead, he was Bud Davis, an oil refinery worker by day, a party animal by night at Gilley's honky-tonk in Pasadena, near Houston. He meets a girl (Sissy, played by Debra Winger). They live together. They dance together. Fights break out at Gilley's, and the mechanical bull takes center stage as a test for manliness.

The double-LP soundtrack to the movie became a hit, as did several of the tracks from it released as singles, especially "Looking for Love in All the Wrong Places" by Johnny Lee and "The Devil Went Down to Georgia" by Charlie Daniels. Suddenly cowboy hats, line dancing, and Lone Star beer filled some of the emptiness in the lives of suburbanites.

The boost for country music was huge: gross sales for 1980 topped those of the previous year by 24 percent. Additionally, there were more country radio stations than ever before.

The Nashville sound (see chapter 2) took a beating as fans flocked to the type of music they heard in the movie. Music Row reacted by scrambling to meet that demand, and perhaps predictably, country music morphed into a reformed pop: not so many strings anymore, but a hybrid of pseudocountry sounds. Many hit songs of the time charted on both the country and pop charts; really, what was the difference? After all, both had devolved into anemic commercialized sounds. Such performers as Janie Fricke, Razzy Bailey, Earl Thomas Conley, and T. G. Sheppard reflected this trend.

As the fad faded, Nashville went in two directions: mixing country with more pop and going "purist." The group Alabama, from Fort Payne, Alabama, embraced the country/pop combo. Critics said their songs resembled commercial jingles and relied too heavily on studio musicians. They certainly played it safe. They were neither experimental nor cutting edge but largely copied the sounds of the Eagles and the Charlie Daniels Band. Yet they were in line with country artists of the past who brought new musical influences into their work, in this case rural South overlaid with laid-back California.

Alabama sold millions of records: between 1980 and 1987, they had twenty-seven consecutive number one hits on the country charts. They continued to have Top Ten records into the 1990s and toured extensively until they retired in 2003.

By the 1990s, however, the most dominant country performer in terms of record and concert sales was Garth Brooks. No one else came close. College educated and the symbol of clean-cut America—no scruffy, bearded Outlaw look for him—Brooks was influenced as much by Journey, James Taylor, and Billy Joel as George Jones, Hank Williams, or Johnny Cash.

Brooks played at huge venues, such as football stadiums, and put on shows that were closer to rock than country. He sometimes appeared amid a ring of fire, under a simulated rainstorm, or, in at least one instance for a show broadcast on national television, flying through the air attached to cables. Brooks sold more than thirty-three million albums and was pointing to country pop as the way for Nashville to make *big* money.

That traditional or purist side, sometimes called "new traditionalism," was represented first and foremost by Ricky Skaggs. While growing up in eastern Kentucky, he was influenced by his family's attachment to traditional country and born-again Christianity and at age fifteen began playing mandolin in a bluegrass band. In the 1980s he gravitated more toward country and recorded twenty Top Ten singles and earned three gold albums. While he maintained a basic bluegrass sound, he replaced the banjo with drums and an electric bass and made the harmonies fuller to evoke a more pleasant rendering than often found in the lonely evocation of bluegrass.

In the 1990s Skaggs promoted traditional country sounds through a television show on the Nashville Network, a weekly radio show, and the annual Ricky Skaggs Pickin' Party at Wolf Trap Farm Park in Virginia. At the same time he returned increasingly to bluegrass and in 2002 was the performing host for a PBS special, *All-Star Bluegrass.*

With his success in the 1980s, Skaggs paved the way for other artists who wanted to emphasize country music's roots. Dwight Yoakam, who was born in Kentucky in 1956 and raised in Ohio, was at first attracted to the rock music coming out of the countercultural era of his youth, particularly the Beatles and the Byrds, whose folk-rock sound came from California. But his parents also influenced him with their preference for country music.

Yoakam moved to Nashville in 1977, but that only reinforced his discontent for Music Row, which he felt had abandoned true country. Consequently, he moved to California the following year, where he found himself surrounded by the Bakersfield sound begun by Buck Owens and continued by Merle Haggard.

In the early 1980s, Yoakam began opening for rock acts in Los Angeles, and Dave Alvin of the Blasters (one of those acts) used his connections in the music business to move Yoakam's career forward. Alvin, in fact, was one of the earliest of the Yoakam enthusiasts. About the first time he saw Yoakam perform, Alvin says: "I was floored.... I just walked up to Dwight and said, 'Order the limousine now! You're gonna be a star.'" Alvin's prediction was fulfilled when Yoakam scored his first hit album in 1986 with *Guitars, Cadillacs, Etc., Etc.* on the Reprise label. "I'm a honky-tonk man," he declares, and proves it with the song of that title, with the title track, and with the way he shapes his music. Guitars, Cadillacs, and hillbilly music—there couldn't be anything more in contrast with flotsam, jetsam, and contrived sounds.

The album proves Yoakam's love for country roots and 1960s rock. Pete Anderson, a guitarist and record producer, helped Yoakam bring together the sounds of both. Moreover, Anderson had complete faith in Yoakam as a performer and shared Yoakam's hopes. Anderson later said: "One person can have a dream. And depending on your age and when you have it, people can beat it out of you. But two people with a dream, that's a lot tougher."

"The rawness had left country music," Yoakam said about his early career, "and I knew I had to leave some rawness in it to make the name I wanted to make." Indeed, his originality has caused him to be labeled a visionary artist. But as his statement indicates, he was ambitious and anxious enough to create an image that went along with creating a name.

Yoakam's *Hillbilly Deluxe* (there's that word "hillbilly" again— say it too loudly on Music Row and your ass will be put in stir), released in 1987, and his *Buenas Noches,* released in 1988, both went platinum. Yoakam's commercial appeal took a hit in 1995 with his CD *Gone.* The effort received plenty of press coverage and good reviews but sold poorly—not because the music was bad, but because it was too different from what country fans expected from Yoakam and too different from what they were more into by the mid-'90s, mainly the commercial dazzle of Garth Brooks.

As Yoakam biographer Don McLeese says in *Dwight Yoakam: A Thousand Miles from Nowhere* (University of Texas Press, 2012), some analysts consider *Gone* to be among Yoakam's best works while others call it his "what the fuck" album. His music becomes transformed with tom-toms, orchestral strings, bongos, and Mexicali trumpets. One reviewer, McLeese points out, called it "hypnotic sonic textures" and said that Yoakam was an artist who "has made a career of defying expectations."

Steve Earle arrived in Nashville in the mid-1970s as a song-writer, with acoustic guitar in hand and fresh from having played anti-Vietnam War songs at coffeehouses. "I was on my way to New York when I first got [there]," he says. "I never got any farther." He adds: "It's where the best songwriters were." He was influenced by such artists as Guy Clark and Neil Young, both of whom played in Nashville, and most especially by Townes Van Zandt. "I ran across

[him] making art with absolutely no regard for how big or small the audience was, or even who was in his audience," Earle says. "He made the art for himself."

Earle turned to playing the electric guitar after he heard *My Aim Is True* (1976) by Elvis Costello, and with Bruce Springsteen's "Born in the U.S.A.," he concluded, "If I make a record that says something about who I am, I'll be able to live with it, be proud of it." Thus came about, in 1986, his LP *Guitar Town* that won the acclaim of country fans. "There would have been no *Guitar Town,*" he says, "without Elvis Costello."

Earle then gravitated more toward rock with his LP and single *Copperhead Road* (1989). Meanwhile, his personal life went down the tubes as addiction to cocaine and heroin cost him several marriages, time in jail, and more time in rehab. After he got clean, he returned to writing country and folk songs for *Train a Comin'* on Winter Harvest (1995). His recordings in the 1990s featured the songs he had written some twenty years earlier and others he had just developed.

Not only did his *style* break with mainstream Nashville but also his *politics*. In the early 2000s, he wrote songs critical of the American involvement in Iraq and Afghanistan. "I'm an unapologetic lefty," he said at the time, "and what I'm pissed off about is this war.... Music is the only weapon available to me." Agree with him or not, he was putting his ideas forward in an industry that usually avoided such controversy and, when political, took more to flag waving than anything else.

Emmylou Harris gained prominence in the early 1970s when she sang duets with Gram Parsons. After Parsons died in 1973, she went on to perform solo and in 1976 had a number one hit single with "Together Again," written by Buck Owens. A true eclectic, Harris has ventured into pop, rock, folk, gospel, and blues, but has seldom strayed far from her country roots. In the 1980s she promoted the careers of Rodney Crowell, Ricky Skaggs, and Vince Gill. She never forgot her time with Parsons, however, and how much his music has meant and still means to her. She has said that she wants to carry on his legacy by bringing together folk with other elements "but always coming back to that electric country blues."

Joe Diffie released *Honky Tonk Attitude* in 1993, which was more commercial than Dwight Yoakam's honky-tonk work but nevertheless raised the banner of traditional country music. He also developed "turbo-tonk," a mix of country with a heavy amount of rock.

The Dixie Chicks stirred controversy nearly from the start of their Nashville career. At first the talk was about whether they were too commercial and shallow, or did they really have substance? Then the group that consisted of sisters Martie and Emily Irwin and Natalie Maines (who replaced original member Laura Lynch) stirred a topical debate in 1999 with their song "Goodbye Earl," in which they sing of a wife murdering a husband who had battered her—and then hiding the body. When there was an outcry over the "violent and lawless nature" of the song, many women reacted by saying those who complained were applying a sexist double standard. At least since the time of country pioneer Jimmie Rodgers, in the 1920s, men had sung about killing women; now when the shoe was on the other foot...

Nevertheless, the Dixie Chicks sold millions of records until 2003, when they were exiled from country radio for a remark Maines made while on a London stage shortly before the United States invaded Iraq. "Just so you know," she said, "we're ashamed the president of the United States is from Texas (Maines's home state)." The comment was honest enough, but it raised hackles at a time of intense patriotic feelings stirred by a president who, in the end, misled the American people about the war. The Dixie Chicks responded to the controversy with their song "Not Ready to Make Nice," so bold and so strongly written that it should end any lingering doubt—if there was any—about their considerable talent.

When Marty Stuart released his first LP *Marty Stuart: With a Little Help from My Friends* in 1978, he displayed his bluegrass background. For an album in 1982, he went rockabilly. Then in 1989 *Hillbilly Rock* fused traditional country with a rock beat. He repeated this style in 1991 with *Tempted* and in 1996 issued *Honky Tonkin's What I Do Best*. In his performances and songwriting, as well as in the several books and magazine articles he has written, he has been a tireless promoter of country music's roots.

In the 1980s and then again in the 1990s, Lyle Lovett confounded country radio with songs of dry humor and memorable characters. But where to place him? He seemed too erudite for country and often too folkish and jazzy. Nevertheless, in the 1980s he scored several top twenty hits, and in 1989 his version of "Stand by Your Man," previously a hit for Tammy Wynette, won a Grammy. But country radio stations ignored his 1992 LP *Joshua Judges Ruth* because it was too bluesy. (It eventually went gold thanks to airplay on the television network VH1.) He was considered one of the more creative artists of the 1990s who was thinking, writing, and performing outside the Music Row box.

Of a similar creative ilk, and even more ignored by country radio stations, was k.d. lang. In the 1980s her honky-tonk band, the reclines, gained a large following in Canada with their LP *A Truly Western Experience*. (Lang was born in Consort, Alberta, Canada.) Her 1989 album, *Absolute Torch and Twang,* went gold, with songs written by her, along with covers of traditional country tunes. Although she has ventured into other musical forms, especially jazz and Latin, in 1994 she wrote and scored the soundtrack for *Even Cowgirls Get the Blues,* which again reached back to roots country.

One of the most successful artists who held to those roots was Alan Jackson. He moved to Nashville in 1985, replete with an education in the school of Merle Haggard, George Jones, and Hank Williams. While working in the mailroom for the Nashville Network, he wrote songs and played in local clubs. His break came in 1989 when he was signed to Arista Records and then recorded *Here in the Real World.* Three singles from the LP reached the Top Ten. Then came *Don't Rock the Jukebox,* which sold more than four million units. But it was *A Lot About Livin',* with the hit single "Chattahoochee," that made him a superstar. Sales of the LP topped six million, and he went on in the 1990s to have a string of other hits. Throughout, he has minimized pop and rock influences to stay close to the traditions of country music.

With Garry Bennett as its leader, the band BR5-49 achieved cult status in the mid-1990s. Johnny Horton, Bill Monroe, Merle Haggard, Flatt and Scruggs, Charley Pride—these were the biggest influences on the group, according to Bennett. (He himself doesn't care for Hank Williams, whom he considers to be too nasally and whiny.) But as a kid in the 1970s, Bennett also listened to the Outlaws, and to him Willie Nelson's *Red Headed Stranger* was "epic" because of its simplicity, because it was old and new at the same time, and because it was real, with a real theme. "There was nothing fluffy about it," he says.

BR5-49 played classic country and ramped up original tunes in a form sometimes described as "country boogie." In 1996 their cover of a long-ago Moon Mullican hit, "Cherokee Boogie," earned them a Grammy nomination. Their music videos borrowed from the intoxicatingly upbeat, fun, exclamatory 1980s pop scene. To many younger musicians, BR5-49 showed that country music could be enjoyable, experimental, and hip.

Bennett says he hated the stuff being turned out by Garth Brooks and similar artists but that there was redemption with Ricky Skaggs, Randy Travis, and Dwight Yoakam. In general, he says, BR5-49 didn't think too often about the Music Row production line because "we loved what we were doing, and we had a frenetic energy." He adds: "We were belting it out from the heart—and when someone is belting it from the heart, you can tell." Their love for their music, their energy, their sincere effort—these accounted for their popularity.

At the same time, Dale Watson (profiled in this book) began cranking out his songs about work, family, and booze, all contained in lyrics dedicated to real people he met in the honky-tonks and in his travels. His debut LP, *Cheatin' Heart Attack* (1995), includes "Nashville Rash," in which he condemns Music Row for forgetting its country roots.

With his commanding baritone voice and handsome good looks, Randy Travis attracted many listeners who would otherwise have ignored anything coming from Music Row. From his father he learned the music of Hank Williams and Lefty Frizzell. When Travis moved to Nashville in 1981, record executives gave him the cold shoulder for being too traditional. Five years later, however, his LP *Storms of Life* reached number one and sold more than three million copies, fueled by such tracks as "On the Other Hand," "1982," and "Diggin' Up Bones." He followed it in 1987 with the even bigger selling *Always and Forever,* which won Album of the Year honors from the Country Music Association. Other hit singles continued into the 1990s, including a notable duet with George Jones, "A Few Ole Country Boys."

John Anderson, who first began releasing hit records in the 1980s, came back with *Seminole Wind* in 1992, an album noted for its title track and "Straight Tequila Night." His music emanated from the honky-tonks by way of Lefty Frizzell.

Junior Brown has always had a hard time winning any acceptance from country radio. But he has been a formidable advocate and performer of roots country since even before his arrival on the Austin music scene in 1979. His command of the guitar, his clever songwriting, and his adept playing of the guit-steel, a combination electric and steel guitar that he invented, has earned him a considerable following from alternative country fans, and in 1996 he won the CMA's Music Video of the Year Award for "My Wife Thinks You're Dead."

From the music fringes, there appeared cowpunk, a blending of country roots with punk rock. The most artistic and prominent of the bands that fit this category was Jason and the Scorchers, begun in 1981 by Jason Ringenberg, the son of an Illinois pig farmer. They released their first LP in 1985, *Lost & Found,* but, as might be expected, it found no acceptance from country radio, for which punk was a completely alien and "unmusical" style. The Scorchers broke up in 1989 but reunited in 1993 and soon released three more albums: *A Blazing Grace* (1995), *Reckless Country Soul* (1995, reissue), and *Clear Impetuous Morning* (1996).

Other artists abound in this period (the Mavericks, the Derailleurs, Wayne Hancock, Blue Rodeo, and so on) to join those discussed above as a subterranean current churning beneath the seemingly monolithic surface of Nashville pop. Together these roots artists or purists or neotraditionalists were assigned a variety of descriptive labels by fans and music analysts. Americana became the most in vogue, although many applied the cumbersome No Depression. (The name likely derives from a song the Carter Family recorded in the 1930s, "No Depression in Heaven," and the album *No Depression,* released in 1990 by the band Uncle Tupelo.) In 1995 a trade magazine, the *Gavin Report,* began issuing an Americana chart to track and rank the airplay of roots artists who usually were ignored by country radio.

Some artists, however, looked at Americana and said it wasn't honky-tonk enough. They wanted more edge to their music, both lyrically and instrumentally. Some derided Americana as "college music," meaning it was too wistful and soft. In other words, it lacked a ballsy attitude. They looked at the 1970s Outlaws for their role models, as artists who sang from the heart a type of music connected to country's roots yet nonetheless creative, topically and otherwise. Those musicians, with their dedication to honky-tonk, had stood up to the Nashville pop machine, had stood on their principles and by their guns, and had succeeded artistically and monetarily while they revolutionized country music.

As the 2000s emerged, these musical dissidents had every reason to believe that roots country had been hijacked by charlatans. Mainstream Nashville, Nashville pop, country pop—whatever it might be called—had come to dominate Music Row more strongly than back in the 1970s. Lady Antebellum, Sugarland, Taylor Swift, ad nauseam. The commercial pandering wasn't without merit, the dissidents argued, for some good songs could be found in the morass of mediocrity, and some good times could be had by listening to them.

But what rankled the dissidents was that Nashville treated the word "country" as if it were its copyright and in the process had ripped country music from its roots. Moreover, country pop threatened to drown all country artists and sweep them into oblivion as radio stations and record studios shut their doors to anything that failed to meet the criteria for selling the Music Row product. *If we could just knock down some of those doors,* the dissidents thought, *much as had Waylon and Willie and Billy Joe back in the Seventies.*

Yet the dissidents know that technology has changed since the 1970s, and with this change the world of music and the rules of the game have shifted. Some observers point to a more fractured setting as redefining what can be done with music and thus creating an environment more helpful to any rebels, a setting in which radio stations have competition from the Internet, YouTube, and music-sharing sites and in which major studios have to compete with indie labels and the "I can cut my own CD in my garage" groups.

So has this made the prospect of a challenge from the music dissidents more or less likely to take hold? That remains to be answered.

In any event, the honky-tonking, edgier, I'm-fed-up dissidents say, "Fuck this; I'm playing country roots, and I'm playing it from *my* heart." They have become the new Outlaws. They have resurrected what it means to be a true country artist. They have resurrected spirits from the 1970s. They have resurrected Outlaw. As Waylon Jennings once said: "There's always another way to do things.... Your way." *That's what today's Outlaws have chosen to do.*

SECTION V

RED-BLOODED OUTLAWS

I've been to church,
I've been to jail.
I've seen heaven,
And I've seen hell.

> Bert David Newton
> "Backwoods"
> From *The Live*

THE PHOENIX ARISES

And so we come to the heart of the matter; we return to the profiles of current Outlaw artists. Jackson Taylor has already been covered in chapter 1. In discussing him, and in discussing the following Outlaw artists, no attempt has been made to be inclusive; indeed, every attempt has been made to be selective. All of these artists know the roots of country music and have been influenced by them to varying but considerable degrees. They have also opened their ears and applied their talent to recent developments in music while remaining honest and true to what they feel within themselves.

If there be a debate over those whom I chose to write full profiles about, or if there be a debate over who more aptly fits the category of Outlaw and who does not, then let it serve as fodder for building interest in these artists and their work and in Outlaw music in general.

The artists profiled herein, and scores of others like them across America, are giving the Outlaw movement its wings. They are giving the movement its energy at a time when, in the words of a reporter for National Public Radio, "country music has more polish than the hood of a truck in a Chevy commercial."

They are breathing life into Outlaw so that it will, like a phoenix born from the ashes of a forgotten but noble past, soar into the minds, the spirits, and the hearts of country fans and reveal the richness of a world beyond the studios on Music Row.

Shooter Jennings, Petal, MS (2012)

CHAPTER 10

SHOOTER JENNINGS

Born Again

Up so high that we could touch the sky,
The heavens unfolding beneath us.
And we knew we were never gonna die,
'Cause the hell that we raised was between us.
"BORN AGAIN"
FROM FAMILY MAN

I had just finished interviewing Shooter Jennings on his tour bus—which was parked along a dirt alley behind a stage at a crawfish festival near Houston, Texas—and was walking near a grove of tall oak trees when I started staring at the night skies. They were glistening with stars and aglow with a moon that seemed to be looking down at me with a grin. Someone had hung wind chimes on the branches, and as the breeze moved, the chimes sounded strangely ethereal.

Clang, tinkle, clang, swoosh, tinkle. I half expected some old Juju priestess to cast a spell, reach her hand down, and lift my spirit to the heavens. Or maybe I prayed that would happen. Whatever the case, I was overcome by a strong sense of kinship—a bond that had brought me together with Shooter, Shooter with his dad, and all of us swirled together in this mystical moment.

Before I interviewed Shooter, I had read the autobiography of his father, the late 1970s Outlaw legend Waylon Jennings. With the story from that book and with what Shooter told me in Houston, it became obvious to me they were touching each other in a deeper and more intimate way than I, as an outsider, could ever grasp, but that I tried, nevertheless, to understand.

On one level, the musician father and the musician mother, Jessi Colter, had begotten a musician son who had turned new Outlaw artist, offering music as creative and original as that of his parents. But more than the physical, more than procreative DNA was at work: despite their separation through death, father and son were still together, united by the essence of their music and the integrity of their souls.

"So Shooter," I said to him as he came offstage after having played three songs made famous by Waylon, "do you feel a connection to your father when you do that?" He replied immediately: "Most definitely. It's more than me pleasing the fans," he said. "I really do sense his presence. I like to pick the songs that relate to me, whether they are his originals or not. I like playing them, and I like giving them back to the audience."

With Shooter's family history and his attachment to his dad, I was a bit taken aback by a friend of mine's reaction when I told him that I was going to interview Shooter for a book on the history of Outlaw country music. "Everyone knows he's a Southern rocker," my friend said. It made me wonder if I had missed something, that maybe Shooter had given up his country roots.

I asked him about this as we sat on his tour bus. He told me that he always felt that his lyrical approach was country, not rock—even when his music had a rock beat. "I would say that I really have more Hank Jr. than I do Lynyrd Skynyrd in the influence, in the songwriting approach," Shooter said, "because [those] early Hank Jr. records, [they were] so powerful, and what was so cool about him is that there was no doubt that he was a country artist because the approach was country. But he brought in those Southern-rock kind of sounds. So when I think of an album like *Put the O Back in Country* [one of Shooter's CDs, released in 2005], Southern rock crowds aren't going to understand what I'm talking about as much as a country crowd is going to understand it. I'm referencing the state of country radio, I'm referencing country artists and things like that."

He added: "I always felt that when we went into the rock form, we did it very tastefully. I wanted to push the boundaries of it being cool *and* country sonically, which *is* like Southern rock."

As I sat across from him, Shooter ran his hand through his shoulder-length black hair, looked at me straight-on through his tinted aviator glasses, and continued with his comments about his music and Southern rock. "I read an article by Tom Petty, it was in *Rolling Stone*," Shooter recounted. "Tom Petty said that when Lynyrd Skynyrd came out, Petty didn't think of them as a Southern rock band but as an English kind of band, like the Who and all those guys, the way the sound of those records were. So for me, what I wanted to do with [my early country records] was pushing the boundaries of, in a way, the taste of music.... I might be drawing from Quicksilver Messenger Service before I'm going to be drawn to an AC/DC vibe."

Because Shooter is only thirty-three, I didn't expect him to count among his musical influences any bands from the 1960s, let alone one of the more obscure psychedelic rock bands like Quicksilver. It turns out, however, that in educating himself he worked his way backwards, first discovering more recent bands, those that were popular when he was growing up, and then delving into earlier works and, in time, going deep into the past.

Question: You mentioned Quicksilver as an influence. What gets you to go that far back?

Shooter: I liked Guns N' Roses when I was younger, and that was mainly because it was intimidating music for me, because I was young, and I remember all these other kids that were listening to it, and it was bad, dirty rock 'n' roll. I didn't like the hair thing [the hair bands]; I was too young for that, really. I got into Nine Inch Nails because I heard the *Broken* album, and they were just about to put out the *Downward Spiral*, and I got them and I started loving them just in time for that record to come out. That record blew my fucking mind. That's really what got me started playing music, because I played piano and drums, and I saw that he [Trent Reznor] was doing everything himself. He was playing all the instruments and programming, so I started doing stuff like that.

Through Nine Inch Nails, I got into David Bowie. And that's where it started, because after that I got into T. Rex, and I got into that whole scene, and after that I got into the Beatles. Zeppelin took me awhile to like.... I got into Pink Floyd big time when I discovered the *Dark Side of the Moon* and *The Wall*...and Blue Öyster Cult at different points in time, I love that band. Even Tommy James and the Shondells got psychedelic on your ass, and the Chamber Brothers. You start into all that kind of shit, and you start learning it and trying to find more stuff. And I love Moody Blues.

That's a heady scene he brings into his music. Add to these influences the country roots at work on Shooter, and the first album he recorded, *Electric Rodeo* (which was released shortly after the CD *Put the O Back in Country),* could as easily have been titled *Eclectic Rodeo.*

Question: Of those Outlaws from the '70s, which had the biggest influence on you musically?

Shooter: My dad, because I feel and relate to and understand my dad's sound. Willie Nelson is one of the best writers in the world. Definitely Kris [Kristofferson], Willie, and my dad, and [Johnny] Cash. But I think I was really, really influenced in the songwriting of Kris and Willie, on top of my dad. I love artists like Steve Young, I'm really a big fan of his music.... I love John Conlee, and I love Keith Whitley.

No one I know of would ever label John Conlee as an Outlaw, so Shooter was including a mix of names toward the end of his comment. Conlee was clearly a man of commercial appeal, but such a musician can have value and substance, and Shooter believes that was the case with Conlee. "Songs like 'Backside of Thirty,'" he says, "for a guy my age means a lot."

Question: Do you get into the earlier country stuff? Like Hank Williams?

Shooter: Yeah, I love Hank Sr., and I love Ernest Tubb, and I love Jimmie Rodgers. But at the end of the day, I listen to far less of that than I do to what was made in the '60s and '70s.

Released in 2006, *Electric Rodeo* reveals the psychedelic rock, Southern rock, and Outlaw country influences that Shooter discusses above. "Gone to Carolina," the most requested song on the CD, displays the strongest attachment to Southern rock by way of Hank Williams Jr., while in "The Song Is Still Slipping Away," which begins with a moaning steel guitar, Shooter goes straight for the traditional country trifecta: "With the *band*, a *bottle*, and this old *guitar*/On the back of some bus on the road."

In "Some Rowdy Women," he sings that he would gladly trade his big-city living for some wild life with the opposite sex "in a honky-tonk tonight." Shooter alludes to Waylon in "It Ain't Easy" when he sings: "When I was just a young boy/My daddy came to me/Said, 'Son, out of this world there's a lot of things/That are going to make you feel like you're supposed to be/You don't have to read the good book/To be a good man just the same/And forget about the money/ Money ain't brought nothing to your daddy but pain.'"

Shooter begins *Electric Rodeo* with the title track, and it both proclaims allegiance to his dad and distances himself from him. It starts with a quick, heavy bass entry, a loud keyboard, and rock-style shouts. "My daddy was a loaded gun," Shooter proclaims, and thus brings Waylon onto the scene. "He said, 'It ain't no fun living on the run, son'/But everywhere I go trouble seems to follow." Shooter later segues into both the title and the lyrics from one of his dad's most prominent songs when he intones: "Oh, this time will be the last time/ Oh, this time will be the last time."

With *Electric Rodeo,* Shooter says, the fun came with "the blending of the rock thing with [country]. That record to me was a really good establishment of that." Clearly, like a happy man at a banquet, Shooter feasts from different genres and from them learns how to create his own musical recipes

Question: When you started your musical career did you feel the need to differentiate yourself from your dad?

Shooter: No.... But if I [start] going into the Waylon territory, it's very apparent that I'm not as good a singer as him and it's just me doing him. If I could nail that thing, maybe I would do more of that sound. I went in the direction to what felt natural for me, which was involving a lot more energy and loud and psychedelic. I was really into that, I always have been. So we always tried to bring that into the records.

Shooter's attraction to rock actually harkens back to his father's early career. Long before Shooter was born, Waylon played bass for Buddy Holly. In 1959 Waylon became part of Buddy's tour, the Winter Dance Party, which also featured Ritchie Valens and the Big Bopper.

Then came a tragedy that redirected the future for Waylon. The rock stars and their bands had been traveling by bus, but as the miles piled up Buddy grew tired, and in February he decided to take a charter flight from Clear Lake, Iowa, to Moorhead, Minnesota, which he booked for himself and some others in the group. Those not taking the plane would remain on the bus. Then, at the last minute, Waylon, who was scheduled to take the plane trip, traded places with the Big Bopper, who was sick with the flu and wanted to fly with Buddy. The fateful decision saved Waylon's life, for the plane crashed in Minnesota, killing Buddy, Ritchie (who was also a late addition to the flight when he "won" a coin toss with Tommy Allsup and thus got to escape the bus ride), the Big Bopper, and the pilot.

Adding more poignancy to the story, before the flight Buddy and Waylon engaged in a joking exchange. "I hope your damned bus freezes up again," Buddy said to him. He responded: "Well, I hope your ol' plane crashes."

By the time Shooter was born, Waylon had already taken his career into mainstream country and then into Outlaw. He had become good friends with Willie Nelson, and the two artists were selling millions of records. He had also married Jessi Colter back in 1969. To Waylon and Jessi, though, the birth of Shooter was special. "Our little Waylon Albright," Waylon writes in his autobiography, "was the joy of our lives." And, more than that, he was "the symbol of our togetherness, from the moment we brought his baby bed into the house."

Yet at this time, Waylon was deeply into cocaine. With the pressure, the money, and the fame he had bought a ticket on the drug train, and he was riding it fast and with reckless abandon around all the steep curves that life presented him.

> *I'd sit behind my desk with two lines of lyrics on the paper in front of me, sometimes for two, three hours thinking. Another two lines, these scraped neatly in parallel white rows and chopped with a razor blade, lay in readiness on the side. I'd have an idea for a song, but my mind would be running and speeding so fast I'd forget the next phrase before I had a chance to put pen to paper.*
>
> —Waylon Jennings[*]

Although Shooter told me that his father's cocaine use never got in the way of his relationship with his dad, Waylon says in his autobiography that the coke had shortened his attention span and that this made his toddler son feel uneasy.

---

[*]All statements by Waylon Jennings in this chapter come from Waylon Jennings and Lenny Kaye, *Waylon: An Autobiography* (Warner Books, 1996).

By 1984, when Shooter was five years old, Waylon concluded that his addiction was hurting Jessi and also Shooter, so he decided to purge his "toxins." He told his wife: "Jessi, my spirit's dying, and there's nothing I can do about it." As he was going through detox, he would sit on the porch swing at his house and watch Shooter play in the yard. Shooter "was my greatest inspiration," Waylon later said.

> *Jessi always wanted me to get off drugs because I wanted to do it, not because she told me I had to.... Through her faith, she had a vision that I would get clean.... "Lord," her prayer used to go, "watch over ol' Waylon 'cause he's so dumb."*
> —Waylon Jennings

Shooter learned directly from his dad about the cocaine addiction. Waylon was always afraid that Shooter would hear about it from some kid or some teacher in school. So Waylon told Shooter that the reason he used to swear so much was because "I was on drugs." "Oh, you mean you drink beer?" Shooter asked. "No, I did cocaine." It had to have been a tough father and son talk.

Shooter loved to listen to what Waylon called the Daddy Tapes. These were the cassettes and vinyl records of Waylon's music. One song Shooter listened to over and over again and that became ingrained in him was "Are You Sure Hank Done It This Way," with the lyrics: "Lord, it's the same old tune, fiddler, and guitar/Where do we take it from here?" Perhaps Shooter was wondering where *he* should take it.

"My dad was a great dad," Shooter told me. "An example I always give is that I was really into Nine Inch Nails, and Woodstock '94 came around, and I was fifteen, and somebody I knew had tickets to go see it. My dad said, 'I'm not going to tell you to go or not to go, but I'm going to ask you not to go because I'm worried about you. But if you don't go, I'll order the whole thing on pay-for-view, and we'll watch it together.' So we sat down and watched it. We watched Nine Inch Nails, we watched all of it.

"Not only did he want to know what made me tick and wanted to understand the music that I liked, but he also found things that *he* liked. He loved Primus [a metal band], and he went out and bought *Pork Soda* [their third studio CD, released in 1993]. He had the *Pork Soda* tape in his car. He was open to me like that."

Shooter grew up surrounded by celebrities. A family photo shows him as an infant being cradled by the heavyweight boxing champion Muhammad Ali. Johnny Cash, Willie Nelson, Billy Joe Shaver, and Kris Kristofferson were regulars in the family household.

Question: How did your parents bring you up so you didn't get big-headed about the family you were coming from?

Shooter: They were just very real. My dad cared so much about music that it never was,... I was never exposed to some type of celebrity culture or something. He had people around him that were famous, but they were people who were real artists. He didn't act like somebody who thought his shit didn't stink. He was very real, down to earth.

Question: What was it like for you in school since you came from a famous family?

Shooter: In elementary school there was a lot of kids, who, because of their parents, were more aware of my dad, his history and the fame and all, than I was. I went to an old-money school in Nashville, so I never felt like I fit in there.

❧❦

On his first day [at school], after he put his little arms around my neck, I stayed outside and waited under a nearby tree....

I had written a story, with Shooter's help, about a racehorse that didn't grow. He was a miniature pony, who reminded me of when Shooter had been the shortest kid in his class. He'd worried about it....

The horse in the story, nicknamed Useless, was the runt of the litter and the pride of the farm.... A lightning storm allowed Useless to become a hero, rescuing the bigger horses from the barn when a fire erupted. "The Little Horse That Didn't Grow" had saved the day.

—Waylon Jennings

High school was more enjoyable for Shooter. He says, "I went to a liberal arts kind of school, and I loved it. I loved those two years. So it took me awhile to find my crowd, but after that I felt at home. My dad always said to me, 'Don't ever try to be one of the boys because you're never going to be.' It took me a long time to figure that out, but once I did, it was 'I'm going to be who I want to be, and I'm not going to be who people expect me to be.'

"It's always been kind of a curse for me; people think they've got me pegged before I walk into the room. But [my dad] encouraged me to be who I was. And he also knew I was never going to be just an average person because of who *he* was, and there was always going to be kind of a thing where people knew about me."

Question: What is your relationship like with your mom, Jessi Colter?

Shooter: My mom is awesome. I love her. She's very spiritual. As a kid, she was trying to make me read the Bible. I was like, "I don't want to read it." But now I'm into theology and all that stuff. I've kind of gotten a grasp on it and explored lots of different avenues and have found my own understanding of it.

The gift of faith. [Jessi] lived it in her daily life, sang it every day at the piano when she turned to the Psalms.
—Waylon Jennings

Jessi was born Miriam Johnson in 1943 in Phoenix, Arizona, and her mother was an ordained Pentecostal minister. Jessi was raised in the church and at age six began singing in the choir. In 1961 she recorded her first record, a country song, "Lonesome Road." Shortly thereafter she took her stage name, Jessi Colter, from her great-great uncle Jesse Colter, who had been a member of the 1800s train-robbing James Gang. Pentecostal thus converged in name with genuine social outlaw.

In 1975 Jessi's LP *I'm Jessi Colter,* which included the hit single "I'm Not Lisa," went gold. Her appearance on the album *Wanted! The Outlaws* in 1976 with her husband, and with Willie Nelson and Tompall Glaser, along with the duet she sang in 1981 with Waylon on the hit single "Storms Never Last," cemented her reputation as an Outlaw artist.

Musically, Jessi's influence on Shooter has, like that of his father, always been around as a source of direction and inspiration. Mother and son even recorded and wrote a song together, "Please Carry Me Home," which appears on Jessi's CD *Out of the Ashes* (released in 2006). The song carries an intensely religious theme that builds to the ending: "Oh Lord, please have mercy/I've nowhere to go/When the temptation's over/Please carry me home."

It's steeped in Jessi's faith, and no one who listens to it can come away without realizing the special spiritual environment in which

Shooter grew up, encouraged much more by his mom than his dad, whose spirituality was less pronounced. That Shooter wrote and recorded this song with his mom attests to their closeness and to the faith that he holds onto and uses in order to help him make sense of life.

Shooter would like to produce a record with Jessi but has yet to find a label that will pay for it. "I always show her my songs, and she always shows me hers," he says. "We work on stuff and relate on a basic level, so that's cool." He says that if it weren't for his mother's spirituality and her strength bringing him stability, "I'd go crazy."

> *Now that I'm paying, I'm running to you.*
> "Please Carry Me Home"
> From *Out of the Ashes*

Shooter first got into playing music as a young boy, when he took to the drums and then learned the piano. He didn't start playing the guitar until he was thirteen or fourteen, and didn't start playing it onstage until 2003.

Question: What makes you want to go out onstage and do what you do?

Shooter: My favorite thing is actually in the studio. I love playing in front of crowds, but like what the Beatles, what they did, when they stopped touring and just made records [a reference to the decision by the Beatles in 1966 to work only in the studio],...that's a dream come true for me…, I just love creating stuff. But you get out here and you meet all the people and you see all these people that are affected by your music, or either come and like it or dislike it or whatever; either way, that gives you this energy. It's like a high when you connect with your audience.

In country music the approach is so much more humble than the approach in rock 'n' roll. It's much more personable. The crowds are expecting to hang out with you for two hours as opposed to just seeing your show. When that happens, it's awesome, man. When we go out there and we kill a show, it's a good feeling.

I'm really fortunate with this band that I'm working with now. I feel like I'm finally in a place where I have guys that I have a lot of respect for, and they have respect for me. We're in a relationship that's free and open. And I love that kinship that happens onstage.

On a good night, and it seemed like they just kept getting better, I could take the crowd with me for a ride. I like to drive.
—Waylon Jennings

Question: Like your dad, you're not a part of mainstream Nashville, and I wonder if in that way he served as a model for you?

Shooter: Sure, him and that crew,... the way they were able to break down those barriers and build an audience by being true to their music is definitely a model anybody should go by. My dad, like anyone else who is an artist who stuck by their guns and believed in their vision, that should be a model that crosses all genres. You can take Kanye West [a rap artist] and use that model; you can take the Beatles and use that model. It's caring about the music more than caring about the success and fighting that battle [for the music].

I've been sinking like a rock in this high society,
'Cause all that means so much to them,
Don't mean shit to me.
"Solid Country Gold"
From *Put the O Back in Country*

Shooter has a stubborn Outlaw attachment to heart, truth, and honesty. "There are people who just cut songs and cut songs, and they may or may not have a relationship with those songs," he says. "But to me, I've always felt it's been about writing your life in a song. Bob Dylan would be another good example of folks who just wrote what they believed and it caught on."

Shooter's CD *The Wolf,* released in 2007, draws from a title used by Waylon for one of his vinyl records, *Will the Wolf Survive?* The album was, for Waylon, a venture into a different sound than what he had recorded earlier, with what he describes in his autobiography as "the heavy undercurrent of rhythm." Waylon had his doubts about whether the record fit him.

Shooter shows his own kind of doubts on the title track to *The Wolf* when he wonders: "Am I country enough or too rock 'n' roll?" and adds "I just can't weather this feeling like I don't belong."

He begins the track "Concrete Cowboys" with Dylanesque harmonics and then quickly launches into a Waylon structure. He sings: "Concrete cowboys eat granite grits/They don't always wear hats/Or sling guns on their hips/They know a song by the taste on her lips."

How's it taste? Sweet and true or cheap and phony? If you're going to ride it, and you're going to ride it to the end, bitter or otherwise, you better love it.

> *We picked a long and winding course,*
> *And we'd do it again.*
> *We picked a dark horse,*
> *And we're gonna ride it to the end.*
> "This Ol' Wheel"
> From *The Wolf*

Question: How do you work in the studio?

Shooter: You get in there with a band, and you work out a song, and it takes on a life of its own once the other players get involved. Sometimes it's quick, sometimes it takes.... But it's very organic, and I don't tell them what to play. We have ideas.... They're excellent musicians, so they're going to do what they do, and I love that. I bring them the song, and they bring it to life.

When Shooter recorded *Put the O Back in Country* in 2005, he took a stand against the commercialized flood of Nashville pop. To put the O back meant put the Outlaw back, with its respect for and attachment to country's roots. He doesn't flat out condemn Music Row—after all, the studios there are doing what they have always been good at doing in developing the sound that they know will sell millions of records. For the Nashville sound to change, he believes, will require other artists to "get big enough on their own" so that the record executives will take note.

Shooter admits that when he says in the title track to *Put the O Back in Country* that "there ain't no soul on the radio," he was taking an exaggerated shot. "Sometimes there is [soul]," he says. "Sometimes a song will come in and out,... like that Ronnie Dunn song, 'Cost of Living.'" He adds: "But I think [we're] in a [different] place now than... when I wrote *Put the O Back in Country,* because those big acts were selling six or seven million records, and they had a firm grip on the radio. It was like, 'We know exactly how to sell six million records.'

"But now with the state of the music business, instead of selling two million the first week, they sell 170,000. It's still a number one record, but there's not that much money being generated off it. That is when [the major studios] will start expanding their borders a little bit, because they're hoping that something else will spark more of an interest." He adds humorously, with a mischievous grin: "So I think that there's a glimmer of hope in the destruction of the music business."

> *We were rebels, but we didn't want to dismantle the system. We just wanted our own patch.*
> —Waylon Jennings

The CD begins with country legend George Jones introducing himself by saying, "I'm just helping ol' Shooter out so he can put the O back in country." Then Shooter proclaims his enthusiasm for the music he loves and was intended to play and provides a little schooling for country listeners when he sings: "Well, I'm rollin' like a freight train/Comin' straight at you/Playing hillbilly music/Like I was born to do/*You know that ain't country music you've been listenin' to."* From there he lays out his roots, with pointed reference to his father: "You take a little country and a little rock 'n' roll/A little Neil Young and a little George Jones/A little Merle Haggard and a little bit of the Stones/Add a little Cash and *a whole lotta* Waylon."

Put the O Back in Country was a revelation to Shooter about the current entrenched state of Nashville pop. "The whole band thought the sound we were getting would actually carry," he says. "But what we didn't realize was that [the mainstream radio stations] weren't going to play the stuff that pushed the boundaries. They weren't going to play that. We were hoping that we could fuel off some success at some point with '4th of July' and be able to expand it." That rousing song, which evokes images of a free-spirited ramble along the nation's highways, reached the Top 30 on the country charts.

Any attachment that Shooter has to his father's musical structure disappears in Shooter's *Black Ribbons* CD. The *structure* but not the *spirit,* the spirit to try something different. Going straight-out rock,

Shooter displays his diverse creativity and declares his coming out from under his father's shadow. "It was like the full rock side of my personality apart from my dad," Shooter says.

"That was like the *Sgt. Pepper's* thing," Shooter adds in reference to the historically important Beatles album from 1967. Much as the Beatles masqueraded as a different band on their LP, Shooter took a fictional pose. "So I was able to do anything I wanted to; it was okay. It gave me free rein to go crazy. But I knew what I was doing with it. I knew I wanted a story. It was all going to be built around this DJ, and the songs would be the best. So me and David Cobb [the producer]...spent six months in the studio designing the music for that.... Doing it was so liberating because...it was not a Shooter Jennings ex-country record." By that he means that he knew that he was going to return to country.

Indeed, there was nothing desperate, indecisive, or exploitive about Shooter's action. It wasn't as if he were straddling the fence between wanting to perform rock and wanting to perform country— and waiting to see which one worked the best. He has set his course on exploring his talent *wherever it might take him*, not from an "I'll do or try anything for the money" approach but from an intense commitment of being true to himself, of being all that he can be as his own man, Shooter Jennings.

> *If we took on the guise of cowboys, it was because we couldn't escape the pioneer spirit, the restlessness that forces you to keep pushing at the horizon, seeing what's over the next ridge.*
> —Waylon Jennings

Shooter never expected *Black Ribbons* to wake anyone up, either on country radio or any other radio. "It's clearly a concept," he says.

The concept: a rock opera. For the CD, Shooter put together as his band Hierophant, (from the ancient Greek meaning "the holy" and "to show"), and for a narrative read between the tracks, he recruited best-selling horror novelist Stephen King. He plays the role of Will o' the Wisp, a late-night talk show radio host in the throes of his last broadcast before an authoritarian government forces him off the air. One reviewer calls the work "an ambitious and delightfully experimental album" with "weird, freak-out music that plays like a studio experiment gone mad."

Just as the Beatles did with their *Sgt. Pepper's* album, *Black Ribbons* relies heavily on studio effects to create elaborate sounds and convey a surrealistic setting. Shooter rejects trickiness, though, and if some might call him over the top, he sees everything he did for the album as essential to creating the atmosphere he intended. (Interestingly, his song "God Bless Alabama" conveys his country and Southern rock tastes even amid the heavy guitar and the trippy effects.)

"Black Ribbons I'm proud of," Shooter says. "I wouldn't change anything about that one. I like that one. I'm just happy we brought it from zero to ten."

Even with the making of *Black Ribbons,* Shooter's attachment to what his dad had done remained ever-present. This was evident in his decision in 2008 to record *Waylon Forever*. Shooter and Waylon had put together some music on tape in the 1990s, and Shooter decided to take these songs, clean them up a bit, and add his country band, the .357s, to them. Nothing could be more of a tribute to his dad; nothing could be more expressive of their closeness. The CD even has Waylon doing a cover of the Cream rock classic "White Room"—yes, Waylon Jennings singing "White Room." The album exudes respect for Waylon's music and having fun with it, and it's no mere repetition of the Waylon sound; the .357s rock.

As Shooter was working on his next CD, *The Real Me,* he released a single, "Outlaw You." He did so in a state of anger over Nashville pop artists who were posing as Outlaws and putting the word "Outlaw" on the titles of their CDs or using it in their songs while their music showed no attachment to the roots and the integrity of the Outlaw movement, either past or present.

"I just got sick of the Outlaw thing and new guys pretending and leaning on that," Shooter says. "I read a couple of articles by some people in that vein and went for it. I was just like, 'Fuck it. Let's write the song and see what happens.' And the guy from CMT [Country Music Television] loved it.... They wanted something interesting to happen; they wanted to stir shit up."

Question: Why was there such urgency for recording that song?

Shooter: Because it was coming to a head at that point. It felt like it just needed to come out now. A lot of people got pissed off about it, but also a lot of people liked it, and they couldn't believe that it was being played on CMT. To them it was, "What is happening?"

Question: You're really attacking the posers?

Shooter: Yeah, it's the posers. It's a poser-hating song. You're not an Outlaw, and don't use the Outlaw name, don't fucking try to stir that up into your shit. You guys write your songs with the Nashville writers and do the Nashville thing, and you just get a little edgy, and you add an Outlaw name here and there, and that's fake. Those guys [the Outlaws from the 1970s] garnered that name because they struggled and fought against something until they won.

"Hey pretty boy in the baseball hat/You couldn't hit country with a baseball bat," Shooter sings. Then he gets to the truth, the inspiration, the engine that keeps running, running, running—running and shaking those honky-tonks: "It's about bein' true to what's inside...."

*The honky-tonk might be low-class and low-rent, but that
means you get lower down with your music, cut it to the bone,
make sure you don't waste a note. You're honing everything.*
—Waylon Jennings

The image created by some studio ain't going to cut it. The Tony
Lamas won't cut it, either, if they're packed with bullshit: "You say
you're an Outlaw with your perfect boots/That you got from your
record label's image group/Sing another man's song with a big drum
loop/Listen, son, you ain't got a clue/You can't buy true, tell you what
they should do/*They should outlaw you.*" There follows a history lesson to show what he means by "you can't buy true," about how many
years of struggle it took for the original Outlaws to make their revolution, which it truly was.

*Let me paint a picture for you, Nashville in '62,
The formula had proven true,*

*They didn't let nothing new through.
When Waylon came to town,*

*And didn't like his original sound,
Tried hard to keep him down,*

*Tried hard to starve him out.
But he kept playin' shows and pressin' on....*

After years and years of struggling strong,

Got his chance and he took it to number one....

And the record labels had the control no more.
"Outlaw You"

I had actually first met Shooter several months before the crawfish festival in Texas. I had gone to a bar in downtown Nashville with Outlaw artist Joey Allcorn, and we all sat there and had a few drinks and talked. Shooter was in town to pitch an idea to CMT: a weekly show, titled *Shooter's Midnight Special*, that would bring together a mainstream artist with Outlaw artists and so build a bridge between the two and expose more people to the Outlaw scene. In his pitch, Shooter told CMT that across much of America an ever-greater number of musicians—modern bards—were loading their equipment into their trucks and vans and taking to the highways to play their music of truth wherever they could.

"A few years ago," Shooter told me at the bar, "there weren't many people that were taking a progressive approach to country, or at least I didn't know about them, and I'm [a person who's] very aware of bands. Now there's hundreds of them. It feels like they're multiplying and making good records."

I said to him: "And the pay is lousy, the hours long, the rip-offs pervasive."

"Yeah, the question to ask them, really, is, why are you even playing this music? Well, it's because that's what they *want* to play."

Question: What do you think of them? Not musically, but about what they are going through?

Shooter: I'm not saying anybody should be hurt; I'm not saying you should leave your family at home and go pack the van up. You've got to be smart and not dumb and just playing all the time and not making any money doing it.... But continuing to make records and continuing to play music inspires other people in droves.... I think it's important that all the bands know that.... Somebody's got to start paying attention to this shit. That's going to happen. It's just undeniable to me.

But he knows the sacrifices. Making money doing it can be painfully difficult.

"He stopped loving her today," George Jones begins to sing on Shooter's *Put the O Back in Country.* Then the music stops, and he asks Shooter, "When do you,... when do you think we're going to get paid for this, you reckon?"

Shooter laughs. "Welcome to the Outlaw scene," says the laugh to George. The time will be never.

Question: Almost always in interviews I find that fellow artists have only a limited knowledge of other current Outlaw artists, and it also seems to be a splintered, regionalized movement. Do you agree?

Shooter: It is splintered to some degree. But because of the Internet, they're all surviving, that's why it's working,... and because it's spread out all over the place, people are now booking shows, playing together and getting closer and going places. I just produced a record with Fifth on the Floor and Rachel Brooke is on that record. It was a cool experience; it was like us getting together and making music. I like working with these other bands. Jamey Johnson always said this: You've got to tie your ships together, because if we all tie our ships together, after a while we'll have a fucking big-ass yacht party going.

Shooter's Midnight Special could bring on that yacht party by cutting through the divisions in country music and the regionalism in the Outlaw movement. It turns out that CMT likes the concept and has recorded the pilot.

Question: What types of music would you play on your show?

Shooter: The first episode would [include] Kelly Pickler. The central point for this is that Kelly, who has a more traditional country record out, as a bigger star, and Joey [Allcorn] and the group Hellbound Glory get to perform a song each. The premise is these are people I like and that they are my friends, because I'm not going to do it when someone else tells me this has to be the person on the show. I would try to make every episode feel special, so there's a point to it. Which is more than there's a mainstream guy and an underground guy, although that kind of looks that way.

We would get someone in from the mainstream that's cool,... and a guy like Jack White together and a guy like Scott H. Biram together.... Then some talk happens, maybe some jamming, putting those people around with some alcohol and talking.

Question: What made you propose this show?

Shooter: Blake Judd motivated me to do it. I had an idea for the show six years ago, but not as focused as now, and having Blake, who is the video director that I work with, help me organize everything... we actually got it moving forward. I knew that CMT at the time, the people that have taken over there are open-minded and cool.

Shooter already has a show on SiriusXM Radio, on their Outlaw station. He programs the music himself, he says, with "no borders to it." He even once read an abridged version of his dad's autobiography with the music to the movie *Blade Runner* playing behind it. "It was really dramatic; it was really cool." (On the air, he has also used some of the works of the Beat writer William S. Burroughs. Shooter, who is well read, especially in quality literary works, has a liking for him and for poet Allen Ginsberg.)

About his radio show, Shooter adds: "I've got in trouble for certain shit, but not because I played something wrong. I'll play anything. I've been using it a lot to try and expose these underground country acts which have really revitalized my faith in what is going to be happening."

As with his proposed TV show, with his radio broadcasts Shooter certainly envisions enlarging his own audience, but he primarily wants to enlarge it for other creative and talented artists. He doesn't want the general population to believe that when they listen to Nashville pop they are listening to a form of music that has an intimate connection with country's roots. Ideally, he hopes he can help raise the desire for the real genre (and make people realize that roots doesn't mean nostalgia or all songs sounding alike) and thus elevate people's tastes above and beyond the commercial fodder that most often poses as country.

Toward this end, Shooter has used his radio show to promote what he calls the XXX Movement. "It was just me trying to get people excited about thinking outside of the box. It was more about turning people on to a large batch of bands at once," he says. "I would like to see a merging of all of this kind of thinking and a web presence and just to know that you could turn on the TV and catch these kinds of bands, and you could go to this website associated with that and find out about other bands. The XXX site is about a cross-pollination effect."

Waylon Jennings died in his sleep on February 13, 2002, of complications from diabetes. He was buried in a family plot at Mesa City Cemetery in Mesa, Arizona. At the graveside service, Shooter sang his dad's hit song "I've Always Been Crazy."

Shooter had lived for years with his father's deteriorating health, which had landed Waylon in the hospital several times. The trial and the pain of it all led to Shooter writing "Daddy's Hands," which appears on the *Family Man* CD released in 2011.

Question: On "Daddy's Hands," you sing that "Daddy's hands keep getting older, reminding us of how much we don't know." How much didn't you know?

Shooter: How much we've still got left to learn. I didn't even think that song was going to make the record, and then it turned out to be one of my favorite cuts.

> *It's been New Year's Eve in a hospital bed,*
> *Daddy's sick, but he's far from dead.*
> *It's holidays like this you never forget,*
> *We'll all drink to that.*
> "Daddy's Hands"
> From *Family Man*

When I first saw Shooter in that Nashville bar, I didn't have him pegged, but I was a bit nervous. There he was sitting in a darkened corner, somewhat ominous-looking as he was dressed all in black, and, at first, paying me only the slightest of attention. I suspected that, like some of the other Outlaws, he was skeptical about what this teacher-type was doing digging around a musician's world.

As it turned out, Shooter was distracted and distant because he was preoccupied with the TV show he was working on, but he proved to be a genuinely nice guy. He quickly agreed to an interview—the one that would occur near Houston—and wholeheartedly embraced this project.

But there's more to Shooter than his friendly personality. There's the Shooter who has to sometimes count to ten when he realizes people think they know him before they even meet him. There's the Shooter whose Jennings name leads to unreasonable assumptions on the part of others. There's the Shooter who has to fight the challenges that come from being on the road. There's the Shooter that no interviewer, and thus no reader, can understand, but about whom he tries to communicate in his music.

Question: In the song "Real Me," on *Family Man,* you sing that the people you've talked to say you're a nice guy. But you go on to add that they're not seeing the real you. What's going on here?

Shooter: The song isn't saying that I'm making shady deals when nobody's looking....

Question: But the song implies that there is a darker side to you out there.

Shooter: There definitely is, and it's the source of all my problems in my life. For me all of my problems have to do with maintaining a relationship with someone while you're traveling on the road—having kids and having to be away from them and doing all of that stuff, and on top of that, you're in this thing. Believe me, there's a lot of problems that can come out of everything that goes on with traveling and the whole package.

Question: Do you get "ornery when you're high," as your song says?

Shooter: Yeah. I find myself pensive. It's weird. I do unfortunately stand by every word. I get myself into trouble all the time. I try to do the best I can, though.

When Shooter was making *Family Man* he had enough songs to create a double CD. Instead he decided to break it up into two records. He released the second one, *The Other Life,* in March 2013. He calls it "the dark mirror of what *Family Man* was." Expect Shooter to go in one direction and he switches to yet another. He discards the homey comfort of *Family Man* to open himself to a psychological vivisection and let his innermost feelings spill into view.

Shooter begins the CD with a Harry Nilsson tune, "The Flying Saucer Song" ("Do you know who you are?" he cries out in distorted plaintive voice, and there's a bongo drum being tapped in the background like a 1950s Beat poetry reading at Lawrence Ferlinghetti's City Lights bookstore.) The song harkens back to what Shooter did with Hierophant. But he then switches gears to reveal an album that veers between *Electric Rodeo* and the more rootsy "Outlaw You," which he includes as one of the tracks. In short he captures all his influences to evoke a creative crescendo, but the crescendo is complex. He builds to the darker than dark ending song "The Gunslinger," that contradictorily, sheds more *light* on who Shooter Jennings is.

With "A Hard Lesson to Learn" he refers immediately to his dad and to Jimmie Rodgers, Hank Williams, and other country artists known for taking to the bottle, and then proclaims himself to be a whiskey drinkin' leavin' kind. "It's the same old bottle, the same old blues, and the same old lesson to learn." The devil collects his toll on that lost highway, and there always seems to be one being built for Outlaws whose lives often appear as dark daggers streaking across grey black skies.

With Scott H. Biram, he covers "The White Trash Song," and it places him in the middle of a loser's scene where his woman runs off with a preacher (Jimmy Swaggert) and the looser winds up drinking himself into jail time. He follows this song with the steel-guitar infused "Wild and Lonesome," which he sings with Patty Griffin. Her voice adds beautifully to his.

How dark is that Gunslinger, though? On *Family Man* Shooter sings about the other side to his nice side, but it's all lighthearted, all tending to evoke a smile or a laugh. But "The Gunslinger" begins with Shooter's *biting voice* and a steady drumbeat, snares prominent, no compromise; he's angry. "You don't know what I've been through . . . you better watch your mouth, boy," he warns. "You need to be scared . . . you think you own this town, huh, I don't care." And: "DON'T CALL ME AN OUTLAW. I'M A MOTHERFUCKING GUNSLINGER. IF YOU WANT TO RUN YOUR MOUTH OFF YOU BETTER KEEP YOUR EYE ON MY MOTHERFUCKING TRIGGER FINGER." He's not taking any shit, and when you look into the black of his eyes you'll see a man "so deep in the red" that it will chill you to the bone. So does the mad tortured saxophone at the end.

In *The Other Life* Shooter comes across as a man grappling with who he is; where all his artistic talent fits in a world that prizes commercial packaging with black and white categories; where his heritage and his uniqueness sometimes blend and sometimes conflict; where he feels the pull from youth into middle age much as the moon in a starry sky pulls a tide without asking it where it wants to go. "I am the outsider," he sings, " a horse with no rider." It's an artistic *tour de force,* an analytic life revealing work that stays attached to roots country and touches enough universal themes to make it both connective and enlightening. It's classic.

As I was writing this profile, a friend of mine, Bret Heim, a classical musician, stopped by my office. He wanted to know if any of the Outlaw artists I was interviewing would sell out to be a part of the Nashville music machine. I said that I couldn't see it happening. "What's with Shooter?" Bret asked. "It seems like he could easily have taken the road to Music Row, given his family name and connections within the industry."

"Maybe," I replied. "I don't know what all is going on with his family. But he has a core set of talent and values that just won't let him be that sellout." A core linked in some way to his father, I thought, as I remembered Waylon's statement: "To us, Outlaw meant standing up for your rights, your own way of doing things."

Shooter has appeared several times on the late-night shows hosted by David Letterman and Jay Leno. In one instance, Leno introduced Shooter as "the son of Waylon Jennings." I asked Shooter if it bothered him to be referenced like that. "No, I'm not offended at all," he said, "because I'm proud of my dad. I know that I'll always be Waylon Jennings's son and I'll always be putting out songs, and at some point that question is going to get old and they're going to have to say either we like you or we don't like you."

He added: "I don't have any fear. I think it's possible to outrun the shadow by producing my own music, making more music. His legacy is still standing there, but I'm building my own catalog, and then at some point there's not a difference." Then he laughs: "Unless nobody bought mine ever."

Question: Where do you want your music to go?

Shooter: I want to keep evolving. [David] Bowie is a good reference in saying that; I really relate to the way he did shit. Every album [of his] was like a reinvention of himself. I'm really into that.

Indeed, why should anyone be so contained as not to be able to reinvent himself or herself? Substitute the phrase "every album" above with "every year" or even "every day" and boundaries that restrict, or even prohibit, growth come tumbling down.

To be real. To sing the truth, regardless of whether we [Outlaws] were walking contradictions or not. We wanted the freedom to use any instruments we wanted, or not use them, whichever the song demanded. Why limit yourself?
—Waylon Jennings

Clang, tinkle, clang, swoosh, tinkle. Maybe when I heard those wind chimes hanging from the tree branches near Houston, the ones close to Shooter's tour bus, I was also hearing poet John Donne from some 400 years ago when he wrote that the bell that tolls for one tolls for everyone—listen to *the bell that tolls for thee.* The strong sense of kinship I felt that night seemed to say so.

Shooter's own sense of kinship makes its appearance in *Family Man.* It expresses a kinship to past music. His dad's, for sure. His mother's, for sure. But also to that from other artists. Revealingly, it also expresses a kinship to his family and, in a much larger sense, to the fans of Outlaw country. The CD's title and the music within make it clear that he is singing about a much greater family than the immediate one—and it becomes clear when Shooter steps out on the stage, as it was that night near Houston, with the stars glistening and the moon aglow, that he needs no Juju priestess to cast any spells. Nor must he rely on any spectral presence; what drives him goes well beyond that surface imagery to draw from a deeper spiritual well. His artistry encompasses it all—*his* artistry, *his* work, *his* decisions, for sure, but blending with the gift from his mom and dad and the musical inheritance received from others. The "bells tolling for thee," if you will.

With Shooter's artistry the turbulence of the world weighs less and we are back to where creativity and honesty reigns—back to the roots, back to where it all began and how it must evolve. We are enraptured by the spirit of Outlaw music at the hands of an artist who uniquely and poignantly bridges Outlaw past with Outlaw present. As with Outlaw as a whole, we are born again.

> *Mama said all I needed was within,*
> *Things were easier back then.*
> *When the world begins to spin,*
> *Feels like I'm shedding off my skin.*
> *And the moon looks like a grin,*
> *Feels like I'm being born again.*
>   "Born Again"
>   From *Family Man*

Shooter Jennings, Spring, TX (2012)

Dallas Moore Posing for Blessed be the Bad Ones (2013)

CHAPTER 11

DALLAS MOORE

Blessed Be the Bad Ones

Drifting 'round from town to town,
To do what I've got to do,
Ain't no more looking back for me.
"BLESSED BE THE BAD ONES"
FROM BLESSED BE THE BAD ONES

ver the years, the Flora-Bama, a bar located on the beach smack dab along the border that separates Florida from Alabama, has gained a reputation as a cool hangout where bikers, beach bums, and trailer dwellers, and even a college professor or two, all get together to drink and listen to country bands. The place is so popular among such a wide assortment of locals that a Baptist preacher friend of mine—a truly fine, upstanding man who lives by his righteous creed and a good forty miles from the joint—uses the Flora-Bama frequently in his sermons as the butt of his jokes. "You know what I mean about those of you who hide your drinking," he'll state in semi-mock accusation. "You go all the way down to the Flora-Bama so you won't be seen. But... you're seen," he says with a smile.

When I heard him preach this, I wasn't sure how he knew, but I suspect through some drive-by sightings or late-night confessions. Unless, of course, he was referring to Jesus himself, watching from above.

When I first checked into the Flora-Bama, it was to see Dallas Moore play. The structure encases two or three stages and three or four bars on separate levels in a maze of wooden decks and wooden walls strewn with graffiti. It's a labyrinth of alcoholic playgrounds, so arranged as to allow any man to flee a pursuing wife or girlfriend, any wife or girlfriend to flee a pursuing man, and any combination of the two to flee an unexpected preacher.

Dallas Moore's band is a bit of a labyrinth itself. Sometimes it goes by the name of the Dallas Moore Band, sometimes by the name Dallas Moore and the Snatch Wranglers. Que sera, sera. Choose which one you want. Neither version of the band is Doris Day. It's sandal-stomping, off-the-books, carburetor-smoking, give-me-another-fucking-beer Outlaw country.

> *Well, when you said you were gone, I thought I could be alone,*
> *So I headed for that old hangout of mine.*
> *I was shocked to find you there, all painted up with your big hair,*
> *Telling everybody how you were going to do just fine....*
> *And darling you're wastin' good whiskey*
> *If you're tryin' to drink me off your mind.*
> "Wastin' Good Whiskey"
> From *Tales of a Road King*

Halloween week had taken hold at the Flora-Bama, and the front of the outdoor stage where Dallas would soon appear was decorated with lighted jack-o'-lanterns. Was it the ghost of Hank Williams I felt breathing down my neck or the light touch of the ocean breeze? Probably the breeze, because it carried with it the sweet aroma of cannabis.

I was early and found Dallas standing and talking to fans out on the floor, amid some picnic tables. Outlaw country artist Wayne Mills was right: Dallas was one scary-looking dude. His long hair, ear piercings, unshaven face, leather vest, and torn jeans declared he was a sinister force. But when we greeted each other, his smile melted me as it would anyone; sinister changed to good. Wayne's other point about Dallas quickly kicked in: he was a terrifically nice guy, one who would make for a great friend.

Maybe the spirit of Halloween was too much in the air, but I felt as if I was about to experience several surprises. One occurred immediately. Near Dallas stood a beautiful young woman. Dallas introduced me to her; it was his wife, Jenna. *Wow!* I thought to myself. *Congratulations, Dallas. Huh, this is probably your trophy in the form of an Achilles heel: a chick so stuck on her looks that she doesn't give a damn about anybody else.* But she greeted me warmly, and a few minutes later she grabbed a pumpkin and began carving its face while engaging me in conversation. It was a spontaneous and tender move. She made me feel as if I belonged. *So,* I thought to myself with some relief, *she doesn't fit the stereotype of her looks any more than does Dallas.*

The second surprise occurred a bit later, when Dallas took the stage. His band included an extra guitarist—Jody Payne, who had been with Willie Nelson's band for many years and had recently retired. I was ecstatic. Here was two generations of Outlaws on the stage at the same time, one from the 1970s and one from today. Dallas topped this by telling me that Jody would be willing to give me an interview after the show. *Jody and Dallas,* I thought. *A kick-ass Outlaw doubleheader.*

Question: How did you get to know Jody Payne?

Dallas: I got to tell you a story about this. And this is no bullshit. I was sitting there opening up for Willie Nelson and the Family as a solo act, and I got my guitar, stringing along, you know.... I'm doing my thing, and all of a sudden I hear all of these notes and the crowd is going ape shit and everything and I'm thinking, *Man, I'm killing these motherfuckers.* I look around and, goddamn, Jody Payne is playing guitar with me. Then like a dumbass,... I [glance at Jody and tell him about one of my songs:] "This one's in G." And he goes, "I'll find it. I play with Willie, man."

Dallas told me this story as we sat at a table with Jody and a couple of other musicians in a beach house across from the Flora-Bama. It was around midnight, and the beer was flowing and the weed was burning. With Dallas and Jody across from me at the same table, I was in Outlaw heaven.

Dallas grew up in Ohio, "adopted by the greatest set of parents in the world," he says. He was named after his dad, James Dallas Moore, who worked in a factory. "He calls me the sequel," Dallas says. His mom, Madgelee Moore, owned a beauty salon and, as an accomplished musician in her own right, played guitar with the country and bluegrass group the Buckeye Belles, which she formed with some friends, who, like her, hailed from the South. In the early 1950s, the group recorded several 78s.

When Dallas was in middle school and high school, he played football and baseball and boxed. He also started playing the guitar and was heavily influenced by his mom's attachment to the music of Elvis

Presley and Hank Williams. From high school, Dallas went to Northern Kentucky University on a jazz and classical music scholarship.

Question: And you graduated from college?

Dallas: Well, I didn't graduate. I took the four-year music course, and I didn't take nothing else. You got to take the other shit if you [want to] graduate. I just took the four years, because a music degree didn't mean nothing but that I could teach high school music and I didn't fucking want to do that, I wanted to go play music. But I wanted the knowledge, so I took the music theory, and I took classical and jazz.

Question: Did that experience get in the way of your country music?

Dallas: No, not at all. If anything, it helped me. Every night I play the solo gig, there's a song that I play where I'm quoting Beethoven and Merle Haggard in the same song. It's just something I put together, but I wouldn't have had that [otherwise]. Here's the bottom line: everybody uses the same twelve fucking notes. Our thing is we usually use three or four or five of them or whatever. But I love all kinds of music—I love jazz music, I love classical music—and that gave me a good insight, you know, into playing everything.

From classical and jazz to honky-tonks and roadhouses, such as the Bent Wrench, located on a country road near Clarksville, Tennessee. When I entered the roadhouse, Dallas and his band were playing songs from their new CD, *Blessed Be the Bad Ones* (2013). Because the bar has no stage for its performers, the band was squeezed into one corner of the low-ceilinged building, with beer signs flashing behind them, one of which was casting a blue halo of light atop Dallas's head. The bar's patrons, a mix of blue-collar workers and bikers, were loud, several of them feeding drinks to the band and having a certifiably good time. This was a typical Dallas Moore crowd, and he was in his element and clearly the blessed bad one that night, playing his songs with passion.

Dallas began earning his Outlaw credentials in places like this. Among his first heroes was the singer and songwriter Billie Gant. As a teenager, Dallas ached to see Billie play, but the singer was performing in honky-tonks in Cincinnati, Ohio, and, at sixteen, Dallas was too young to enter them legally. Through Billie, however, Dallas got his chance. He recalls: "I went in and seen [Billie], you know, black hat and black leather all the way from head to toe and just standing on his head playing upside down, playing the harmonica, and singing and entertaining the crowd, holding the crowd right in the palm of his hand, you know. It came to be a little honky-tonk, but in [my and my friends'] eyes it was a fucking Astrodome. We weren't allowed to be in there, but he never made us not be in there, and he would always get us up to sit in and play."

For Dallas it was a time of excitement and impatience, of desires that needed to be quickly gratified in the burning furnace of his youth. "Me and the guys in my first little band, when we first started playing," he says, "we just came up learning, playing in bars. Most bands get together, you know, get a band together and go rehearse and then do stuff. We didn't do that. I had me and a drummer and our hero [Billie, who jammed with us]....We were playing "Okie from Muskogee," and it probably sounded punk rock, but we thought we sounded like the Hag [Merle Haggard]."

Dallas was also heavily influenced by Southern rock, which shaped the first band he put together. Several of the Southern rockers left a stylistic imprint on his music, in part because he covered their songs and played with the groups. Dallas remembers that his band got the honor of being an opening act early on, not because they were particularly good but because they were one of the few bands in lower Ohio who fit in with the Southern rock sound. Among musicians from that genre, the greatest influence came from the Allman Brothers, the Marshall Tucker Band, and Lynyrd Skynyrd. Dallas says that with his first band, the music was pretty much evenly split between Southern rock and 1970s Outlaw country.

Indeed, Outlaw was another big influence. Tellingly, Dallas's early CD, titled *My Heroes Have Always Been Cowboys*, was dedicated to Waylon Jennings, Willie Nelson, and David Allan Coe. Dallas respects Coe for being a versatile songwriter who could switch from a tender song at one moment to a brash one the next. (Later, Dallas opened for Coe at many venues.)

Dallas calls Billy Joe Shaver, who provided Waylon Jennings with many songs at the outset of the Outlaw movement, "one of the greatest poets of all time." He says, "We got to do shows with Billy Joe and be friends and everything. I guess for me it comes back to this is the music I was into before I ever started playing music. And then to get a guitar, and then to get to meet—and in some cases become friends and family with—people that you idolized your whole life,... it inspires you. It makes you take things to a different level. It makes you try to do your best."

Dallas was also drawn to several artists who, although not a part of the 1970s Outlaw movement, nevertheless followed their own musical beat. Merle Haggard was one; Johnny Cash was another.

"Johnny Cash's music," Dallas told me, "it's just timeless. It's unconditional. If you're going to pick up a fucking guitar..." He didn't complete the sentence because it was quite obvious what he meant: you know Johnny Cash, or you don't know country music. Dallas even named his dog Johnny Cash. He calls it his "Lab in black."

But Dallas's musical lineage goes much further back; it reaches into America's own deep roots across the Atlantic, to the Old Country.

"For my mom," Dallas says, "a lot of the Appalachian music she plays is the stuff that came over on the boat"—boats that plied the Atlantic in the time of masts and sails and pierced the darkness, the mist, and the fog while following the compass points of hope toward a fresh start. She played much of that music, which was passed down through her family, on a dulcimer.

She also liked traditional songs from other parts of the country, whose lyrics were reinvented over the years, such as "Wildwood Flower."

> *Oh, he taught me to love him and called me his flower*
> *That was blooming to cheer him through life's dreary hour.*
> *Oh, I long to see him and regret the dark hour,*
> *He's gone and neglected this pale wildwood flower.*
> "Wildwood Flower"

Simple. Touching. The beauty of meadows and streams mixed with the shadowy gloom caused by a man who has left his lover behind. These were mountain songs and traditional songs for the soul, passed down to Dallas as a commentary about life's heartaches and about how pure music can be. His mom also had an old Victrola with a bunch of records that featured Jimmie Rodgers, the Carter family, and Hank Williams. Perhaps often unknowingly, all of this music still plays in Dallas's mind as he reaches back to write new songs.

In 2011 Dallas released *Hank to Thank* as a tribute to Hank Williams. Dallas made the CD at Herzog Studios in Cincinnati, the last known standing structure that Hank recorded in. The country music legend came there on two different occasions with the Pleasant Valley Boys. The project came about when the Cincinnati USA Music Heritage Foundation contacted Dallas about celebrating the sixty-first anniversary of Hank having recorded there.

Herzog Studios was actually no longer a studio. It had been converted into a museum. Dallas and his band decided to return it to what it had once been by bringing in gear and inviting a small audience to come listen to them play. Jody Payne, who graduated from high school in the Norwood section of Cincinnati, joined the band for the occasion, and Dallas's mom played her dulcimer with the boys for a rendition of Hank's "I'm So Lonesome I Could Cry." Dallas says about the project, "It was a natural fit for us to be the ones to do it. So when the time came about, we just hit the record button and let it fly. That's what that whole disk is: that show in its entirety."

"I'm So Lonesome I Could Cry" is the only song on the CD written by Hank Williams. Rather than cover Hank's music, Dallas decided to go his own way mainly with tunes he composed himself and reflective of Outlaw country. In doing so he proclaims that the originality and creativity found in Hank's music of the 1940s and early 1950s—an era before Nashville had become heavily commercialized—remains vibrant at a venue far from the studios associated with Music Row.

Hank to Thank opens with the title track, written by Danny Frazier. The CD also includes "Outlaw Country" (written by Dallas with his friend Billie Gant), which has become an anthem for the Dallas Moore Band. Dallas introduces the song by saying: "This is a little something about our kind of music here." It celebrates Cash and Coe and Shaver as influences on Dallas and puts them straight into the Outlaw statuary, footlights ablaze and engines revving. Dallas recalls: "Billie kind of got out of playing music…and during that time I started recording, traveling, and getting to do my thing. And several years, many years later, we came back together and he had half that song, 'Outlaw Country,' [done], which he had written in 1976. Then I finished out the other half and we ended up cowriters on it. It was a great thing to write a song with one of your heroes. It was pretty cool."

The CD closes with a rousing rendition of "Are You Sure Hank Done It This Way," written and originally recorded by Waylon Jennings. And so what opens with a salute to Hank closes with a tribute to a 1970s Outlaw, creating, in terms of lineage, an unbroken circle.

Question: So do you really have Hank to thank?

Dallas: Yeah, shit, everybody does. If you ain't got Hank to thank, you're a pussy communist. Or something. [*Laughter.*]

୬ଈଈ୬

To Dallas, in terms of country music, Nashville is Trashville. While Nashville pop may appeal to millions of fans who buy millions of records, it does so through largely bad music torn from its country roots without any respect for the traditionalists, such as Hank, who made it great in its early years, or the original Outlaws, such as Waylon, who returned it to a creative era.

When I asked Dallas to define Outlaw country, he stressed his independence from the constraints imposed by the big Nashville studios. "You get back to an artist using their own band, their own crew, producing their own records," he says. "We're on Sol Records, an independent label out of sleepy little Bright, Indiana. You would never see us coming. And yet you have three artists on the roster that are getting national tours, lots of play on SiriusXM. Of course, we don't see the light of the day on Top 40 country, but that's not what these acts are."

Since the time of the 1970s Outlaws, who Dallas says are artists that make up "the fiber of my being," Nashville has regressed. He observes: "All of the doors that were originally kicked down by Waylon Jennings, Willie Nelson, David Allan Coe, and everyone in the original guard are, as far as modern popular country music, put back up twentyfold. So a band like us wouldn't fucking exist [in Nashville today]."

Question: Do you want to be in the Top 40?

Dallas: Well, if they come around to us, that would be okay. But we do what we do, all of us in our own respect, you know. If we do something that they happen to like, great. But we do what we do, and pretty much that's it. And what we do is entertain people. The thing of it is, we're glad to be playing our songs and the songs that influenced us, [that] came before us and shaped us.

At one point, Dallas went to Nashville and was offered what he calls "three bad record deals." The companies wanted to buy his songs and completely own them. They could then do what they wanted with them, including shelve them, meaning they would likely never be heard from again. The deals, he says, "just weren't the right fit for me." He adds: "I would have to completely change what I did, and I just chose.to stay with what I know and just be myself."

Dallas would love to expand his fan base, sell more records, and make more money. But above all, he wants to do music as *he* wants to do it. He's country to the bone.

Question: Isn't there a happy medium? Isn't there a place where you can perhaps not sell out to pop but move a bit to widen the audience?

Dallas: I don't think it's necessarily the effect of moving.... There's an audience for it, and sometimes that's going to vary in degrees of popularity across the scope. We just keep making the music. It lands where it lands.

I don't give a damn who you think I am,
And I could care less what you think.
And you can come unglued with your bad attitude,
I'll just stay here and drink....
Well, it might not be your way of life,
But it damn sure works for me.

"Damn Sure Works for Me"
From *Can't Tame a Wildcat*

If freedom for Dallas comes through being at one with his music, whatever might be going on in Nashville, it also comes from jumping on his Harley and heading out on the road: man, machine, and the wind. Maybe Jenna behind him on the rider's seat, her arms around his waist. And as he cruises away from the cities, onto the rural roads of the Midwest where a carpet of farms lays gently across the hills, he empties his mind of worries and allows it to fill with music.

When he rides his bike, he is mentally alone. "I have no distractions," he says, "so for all the miles, as you're listening to your bike run along, all of these different ideas come. Half the time you're praying, half the time you're thinking of words, half the time you're going, 'Man, goddamn, look at that fucking bunch of butterflies over there.' Now, you see what I'm saying? All of that stuff comes through your mind, but that's where I come up with most all my songs. Not all, but ninety-nine percent of them, and then when I get off my bike, at some point I'll have a guitar and write."

A good song, he believes, will stick with him until he gets back home. He finds it impossible to sit in a room and write under pressure or on command. He told me while I was with him and Jody Payne that if I asked them to take out their guitars and "write a song about these two dying flowers [on a table in front of us], my lines would be the worst ones because I can't just do that." He adds: "I'll go months without writing anything, and then all of a sudden, when I'm on, I'll write the five best songs I ever wrote in my life in a day. I can't turn it on and turn it off. Everybody's different, everybody does it different. That's just what I do."

Like most Outlaw artists, Dallas tours a lot, heavily in the Midwest and upper South but ever more so elsewhere as the appeal of his music spreads and the economic pressure to find more audiences mounts. In one of our first conversations, I asked him if he would prefer to slow down and tour less. He looked at me as if I were crazy. "Less?" he said. "I want to tour more!" The road has him hooked, and it shows in his performances, where it appears that he would rather be pulled from the stage than end his set at a prescribed time.

Question: Is it rough for you to be on the road so much?

Dallas: Well, you meet a lot of people, and you never know when you're going to meet someone who will be a lifelong friend or a business associate. The thing of it is this: we're going up and down the road doing what we love. We're averaging around three hundred dates a year, between my solo shows and the band. It's pretty nonstop, but that's what I live to do. I love it. There's nowhere else I'd rather be.

> *But I wouldn't change a thing if I had the chance.*
> *You've got to pay the band if you want to dance,*
> *And I love to dance on the high wire without a net,*
> *And that's as good as it gets.*
> "As Good as It Gets"
> From *Hank to Thank*

To Dallas those flashing neon bar signs in the towns and on the highways, where tires burn the asphalt in search for destinations that offer purpose or escape, are like a second home where the beer is cold, the fans are warm, and the music is real. He doesn't believe the world of honky-tonks and roadhouses will disappear anytime soon. "I've seen it go through all the worst. The worst was the line-dancing years. No bands could get any work. Everything was the DJ, or they wanted you to play the Top 40 line-dance hit."

Dallas changes the personnel in his band as frequently as thunderstorms rise up in Chile's superdry Atacama Desert. His lead guitarist, Chuck "Lucky Chucky" Morpurgo, has been with him for seventeen years. Dallas says that while he had to labor at learning the guitar, for Chuck it came as if he were "touched by the hand of God." Dallas calls him "a magical player" and says that onstage he and Chuck trade riffs. "We're like jazz players; every night is different. No doubt about it, Chuck has made me a better guitar player."

Bob Rutherford, who is a bona fide reverend through an online certificate and who married Dallas and Jenna, plays bass guitar and has been with Dallas for the same amount of time as Lucky Chucky. Mike Owens has been blowing a harmonica for Dallas for five years. (Multitalented, Mike, if he wanted to, could also play a mean sitar, but there's not much call nowadays in Outlaw country for Indian music.)

Rocky "The Cat" Parnell, the band's drummer, joined the group eight years ago. He got to know Dallas when Rocky was nineteen, and they were riding their Harleys and drinking beer together. After the band's previous drummer was fired, Dallas said to Rocky, who had played with the band on several occasions, "How would you like to be a Snatch Wrangler?" Rocky answered, "Are you shittin' me, dude?" When Dallas assured him he was sincere, and that it would be for the long term, the two men went and sealed the deal with a handshake and some chicken wings. (The handshake, I assume, occurred before the handling of the wings.)

The band is about as tight as a virgin with an aspirin squeezed between her knees. Rocky says, "We're brothers from other mothers, and you fuck with one of us, you mess with us all. We've got each other's back. We get into it all the damn time, but the next morning it's like 'Hey, man, I'm sorry, dude. My fault.' At the end of the day, we're brothers. We all love what we do. We're best friends, brothers; that's about it."

Rocky admits that life on the road sometimes wears on him: "You get tired, you're human, there's sometimes [when] you don't feel like doing the donuts, you know. You gotta get up there,... it's your job, it's your profession, it's what you chose to do. It beats swinging a hammer." He likes to put on a show, and as sweat drips from beneath the bandanna wrapped around his head, he will smile unabashedly and twirl his drumsticks in the air.

Dallas sees a bright future for Outlaw country. It might not ever grow bigger than Nashville pop, but the niche it occupies will attract more people.

Question: What do you think will happen to your type of music?

Dallas: I think it's definitely expanding. I see more people doing some version of it; it's a pretty big umbrella, as far as what the parameters are.... But I see the audiences growing. One night you might be at a roadhouse, the next night you might be at a beach bar, the next night you might be at an amphitheater. I think it's just there's a lot more people doing it and getting the music out and turning more people on to it. It's like a loose community or family, where everybody kind of really supports each other and tries to turn people on to different friends in the scene.

I asked Rocky if Dallas was always so upbeat. He said, "Yes, and I know he can't be that way twenty-four-seven. But when he walks in the damn bar, in front of our [fans], it's that way." I prodded him:

certainly, Dallas must lose his temper in the studio. Rocky replied: "He's cool to work with, man. We could be recording and he'd say let's all have a drink and settle down and come back in an hour and not just fuck around."

Dallas said to me: "My worst days picking guitar I'd say are better than a lot of people's days." When he admitted that difficulties could on occasion get to him, he put it in the form of a joke: "Obviously there's sometimes when something could go wrong. Everybody has one of those days where it could be raining pussy and you suddenly get hit in the head with a dick. You just make the best of it and go on, and you just might get a song out of it."

Enter Dallas's website or his Facebook page and you enter a world of unbridled enthusiasm, self-promotion, and folksy talk. A typical entry: "Up early and kickin' off this week with EXCITIN' NEWS! 1st up, our debut video for 'Crazy Again' has moved UP from #34 to #13 on the YALLTURNATIVE Chart and made it's respective entry into the Top 100 Country Chart at YALLWIRE.COM!" Or this one: "Locked and Loaded and Rollin' SouthBound! Join us TONIGHT at The Emerald Lounge in Asheville, North Carolina with Waylon Speed! And Tin Cup Gypsy. Thursday finds us hittin' 'em up at 3rd & Lindsley Nashville,Tennessee with Rick Huckaby. All fired up for TWO Great Jams in Two Great States."

Locked and loaded and rollin'. Looking forward, not back. Probably the only way to survive life on the road, where urinals and troughs reek and sound systems may or may not work, where fans might hug you one minute and in a drunken state throw a beer bottle at you the next.

When Dallas Moore and Jody Payne were sitting with me in the beach house near the Flora-Bama, a generational net was cast over them and their experiences, their thoughts, and their music that spanned some hundred years. And I was holding onto that net and pulling it in for a big catch.

At one point during our conversation, Jody, who had been silent while he looked up at the ceiling and reflected about something I had asked earlier, turned to me and said: "Our music don't have nothing to do with Outlaw or old country or new country or nothing like that. It has to do with what you have inside of you."

With that, Dallas interjected: "I always believed in me and my band more than I believed in anybody that is going to offer us any-thing. So I chose that. I chose to stick with me and my guys rather than what would have took all of that away." Nashville pop would take that away, where many bands perform as corporate entities and drummers onstage, in live performance, wear headsets and listen to a click in order to keep a precise beat and make sure they replicate a song *exactly* as it is on the CD.

I asked Jody to offer his definition of Outlaw country. "It's just guys taking their band and playing their music. That's what Outlaw is.... You see guys all over the country, they have a band and they play their songs, that's what Outlaw country is. And they've learned, with the Internet and things like that, to do that by their self, and they've learned to sell it. They don't have to deal with a record company and somebody that don't even know you, trying to tell you what to cut.

"Outlaw country wasn't the thing that meant guns and shit. We're not talking about Jesse James. We're talking about guys that wanted to do their music. David Allan Coe presents his music one way. Dallas presents his another. Willie presents his another. But it's still that defined thing that was against the establishment."

Outlaws 1970s as a bridge to Outlaws today. Fuck the establishment.

Dallas jumped back into the conversation. "I grew up knowing every word Jody Payne said in the movie *Honeysuckle Rose,*" he said.

"I guess one reason that I've been lucky enough to be on the level that I'm at and have guys like Reverend Bob and Chucky stay with me as long as they have and Rocky and Mike Owens...[is] I wanted our outfit, I wanted my outfit, to be like [Willie's]. [Willie] made everybody their own star in their own right. Everybody contributed, everybody added to the whole thing. It wasn't like a guy standing up there in a fucking light and your fucking band's back here and, fuck, you don't even know their fucking names, some monkey-ass shit like that. It's like playing music together—you're a family, and you're a brotherhood."

Brothers from another mother, but all the sons of Outlaw. Fuck the establishment.

Question: Can I ask your reaction to some names that I'm going to throw out at you?

Dallas: Okay.

Question: Garth Brooks (Nashville star from the 1990s).

Dallas: Is he still alive?

Question: Justin Moore (Nashville pop singer).

Dallas: No relation. (When I asked Dallas if he was just kidding around or if he could tell me something about Justin Moore, he again said, "No relation.")

Question: Jason Aldean (Nashville pop singer).

Dallas: Is that like a designer set of panties? Are you trying to trick me? [*Laughter.*]

Question: No, he's a Nashville kind of now-sound guy.

Dallas: Ah, my old lady likes all kinds of fancy clothes. [*Laughter.*]

When Dallas Moore released the video to the title song from *Blessed Be the Bad Ones,* I was a bit taken aback by its dark, Goth-like imagery.

At times it's a bit too melodramatic, but the story mesmerizes. Dallas layers onto the song a fictional account of a hurt, jaded man hunting down the person who did him wrong and letting loose with his gun. But the strength and defiance that Dallas displays reveals his own determination and fortitude against obstacles: Nashville pop, critics, the economic realities of life on the road. He flashes hints of another Dallas, the one beyond the nice, smiling, buoyant Dallas. He has his dark thoughts, his dark moments—and that's good to know, for the best creativity comes from a complex pool of emotions.

And whatever generated the idea for "Blessed Be the Bad Ones," the song shows Dallas at his best and showcases so much of his band's talents. In the video to the song, Dallas stands with arms outstretched, looking up at the heavens, as if to implore "This is me, this is who I am, take me for what I am." When Dallas sings: "To the nights I can't remember/And the things I won't forget/Should have been dead a long time ago/But they ain't got me yet," he's saying, "Yeah, it's the bodily Dallas who should be dead, but it's also the *musical* Dallas who should have died a long time ago at the hands of all those obstacles. But I'm still around, so suck on that."

> *Drifting 'round from town to town*
> *To do what I've got to do,*
> *Ain't no more looking back for me.*
> "Blessed Be the Bad Ones"
> From *Blessed Be the Bad Ones*

While *Hank to Thank* is a good CD—very good, in fact— *Blessed Be the Bad Ones* is where a fan should be to hear Dallas at his best. It all gels there—the songwriting, the musicianship. Mike Owens blows mean on the harmonica, Chuck cranks it up, as do the Reverend and Rocky and good ol' Dallas. They come together more seamlessly than ever before. Dallas's voice penetrates rough and full of expression as he fits it in nicely with the music. His voice can be dark, it can be light; it can have the feel of quality leather that has been well worn and grooved to its owner's comfort. While some of the band's earliest CDs had a few fast-forward moments, this one makes redemption for any past omissions and shows by how many notches Dallas can crank it up. It also reveals the number of notches he can put in his gun belt as he takes aim at all that mundane Nashville shit that has tried to grind roots country into the dirt.

The CD ranges from the fun, Southern-rocking "Slippin' and Slidin'" (which Dallas co-wrote with Rocky), filled with sexual connotations, to several songs with a definite cowboy flair (has Dallas been watching the Western movie channel?), such as "Somethin' Changed" and "Texas Tornado." And Mike Owens on "Somethin' Changed" creates with his harmonica a floating eerie presence akin to the haunting sounds heard in Sergio Leone's classic movie "Once Upon a Time in the West" (1968), where gunslingers do battle in a dusty, desolate but also majestic setting.

"All Those Good Times" has a Bruce Springsteen sensibility to it and a bit of a beachy calypso feel that makes you think of hanging out at that Flora-Bama shoreline with sand between toes. As with the CD's title track, in "Last Man Standin'" Dallas flexes his commitment to do his music his way (this time couched in a honky-tonk metaphor): "I took it to the edge/Then I rolled that extra mile/I'm the last man standing."

In "The Ballad of Sweet Marie," Dallas begins by singing how he left "my sweet, sweet Marie" at the river to drown. He then moves slowly, hauntingly past that statement of fact (the pace of his music resembles the pace of a determined killer) to the details of why he killed Marie. They're not pretty, and Dallas exudes all blacks and grays and reds in painting the picture with an indelible brush. The chilling story is darker than Jimmie Rodgers's "T for Texas" but thematically in that tradition. "Little did I know," he sings, "that it would take murder to make Marie mine." And maybe little did he know, years ago, that it would take this CD to bring him to his fullest artistically. It's a gem.

As the interview at the Flora-Bama began to wind down and the night was becoming as comfortable as a well-worn sandal, I was taken aback when Dallas and Jody decided to take out their guitars, swap songs, and transport me to Outlaw Heaven. Jody played several of Willie Nelson's tunes, stopping occasionally to tell stories about life on the road. He was seventy-five years old and had seen honky-tonks, roadhouses, stadiums, and Hollywood movie sets. Jody and Willie had pretty much done it all.

Dallas joined Jody on some of the Willie songs and on a stirring rendition of one that Coe had written and Jody had recorded years ago, "I Still Sing the Old Songs." Then Dallas chose to sing songs he had just written but not yet recorded. He dove deep down into his gravelly voice, his throat quivering with each note.

Perhaps it was because Jody had said to me about "Wildwood Flower," "Have you ever heard the words to it? It's beautiful." Or perhaps it was because of my own liking for such traditional music, but the acoustic performance at the beach house made me think later of a track on *Hank to Thank.* It's the one where the Dallas Moore Band and Jody cover Hank Williams's "I'm So Lonesome I Could Cry" and are joined by Dallas's mother, Madgelee, on the dulcimer. I thought that if she were only present that night at the beach house with Jody and her son, the acoustic set would have created its own unbroken circle, a connection formed by the songs that she knew, the 1970s Outlaw music that Jody knew, and the current Outlaw that Dallas knew.

But then I realized that Dallas was right when he talked about his going "way back." When he sang, he brought with him a treasure chest filled with more gold than ever could be made by performing Nashville pop, than ever has slipped through the fingers of stars on Music Row. The gold was the songs he had inherited from his mom, and she from her ancestors, and the music he had learned from Jimmie and Hank, from Merle and Johnny, and from the Outlaws back in the 1970s. Dallas was refusing to let that heritage pass into oblivion. He was determined that it would not. When he sang, so too did Madgelee, and so too did all those other artists—all of them performing for "these people out there," as Jody had put it, and for the soul that emanates from the roots of country music.

"You should come with us to church service tomorrow," Jody said to me as I got up to leave the beach house.

"Where's it at?" I asked.

"Right across the street," Dallas said. "At the Flora-Bama."

For a moment I thought Dallas was joking, but he explained to me that every Sunday morning the Flora-Bama closes its bar and has a nondenominational preacher give a sermon against a backdrop of ocean and sand. I was surprised to hear it.

"You can come by motorcycle, car, or even donkey," he smiled.

"I might stop by," I said.

"You should," Dallas said. "It's a nice little service. That's where you'll see me, with all the other bad ones."

Ha! I thought. *Blessed be the bad ones, Dallas. Blessed be you for soldiering on.* The rest of us can do it too, even if it means that we wind up being "the last man standin'."

> *Finish what you started,*
> *I'm here to do just that.*
>> "Blessed Be the Bad Ones"
>> From *Blessed Be the Bad Ones*

Dallas Moore aboard his tour bus, Silas, AL (2011)

Charlie Starr, Hard Rock Casino, Biloxi, MS (2012)

CHAPTER 12

BLACKBERRY SMOKE

The Whippoorwill

In the tiny town where I come from,
You grew up doing what your daddy done.
"ONE HORSE TOWN"
FROM THE WHIPPOORWILL

Back in the era of the original Outlaws, in the 1970s, Gary Gentry wrote a song titled "The Ride." It's a story about a musician, guitar strapped to his back, hitchhiking along a highway in Alabama on his way to Nashville, who meets up with a strange man driving an antique Cadillac. The driver looks "half drunk and hollow-eyed." The hitchhiker learns he has encountered none other than the ghost of Hank Williams. Hank gives the drifter some advice: bend your guitar strings and make people feel what's inside of you, make them moan and cry and weep to your music.

The ride I was staring at behind the Hard Rock Casino in Biloxi, Mississippi, was a giant RV with a tail of an equipment trailer attached to it. The RV looked like it gulped down wads of twenty-dollar bills as quickly as it did gallons of fuel. This was no antique Cadillac but a powerful modern machine that could speed down the highways and create enough wind turbulence to easily lift and swirl the dead leaves of autumns past and make invisible any hitchhiker on his way to Nashville.

I was a bit apprehensive about entering the vehicle. I had come to interview the band Blackberry Smoke, who had begun to experience the material rewards of their musical success, and I had just finished a string of interviews with Outlaw artists whose lives were spent inside cramped vans and beer-drenched honky-tonks. Because of the band's fame and the contrast in setting from my recent experience, I felt uncomfortable and wondered how Blackberry Smoke might receive me, whether they might be snobbish or arrogant.

The door to the RV opened. Trey Wilson, the band's manager, greeted me and told me to come in. As I entered, Brit Turner, the drummer and a graphic design artist who draws up the band's T-shirts and other merchandise, was easing himself onto a cushioned bench near Charlie Starr, guitarist and lead singer for the band and also its spokesman. Charlie was sitting on a sofa while looking intently at his laptop. (Richard Turner, Brit's brother and the band's bass player, joined us later.) Paul Jackson, who plays guitar and does backup vocals, was seated across from Charlie. Brandon Still, the keyboardist, was standing, leaning against one wall of the narrow hallway that led to the beds located near the back of the RV.

Charlie closed his laptop, smiled, shook my hand, and motioned for me to take a seat next to him. The other members of the band introduced themselves to me, greeting me warmly.

I likened Blackberry Smoke to a vision I conjured up while I was listening to one of their early CDs. I saw through a cerebral haze a white country house, the kind you can find in any number of small Southern towns. Surrounding the house were stately trees that provided just enough shade to make the swing on the front porch an appealing place to rest. Off to one side was a garden and a rain barrel ready to catch the runoff from the roof, while on the other side some laundry on a clothesline fluttered in the breeze. It looked so tranquil, so reminiscent of a bygone world. Yet near the house I also saw a muscle car waiting for its new coat of paint and a satellite dish pointed to the sky.

Then, as I focused on the front porch swing, I noticed an object that helped bring this contradictory picture together. It was a patchwork quilt, but one that textile artists call a crazy quilt, made up of patches cut into different shapes, with many different colors and designs. In its busy appearance, the quilt for me symbolized a complex world, what I saw as the mix in my imaginary scene of tradition and modernity.

Blackberry Smoke's music can be understood by this crazy quilt pattern: rooted deep in the past—the house and the trees—but also reflecting the recent—the muscle car and the satellite dish. As such, their songs make up a harmonious whole through distinct patches stitched together by their own unique talent and steeped in the era of Hank Williams and Appalachian bluegrass, the Outlaws of the 1970s, and the Southern rock with which most people associate the band.

By its lead song, "Good One Comin' On" (written by David Lee Murphy, Gary Nicholson, and Lee Roy Parnell), the band's CD *Little Piece of Dixie* might lead a listener to think the entire recording is pure Southern rock. "Good One Comin' On" opens with gritty riffs, in the tradition of the Allman Brothers and Lynyrd Skynyrd, and lyrically hits every redneck emblem to the point it comes perilously close to being cliché. "Two six-packs," "throw in Ray Wylie Hubbard," "skinny-dipping in the bright moonlight"—the lyrics can be criticized for following a commercial formula, but the song is catchy, rockin', and lets the band display its superb guitar work.

Other tunes on the CD, either musically or lyrically or both, reinforce the Southern theme. But add this patch to the musical quilt: "Yesterday's Wine," a Willie Nelson song in which Charlie Starr is accompanied on vocals by country legend George Jones and Jamey Johnson. Johnson starts the first verse, followed by Charlie, whose phrasing gets pleasingly Jones-like, then Johnson, then Jones himself. As an anchor to the CD, it's Blackberry Smoke standing up and declaring, "Hell, we're this too, and don't you forget it."

An earlier CD, *New Honky Tonk Bootlegs,* is all country, and Charlie told me how it got to be that way: Blackberry Smoke had recorded these songs thinking they would appear on other albums, but they never made it. The band then got the idea of bringing them together collectively as a separate CD to showcase their country dimension. Charlie describes it as "honky-tonk music, real country, not what's on the radio now coming out of Nashville—not glitzy guitar pop."

Question: Where does the tapestry of your songs (country, Southern rock, and bluegrass) come from?

Charlie: Good music. You don't have to look hard to find a lot of good music to be influenced by, and if you're lucky enough to have access to all that when you're in your formative years, when you're sort of creating your identity as a musician.... Some people could just as easily go play classical music as they could pick up a Les Paul. We were lucky enough to pick up Les Pauls and drumsticks and Hammond B3s and what not.

As for the bluegrass element, such as in the start to "Scare the Devil Outta You" (on the CD *Bad Luck Ain't No Crime,* released in 2003), it comes from the influence of Charlie's father. Charlie calls his dad "a died-in-the-wool bluegrass picker" who has no patience for rock 'n' roll, let alone a liking for it. Charlie claims that although his dad gets into gospel and some roots country, he's "kind of like a jazz musician" in that he "doesn't want to hear anything else."

Although Charlie's father has never played bluegrass professionally, it's been a hobby for him, one which in years past gave him relief from long days working in the body shop at a Chevrolet dealership. Charlie remembers how his dad taught him to play the banjo and guitar despite being exhausted from his job. "He's a great father," Charlie says. "He's my hero." Charlie also worked in a body shop. "That's what he taught me," he says about his dad, "cars and guitars."

Charlie's mom didn't play any musical instruments and preferred listening to rock, and this became another influence in Charlie's musical upbringing. She liked the Rolling Stones, the Beatles, and Bob Dylan. ("I am not an abstract lyricist by any means," Charlie says. "I'm not going to write something that might be on *Blonde on Blonde,* the Dylan album.") He remembers an LP from her musical collection, *Taste of Honey* by the Ohio Players. Open up the cover and there appears a naked woman covered with honey being poured from a crystal ladle. For Charlie, it was a jolting contrast to his dad's religiosity—he was and remains a devout Baptist—and strict views about what should be considered moral and what immoral. "Those might have been my first dirty thoughts," Charlie recalls with a laugh.

Charlie's parents divorced when Charlie was two years old, and even though his folks stayed on good terms and he remembers his childhood as a happy one, he felt the awkwardness and sometimes the loneliness that came from the situation. It's one reason he wrote the song "Prayer for the Little Man," in which he sings: "I remember my daddy's phone calls/Just a kid, I'd always talk to him out in the hall/ To keep from settin' mama off."

In his youth Charlie found in some Southern rock bands an "economic" song structure and a discipline in performing that attracted him. Lynyrd Skynyrd and Tom Petty and the Heartbreakers were "verse, chorus, verse, chorus, bridge, solo, chorus, out. But they also were very rehearsed. If you've ever read stuff about what Al Kooper said [Kooper was a songwriter, musician, and record producer who performed with Lynyrd Skynyrd in the band's early years], solos were worked out completely, every single part, and they were as rehearsed a band as I've ever heard."

But Charlie also found attractive the long jams that Southern rock bands reveled in back in the '70s. "The Allman Brothers would stretch out and play a thirty-minute song. [And] that's fucking fantastic too. So you take the best of them. Marshall Tucker would be an example of a band that had both of those elements." He meant the tightness found in Lynyrd Skynyrd and Tom Petty and the extended-jam style characteristic of the Allmans.

Question: Lynyrd Skynyrd in its current state says what it is trying to do is to carry on the tradition of Southern rock. Do you see that as part of what you're doing?

Charlie: I think so. It doesn't bother us if people say that, if that's the way it makes people feel. I don't think we ever set out to be like "We are going to carry this flag forever. This is what we are and this is what we do." We just play the music and it sounds as it sounds.

We've never sat down and said, "All right. We're going to play this new song and we want it to sound exactly like this Marshall Tucker song." We've never done that about anybody. It's just...you play the way that you play; you sing the way that you sing. It is what it is.

All the talk about Southern rock made me think that I was wrong to be interviewing Blackberry Smoke after all, that they in no way fit into a book about Outlaw *country*. But at this point in our conversation, Charlie mentioned Hank Williams and insisted that they not only reach back to him but also to the "father of country music," Jimmie Rodgers.

Charlie's reference to Jimmie and Hank made me start thinking about Willie Nelson and Waylon Jennings, who had not yet been mentioned. Visions of the 1970s album *Wanted! The Outlaws* flashed through my mind with its cover, a wanted poster in tan. I despaired that the band might never have heard of those Outlaws. Post the cover on the brown walls of the RV, it seemed to me, and it would blend chameleon-like into obscurity, lost amid the plush surroundings of the ride.

But the band's drummer, Brit, pushed my despairing thoughts aside when he interjected: "Then there's those Outlaws from the 1970s who had so much power, so much feeling. It was real music. It told true stories. Some people can't relate to that type of music, and I understand that, but *I* can relate to it."

"Those guys too, you know," Charlie added, "at the time, they were really stepping out on the edge by moving away from Nashville and that box Nashville [is] guilty of trying to put everybody in. Waylon and Willie were definitely like screw that,... we're not going to stay here and be pasteurized for all the sheep."

"Pasteurized for all the sheep" was a humorous descriptive but also a revealing one. Here was a young band aware of the Outlaw legacy—aware of what it meant to be creative and independent and aware too of the other side, of what it meant to be a performer packaged for mass consumption, to lose one's creativity in order to bleat whatever Nashville wanted. Their statements reassured me that Blackberry Smoke really knows good music and made me think again about how country music has become victimized, as well as many of the mainstream artists themselves, by the pop machine—as victimized as stray sheep in a town of sexually depraved men.

Question: Did any one of the Outlaw artists have more of an influence on you than the others?

Charlie: Willie. I think Willie to me because Willie did so much. When you talk about really fearless, Willie Nelson is the real, real fearless one—not taking anything away from Waylon because Waylon was a trailblazer too. But Willie—think about what he did—after *Red Headed Stranger*, what does he soon follow it up with? An album of standards [*Stardust*]. Only he would come up with some crazy shit like that.

❧❧

Charlie calls Willie a fantastic writer. "His songs, like [those of] Hank Williams," he says, "are timeless; they'll never get old. Each generation will discover them and love them, just like the generation before did."

Charlie also heaps praise on Townes Van Zandt, Guy Clark, and Billy Joe Shaver as songwriters. "Townes," he says "is so poetic and aching and is so intelligent," whereas "Guy's always been a little bit of a more real-life type of lyricist. Townes seemed like an escapist to me, or maybe he was so complicated and had so much going on in his brain." Charlie adds: "Guy and Billy Joe Shaver are able to turn a phrase that is so simple but it sticks with you. And me personally, when I hear it, it stops me in my tracks, and I'll be like, 'Wow, why haven't I heard it said that way before?'"

Charlie believes that today there are too many pseudo-Outlaws. "There are a lot of people now that are like 'Yeah, Outlaw, we're this and that,'" says Charlie. "That word tends to get overused. No you're not; shut up. That's been done. Those guys [in the 1970s], they laid the groundwork for that. So if you really want to be Outlaw about it, do something that people ain't expecting you to do."

Brit adds: "I think a good amount of the public can see through bullshit. No matter what type of music it is, you can tell if it's real or coming from the heart."

Question: If they can see through bullshit, why are so many people listening to pop Nashville?

Charlie: There's always going to be shitty pop music.

Brit: Well, those aren't people to me. [*Laughter.*]

Charlie: They don't become people until they turn twenty-five.

Brit: But you know what I'm saying, though. I guess...our musical peers, they can tell—if its rap or whatever—they can tell if it's coming from the heart or if it's somebody just saying, "That did well, let's go do that now." You go see somebody play live, you can tell. Can't you tell if it's coming from the heart when somebody's playing live music, and they're feeling it?

His plaintive voice had a twinge of desperation to it, as if he were looking for reassurance, as if he were saying, "Please, please, tell me I'm right." If I were to answer him, I would say yes. But that would beg a question: What if the heart is really a beating cash register and has been totally conquered by materialistic impulses and commercialized schemes? If so, we're doomed.

Question: Do you guys see yourselves in any way on the cutting edge?

Charlie: I think we're just doing what comes naturally, and we're not following anybody's template, because there's really not one. Well, there are templates to follow, but we couldn't do that because we're too goofballish and stubborn and old.

Question: But in doing what comes naturally, aren't you on the cutting edge?

Charlie: Well, yeah. But at the same time, what I'm saying is we're only doing what we know how to do, which is to go out and play this music. It's not about how cute we are or where our jeans came from. It's all about the music being real first. We don't want to go up there and play a bunch of shit that doesn't move us every night. That would be pointless.

✂ ✂

The band has been together in its current form for about ten years, except for the keyboardist, Brandon Still, who joined the group some three years ago. Brit admitted that there has been friction at times, but he says they all have benefited from the experience of having played in other bands before. Moreover, he says, "We know what's important. It's not really about us. It's about the music and what it feels like when we make it. It's worth more than any argument and worth more than any bad vibe."

Indeed, there could have been arguments over choosing the band's name, but it turned out to generate only frustration. Brit said: "We had another name [in mind], but somebody else had it. Everything's been thought of, you know. So we were getting a little bit desperate because we had some offers to do some touring and some shows, and obviously you need a name. So we asked our friends, we asked Chris and Steve from the Black Crowes, 'Hey, have you thought of any name that just hits you, like we should have named our band this rather than the Black Crowes?... Have you thought of anything like that since you were established?' And they started sending us names. Most of them were just jokes and funny stuff. Finally, Chris sent Blackberry Smoke. We were: 'That seems like something no one else will have, and so it seems safe.'"

Like most Outlaw artists, Blackberry Smoke adheres to a grueling road schedule and has built its fan base primarily through travel. At first, they lived on a steady diet of honky-tonks and roadhouses, breathing in cigarette smoke and gulping down drinks bought for them by their fans. Today, they still play many small venues, but their schedule contains more dates at stadiums, auditoriums, festivals, and casinos.

The early years made the group tighter musically and closer personally, for they could see in every honky-tonk the remains of broken bands and the traces of shattered dreams. Survival and advancement required more than getting drunk together; it required cooperation, growth, and hard work—and Blackberry Smoke works exceptionally hard. In fact, probably because they have been screwed over too often by people who made big promises but failed to follow through, the band grows impatient with those who lack a strong work ethic.

Blackberry Smoke learned lessons they thought would never need to be learned. In that early period, Charlie was drinking heavily. Then one day after a binge in New Orleans—when he was hung over "with bloody eyeballs and with the harsh light of day hitting me"—Brit took him aside and told him that his reckless behavior was hurting everyone.

Charlie has since given up alcohol, and his song "Lesson in a Bottle" comes from the words Brit said to him in New Orleans. ("There's a lesson in a bottle that never gets fucking learned," Brit had told him.) "Blue lights and fistfights,... sloppy drunk and a drug abuser," Charlie sings. Maybe the cross from the Baptist church was casting its shadow over him.

> *There's a lesson in a bottle*
> *That never gets learned.*
> *Sweep out the ashes*
> *Of the bridges that I've burned.*
> *White lines and wild times,*
> *Passed out cold and left behind.*
> *Then I'm right back*
> *In the saddle again.*
>> "Lesson in a Bottle"
>> From *New Honky Tonk Bootleg*

"Puff the Magic Dragon," Charlie said. The band had turned on the TV as they were getting ready to head into the Hard Rock and was watching *Wheel of Fortune*. Charlie was blurting out his answer to one of the puzzles. "It's really not hard to figure it out when it says 'magic dragon' on it," he said. "Let's see...," Brit added, "there's only a couple of magic dragons. There's Puff, there's—"

Before he could finish his sentence, their manager, Trey Wilson, reminded them that the eight o'clock show time at the Hard Rock was indeed a "hard start"—meaning that by the terms of their contract they had to be punctual. He invited me to accompany the band, and a few minutes later, we left the RV and walked through the parking lot toward the back of the building.

As we did so, we trodded on ground that six years earlier had been devastated by Hurricane Katrina. The ocean, the river, and the creek had gotten higher, and the recently constructed Hard Rock was totally destroyed just two days before its scheduled grand opening. It had to be completely rebuilt. The new Hard Rock is a middle finger aimed at the nasty side of Mother Nature but promises to be no more effective than a bouncer throwing out a still-determined drunk; it's easy to sense there will be another fight. A good one comin' on, at that.

Trey opened the door for us, and we walked along a maze of hallways to a dressing room. Once there, the band sat down and made small talk, while I marveled at the selection of food and the open bar that had been made available. The band pretty much bypassed the goods. They were focusing on the upcoming show and also had to meet some of their fans in a meet-and-greet.

Brit had earlier told me that they like to hang out with those who follow them. They marvel at the extent to which some of their fans travel to see them—in some cases, hundreds of miles. "They've started having friendships where they go on the road together," Brit said. "That's nothing that the radio can get you."

As the band approached the backstage room for the meet-and-greet, Trey told them to slow down. "Let it build," he said, referring to the anticipation of their arrival. "Wait for it." That is, wait for the crowd to sense that Blackberry Smoke was about to walk through the door. Charlie stopped only for a moment, and then, either because he didn't like Trey's instruction or he was unfamiliar with acting that way, he quickly entered the room.

There were a couple of dozen people there who had VIP passes. The band talked with their guests, laughed, signed autographs, and posed for pictures.

About twenty minutes later, we walked to the stage and stood behind the curtains. The band was a bit tense as they waited for Trey to get the word to begin. Paul Jackson, the guitarist, yawned as he paced about. "I don't know why I do this, but it happens every time right before I play," he told me. He wasn't yawning from boredom; he was yawning from anxiety.

Trey heard from the stage manager at eight o'clock sharp and waved his arms to motion the band out. As soon as Blackberry Smoke appeared, a loud cheer went up from the crowd. "Hey, Charlie!" several people cried. The elaborate stage lights flashed blue, red, and orange, and the band began rocking the house.

The material drive is important and in many ways commendable. So too is the artistic drive. They clash, they merge, they move on, taking the Outlaw artist on a ride that he must ultimately define, generating choices that *he* must make.

Question: Do you guys feel that you can relate to the Outlaws who are still in those vans?

Brit: Shit, more than I want to.

Charlie: Yeah, Brit's going to get VAN LIFE tattooed on his stomach.

Question: I thought your success happened overnight.

Brit: Well, sure! [*Laughter.*]

Before Blackberry Smoke finished their show at the Hard Rock, I went into the crowd to take photos and get a feel for what was happening. Onstage, Brit was focused on his drumming and Brandon glided his fingers smooth as silk over the keyboards. Richard played the bass (his instrument of choice is a Fender or Zemaitis) with such acumen I wondered what it might be like if he got to underpin a long melodic set similar to what the Allman Brothers did. And Paul harmonized his voice sweetly and strongly, never overpowering Richard or Charlie. (A fan standing next to me turned to me and said emphatically, "They make it look so easy.") As Charlie talked to the crowd in between songs, he was upbeat, friendly, a front-porch type of guy.

Blackberry Smoke had arrived at the midlevel of monetary success by making their fans happy while producing good music still rooted in country and rock traditions. They were able to bend their guitar strings and make their fans feel the artistry, the emotion, and the commitment they felt inside.

When I interviewed the band, they had just finished recording *The Whippoorwill.* In a subsequent telephone conversation I had with Charlie, he called the CD "beautiful." Their previous albums, he said, had been recorded under duress, where they would lay down a track and then have to go out on the road before being able to go back into the studio. "Finally, we got five days instead of one," he said, "and it turned out exactly, *exactly,* like all of us wanted it to."

He said that he was especially excited "because one of the co-producers, Clay Cook, who used to be in Marshall Tucker, actually said, 'No click.' The click will suck the life out of a song. It's robotic. Not many [artists] say that because it makes an engineer's job easier, because everything is to the click, so if he's got to make edits, he can do it."

Click tracks are potentially the bane to an artist's music. Often in the studio and sometimes onstage, a musician will use a click. It's no more than a modernized metronome, which provides metrical beats measurable per minute. The metronome, which looks like a tail wagging from inside of a box, was patented in the early 1800s in Europe as a "musician's helper." It allows the musician to keep a consistent tempo. In 1817, Beethoven provided metronome markings in his compositions, and the device was soon widely used by other classical composers and musicians, such as pianists.

Today the metronome has been replaced by an electronic click, often handheld, and the click can be created on a computer with an MP3 file. Advocates say that the click keeps rhythms even and clear and the meter consistent. Opponents say it turns the musician into a machine. Imagine a single beat repeated twice every second to produce an overall 120 beats per minute. Imagine listening to this mechanical beat through a headphone—with this device, you can know precisely when to hit a drum, for example. So you can play exactly the same way all the time. Now take it to the stage, and you can play exactly as you did in the studio—conceivably, and perhaps with good reason, a person could consume a pint of whiskey and remain true to the beat.

For *The Whippoorwill* Blackberry Smoke uses no click, no metronome, no mechanics—only emotion. They also turned to a new record label. Their previous one, the independent Bama Jam, went belly-up about the time the band was ready to go back into the studio. Just as they thought all was lost, they received a call from a friend, Zac Brown. "We played some shows with him and his band," Charlie says in an online magazine interview. "We watched his rise to stardom. You know, everybody in Georgia did. Him being a Georgia boy, we were proud watching him take the world by storm, so to speak. So, Zac [said to us]: 'If you guys need a home, you've definitely got one.' He actually did something, and it means so much, and it speaks volumes about Zac as a person." As a result, the band signed with Southern Ground Records, which Zac had recently started.

I prodded Charlie to imagine himself writing an e-mail to a record executive on Music Row. "What would you tell him?" I asked. He responded: "I would want to say, 'You should be ashamed of yourself for the crap that you shove down people's throats.' But it's always happened. There's been good stuff and then there's been shit.... I would say, 'How do you find that middle ground where you let country music evolve, but it doesn't lose its identity?....' The only identity it seems to have is a cowboy hat from time to time. It doesn't sound anything like what we love about country music."

Once back home, I again envisioned that Southern house, the one with the muscle car, the clothesline, and the satellite dish. The breeze was stirring some lace curtains in a window and making the front-porch swing move gently back and forth. The crazy quilt was still there, draped over the swing, but perched on it, and enjoying the night air, was a whippoorwill, singing loudly and moving its head around as it eyed its surroundings.

When I started writing this profile, I had not listened to any of the band's songs from *The Whippoorwill*. The vision of the patch quilt on the front porch that I recounted earlier in this chapter had come to me from my imagination, created in a blessed moment.

Only later did I play the title song and decide to include these lyrics from it: "I dreamed I heard that whippoorwill sing/Yes, she sang my song and called me by name..../You sewed my years together *like a patchwork quilt....*" With those words, my jaw dropped. My imagery and the band's had merged.

We were on the same road, and although we had gotten there differently, we were moving forward, refusing to let the past bind us and inhibit our progress while at the same time realizing that the past meant more than a cold shackle around our souls, for there was much to learn from it, much to embrace and hold dear, and much to cherish rather than regret.

For Charlie the inspiration behind the title song to *The Whippoorwill* came from his grandmother. She had an enormous influence on him when he was a boy. A widow for years, she committed herself to taking care of her family and living a godly life. A devout Southern Baptist, she took part in many charitable works, and the many losses she suffered in her life only deepened her faith. Charlie was brought up in the church and remembers well the preachers who implored him to live the righteous way. Charlie remembers, too, his grandmother as an "old-school" woman who would cook for the family and not eat until everyone else had eaten and then would do so alone, in the kitchen.

She was an avid musician. She taught Charlie his first chords on the mandolin. He became so excited about learning to play the piano that she taught him how. It's easy to imagine Charlie as a little boy at his grandmother's house, sitting barefoot next to her on a worn bench, their fingers tapping the keys, also worn from use, and both of them smiling as they brought to life the music they loved. As much as the tantalizing aroma of home cooking permeated the house and carried with it feelings of security, comfort, and love, music was always present and did much the same. Charlie fondly likens the setting to what one of the characters on *The Andy Griffith Show* once said, that music is just as important as breathing.

Charlie's grandmother loved flowers. She loved the bougainvillea and the sweet fragrance from the honeysuckle. One day, she took Charlie aside and showed him how to suck from the honeysuckle bloom, how to pull the stem through his teeth to extract one precious little drop.

She also taught Charlie the different sounds made by birds, as she whistled their tunes and brought alive the bobwhite and the whippoorwill. Maybe he even imagined the whippoorwill calling his name. In some folklore, the whippoorwill portends death. For Charlie, the whippoorwill symbolizes life—the beauty found in life overall, but most especially in the life of his grandmother.

Several songs on the CD, which was recorded in a former church—Echo Mountain Recording in Asheville, North Carolina—reach into the deep ferment of Southern religious experience. The back cover even consists of a black-and-white photograph, circa early 1900s, of an outdoor baptism.

The lyrics from the different songs brim separately and collectively with the confluence of past and present, religious spirit and secular senses: "Well, my fall from grace was a sight to see..., I've danced with the devil 'til I'm in debt," "I may not get to heaven, Lord, for the wicked things I do," "Good Lord's smiling down on me/I ain't got a worry on my mind." Then there's the instrumental beginning to "One Horse Town," a melody wrapped in a consecrated veil.

The title track drips Deep South and conveys the experiences Charlie shared as a child with his grandmother; the bougainvillea comes together with the honeysuckle juice that Charlie had learned to extract. As Charlie's friend, Zac Brown, put it when he first heard the lyrics, they convey the sense of how a person finds more to savor from a little bit than a lot.

Charlie also sings of going down the Jericho road—perhaps sent that way by a preacher, by his grandmother, by his deeply religious childhood, by all of those and more—while standing barefoot and smiling by a piano, one from today, maybe, but more likely the one on which his grandmother taught him how to play. And he seems to lament his failure to live fully the righteous way, as his preacher had said and his grandmother had done, and so he sings: "I hung my head in shame." ("Lord above," he agonizes.)

Blackberry Smoke has posted at its website a headline about *The Whippoorwill:* HAUNTING BIRD FOREBODES LOST LOVE, MADNESS, SOUTHERN ROCK. Haunting bird, haunting CD, and haunting imagery. Charlie lost much when his grandmother died: she was no longer around to sing with, to smell flowers with, and to smile with. But she remains in his heart—"she's always here with me"—her love quilted into what he plays, what he sings, what he writes and then offers to others song by song, lyric line by lyric line, drop by drop, extracted from the sweetness of the musical vine.

The Whippoorwill from today might well shape Blackberry Smoke's future, and maybe the whippoorwill—in a dream or in a song, or in the love given from one person to another—will call out our names, capture our souls, and help reveal to us who we are. "Could the whippoorwill look into my eyes and be bold?"*

> *Going through life the righteous way,*
> *The only way, so the preacher would say.*
> *You put me on the Jericho road....*
> *Well, I dreamed I heard that whippoorwill sing,*
> *Yes, she sang my song, and called me by name, Lord.*
> *Starting all over again,*
> *Starting all over again.*
>
> "The Whippoorwill Song"
> From *The Whippoorwill*

Help me remember my lesson. Sing for me, show me *the way*, and help me live. Help those on the Jericho road start all over again.

---

* From "The Runaway Slave at Pilgrim's Point" by Elizabeth Barrett Browning.

Charlie Starr, Hard Rock Casino, Biloxi, MS (2012)

INTERLUDE: HARVEST FUGUE

By Neil Hamilton

Don't leave me, don't forget me,
Plant me a cherry tree and build me a nest.
Make the juices flow and disregard the rest,
For the storm has come and the harvest has passed.

If a river courses through life and leaves alluvial sands,
Then I've been shaped by something I can't understand.
But don't leave me floating,
And don't let me drown.
Save me instead with what I have found,
And the heart to which I am forever bound.

Elizabeth Cook, Levitt Shell, Memphis, TN (2012)

Chapter 13

ELIZABETH COOK

Mama's Prayers

Not everybody has a mom,
And no one does forever long.
And I used to think, "Well, Lord, that's just not fair."
But I believe the words are for always,
And they won't end with her days.
I'm grateful to be in my mama's prayers.
"MAMA'S PRAYERS"
FROM BALLS

In Smith County, in eastern Tennessee, a two-lane country road jumps up and down the valleys and wraps itself around the mountains and hills before it reaches a gravel drive seemingly in the middle of nowhere. The drive extends across a cleared swath of land and ends at a single-wide trailer perched on a hillside. In the front, a covered wooden porch extends down the length of the trailer, and a swing hangs from the rafters, making a cozy spot for relaxation and thought.

Many a time Elizabeth Cook would visit her mom, Joyce, at this trailer—Joyce's home—and they would sit together on the swing and gaze at the bucolic scene that surrounded them. The forty acres of land on which the trailer was perched held a pasture for goats and a big barn. The trees on the land provided shelter for the birds, which added their melodies and flights of fancy to the country setting.

The trailer itself was surrounded by flowers, many of them planted lovingly by Joyce. This natural skirting made it seem as if the porch were a colorful ark, with Elizabeth and Joyce afloat in the complicated flood of life as they talked about their music and their family, an unusual and sometimes perplexing clan. Mother and daughter often recalled the stories that Elizabeth's dad, Thomas, had told them. He was a larger-than-life man, adventuresome and strong-willed, and with a captivating sense of humor.

As they sat and reminisced and the sky grew dark at the end of the day, moonbeams painted rivulets of light that sparkled and danced on the moist grass and made it feel that much more wonderful to be alive. The serenity made the two women grow quiet and caused them to wander deeper into Thomas's stories, reaching for a palette of hues whose mix depended as much upon the listener, the format, and the setting as it did on the storyteller.

Elizabeth once said to me: "Any writer who writes something is always writing their truth, for that moment, even if it's fictional." With that statement she gets at one of the contradictions of art, bound in human existence as securely as parchment papers inside leather covers: truth can be fiction and fiction can be truth.

For this moment, imagine Thomas as a young man, bumping along the sandy back roads of Florida and kicking up clouds of dust as he drives an old truck under a moonlit sky. He wasn't about to break a sweat, not at all. He had done this many times before and had never been caught. He was hauling moonshine as part of an illicit network that ran along the eastern seaboard, and his market was Jacksonville. Thomas liked the action, and the money was pretty good. This night, however, as he came to the point where the back road joined a paved highway, a bright light tore into his eyes, and he soon found himself peering down the barrels of several guns. Commands were shouted; badges were flashed. Thomas was busted and busted good. The feds shut him down, and he was sentenced to three years in the Atlanta penitentiary.

The details of this scene, as I present them here, might be imaginary, but the arrest was real.

Question: How autobiographical are your songs?

Elizabeth: They are pretty autobiographical. I would say they are pretty accurate. They're an accurate reflection of my reality.

My reality and no one else's, certainly not that of some anonymous writer whose thoughts connect to the performer only as a ledger book connects to a bank account. For Elizabeth country music has its roots primarily in her experiences, her soul, and her grounding in the legendary artists of the past.

I was speaking with Elizabeth inside a cramped van parked beneath a blazing sun in Memphis, Tennessee. The engine was running, and the air conditioning was on full blast. She was waiting to take the stage as part of the What the Folk Festival, an annual event put together by alternative country artist Todd Snider. The festival occurs at an outdoor band shell, called Levitt Shell, known as a historic site for rock 'n' roll and country. Here in July 1954 Elvis Presley gave his first paid performance when he opened for country star Slim Whitman. Among other early country artists, Johnny Cash also played at the shell.

Elizabeth was excited about singing where these legends once had and excited, too, about being on the same bill with Todd and fellow country artist Hayes Carll. "It's a huge validation for me," she said. "I still feel like I've got a long way to go. I'm nowhere near as good as I'm gonna get,... but being around these guys is inspiring, and the fact that I get to play ball with them on their field, even if I'm in the outfield, is encouraging to me."

To say that country music ran through Elizabeth's blood at an early age would be an understatement. Her parents were both musicians: Thomas played standup bass, and Joyce played the guitar and mandolin. When Elizabeth was four years old, they recruited her to sing with their band. "I could sing a Buck Owens song on key," she jokes, "and that excited them."

When she was nine, her parents created a backup band for her. "My dad bought a PA system and hired a drummer, bass player, keyboardist, and guitar player," Elizabeth says. "He put together a list of covers and songs my mom had written, and we put on a show."

They played honky-tonks in the Southeast, and Elizabeth found herself singing plenty of roots country. She grew up fast, not only in learning about the adult world, but also in learning about music. Yet as a child she still needed to discover the spirit behind the songs. "I was singing Hank Williams before I understood what it was like to have pain," she says, "what it was like, you know, to have all the things that are necessary to make that kind of music in a convincing way."

Elizabeth was born in Wildwood, Florida, in 1972. By that time, her dad had been arrested twice more for trafficking in moonshine and had served additional sentences in the penitentiary. Not long after his release, he met Elizabeth's mom. As Elizabeth described it to David

Letterman on his late-night TV show, when Thomas got out of prison, he moved next door to Joyce. The two talked from time to time, but Thomas had a girlfriend. Then the girlfriend left him, at which point Joyce, who was from the mountains of West Virginia and used to country ways, decided to cheer him up by bringing him a "big ol' pot of beans." As Elizabeth told the story lightheartedly, Letterman and the crowd, and even Elizabeth, thought it funny and laughed loudly.

Thomas and Joyce each had five children by previous marriages, so when Elizabeth was born, she became part of a large family. She joked on *Letterman* that she had yet to meet all of her half brothers and half sisters.

Thomas played his standup bass for a prison band and earned a welder's certificate. He was planning to use his newly acquired trade to make moonshine stills when he got out but changed his mind. "Prison shaped my dad's life," Elizabeth says, "like wars shaped a lot of my friends' parents." It turns out, she says, that "jail is where the roots of his long recovery began." He still wanted to weld but not to make stills. So on his release, he bought a mobile unit, attached it to his truck, and became a traveling welder, going from farm to farm in central Florida.

According to Elizabeth, when her dad and Joyce began their honky-tonk band, Joyce was the more serious musician. Thomas would play, but "he never messed with instruments much. He was more of an entertainer. He was a comedian, and he was funny and outrageous."

Question: Were you as close to your dad as you were to your mom?

Elizabeth: Our relationship was a little more contentious because he was a bit of a hard-ass character. He was a dad, he was tougher. Mothers can be a little gentle. He raised me like a boy. He raised me to be really independent and fierce. He would tell me, "You're the only boy I've got." He would throw a fifty-pound bag of feed over my shoulder. [I was] a tiny, tiny thing and he would just treat me like a boy. I went fishing, I baited my own hook, and I had to take my own fish off whenever I caught it. He was a great dad; we were deeply bonded.

In her love for roots country, Elizabeth's mom hoped one day to go beyond the local honky-tonks, make it to Nashville, and perform at the *Grand Ole Opry*. When Elizabeth was a child and showed that she could sing, both Joyce and Thomas saw in their daughter the possibility of fulfilling a dream—either through her talent taking the family band to the top or by her becoming an accomplished performer on her own.

> *Saw the look in your eyes when you showed Tammy's house*
> > *on TV,*
> *And you can't believe Loretta has her own town.*
> *And the way you get lost when you play and sing, well, it's easy*
> > *to see*
> *Your dreams had to be bygones because life pinned you down....*
> *But from time to time when I play a song,*
> *No matter what you say,*
> *I know you see yourself up on the stage.*
> > "Mama You Wanted to Be a Singer Too"
> > From *Hey Y'all*

From her mom's music, Elizabeth learned more than the notes, more than the lyrics, more than the beat. She tapped into the spirit. "She had all that strife in her life," Elizabeth says. "All that pain." Elizabeth could see that when her mother sang, it healed her. In time, that connection to the pain of life, and to the joys and to the healing—to what was missing when Elizabeth first sang those Hank Williams songs—became the most important feature of roots country that she learned from her mom.

Elizabeth went to college, although her parents were of the mind that in doing so she might actually be ruining her life by becoming too educated and too removed from her country roots, musically and otherwise. She graduated from Georgia Southern University in 1996 with degrees in accounting and computer information systems.

Elizabeth then worked in business for a while, but with her childhood background in country music, her voice, and her desire to write songs, Nashville beckoned. She soon signed with a major record label, Atlantic. Her contract was then sold to Warner Brothers, and in 2002 they released her CD, *Hey Y'all.* It went practically unnoticed.

Warner didn't promote it, Elizabeth says, but she then adds that it didn't deserve promotion because it wasn't any good. In truth, the CD has a lot going for it, especially the track "Mama You Wanted to Be a Singer Too." That song pulls at the listener's heart as it unveils Joyce's tough times in West Virginia and shows how the sometimes-cold blizzard of life ("Had babies from a deadbeat dad," the song goes in reference to Joyce's first husband) demolished her dreams of country stardom. Moreover, Elizabeth's voice carries with its range and charm the proof of her considerable talent.

The album actually failed because Warner Brothers was caught in a merger between Time Warner and AOL, and the company's record executives didn't want to risk their already shaky jobs on a CD that didn't follow the formula for Nashville pop. "I just did not fit in," Elizabeth says. "Blake Shelton and I were signed at the same time. We were coming up together, and if we were at functions, I would just hang out in a corner. I couldn't even fake having anything in common with any of them. It was really weird."

When Elizabeth signed her record contract, she tried to write for the Nashville mainstream scene. "I was getting paid a lot of money to do it, and I was just not good at it," she says. "It was like Johnny Cash being a carpet salesman or whatever kind of salesman he was here in Memphis. He just wasn't good at it. I was just not good at sitting down and trying to write a power ballad for Martina McBride, for her new record. I tried because I was being paid to do it and I felt like it was my job, and I was raised that when you have a job, you're lucky to have a job, and you do your job to your damnedest ability, for your bosses' pleasure and their needs. I really tried, I really did.... Finally, it got so bad that I woke up sick to my stomach every day."

So she quit writing pop country and went to the president of Warner Brothers and asked to be released from her record deal. He agreed and, she says, "I just went to waiting tables and started putting out indie records."

Question: How does a song idea come to you?

Elizabeth: I wish I knew. You sort of have to spend some time dwelling over the right lobe, over your right ear,... spend some time dwelling there, and if you can do that in an undistracted way, usually there's some thoughts that are floating around in there that are interesting. Then you start putting them down on paper, and you get some sort of flow going out of something that's original.

Question: Do you write with a guitar? At a piano?

Elizabeth: It usually starts with a lyric, and if it feels like something's got legs, it moves to a guitar pretty quick.

The right lobe, the right brain—Elizabeth is referring to the psychology-based right brain/left brain theory as it emerged from the work of Roger W. Sperry (a winner of the Nobel Prize in 1981) and then became popularized. In studying the effects of epilepsy, he discovered that cutting the structure that connects the two hemispheres of the brain could reduce or eliminate seizures.

When the patients he worked with experienced other symptoms—such as being unable to name objects processed by the right side of the brain but still able to name those processed by the left—Sperry claimed that this showed a cerebral split in the handling of specific activities. From this conclusion, others advanced the view that the right side of the brain best handles expressive and creative tasks—such as music, painting, and writing—while the left side best handles logical and analytical tasks, such as business, math, and science. Some people might be more right- than left-brained and vice versa. Understanding this, of course, involves a left-brain exercise. Writing it involves a heady right-brain moment. (And if there is any truth to this theory, it perhaps helps to explain the clash between record executives—the business people—and artists—the music people—as an ongoing *war of the brains*.)

But Harold Gardner, a professor at Harvard University who has studied creativity, offers a different analysis. "There can be no such thing as a hermit creator," says Gardner. "Psychologists tend to view Picasso as a solitary genius who created Cubism [an abstract form of painting] in isolation. In this view, the artist was born with creativity, and if we knew enough about the brain, we'd know exactly where to look for it. But it's simplistic to try to locate artistic creativity in the brain." Gardner sees the situation as one where the environment plays the crucial role in a person's development. After all, Picasso worked within a craft shaped by society, he was judged by others within the craft, and he came from a time and place specific to his life.

While Elizabeth owes much to her "right lobe" for her creative talent, the environment has worked its influence as well, such as in her at-odds relationship to Nashville pop and the record companies that produce it, both of which are a part of her own specific time and place. Like Picasso, she paints. She paints with songs, and she paints from something that bubbles up inside of her. No revolutionary Cubist, she nevertheless keeps reaching back to country roots (themselves shaped by a particular time and place) and reassembles those roots to reflect her life in a modern-day world.

Yet Elizabeth evoked the workings of another influence on her music when she told me that, for her, songwriting becomes largely *spiritual.* So where does this fit in? And where does the *sense of the spiritual* fit in? It's certainly something beyond any *rational* analysis of right lobes, left lobes, and the environment.

In Elizabeth's case her connection to her mom shapes her art and even more: *it shapes her life.* Elizabeth's hands and those of her mom grasp a gospel plow together; in doing so they are yoked as one with the Holy Spirit, who guides them through their effort as they turn one row and then another, here a work of art, there a work of survival.

Question: How does spirituality affect your songwriting?

Elizabeth: When it's good, it's deeply spiritual. When I'm more present in it, it's not as good.

Elizabeth told me that she doesn't adhere to any religious doctrine. "It's not my style," she said. "Any spirituality that I have comes from being an observer of a higher plane. And I'm not always there. But when I am, I know it."

Question: You sing that you will forever be in your mama's prayers. Do you really believe that?

Elizabeth: Yeah, because spiritually she's still our mother. She's still got that same protective arm around us that is so special. Once you've had it, it doesn't go away.

❧❧

We were still in the van awaiting the start of Elizabeth's show in Memphis when I asked her to tell me more about her relationship with her mom. As she did so the intimate connection became more intense.

Question: You think your mom looks after you?

Elizabeth: Yeah, I know she does.

Question: How do you know that?

Elizabeth: Because she's talked to me a few times.

Question: How?

Elizabeth: In my ear. I've heard her voice say something.

Question: I'm interested in this partly because my mom passed away two and a half years ago, and I feel something similar.

Elizabeth: She told me where her skillet was once, [the one] that I was looking for in her kitchen. Her voice, in my ear, said, "It's in the oven, it's in the oven."

❧❧

But much more than the location of a skillet has affirmed her mom's presence. "I was just doing a gig at the Station Inn a few weeks ago," Elizabeth says. "It's a bluegrass club in Nashville; it's on Twelfth Avenue South, and it's down in the gulch. All this urban, yuppie thing has happened around it. It's this hilarious old shack in the middle of condos and Urban Outfitters and sushi bars. It's a bluegrass place where Ralph Stanley and Bill Monroe used to play. It's got that sort of legacy."

She paused for a moment, sipped from a bottle of water, and then looked directly at me and continued.

"Anyhow, it's where my mom would come to see me play in Nashville, and she would sit at a certain table tucked back by the soundboard. I haven't played there in several years; I've been on and on the road. The time that I used to play there, and she and Dad would come, was a certain chapter of my career, and I have certain memories there with her. And my dad's passed on too, so this was my first time back there since all that's happened. So I was partway through the set list. I don't usually write out a set list, I just wing it as I go, and she asked for that song."

"What song?" I inquired.

"'Mama's Prayers.'"

As she ended her story, a gust of wind shook the van and moved the tree limbs above it. The disturbance couldn't have lasted more than a few seconds, but it startled me and made me feel the strong spiritual presence that I often get at special times.

> *Things go right and things go wrong,*
> *Sometimes you hear me sing a song,*
> *But you'll always find me in my mama's prayers.*
> "Mama's Prayers"
> From *Balls*

Elizabeth took the stage in the early evening. "Come on, Jesus," one of the event organizers implored as rain clouds gathered, "don't let it pour." It didn't. Instead, as the sun dropped lower, it enveloped the crowd and the grass on which the crowd was seated in a blanket of gold and orange colors. I sensed that when Elizabeth began singing, her mom was there with her, as surely as if she were still alive and sitting by a soundboard or standing backstage to watch her daughter perform the country music that owed so much to the past.

Question: Do you think you're making your mom's dreams come true?

Elizabeth: Yes.

Question: What would she have wanted for you?

Elizabeth: I struggled so hard outside of Music Row to find my place, and I was always such a freak and such an outsider, yet I loved country music, and I had these deep, deep ties to it, and so it was frustrating to not be able to connect to what was right before me and even offered to me. I was playing the *Grand Ole Opry* a lot. That was a bit of an anomaly in my career, that they came along when they did and would have me on all the time. [My mom] got to go watch me. It was the most favorite thing, I think, that ever happened to her. She saw me stand on that stage hundreds of times, and she would go out front and watch, and then she'd come back [behind the curtains]. She knew the door lady. And she had her little place where she would sit, and I think it was a big dream come true for her.

> *God grant me strength to see in you,*
> *I hope I make your dreams come true,*
> *'Cause mama you wanted to be a singer too.*
> "Mama You Wanted to Be a Singer Too"
> From *Hey Y'all*

I was once bemoaning to her on the phone how frustrated I was with some deal, and I wish that I could do better. And she said, "As far as I'm concerned, if you never do anything else, the fact that I've seen you play the *Grand Ole Opry* so many times and be loved there has been just wonderful." I think that nothing else that's come since would be as important to her—not *David Letterman*, not anything else that I've done, not playing world stages. None of that's as big a deal to her as playing at the *Grand Ole Opry*.

Question: On another level, which country artists have influenced you the most?

Elizabeth: The obvious: Loretta, Dolly, and Tammy were the trifecta. Willie, Merle, Waylon, Jessi Colter....

Question: Was that because of their songwriting?

Elizabeth: I don't know. I can't really say I used this person for this and I took that from this person. I don't think about it in those terms. I don't define it. It's just, I take all that in, and it washes out in some form. So it's just everything that I've ever heard has influenced me, some good and some I've heard like, "God, I don't ever want to do that, please don't ever let me do that."

In the band with Elizabeth is her husband, Tim Carroll. An accomplished singer, songwriter, and guitarist in his own right, he too walked away from big record deals to become an indie artist. "His guitar playing is really, really special," Elizabeth says, "and I've been able to apply that to my songs, which has been so fun for me. It's like a dream come true. Like getting to have whatever your favorite guitar player is to play. I feel like I've got Neil Young because that's how he sounds to me."

Question: Do you and your husband write songs together?

Elizabeth: No. We write songs in the same space as each other, but they're always an independent effort. He can see [mine]; he's the first one to hear anything that I'm working on.... We're gentle and sensitive enough that we know when to encourage each other and when to get out of the way. We know when to be quiet. We know when to say, "Hey, that sounds like one of these other songs" or "That sounds really cool." Sometimes that's the encouragement I need to keep working.

He'll see a lyric I've got up, laying around somewhere,... so it's more like we are consultants for each other. So we don't cowrite, but we consult-write. It's cool.

Elizabeth's heavy Southern accent, when combined with her sense of humor, can make her come across as a backwoods hillbilly and somewhat of a ditzy blond. She's anything but. She knows what she's doing. She's savvy, and her combination of talent, determination, and wit makes her a joy to be around. When I asked Elizabeth how she became a guitar player, it turned into a lighthearted exchange.

Question: So how did you get to learn to play?

Elizabeth: Self-taught.

Question: What drew you to it?

Elizabeth: I can't dance. I used to clog. Oh God, yeah. You haven't seen that on YouTube?

Question: Really? There's a clogging thing of you on YouTube?

Elizabeth: Many. I used to do it until touring wore my knees out from sitting like this [cramped in a van] every day, so I can't clog in my shows anymore. So my clogs are retired. They're these scuffed-up white shoes with clogs on their bottom, and they're on our mantel in a place of honor.

They're retired.

Question: When did you give it up?

Elizabeth: About two years ago.

Question: So you're clogging history now?

Elizabeth: I had to let go.

Just as men dominate the world of record executives, they dominate the world of Outlaw artists. When I asked Elizabeth to explain this, she said, "Because it's true in everything. You know, good old-fashioned sexism, but we're working through that, and it's fine. Probably because I was raised more like a boy, I'm able to exist in this world a little bit better. A lot of girls with a softer spirit just end up marrying one of the Outlaw guys." She says that being a female artist means, "I have to write twice as good, be twice as good. I have to be way better to get the same amount of respect. Way better."

Question: Is this because of the audience? Or the record people?

Elizabeth: It's just because of people's gender bias. It's, like, she's a girl, what could she possibly have to say? She probably can't play good. Maybe she can sing okay, stand there and look pretty. But the thought that I might have something to say that wasn't some sort of record label's marketing idea for me to say is...

As she let her statement trail off, she left me thinking of her song "Sometimes It Takes Balls to Be a Woman" (which she co-wrote with her husband): "Oh, sometimes it takes balls to be/Big, big, big, big balls to be/Sometimes it takes balls to be a woman."

When Elizabeth concluded that *Hey Y'all* was a disappointment artistically, she worked hard to improve her songwriting and performance. *This Side of the Moon,* released in 2005 and with many of its songs co-written by Hardie McGehee, ranges from the upbeat "Cupid," replete with a honky-tonk piano, to the similarly arranged "Hard Hearted" and "This Side of the Moon," with its prominent steel guitar and tender lyrics: "How did we get on this side of the moon/Did we dance across the sun?" As an established songwriter, McGehee reaches back heavily to roots country, and it shows in the CD.

Balls, released in 2007 as pretty much a live album in the sense that it has little overdubbing or layering, really has two levels to it. On one level appears a kick-ass, don't-get-in-my-way woman. But it's Elizabeth Cook, after all; it isn't a truck-driving, boot-stomping, I'll-maul-your-face-and-then-sit-on-it femi-toughie.

So on another level her country twang holds sway, and her sweet demeanor never gets completely tucked away. She even becomes sentimental with "Mama's Prayers." Some reviewers criticized her for including this song in an otherwise rousing album. But far from being cutesy, it gets to the heart of what Elizabeth feels—what moves her— as she writes and plays her music. And if it sometimes takes balls to be a woman, it sometimes takes a mother's prayers to make the art come together; to make the day more tolerable, even enjoyable; and to keep the gospel plow righted.

> *When I'm down and think nobody cares,*
> *I remember that I'm in my mama's prayers.*

Elizabeth shifted gears for her most highly acclaimed CD, *Welder* (whose title refers to her father's occupation). In it, her voice sounds less sweet and more edgy. She combines personal stories with her humor, which erupts full-tilt for the songs "El Camino" and "Snake in the Bed." In "Yes to Booty," she lets loose a raucous tune from a woman's viewpoint: "If you say yes to beer/you say no to booty," she cautions her man.

Question: What do you think of *Welder?*

Elizabeth: I was not going to be satisfied until I made *Welder.* It took me three indie albums even for me to be able to evolve and have my own culmination of my own artistry. That's the payoff. It's the only reason for me to do it, because that's what I'm motivated by. I'm motivated by my own self-fulfillment and trying to do good work and satisfy my own tastes.

If I was gratified by prancing around on a stage in an expensive cocktail dress and having somebody put together my band for me and having somebody give me the song I'm to sing and [I'd] show up at the session and do my vocal and then leave,... there are people that are satisfied by that. And that's what they do, and they have an excellent business arrangement with their record label. And it's valid. I don't necessarily speak to "Well, that's not the right way" or whatever because there's people that consume it, there's people that buy it, there's people that don't mind it, people that love it. So you can't argue that. It just was not what *I* wanted.

I don't want to be famous. I don't give a shit about being famous, although I would like to make money. [*Laughter.*] But I've got to do it on my own terms or I'm miserable. It doesn't matter to have money. If I'm having to act like an idiot [or doing] what [to me] looks like acting like an idiot and humiliate myself and patronize music fans, I don't want to do that.

❧❧

On *Welder* Elizabeth rocks electric in the tune "Rock N Roll Man." Indeed, rock and pop have been big influences on her. She listens to Hole, Lady Gaga, Madonna—"I just sing along," she says. For Elizabeth rock provides another emotion. "It often calls out anger, angst, sex, a party," she observes, "through sound, usually." She mostly listens to music for mood. "Sometimes I need Courtney Love, sometimes I need Patsy Cline."

With a song like "El Camino," a fantasy about Elizabeth and a guy in a 1972 "refurb"—a "funky ass car"—who picks her up, *Welder* contains an eclectic and exciting mix of music. It displays Elizabeth's songwriting, voice, and guitar work at its finest.

Midway through her show at the Memphis band shell, Elizabeth switched from the songs found in *Balls* and *Welder* to the music she he had just finished recording for her EP *Gospel Plow*.

Onstage Elizabeth prefaced her gospel music with a story about how, when she was a child, her parents would take her to the honky-tonks on Friday and Saturday nights. Then on Sunday they would head for the Sunset Church of God. There a Pentecostal preacher pounded the Bible and laid hands on the worshippers. Elizabeth said that a band played gospel songs "until the smell of fried chicken wafted over the neighborhood" and lured everyone away.

In 2007 Elizabeth received an offer from SiriusXM Satellite Radio to host a show on its Outlaw music station. On *Letterman* she joked about how, on many occasions, she does her broadcast while on the road, which means from motel rooms. While in her bathrobe and sipping "a bad cup of Styrofoam coffee" to fight the grogginess from her previous night's stage show or the arduous travel schedule, she often winds up "dropping things and sneezing on the air." She joked: "People would not be impressed if they saw what's going on behind [the scenes]." To which Letterman responded: "Well, maybe that's what they enjoy and find so engaging and compelling." Elizabeth stopped him and interjected: "Yeah, that this show is a wee on the under-produced side."

Question: In one of your *Letterman* appearances you said that initially you didn't want to do the radio show. What made you change your mind?

Elizabeth: They let me ease into it. They let me do one day a week. At that point they needed a girl to be on the channel, they needed a little estrogen because it was all dudes. They needed a girl that had a Southern accent, that knew who Johnny Cash was. I don't think they foresaw that I would make some radio fans out there. I didn't, either. I thought, "I'm an artist and that's what I do, but we'll just see how it goes." So it was loosely entered into, and that was the slippery slope that four years later [has gone from one day to] five days a week.

Question: If somebody comes up to you and says: "Elizabeth, you have this show on Outlaw country radio; what in the world is Outlaw music?" What would be your response?

Elizabeth: It's really difficult to define. It depends on who you ask. My viewpoint of it is limited because my experience of it is limited. But when I think about it, I think Willie and Waylon didn't want to be told what to do, they could not reconcile the music they wanted to make with what was coming out of Nashville at that time, and they defected. So it's almost anybody that's operating [like] that.

I defected; I literally defected. I had the exact same scenario in a lot of ways. I made the decision that I'm not going to work with these people anymore. I wanted to make my own music.

Free once more. She went over the prison wall to the freedom of her art, and her body and mind reconnected with her soul. She adds: "What comes out of Music Row [today] is preconceived by a committee of fifteen marketing executives that micromanage everything from the photo shoot to the bridge of the song. It's prethought out; it's a huge business for them."

Question: How did you get to be on *Letterman*?

Elizabeth: From what I understand, David listens to [my show] *Apron Strings* on Sirius every day as he drives into [New York City]. He's a big fan and particularly of the kind of stuff we play on Outlaw country. He became interested in me and requested an interview for his show. It was shocking and [came] out of nowhere.

A huge chunk of Elizabeth fell away from her when her mom died. After all, her mom had taught her music, had taught her how to sing and how to caress a song, had taught her how to express her own feelings. Her mom had been her most enthusiastic supporter, her coach, her confidante.

> *When I'm down and think nobody cares,*
> *I remember that I'm in my mama's prayers.*

Whenever Elizabeth and her mom sat together on the porch swing at the trailer, the one perched on the hillside in Tennessee, and watched the rivulets of light dance on the grass, the silence of the stars would confirm their love for each other. That love held them together—a flowing river, joyfully eroding the banks of solitude. The essence of love, the great bond of human existence, the great hunger in our lives, has the power to destroy, but most assuredly, and most prominently, it has the power to create, and it has the power to mend broken hearts and save lost souls.

> *Sure as the skies will turn dark*
> *At the end of the day,*
> *The angels must count*
> *On what she's gonna say.*

Elizabeth chose to hold her mom's funeral where the sounds of guitars and mandolins still roam the mountains and hills, and where her mom was most comfortable. She chose to hold it at the trailer, next to the front-porch swing. "She is a non-pretentious person," Elizabeth says about her mom. "She didn't like ceremony; she didn't like formality. She was a hillbilly singer that came from the Appalachian vibe of musicians."

Elizabeth adds: "It came to me as soon as she passed, and we were all in the room with her, and I don't think she was even cold yet, and there was all my siblings and everything, and I said, 'No funeral parlor,' because I knew she would hate that. All those velvet drapes and carnation oil—that's just not my mom's style."

No funeral parlor. *Because I knew she would hate that.* There was Elizabeth, doing what her mama would want and knowing in her heart that it was right, just as she knows that her mom still walks with her.

> *At mama's funeral, organs didn't play,*
> *But you could hear the lonesome sway*
> *Of a local guitar man.*
> *He played Hank Williams songs,*
> *We all did "Further Along"....*
> *Oh, the birds showed up to sing*
> *As we gathered round the ol' porch swing*
> *Where her feet had worn the paint off the boards*
> *And her pillow sat all faded and torn.*
> *Her children all took turns*
> *Trying to find the words,*
> *Just wantin' to say somethin' right*
> *'Bout the best friend they'd found in life....*
> "Mama's Funeral"
> From *Welder*

When I first heard Elizabeth's song "Mama's Funeral," it reminded me of the day *my* mama was buried. It was a sunny morning. The breeze was blowing strong, but no wind could dry the tears in my eyes. Nor could any consolation. Yet amid the sadness and despair, I was touched by friends around me who reached out and provided me with support where I feared there would be none.

Much as with my friends, Outlaw music helped me in the darkest of times. As I face each day, Elizabeth's music reaches into my own shadowy dwelling place—filled with fear and confusion and desire and with love and happiness and hope—and brings me and the artist together as one.

"What do you think is the meaning for us being here and doing what we do, Elizabeth?" I asked as I still thought of that gust of wind that had rattled the van, stirred the trees, and lifted the spirit.

"To be challenged," she responded. "To learn and grow and rejoice and mourn. It keeps the ball spinning."

For this moment, imagine Elizabeth and her husband, Tim, at the end of the day, packing their van to leave Memphis. Once they finish, Tim slips behind the wheel and begins driving along a bumpy asphalt road pointed toward the interstate. Next to him in the front seat sits Elizabeth, and as the lights from the oncoming cars flash in her eyes, she begins to hum a song she has just finished writing.

She thinks about the radio show she will be doing in the morning and another appearance she will soon be making on *Letterman*. Suddenly a voice speaks to her—she hears it in her ear. Elizabeth smiles because she knows that she is in her mama's prayers. She looks out the window, and despite the traffic, she couldn't feel more at peace. Contented, happy even, she grasps Tim's hand, holds it tenderly, and goes to sleep.

The details for this closing scene, as I present them here, might be imaginary, but the artist and the sprit are real.

Elizabeth Cook, Levitt Shell, Memphis, TN (2012)

Bert David Newton, 2ⁿᵈ Street Music Hall, Gadsden AL (2012)

CHAPTER 14

BERT DAVID NEWTON

Names on My Guitar

Some friends and some foes,
So many faces in all the places I go.
And those who took country oh so damn far,
These are the names on my guitar.
"NAMES ON MY GUITAR"
FROM THE LIVE

"I insist," Bert David Newton says, "that my lead guitar play a Telecaster."

With that he stamps his allegiance to, his complete dedication to, and his unending, unloosening, unshakeable embrace of and alliance with the 1970s Outlaw movement as embodied in the music of Waylon Jennings, who made the Fender Telecaster an iconic part of his performances.

"Bourbon and rocks to start him off," Bert sings with his alluring baritone voice in "He Plays Country but He Lives Rock 'n' Roll." "A life of licks that he never lost/He writes from the heart and sings from the soul/He plays country but he lives rock 'n' roll." Then in a performance for his DVD *The Live,* he kicks out his left leg and growls out:

"AHHHHHHHH, LIVE IT!"

And Bert wants *you* to live it. He wants his music to be straight-from-the-heart good times. When he lets it fly from the Waylon-Jennings-roots side of country, from the Fender-Telecaster-be-my-master side, he lets it fly straight at you, as in take-no-prisoners style. He has little tolerance for what Music Row cranks out.

Question: How did you get into Waylon's music?

Bert: My dad listened to a lot of Willie Nelson, so I got turned on at a pretty early age to Willie. Then I started listening to the Highwaymen. To me it wasn't really Outlaw country music, it was just country music. Back then we were having that Garth Brooks bullshit that kind of brought everything down in the '90s. You can quote me on that, I don't give a shit.

Then I got into listening to Kris Kristofferson a whole lot. I got to where I was listening to Kris in my early twenties. It got to where I was just,... I would sit back, smoke pot, and listen to Kris. It got to be where I just understood everything he was saying. I was listening to it over and over, only old stuff, and it was amazing, simply, totally amazing. And then I hear Waylon covering a lot of Kris songs. I know everybody did, of course. I know Ray Price did and Janis Joplin. Kris wasn't making them [become] hits, everybody else was.

When Waylon did it,... they say the songwriter sings them better because it's his or her song and they put their soul into it, and that's pretty true, and I've never heard anybody else do a song of somebody else's and make it feel like it's theirs better than Waylon Jennings. He was unbelievable. I mean, just like he did Billy Joe's *Honky Tonk Heroes* album,... it changed country music itself,... that made a revolution within itself. You know what I mean? That made a revolution.

Know what you mean. Absolutely a revolution. Waylon and Willie and all of the 1970s Outlaws shook Music Row to its foundation and threatened to end forever its love for pop content. But time has its way of swinging pendulums—first one way and then another—and musical tastes change, so a subsequent Thermidorian Reaction (a name most often attached to the French-style, derringer-firing, baguette-swinging, tumultuous early 1800s in France) has restored pop to its Nashville throne. Certainly not Thermidorian as in a reaction to a reign of terror (although David Allan Coe did strike a few fears of bodily harm in some people), but Thermidorian as in a Music Row reaction to the excesses of artists being too independent of studio control.

I asked Bert how he would define Outlaw country. "It's something that these days won't sell," he said laughingly. Then he went on to say: "It's nothing more than just different. It's good times and truthful songs that aren't depressing or all about love. There's nothing wrong with that, not with either one of them. But with Outlaw all the songs don't sound the same, none of the artists sound the same. Me and [Outlaw artist] Whitey [Morgan], we're high-octane honky-tonk."

Then he hesitated and decided to stress the last point: "Both my band and his are *high-octane* honky-tonk. But we don't sound anything alike. We sound nothing alike, but our music is much alike. If you heard us both on the radio, you'd go through [our real experiences], too, unlike what you hear today with the mainstream stuff. Honky-tonk or Outlaw music is just that: being out[side] of the laws of mainstream country. It's Waylon doing things in his own way. It's why [Outlaw artist] Shooter Jennings [son of Waylon] is still doing things his own way."

When I asked Bert if he had ever tried to sell any of his songs to the studios in Nashville, he said that he had, back in the 1990s. But the studio execs said to him that they were looking for something more standard, more commercially viable. "I remember they had me start playing some shit about some rodeo," he recalls. "And instead of sounding like some twenty-something-year-old guy, which I was, it sounded like Garth Brooks. I said to the studio person, 'But you've already got that. You've already got that. You've got a Garth Brooks!'" Bert says he couldn't believe that they wanted a carbon copy. But money talks and creativity often walks. *Stomp, stomp, stomp.*

As it turns out, I met Bert in Fort Payne, Alabama, *the* home of *the* country super group Alabama, who sold millions of records from about 1980 to 1995 with a heavy *overlay of pop* sounds. Bert lives in Fort Payne, and being on the Outlaw side of the musical tracks, he was playing at a small local bar called the Mainstream Deli. Until recently the town—nestled in the hills and mountains in the northeastern corner of the state, near Chattanooga, Tennessee—was dry, so because the local ordinance requires the sale of food in order to also sell alcohol, the word Deli stands in place of Bar.

Bert's band had set up on a cramped stage in the corner of the "deli," and a crowd was streaming in to fill the place to its capacity of about one hundred. The beer and whiskey were flowing, the voices were getting louder, and the locals who know Bert well and love his music were getting ready to party their way through his songs. Fortified with alcohol, it seemed as if they were getting ready to storm the Bastille of Nashville pop.

In country music circles Fort Payne indeed may be famous as *the* home of *the* band Alabama, but the town once held the distinction of being the sock capital of the world. In the early 1900s more than one hundred hosiery mills employed thousands of workers. Then in the 1990s trade agreements ravaged the local industry when they resulted in a flood into the United States of low-cost imports from Central America and China. Many mills closed and hundreds of workers lost their jobs. On top of that, in 2010 the Alabama legislature passed a law that cracked down on illegal immigrants in the state—some called it the harshest such law in the nation—and this took away cheap labor and further decimated the sock industry.

Together, Bert and his brother manage their family sock factory, one of the few left in town. Bert has been able to survive because he doesn't actually make socks; rather he bleaches those that have been manufactured elsewhere. Even so, his business has declined dramatically over the last few years and hangs by a thread, or more accurately, several barrels of chlorine bleach.

Before his show that night, Bert took me on a tour of the factory, housed in a modest-sized building on a side road in town. We pulled into the parking lot and entered through a door in the back. It was late at night, so we found only one man working at the time, under the glare of fluorescent lights. Huge cardboard boxes stuffed with socks surrounded him. I had never seen so many socks in one place, and, like the ones from my laundry at home, they still had to be paired. "These are the ones we have yet to bleach," Bert said as he pointed to the boxes. The socks were off-white rather than the bright white displayed in stores.

We walked into another room and Bert motioned toward several tall machines made from gleaming steel and looking like oversized front-load washers. "These are the machines we use to bleach the socks," Bert said. "Once upon a time we had all of them running constantly, but now we only use two of them, and even those don't run as often as they used to."

Bert lives in an attractive house perched on several hilltop acres, but his finances have taken a hit from the unraveling of the sock industry. Moreover, he dislikes being in the business. The country music muse has him firmly in her grasp, he loves being there, and he finds socks to be mundane. His career as a musician, though, has been difficult—as much under assault from foreign predators, in this case Nashville music chiefs who are aliens in the land of roots country, as has been the sock industry.

Bert, who is in his late thirties, says: "I've played in every honky-tonk in forty-four states. Lord, have mercy. It probably put about twenty more years on me than it should have."

> *He plays and sings in the midnight pubs,*
> *Women love it when he does.*
> *And I don't guess he'll ever get enough,*
> *To ever do him in.*
>> "He Plays Country but He Lives Rock 'n' Roll"
>> From *The Live*

Bert recalls that as a kid, well before he could play a musical instrument, he was writing songs. "When I was six, seven years old, I was sitting down in the driveway writing them." He connects that musical ability to his being able to read and write well. "I was like at a twelfth-grade English level when I was in the third grade," he says. "I was always very good at literature. I suck at math, but I was always good at literature."

He adds: "My teachers told my mom that 'Bert's doing real well, he's a real nice young man, he's a real good student, but he's lost in another world when he's in this class. We're worried about him. It's like he's not even there.' Hell, I *wasn't* there. Who wanted to be there when you can be off somewhere else? I was always kind of a loner.

I liked to be out just writing songs in my head, and I got to singing them in my head. Then when I learned three chords on the guitar, I wrote a song to it."

Bert moved with his family from Waco, Texas, to Fort Payne when he was seven years old. All the while, he grew up with country music records being played around his house. He heard everything from Ronnie Milsap to Merle Haggard to Willie Nelson to Waylon Jennings.

While he was still a kid, he went to his first concert to see the band Alabama. At that time, he observes, they were less pop than they were later. When I asked Bert how he became a country artist, he laughed, and in reference to a song made popular by singer Barbara Mandrell, he said, "I guess I was country when country wasn't cool."

"But I loved rock 'n' roll, and I still love it," he says. "I love some crazy shit that makes people say, 'Man, you know that?' Hell, I do know it. Prince and other shit like that. I love it."

"I actually started playing pretty late," Bert says. "I was eighteen when I started playing." That ultimately led to his forming a country band, the Skeeters. They released their CD *Easy for the Takin'* in 2006 and began getting airplay on the SiriusXM Radio Outlaw station. "We were signed up with a booking agency, which is Paradigm now but was Monterey Peninsula back then," Bert says. "It's right when Sirius Radio came out, and we were the first ones to be played on Outlaw country. Shooter Jennings [who has a show on the Outlaw station] was with Monterey, so that's how I met those guys at Sirius."

The Skeeters were rapidly climbing the music ladder as they opened for acts in larger venues. "We played the Houston Astrodome," Bert says. "We did a show with Travis Tritt. We did a tour with Junior Brown, two tours with Billy Joe Shaver,... whoever was hot then: Gretchen Wilson, Robert Earl Keen, and, hell, it goes on and on."

Question: So what happened? Why didn't you guys continue?

Bert: It was a real tragedy. My guitar player, Matt Martin, who is still a good friend of mine, his daughter passed away. She was like nine years old. She had a brain aneurism. She was at the high school running track, and he lost her, and that was the end of the Skeeters. We went back to the Skeeters out of respect and kind of started over. Then we all took another year off and started back up as the Bert David Newton Band. It was kind of like starting over. Older and wiser, but what he lost could never be, you know…. I hate the way that went down, but we didn't feel it would be right to go on as the Skeeters anymore.

> *It's so much easier*
> *Just to take it all in stride.*
> *So I'll keep my wheels a turnin'*
> *'Till I can figure out how to fly.*
>> "Keep My Wheels a Turnin'"
>> From *The Live*

On the first Skeeters CD, Bert begins carving out his Outlaw niche with music that proclaims, "We ain't Nashville." The songs "Easy for the Takin'," "Jester of Life," and "Mother Trucker" (written by Billy Joe Shaver) clearly present the gospel according to Waylon, and they remain a part of Bert's repertoire today. In "Honky Tonk Keep on Honky Tonkin'," he sings: "Promised another pocket of cash/Another beer joint we had to play." And when the bar changed its mind about settling up, "we had to kick their ass to just get paid." Such are the venues on the road and the characters and travails that go with them.

By the time *Easy for the Takin'* appeared, the Skeeters were in such demand that they released another CD, *Rhythm of the World*, the songs for which had been recorded four years earlier. Bert recalls: "We were 'Well, we already have this one in the pocket, we've already got this old CD, so let's release it as our second one.' And that's what we did."

Like many other Outlaws who have been constrained by the monolith known as Music Row, the Skeeters offer an in-your-face anti-Nashville tune, in this case "Country Pop," written by Bert. It's part strident "I won't concede," part homage to Waylon Jennings, and part "Fuck you, Nashville, we will *prevail*."

> *It's tough to be a honky-tonk hero,*
> *I guess we'll never make it to the top.*
> *I'd just as soon as stay at ground zero,*
> *'Cause I'll be damned if I'm gonna sing that country pop.*
> *Waylon once said, "Where do we take it from here?"*
> *Hell, I think some people took it the wrong way.*
> *So we are taking back country music,*
> *And we don't care what Nashville's gotta say.*
>
> "Country Pop"
> From *Rhythm of the World*

Question: What's wrong with mainstream Nashville country today?

Bert: Man, I don't want this to sound a bit out of spite or jealousy or anything like that, but I can't tell who the hell is who when I'm listening to it on the radio. It sounds the same. I can't tell which artist is different from.... Who's who? You know what I'm saying? It just sounds too damn the same. It's too neat. It's too neat. There's no looseness to it. It's all neat, and all their voices sound pretty much the same.

Question: Why is mainstream Nashville able to sell so much country pop?

Bert: Nobody around here listens to [Outlaw country], and that's sad to say. I think [country pop] sells to old-century women. No offense, but to a Yankee audience maybe, some of them. [Pop performers] sing a song that makes you somewhat emotional, and that's what they prey on. That's what they prey on, the emotions of these women. And they're out there to sell albums and to sell tickets, and that's understandable, it's a business. They know that they can sing a song about something so damn sappy, so damn sad, somebody's freakin' dying, somebody's died of cancer, or somebody's doing this and somebody's doing that. Of course, something like that's going to hit home. Everybody knows somebody with cancer or somebody that's lost somebody with cancer. You know what I mean?

I've listened to some of those songs, and you get emotional, even if you don't intend to. But I don't want to hear that shit all the time. I think there's room for more. They don't need to block everybody else out.

Question: Do you think Nashville is actually blocking out alternative country artists?

Bert: I do feel they're doing that. I feel like Jamey [Johnson] kicked out a big door, but I don't see Nashville letting a lot of people walk through it. I know he did. He had to write some of those songs in order to do it,... "Honky Tonk Badonkadonk." Then he wrote "Give It Away," which is a good song, and then when he got his own chance, he invested his own.... Hell, "Sunshine through my Chevrolet/Whiskey eyes/Ashtray breath."[[He quotes the lyrics from a Jamey Johnson tune, "That Lonesome Song."] He started writing about Outlaw shit.

I'm not sure of the statistics, but I would say that women probably buy more music than men. The most country music for sure. I wouldn't say there aren't any honky-tonk women out there, but if they're downloading music, it's probably from the seventies.

❦

Despite his comment about "Yankees," Bert expresses dismay and frustration over the South being the region of the nation that appears least receptive to Outlaw country. "I don't know why it is," he says.

"You know, Texas is,... it's hard to compare yourself to Texas [where Outlaw has a lot of fans]. You've got a Texas, and then you've got a Nashville—that's two different worlds.

"But you know, up north they love that shit. They love it. They love Outlaw country. We get a better response in freaking Detroit and freaking Ohio and Michigan,... they love it. We did a lot of shows with Junior Brown. He does a lot of shows in the Northeast, up that way. He knew what he was doing because they love that shit."

Bert particularly gets ruffled by the Outlaw "posers" who claim they know country roots, and claim that their music even draws from it, when they neither know it nor play it. He says, however, that by creating the posers, Music Row admits there's a movement out in the husking that they are too afraid or too incompetent to embrace. "I think they know there's a market [for real Outlaw]," he says, "but they're skeptical for some reason."

Then he hesitates and says, "Don't get me wrong, I'm not trying to dog everything that comes out of Nashville, but it's hard to say I'm not dogging everything that comes out of Nashville." After thinking about his statement for a few seconds, he begins laughing. "That's the way it is," he says.

Question: Do you think there's a future for this kind of music?

Bert: I think there's a big audience out there wanting it, more than [Nashville] realizes. And they [the audience] don't know where to get it.

Question: If there's a big audience out there, and that obviously means there's some money to be made, then why doesn't Nashville tap into it?

Bert: I don't know if they fully believe it. I think they're starting to come around to believe it. Even if [Outlaw] is about being hung over, being drunk, having a one-night stand, having your heart broke and then getting drunk. It's not all about live like you are dying, you know what I mean? Not everything has to try to make you cry. Hell, [not everything should be] "I'm going to try to make you cry; what we're going to do is write a song, put it on the radio, and try to make you cry." Not everybody wants to cry [while listening to] the radio.

You know, you're having folks over, you want to put on the radio, you want to crank up the music, have some beers, cook some ribs. You don't want to turn on to some crappy-ass shit. That's why I'm sitting here, much like a whole lot of other people. Trust me, a *whole hell of a lot of other people*.... They don't know Waylon Jennings while I'm cooking my damn ribs. That was music from thirty, forty years ago, but we're out here jamming to that stuff.

There's a market for it. There's a lot of hungry people wanting to buy it, wanting it, and they just don't know where to get it because it's hard to get.

Question: What about the honky-tonk scene itself? Do you think that's fading, or does that have a future? Or with Outlaw and honky-tonk are we talking about basically the same thing?

Bert: I say that they're the same thing. I know they can be extremely different. I say honky-tonk a lot more than I say Outlaw, but there's a future for Outlaw music. Yet if [Nashville] would accept it up there, it really wouldn't be Outlaw music, would it? That would be okay with me, but they're not going to.

People ask, "What's this guy play?" He plays Outlaw country. It's because that's what I do play. It's not because "Well, I'm going to play Outlaw country." I don't put myself [in that category]. I'm just there because that's what I play.

Although Bert counts Waylon Jennings as the most prominent influence on his music, other country artists from the 1970s enter the picture as well. He likes Kris Kristofferson for his poetry. And Billy Joe Shaver, well, he's the tireless songwriter, one of the founding fathers of Outlaw who's "still riding around in that white van at his age doing the same thing because that's what he does. He doesn't, as far as I know, sing anybody else's songs but his."

To Bert, a story about Billy says a lot about Billy and about Kris: "I think Billy Joe Shaver recorded one song, to my knowledge, that wasn't his, and I think it was a Kris song—in his whole career. Now, I may be wrong about that, but I've got a lot of wax; I've listened to a lot of records. To my knowledge, it was a long time ago, but I think that's the only one that Billy Joe has ever recorded that wasn't his. It was a Kris song." This story says that Billy Joe is a genuine, straight-from-the heart country guy and that Kris must have written some powerful songs for him to break through Billy Joe's preference to record only Billy Joe's stuff.

Bert calls 1970s Outlaw artist David Allan Coe "one hell of a songwriter" and describes Coe's contemporary, Johnny Paycheck, as "underrated." Then there's Merle Haggard, who Bert "[doesn't] think has ever written a bad song," and Johnny Cash, whose legendary status speaks for itself.

Bert didn't begin listening to Hank Williams until he had already listened to these other artists. Still, he considers Hank to be the "godfather of country music" and really "the first Outlaw" for his singing straight from the heart, wherever that might take him.

But even in talking about these musicians, Bert gets back to Waylon. "With Waylon, he says, "it was soul and that voice and that sound, that sound that he had with Ralph Mooney [the steel guitarist, who was a graduate of the Bakersfield sound] and himself going back and forth, and with Richie Albright [the drummer]."

Bert takes exception, however, to those who say about him and his music "You sound a lot like Waylon." He says: "No, the hell I don't. I wished I did. I appreciate it. But no, I don't.... I'm just a baritone. You don't hear any baritones anymore. You don't hear Outlaw country anymore, so you throw me over there and say I sound like Waylon. That's a compliment, but it's not true."

Question: How do you go about writing a song? How does the idea come to you?

Bert: That's the hardest question to answer. A lot of it is truth, and a lot of it is imagination. I'm blessed with a lot of imagination, I guess. Driving around, with the radio off, is when you write some of your best songs. When you sit down and say, "I'm going to write a song today," well, it's very unlikely. If you're just hanging out, not expecting it—*bam!* Then you're going to write one. Two lines are going to get you, and the rest is going to flow right along with it.

Bert sometimes adds complexity to his lyrics by suspending or shifting the point of view. In this stanza from "Nothin' to Lose," for example, he leaves it unclear as to who might be doing the talking: "Repercussions of Cuervo from a party last night/Discussions of all that she said out of spite/Thinking about what she did as the morning goes by/With a beach bum from 'Bama that lays by *her* side." It would be more precise but less interesting to put the words "he was" or "she was" before the word "thinking." The wording is a nice touch on Bert's part.

When I was in Fort Payne to see Bert, the weather was cooling down from the hot summer days, and the hills were starting to come alive with the bright hues of autumn. Bert took me to the show in his pickup truck, with his equipment trailer latched to the back. "Geez," he told me, "after the Skeeters ended, it was back to these hole-in-the-wall places. I tell you, that took some adjustment, a big adjustment. I went from playing the Astrodome to this. It was hard, real hard."

Once we got to the Midtown Deli—the bar in deli guise—he and the other musicians in his band unloaded the trailer, set up the equipment, and did a sound check. Bert groused about the police station right across the street. He and the cops don't see eye to eye, and he particularly complains that they harass customers from the bar to discourage his fans in this newly "wet" city from enjoying themselves.

Around ten o'clock the musicians stepped onto the small stage. The Bert David Newton Band, or BDN as it likes to call itself, consists of Bert on rhythm guitar and lead vocal, Rick Eller on bass guitar, Chase Armstrong on drums, and Phillip Haushalter, "Cowboy Phil," on lead guitar—the Telecaster. The band played tight, with more energy and speed than the Skeeters, as if BDN wanted to drive home their 1970s Outlaw sound with an urgent declaration of independence and feistiness. They took command of the room, they took command of the music. They stuck their musical fork in the lard-ridden pig of Music Row, twisted it with talent and honesty and glee, and got that animal to squeal. Outlaw ruled the night.

The BDN playlist followed closely the songs on their recently released CD/DVD set, *The Live.* The crowd wanted four-to-the-floor, foot-stomping, beer-drinking honky-tonk, and they got it. They got a double shot: a rousing time set to honest music. There was nothing sad, nothing about "somebody freakin' dying." Yes, Bert's lyrics dealt with lost love, but in the context of a woman breaking a man's heart and sending the man to drinking, and all accompanied by the relentless, driving Outlaw beat.

I do everything that I can do,
But it never seems to be enough.
They say that the going is getting that way,
Hell, for me it's always been tough....
The young men talk about what they're going to do,
And the old men about what they've done.
But I see in their eyes that it ain't no surprise,
You can lose as much as you've won.

"The Handle"

From *The Live*

For *The Live* Bert provides liner notes in which he says about his band's music: "The truth. The real deal. No bells and whistles. No overdubs or fill-ins. Just hammering down the raw Outlaw energy that is genuine in what we do." In doing so he provides the words essential to his work and indeed at the heart of Outlaw: *truth* and *genuine.*

The DVD was taped at the 2nd Street Music Hall, a blues club in Gadsden, Alabama, near Fort Payne. It comes as close to "being there" in showing the intimacy of the setting, the raucous fun, and Bert's shouts and kick-outs as any DVD can. Cowboy Phil sizzles on the Telecaster, and the band comes together as effectively and as dedicated to its art as that which played behind Waylon in his prime Outlaw years. The only disappointment comes when we don't get to see Bert play his classic song "Clydesdales."

But it's on the CD. Bert sweeps into the album with "Cold Front": "Well, I ain't missing life/I'm still standing in it/I still do what I do/ Just more from the forget it." He's leaving behind his broken heart, yet the woman who has hurt him "time and time again" is coming back— "there's a cold front moving in." When she says she's returning, "I'm back on the whiskey/It's a warm place to begin."

"AHHHHHHHH, HERE IT COMES!"

And here comes "Clydesdales." Pure honky-tonk images uncorked straight from the whiskey keg.

> *I've seen love, I've seen dreams,*
> *I've seen times when I thought I could change some things.*
> *I've seen how, I've seen why,*
> *But since you left me all I've seen is how I'm goin' to die.*
> *'Cause I've got Clydesdales pulling my casket,*
> *Jack Daniels, he's digging my grave.*
> *And the Marlboro man, hell, he's doing the preaching,*
> *And I'm wonderin' if I'd be around if you had only stayed....*

"AHHHHHHHH, HERE WE GO BOYS!"

> *I've had time to think things through,*
> *I've had problems gettin' over you.*
> *I took chances to start again,*
> *And no girl wants an Outlaw that's headed for the end.*
> "Clydesdales"
> From *The Live*

The CD also includes a tribute to African American folk singer Huddie William Ledbetter (1888-1949), better known as Lead Belly. I asked Bert how he became interested in Lead Belly, and he told me that he had studied the artist in a course he had taken on folk music. Lead Belly was in and out of prison most of his adult life, and because of the style of his music, he was not popular with black audiences. He found his greatest following among leftist "folkies," although Lead Belly himself displayed little interest in politics and may even have been a conservative. Musically, he was called the King of the Twelve-String Guitar.

Bert identifies with Lead Belly's musical talent and his determination to play what to Lead Belly was true. Moreover, there's Lead Belly's underdog status, something that every Outlaw can understand, often identifies with, and often finds romantic.

> *He was convicted of murder in the early 1900s,*
> *Huddie Ledbetter was a folk lord of our land.*
> *Down in Huntsville, Texas, doing time behind steel bars.*
> *Huddie, there's only one way out,*
> *So tune up your guitar.*
>
> "Leadbelly"
> From *The Live*

Lead Belly fits into the definition of Outlaw that Bert has appear on the screen at the beginning of his DVD: "A person who refuses to be governed by the establishment rules or practices of any group; rebel; nonconformist." (Notably, given the number of times Lead Belly frequented jail, his Outlaw status went well beyond music rebelliousness.)

Bert's rendition of "Rusty Cage"—a song written by Chris Cornell and with its narrative chorus reminiscent of the 1960s rock group the Doors—once again has Cowboy Phil excelling on his Telecaster and Bert declaring his intent to gain freedom: "I'm going to break/I'm going to break my rusty cage and run."

"Well, here's what I think about this whole year," Bert declares as he goes into "You Can Have Her," a song written by Bill Cook and played often by Waylon Jennings. "You can have her,...she didn't love me anyway." The girl left him and ran away with his best friend. Bert comments at the end of the song: "It [the year] wasn't a total loss. My beautiful wife gave me a precious baby girl."

When I visited with Bert on that autumnal day, he was gracious enough to let me stay at his house. His wife, Suzie—pretty and lively and smart—and the couple's sweet sixteen-month-old daughter, Ansley, live with him on the hill. Bert's parents live next door. It's a picture of a close family and loving domesticity, and although Bert itches to be on the road more, he has a happy home life. While I was there, Suzie made a favorite Bert breakfast of bacon and eggs and Ansley scrambled around the floor, a bit perplexed as to why this stranger was invading her territory but outgoing and happy about rolling a ball back and forth with me.

"You know," Bert told me, "when you listen to Waylon's 'This Time Will Be the Last Time,' there's no other sound like it. That Telecaster gives a unique sound to Waylon's music." Bert has chosen as the logo for BDN the image of a guitar that has on it a modified version of Waylon's own phoenix-like logo.

The Live was the title chosen by Bert for his CD/DVD to emphasize what he calls "the real deal," a band playing with "no overdubs or fill-ins." What *The Live* means to Bert, and where it places him in the Outlaw movement, becomes revealed with his liner notes, his lyrics, and his melodies: he's smack dab at its essence. Ground zero. The pulsating honky-tonk. The honest roots. The beer-guzzling, whiskey-drinking celebration. Bert playing for us to forget our problems, the problems from our work—the sock factory, the fast-food joint, or wherever it might be—the frustration and disappointment. Let loose, man, let loose. *High octane*. Pour it on.

As Bert played his acoustic guitar during the show, I noticed that it had been signed by a number of country artists. There are the members of Waylon's old band, there's Willie Nelson and Kris Kristofferson, there's Billy Joe Shaver and Jamey Johnson. They have all helped to keep alive country's roots. So too has Bert—his chosen course determined, his Outlaw art enlivened, and his sights set on getting everyone to AHHHHHHHH, LIVE IT!

> *Most of the photos I've got are the ones in my mind,*
> *Sometimes even those pictures can be hard to find.*
> *But I can be just as sure as one hundred proof,*
> *'Cause they're all here on this six-string in black and blue....*
> *These are the names on my guitar.*
>> "Names on My Guitar"
>> From *The Live*

Bert David Newton, The Riverbend Music Festival,
Chattanooga, TN (2011)

Chapter 15

JUST AS I AM

About a third of the way through my interviews with the Outlaws, I was beginning to realize what was bugging them so much. It's true that every one of them would like to make more money; none of them wanted their lives of worn shirts and torn jeans onstage to be duplicated by lives of sackcloth and ashes at home.

But what they most disliked were the huge signs that have been placed at both ends of Music Row. The signs that say to them NO TRESPASSING.

All of us feel alienated about something. Maybe we feel alienated toward our jobs, toward politics, or toward another person. There can be no more intense alienation, however, than that which comes from feeling like an outsider in a land you love, and whose heritage and history you embrace for its legitimacy and its sense of rootedness.

That's what these Outlaws are feeling. The land that they love, the land of country roots, has been taken over by an invading army of marketers (or reinvading, given what Nashville has done so many times) who have planted themselves behind the NO TRESPASSING signs, behind the chain link fence, and have declared, "You are not wanted here."

You are not wanted here unless you conform to our way of doing things. So the Outlaw feels disowned, rejected, and scorned. To them, Nashville works in mysterious ways because its commercialism seems overwhelming and unbreakable. Undoubtedly, what Music Row does crank out fills a need, musically and economically, and it isn't all bad, and it's people aren't all evil.

Nevertheless, the Outlaws who embrace country roots have become the unwanted. That's right: Outlaws on unwanted, not wanted, posters. If an Outlaw agreed to what would gain entry to the land behind the fences, it might bring him or her material gain, but it would hold little potential for solving the problem of alienation. Ultimately, the Outlaw would still be a stranger and would become just another disposable product coming down the assembly-line chute.

Illogical? Maybe, but logic is not a strong point among artists, and feelings often defy logic; in fact, they can even prevail over logic. Insensible? Maybe, but feelings can defy sense, and logic itself often makes no sense.

Disingenuous? No. Whatever might be the flaws in the views of the Outlaws about Nashville and their current standing in the world of country music, they are sincere about what they think. "Stop it," they say with a unified voice. "Stop saying you are the true country. Stop corrupting the word, stop corrupting the music. If you do this and if you accept me just as I am, more people will realize that there's something more going on, something beyond the assembly line."

Joey Allcorn posing for All Alone Again (2009)

CHAPTER 16

JOEY ALLCORN

Nothing Left to Prove

> *I never met Ernest Tubb,*
> *I never shook Roy Acuff's hand.*
> *I never got to hear Hank Williams play*
> *With the Drifting Cowboy band.*
> *I never got to hear Webb Pierce sing on WSM,*
> *And I don't like it but I guess it's fate,*
> *I was born fifty years too late.*
> *"50 YEARS TOO LATE"*
> *FROM 50 YEARS TOO LATE*

On Boscobel Street in Nashville sits a small, unassuming clapboard house pockmarked with peeling paint and surrounded by an unkempt lawn. As with most of the houses in the neighborhood, this one dates back many years, but unlike the others, it serves as a sound studio. When I arrived, Joey Allcorn was recording his new

CD, *Nothing Left to Prove.* Joey had invited me to watch him work. He had begun making his CD several weeks before, and he was almost finished with it. He and his engineer/producer Eric McConnell were smoothing out tracks.

Joey was troubled that one of his songs lacked something. He thought it over and then told Eric that he was going to call in Hank Singer, who would add his fiddle as another track to the recording. In today's world of computers and digital technology, multiple tracks—a number limited only by the size of the hard drive—can be added to a recording with relative ease. This process, called overdubbing, existed before the digital age, but it was more cumbersome and limited.

The fiddle appears in many of Joey's songs, and Hank Singer played on one of Joey's earlier CDs, *All Alone Again,* released in 2009. Singer started out with Faron Young back in 1964, and since then he has worked with just about every artist in the music business. Singer was a nice fit for Joey, who preferred a roots sound coming from a seasoned master, one firmly planted in the traditions of country music.

For Joey, Hank Williams rules. Joey has immersed himself in the country legend's life. Many experts would claim that Hank's artistry remains unsurpassed and that his influence from the late 1940s and 1950s continues to be critical and massive. Historian George William Koon says that "Hank thrived with the [country music] industry and died just as rock and roll was beginning.... But to see him as a creature of history would be a mistake, for he shaped and substantiated country music at least as much as it shaped and substantiated him."

Joey's admiration applies to other artists from Hank's era—particularly Roy Acuff, Ernest Tubb, Lefty Frizzell, Faron Young, and Johnny Cash in his early career with Sun Records. Along with Hank, they have come to possess Joey's music, like guitar-bearing ghosts looking for a ride along some lost highway of musical roots.

There's something about a dead man singing
That sure makes me feel alone....
And Hank sings those sad songs about leaving,
Johnny Cash is singing songs about jail.
Ernest Tubb will sing you a song about Texas,
But they're all down here in honky-tonk hell.
                    "Honky Tonk Hell"
                    From *All Alone Again*

Because Hank and the other ghosts of country's past occupy so much of Joey's life, it seems appropriate that the studio where Joey was recording resides on the same street as did the house of Delia "Mom" Upchurch. Many a musician arriving in Nashville back in the 1940s or 1950s and into the 1960s—carrying a guitar or fiddle or banjo, along with high hopes but low funds—survived by staying at Mom Upchurch's boarding house.

"They were coming into town with...no jobs and no friends," Mom once said. "They needed someone to give them a place to stay,...someone to give them a home." She rented only to musicians, and she often rented not entire rooms but beds. As a renter, you could use one bed, slide your guitar under it, and lay claim to one dresser drawer, where, with your clothes, you might store some sheet music or old records. One musician later observed that if you went out on tour and someone else showed up looking for a place to sleep, Mom "had the habit of renting out your bed to them." There was always, after all, somebody else to help and a boarding house to keep up. The musicians loved Mom. The floors might have creaked, but the home-cooked meals nourished them, and the companionship fought back loneliness.

I first learned about Mom Upchurch from Joey. In studying Hank Williams, he has delved into most every part of Hank's life: friends, other artists, the music industry, the *Grand Ole Opry*, and, of course, Mom herself, the guardian angel for those hopeful musicians.

Musically, Joey Allcorn met Hank Williams at an early age. One day he went to Kmart with his mom, and while she was there, she bought a Hank Williams greatest-hits CD for herself. In the car going home, she played it. Joey was so impressed by the music that he asked to borrow the CD. He kept it, and as he listened to it over and over, Hank etched deeper into Joey's soul; with each year of Joey's adolescence, Joey and the long-dead music legend grew closer. For Joey, the songs touched him so deeply because of how he related to girls: as he sought out relationships, they invariably ended in a broken heart.

"A song like 'Your Cheatin' Heart'," Joey told me, "is just as relevant today as in 1953 because it's purely about emotion." In that song Hank sings about a woman who has cheated on her man. It's the only detail we get, and, Joey says, it's the only one we need. The essence is Hank crying throughout the song, with a mournful steel guitar wrapping around many of his words. Any listener can embrace the way he cries, no matter what the romantic hurt might be.

> *Your cheatin' heart will make you weep.*
> *You'll cry and cry and try to sleep.*
> "Your Cheatin' Heart"
> Hank Williams

Hank's broken heart became Joey's broken heart. By calling forth the specter of the music legend, Joey has allowed Hank to substantiate country music once more. In reaching into the past, Joey picked a musician from the 1950s whose songs back then could be embraced by parents and youngsters alike. He chose not a symbol of rebellion, such as Elvis Presley, but a man symbolic of a quieter, less tumultuous time than today.

Question: Where did you grow up? Where were you when you were fourteen, fifteen?

Joey: Columbus, Georgia.

Question: Would this be typical for a fourteen-year-old, fifteen-year-old in Columbus to listen to Hank Williams?

Joey: Not at all. Anywhere, any city, really. But it's amazing because you meet so many people like me that did get into him at that age. For some reason that's just the age Hank kind of comes into play.

Although Joey's mom was present in his youth, Joey was raised by her parents, so his first musical exposure was to whatever they listened to. He says that on the radio, "It was like Randy Travis, 'Digging Up Bones,' and Johnny Cash had the 'City of New Orleans' out, and growing up I remember listening to that in the car. My grandparents were more just kind of 'Let's turn on the radio to whatever song.'" It was as if Joey were traveling with them in a big-finned 1950s-style car, windows rolled down and the breeze carrying the voices of modern singers, but singers whose music flowed effortlessly around the contours of a sheltered life.

Joey's mom was only nineteen years old when Joey was born. She was also unwed. Joey's father, a race car driver, was thirty years old, married, and already had a couple of children of his own. Joey has never met his father and has no desire to. "I would have nothing to say to him," he says. He believes that what happened is just another blip in an imperfect world, so it's best to move on. But the blip is similar to what Hank Williams went through in being fatherless, something that bothered him throughout his short life. If Joey has moved on, he, like Hank, travels with an empty spot in his soul, perhaps hidden, but still there.

Joey comes across as calm and controlled but melancholic, creative and talented but staid. He would never don the braids worn by Dallas Moore or display the array of tattoos found on any number of Outlaw musicians. In fact, for his stage appearance he tends to wear long-sleeve shirts decorated with a traditional Western-style yoke; sometimes he even wears a Western-style dark suit. He refuses to use cuss words while performing because he hates to turn anyone off to his music. He wants to be able to play at a honky-tonk one night and, without missing a beat, at a university art and culture show the next.

When his grandparents raised him, they did so with plenty of love and care. He also had much of the material stuff a boy in mainstream America might want. He says: "I didn't get everything I wanted. But I didn't starve or [lack] clothes or anything." Joey was a good kid, obedient to his grandparents and mindful of the rules they set out for him. He spent hours at home playing video games and fooling with computers. "I never went through a drug phase or drinking phase or any of that," he says. "I knew from the time I was sixteen, seventeen years old, when I started being good at playing music, I was like, 'Man, this is what I want to do.' Since that time, I've planned my life completely around that, and I'm just fortunate that it's worked out. I tell people all the time that if I died tomorrow, I accomplished way more than I ever thought I would."

Joey was first attracted to playing music in elementary school. One day he walked into a classroom and there, in the back, stood a row of about thirty guitars. He stared at them. They might as well have been magical, able to dance with him and his music, make him feel wanted, and then lead him by the hand into a world where he could escape from his troubles—a world of creativity, imagination, and reward. Soon he began making those guitars come alive. "When you get into sixth grade," he told me, "they actually let you play [the guitar] and learn three chords. We learned some old kind of hobo song, something like 'Pallet on the Floor.' That was the first thing I ever learned on a guitar."

In fact, Joey learned to play those guitars of his childhood by listening to Hank Williams. It was a case of simple chords combining with the appeal of what Hank had to say.

Even as an adult, Joey has turned to Hank and his music for help in dealing with the outside world. He says: "When I broke up with my girlfriend last year, first thing I did was go listen to Hank because I knew that he had been there before, and he pulled through, and he's been sad about it too."

Two broken hearts again became one, and with such a strong connection to Hank, Joey feels committed to helping others in the same way his musical hero helped him. Joey told me: "I always said [that] whenever I get to make records, if I can help people the way he helped me, then...I just kind of always wanted to be like that."

He has accomplished this by channeling Hank's emotion. "On my Facebook," he observes, "some guy posted something on there, and he said, 'Man, your music's helped me through some tough times here lately. I love you and your music.' To me that means more than anything because that dude was probably upset about something or sad, and I helped him feel better."

> *It's another lonely night in the barroom,*
> *Someone just turned the jukebox on.*
> *It's playing all those sad songs I remember*
> *That I haven't heard in so long.*
> "Honky Tonk Hell"
> From *All Alone Again*

Sadness. Joey has a preternatural attachment to it and must fight to keep it under control. The sadness within Joey leads him to project a sense of detachment, as a way to keep from being hurt, but also a sense of commitment, like he knows his values and will stick by them.

He seems like a smooth-running river, but beneath the surface run rivulets of anger that are observable when carefully discerned or when Joey gets disturbed. What gets Joey-the-river bubbling and frothing and agitated? Those who don't trust him (interesting, because Joey himself is cautious and guarded, even distrustful), those who betray him, and those who lie or cheat.

Every river has a source, and over time, over distance, over the miles traveled on a long journey toward its end, tributaries enter into the river and make it bigger. The *source* for Joey goes back to his childhood. But Hank Williams has *become the river* that courses through much of Joey's life, like the phantasmal Greek river Styx, but in reverse. In his case it serves as a conduit not from the living to the dead but from the dead to the living and in this way energizes Joey's talent. Joey has taken his oath to Hank, and as the ancient Greeks say, an oath sworn by the river Styx can *never* be broken.

He says: "I want to be the guy [who], when you're fucking heart-broken sad, you put on my record. When people are feeling bad, I want to help you through that. So most of the stuff I write is like that. I try to write more upbeat things, but it's not in me. I can do it a little bit, but I'm just more of an old-school sad-song and love songwriter."

Fucking heartbroken sad. Listen to Joey Allcorn on "South Montgomery Blues" from his yet to be released CD *Nothing Left to Prove*, and you will hear him delve into a bluesy style, a cross between Hank Williams and country pioneer Jimmie Rodgers. That Joey is going to jump a freight train heading to another town to escape the south Montgomery blues comes straight out of a scene from the 1950s, with a chord progression and simplicity akin to that of Hank. In fact, Hank and Lum York, who played upright bass for Hank, would hang out among blacks in south Montgomery, absorb their music, adapt it, and take it to white people. (Haven't some observers called country the "white man's blues"?) Several of Hank's bluesiest numbers, the ones that display this black influence the most, attract Joey, songs such as "Lovesick Blues," "My Bucket's Got a Hole in It," "Mind Your Own Business," and "Long Gone Lonesome Blues."

Case closed. Joey so adores Hank, and so adores the era of Hank, that he has no other musical attachment.

But the story continues.

Joey admits to being 80 percent Hank style, roots style, old-school style. Another 20 percent, however, comes from a tributary that flows into the main river, which on a map of Joey's personality should be labeled the Tributary of Darkness, Anger, and Grunge. It is Joey's Cocytus, the tributary of the river Styx. Translated from Greek, the name means "wailing."

Question: You have at least a couple of songs that really are pretty heavy with the death and funeral scene. What gets you to that?

Joey: The two strongest emotions that people in life go through, things that will wear you to the core the most, are love and death. One day I want to make an album called *Love and Death*.

> *It's a long, lonesome road that I'm walking,*
> *It's a sad way of life that I live.*
> > "Son of a Ramblin' Man"
> > From *50 Years Too Late*

Joey's sadness leads his music to the wailing which echoes throughout human existence. On a CD Joey titled *All Alone Again* (which as an outsider he has frequently been), on the cover of which he wears black, his "Six Feet Down" steeps in gloom. First comes the burial: "A preacher dressed in black/Just sent my baby back/To the Lord just yesterday." Then comes a haunting lamentation that gives life to the dead and, as with Hank, connects Joey to the grave: "Six feet down, I know she's crying/As I stand here at her grave.... Atop that lone blue casket there sat a flower basket/That I just know she would love."

Or this from "Graveyard Bound" on Joey's CD released in 2006, *50 Years Too Late:* "Well, I woke up on Friday lying on my cooling board/It seems I somehow wound up down at the city morgue." The song has an arrangement whose sounds go beyond anything Hank would have done. There's a tolling bell, people sobbing, ghastly cries, and a commentary about how Hank and Jimmie Rodgers died, but it matters not because once they are buried you can't tell the two men apart. The ghastly cries are provided by the group Those Poor Bastards, who had been working with country artist Hank Williams III and whose metal-like music of doom Joey describes as similar to what would result if Tim Burton (the film director known for the macabre) performed country music. That Joey praises Those Poor Bastards again reveals his own dark side.

What Joey does lyrically in "Six Feet Down" he does instrumentally in "Like I Never Will Again" (also on *50 Years Too Late)*. The song begins with Joey strumming his acoustic guitar softly and a steel guitar playing tenderly in the background. But on the second stanza, an electric guitar erupts when Joey strokes three power chords. The listener once lulled into repose suddenly wonders, "Where did this Hades come from?" Because the drumbeat remains steady, as does Joey's acoustic guitar, sadness prevails, but tremendous anger explodes from beneath—a psychological stacking more powerful than any musical one could be.

Joey told me that the power chords were Nirvana-like. He says: "That song was...if I make this part really heavy and kind of sound like [grunge rock group Nirvana's anthem] 'Smells Like Teen Spirit,' that would be a little tip of the hat to [the late Nirvana lead singer, guitarist, and songwriter] Kurt Cobain." The anger and the grunge wail, causing Joey's river of calm to bubble and froth and become agitated.

Joey was born in 1980, and so as a youngster, in addition to roots country, he listened to the grunge music that his peers liked. In fact, even before he found Hank Williams, he was attracted to Nirvana. When Joey told me this, I thought it was a complete one-eighty from Hank. But Joey explained that, like the country legend he grew to love, Cobain sang about what an adolescent such as Joey felt: pain, loneliness, and heartache. "I was not a popular kid," Joey says. "I didn't play football or other sports. I didn't do drugs. I was an outsider." So Kurt Cobain nailed loneliness with his grunge, Hank Williams nailed it with his country, and Joey Allcorn absorbed both while growing up in Columbus, Georgia, as that outsider.

With *50 Years Too Late* and *Alone Again,* Joey also displays the influences of the 1990s country band BR5-49 and of Hank Williams III, Hank Sr.'s grandson. In those two recordings, Joey tries to combine roots country with the "modern traditionalism" of BR5-49 and the edginess of Hank III.

To Joey, BR5-49, in its original shape with lead singer Gary Bennett, showed how creativity could still survive in Nashville. The innovative group reached back to honky-tonk, Western swing, rockabilly, and the Buck Owens/Bakersfield, California, sound to create its music, which also has overtones of 1980s pop. Joey sees BR5-49 as the modern version of Hank, with their use of a fiddle and a nonpedal steel guitar and with their appearance in suits reminiscent of the careful way that Hank dressed.

When it comes to Hank III, Joey becomes easily irritated by those who accuse him of having tried to be like the man who for years was his mentor. Hank III influenced Joey as he began his career. Joey was only in his late teens when he first met Hank III.

Question: How did you get to know him? Was it because of his being on your record, or how did that materialize?

Joey: I met him when I was about nineteen years old. That was through his great-aunt, who was Hank Sr.'s half sister. I went to his show with her in Mississippi, and that was the first time I ever met him. [We] became friends playing video games online and stuff. Of course, I went and saw him every time he played Birmingham or Atlanta or something. He'd always let me come up on the bus and hang out with him before and after the show, and we kind of got to be friends.

❦❧

Musically, Joey was attracted to Hank III's ability to blend punk with country. In songs such as "Smoke and Wine" and "Crazed Country Rebel," Hank III shows this artistic combination. Joey was particularly curious about the punk element because he had hardly ever listened to it. With Hank III, he saw how roots country could be taken to another level without losing its origins.

Joey's *50 Years Too Late* contains the song that he wrote and recorded with Hank III, "This Ain't Montgomery." And Joey's "Graveyard Bound" (on *Alone Again*), with its experimentalist technique, has something of a Hank III feel to it. If those two CDs show Joey's attachment to Hank III, he nevertheless remained true to himself, certainly influenced by his mentor but not replicating him.

Since the recording of *50 Years Too Late,* Joey and Hank III have "disengaged." Joey seldom listens to Hank III's music anymore—although this appears to be a case of having developed other interests and of Hank III having moved away from country rather than any animosity at work—and the two men seldom talk. Hank III, meanwhile, has accused Joey of copying him. Despite this rift Joey says he appreciates everything he ever did with his former mentor and calls him "the genesis of my career."

Unlike other Outlaw artists, Joey has for a long time paid little attention to the 1970s Outlaw movement. For example, it's only recently that he has begun listening to the Outlaw Waylon Jennings and to the renegade sound of Merle Haggard. It's as if he didn't want these influences to make impure the older roots country by which he lived.

Joey might be criticized for having ignored huge chunks of such heartfelt country. And his immersion into Hank Williams and into Hank's contemporaries might seem excessive. But whatever the case, Joey has contributed significantly to keeping roots country alive.

Joey's music strikes out with mainstream Nashville on three counts. First, he is too traditional, too connected to the past. Second, he is too creative and innovative. Third, he plays from his heart.

Question: Some people might say that with your music you have a nostalgic look to it. Would you agree with that?

Joey: Yeah, I love it. I mean that whole retro and nostalgia, that's what I'm doing. If someone tells me that, then I'm like, yeah, success!

Success. In June 2006 Joey testified before a congressional committee in Washington on behalf of his fellow roots country artists. A company called Sound Exchange was at that time trying to get Internet radio stations to pay a higher royalty rate for the right to play music. The increase would have devastated those musicians such as roots artists who, because they were getting little airplay in mainstream radio, relied heavily on the Internet stations for exposure.

Joey told the committee: "Internet radio...helps fans find new music, it helps artists find new fans, and it leads to new and unexpected performance and touring opportunities." He went on to say that the higher royalty rate would decrease the number of webcasters and that only "a few big artists" would benefit from the hike in fees. Just like with broadcast radio, the independents artists would be left "high and dry."

Joey's testimony aided in defeating the push by Sound Exchange for the higher royalties. "I'm quite proud of having done something to help everybody," Joey says.

For Outlaw artists, Nashville represents the despised third rail. Touch it and you will be fried by the money machine and turned into pop ashes. So Joey begins his song "In Nashville, Tennessee" (on *50 Years Too Late)* with a casual I'm-just-plugging-in-my guitar static and feedback sound and then sings: "Some people tell me that I ought to be in Nashville, Tennessee/They just don't understand or they don't know it ain't the place for me/When I went to Nashville they told me to pack up and go back home/They said we don't like your sound and we don't like your style/Son, you just don't belong."

Question: I'm really referring to one of your songs, "In Nashville Tennessee." In it, you say "I'm a little too country, you see, for Nashville, Tennessee." A little too country. How do you mean that?

Joey: To me, Nashville's version of country now, it's just a real homogenized version [of country]. But it's their demographics. That's who they're trying to sell to. Walmart sells more country records than anybody else, bar none.

❦

Walmart, where America shops in sanitized style. When Joey's mom bought that Hank Williams CD at Kmart, it was an oldies record. Go today to Kmart or Target or Walmart or any other conventional retail outlet to find old-school roots country music recorded by a current artist such as Joey and you will likely walk away empty-handed. It would take a sizeable change for it to be otherwise, and Joey knows it.

Although Joey doesn't really care about how his music is labeled, he said to me that he prefers the word "roots" to "Outlaw." Yet he realizes the problem with terminology and so will accept either word. "You know, you can call it alternative country, you can call it Outlaw," he says. "I don't really care."

For the Outlaw artists such as Joey, commitment goes to the heart of why music should be made, the belief that what courses through the artist should course through the art. "God knows," Joey says, "nobody's getting rich off of it. And it's hard to do. It's very difficult. It would be much easier just to go and get a job doing whatever."

When I was in Nashville with Joey and we were waiting for the recording session to start on Boscobel Street, we decided to visit the Country Music Hall of Fame. Joey had been there before, but I had not. I was impressed by the mix of old movies, still shots, and guitars, clothing, and song sheets that make up the artifacts. As Joey said while we viewed the movies or "shorts" from the 1930s—which in that era were meant to precede the main shows in theaters—none of the promoters "back in the day" knew what to make of these hillbillies or exactly what to do with them. Sophisticated urbanites saw them as country rubes posing as novelty acts, and they laughed at them. Those city dwellers who had recently left their homes in the country, however, saw them as cultural connections to a fading rural world.

As we wandered along the museum's time line, coming closer to the present, we both noticed how little was being said about the Outlaws from the 1970s, such as Waylon Jennings and Willie Nelson. We thought it was a serious mistake given what those Outlaws had done to make country more creative. We did notice that the museum had on display some of Jason Aldean's clothing, along with Taylor Swift's laptop. It wasn't just the museum's inclusion of the present that disturbed us, it was the pandering to the Nashville pop audience and the singers they idolized, the crass attempt to be "hip."

With all this being said, Joey insists he will not be a radical absolutist about Nashville. He likes the city and many of the people in it. He pointed out to me that many small clubs in the city host artists whose music stands at odds with commercialized pop.

Question: Is it that some artists are so critical of Nashville because they haven't been able to make it there?

Joey: Truth be told—and I was one of them when I was twenty-one years old and wrote "Nashville, Tennessee"—most of those people that say that stuff and bash Nashville—and like I said, I was one of them—have never even come here and tried. I'll tell you, the people here have been great to me. That's why when I put the vinyl out of *50 Years Too Late*, "Nashville, Tennessee" is not going to be on it because I feel hypocritical singing that now. The people I work with, they've become my best friends. They like what I do, they support what I do, and it just means more to me to be doing it in Nashville knowing that this is where all my heroes did it.

Joey hasn't smoked a peace pipe with the big record executives, nor does he even listen to Nashville pop. Yet he says: "Some of the people who are the worst singers, musicians, or whatever, they can still be the best people in the world to you; they can be your friends."

Question: Many of the artists I've talked to, they emphasize doing their own music. But sometimes that might, in turn, restrict their audience. So do you think there's some sort of a compromise?

Joey: I think so. Like Jamey Johnson, you know, he did it, and by virtue of him writing a song as silly as "Honky Tonk Badonkadonk," he made enough money to produce his own record. And that's the thing about Nashville versus Texas,...nobody else has the business means that is here in Nashville. People can say what they want about it, but at the end of the day, if you want to be in the movies, you go to Hollywood. If you want to be in the casino business, you go to Vegas. If you want to do country music, you still got to go to Nashville.

> *Well, I sure didn't get my start from MTV,*
> *They won't ever play my songs on CMT.*
> *I'm just a hillbilly singer with a five-piece band,*
> *I'm a real honky-tonkin' ramblin' man..... .*
> > "Honky Tonkin' Ramblin' Man"
> > From *All Alone Again*

Even though Joey sees room for compromise, he insists that an attachment to country's roots must be kept. "To me," Joey says, "Allan Jackson is the natural progression of country music. You can listen to him and say okay, I can understand how Hank Williams led to this. But you can't do that with Jason Aldean or Eric Church or Justin Moore." He congratulates them for making their own genre of music, but it just ain't country. "They're selling millions of records," he says, "and they've got bunches of people fooled into buying that stuff. But five years from now nobody will give a shit about them."

On one of my journeys to interview Joey, I drove south of Miami to meet up with him. South of Miami—who would have thought that country music would have any following even a short distance south of Orlando, let alone beyond Miami, where the towns and cities melt together to form a Hispanic megalopolis unfriendly to Joey's type of songs?

Joey wanted me to meet him in the Everglades, where he was performing at the Miccosukee Indian Reservation. As I drove farther south, "Seminole Wind," a tune by country singer John Anderson, began running through my mind, particularly the part where he blames white America for draining much of the Everglades and hurting Indian culture.

Several years ago, the Miccosukee also changed Indian culture by building a casino on land they owned on the eastern edge of the Everglades, near where the expressways and state roads creak and groan beneath endless trucks and cars often frozen in mechanical copulation. I had misunderstood Joey and thought that he would be playing at the casino, so I called him when I got there. "No, no, no," he said. "That's not the main reservation. I'm on the main reservation. You have to go about another twenty miles."

"Oh," I replied wearily. I had missed the cutoff to the casino and was already running late for his show. And the sun was setting. I didn't relish driving into the Everglades in the dark.

But I left the megalopolis behind and entered a land of saw grass, alligators, and mosquitoes that seemed an even more uninviting place for country music than did the land of Cuban sandwiches, dark coffee, and habanero shirts. I was having a tough time figuring out how Joey could be way down here.

The sunset painted streaks of orange across a darkening blue sky. But I had no time to enjoy the scene for I was clinging to the steering wheel of my car while plunging deeper into the dark along Tamiami Trail, a tight, two-lane road with narrow shoulders on either side. The bright lights from oncoming traffic cut into my eyes, and one rum and coke and one blunt into the wind, I envisioned gator jaws jumping the road, grabbing my ankles, and making a meal of my feet. But I knew that if I were to be devoured here, it would be in the service to Outlaw, which I could accept.

On and on; it seemed like a hundred miles. Then I hit a stretch where the road came down to one lane as construction workers let traffic through, first one way and then the other. Pebbles and dust rose from the ground and mixed with the headlights to disorient me even more.

As the road again widened to two lanes, I encountered an Indian police officer. I asked him if I had passed the entrance to the main reservation. He said that I still had another three miles to go. Look for the two tall towers, he told me, the ones with the flashing red lights. They were near the entrance. By now I was wishing I had never come. But I was so close I decided to go on.

I drove past the towers the officer had referred to—they seemed like five or six, with the red lights taking the shapes of bloodshot gator eyes—and finally reached the Miccosukee Reservation. I asked the guard at the main gate if he knew Joey Allcorn. He looked at me with surprise, as if to say, "Are you crazy? Everyone around here knows Joey Allcorn." Then he directed me to a house about a mile away. The street that ran in front of it was lined with cars. The gathering looked like a block party, but it turned out to be more than that.

Hundreds of Indians had converged for a huge birthday celebration. They presented a swirl of orange, red, and yellow with their traditional shirts, dresses, and jackets. An expansive grassy area between two houses held several shelters with concrete floors and roofs made from palm fronds.

Beneath one such tropical covering stood Joey and his band, well into their gig. The Indians were enjoying his old-school country music. A short distance from Joey, the flames from open grills shot upward, and the aroma from barbeque beef, pork, and chicken filled the air. A long table held so many different items of food that it would be impossible for me to list them, or even recollect them. I do clearly remember, though, the hospitality of the Miccosukee as they invited me to join in their feast and eat what I wanted.

As Joey took a break, unstrapped his guitar, and looked for a beer, an Indian came to the microphone to announce a raffle. He spoke first in English and then repeated himself in Seminole. It seemed as if I had entered another time and another world—not a third-world country economically, because the Indians had acquired too much money for that, but a different world culturally. As I enjoyed the experience, any regrets I had developed about coming to the Everglades at night and braving the threatening gator jaws quickly dissolved.

I was anxious to ask Joey about his connection to the Indians, but too many people had gathered around him. So I fiddled with my camera as I got ready to take pictures, and I walked about in the night breeze, watching as children rolled on the grass and family members giggled and laughed at each other's jokes.

At one table I began speaking with a middle-aged Indian lady, who was wearing a traditional dress and, to my surprise, told me that she was the queen of the Miccosukee. I found that odd, for I was under the impression that the Miccosukee had no queen (which Joey confirmed for me later). But as I told her that I was a bit unsettled and worried because I had arrived at the reservation late, she shared her wisdom with me, wisdom that didn't come as much from owning or not owning a title as from having lived a full life. She calmly responded: "You got here when you were meant to."

After Joey finished his show, the Indians invited us to have a few drinks at the casino, the one I had mistakenly gone to earlier that night. There we sat in the lounge, and Joey told me about how he came to know the Miccosukee. It began at a show in Tallahassee, Florida. One of the Indians had stopped there to see Joey perform. Joey knew that the man liked his music when he started buying a bunch of CDs, which were on sale at a table.

But Joey didn't think much more about it. Then one day he got a call from a Miccosukee who asked him to come down from Georgia to the reservation and play at a party. Joey agreed. Apparently, he had been at the right place at the right time.

The relationship deepened when the Miccosukee decided to back *50 Years Too Late* with money. Old-school country and the Indians thus came together. Ever since the encounter in Tallahassee, Joey has played at numerous gatherings on the reservation.

While I was in Nashville, I agreed to meet Joey a second time at the house on Boscobel Street. Either I was early or he was late; whatever the case, I stood on the porch for nearly half an hour waiting for him, while a "guard dog," clearly used to getting hugs rather than giving bites, sniffed at the locked front door from inside.

I looked up and down the street and tried to imagine Mom Upchurch standing on *her* porch—her white hair tied into a bun, her eyes still sparkling despite the wrinkles of age around them—and watching as one of "her" musicians left for the *Grand Ole Opry* and that moment on the big stage. Maybe the musician was Faron Young or Lloyd Green or Roger Miller; maybe it was a member of the Carter family, all of whom at one point stayed at Mom's. I imagined them as they left their rooms, grateful for the comfort Mom provided, and then walking in the summer heat, guitar cases in hand, thinking about the music and the show that night.

It would have been neat, I thought, if all of them—Faron and Lloyd and Roger and the Carters—could have walked down the road together. What stories they could have told about their pasts and about what they wanted to make of themselves. Maybe they would be swapping stories about Jimmie Rodgers and Hank Williams.

When Joey arrived at the studio, he went right to work, refining some of the vocals on *Nothing Left to Prove.* I remembered a comment made by one of his fans at a recent show, that he had the same kind of nasally voice as did Hank Williams. Indeed, the fan said, if you closed your eyes, you would think that it was Hank himself singing.

Nothing Left To Prove tops Joey's other CDs. He seems more confident, whether it be at the beginning with his take-command song "When You Start Back to Wanting Me" or deeper into the selections, when he offers a cover of "Little Ol' Wine Drinker Me." That song conjures up thoughts of lazy, laid-back days filled with the juice from grapes whose stream of sweetness erases a person's woes.

In the CD's title cut, Joey proclaims that he has been kicked around, but he draws a line in the sand: his music remains true to himself and to his fans, and so it will remain. He displays bravado, but he does it with class, as Joey, unlike some other artists, knows how to do. It's a great fuck-you song without coming right out and saying "fuck you." He's all attitude.

> *Living on the road ain't everything I thought it would be,*
> *It's just trying to get paid and looking for a place to sleep.*
> *But we've had some good times in places that we don't know*
> *that we've been,*
> *And if I could go back, I'd damn sure do it again.*
> "Nothing Left to Prove"
> From *Nothing Left to Prove*

Joey might answer his critics by saying he has nothing left to prove. But as an Outlaw musician, he will always have something to prove, namely that amid the tsunami of Nashville pop his artistry can grow and his oath to Hank can survive. Maybe he will even have to compromise at some point, or feel as if he must compromise, and if he does, he will have to prove that he has not sold out, that he remains true to his word.

The title to Joey's first CD describes Joey as an artist "fifty years too late." That indeed may be true in the context of a Nashville music scene more pop than roots country. But it's not true in the context of what many people need: a creative music that touches, and can even help heal, the hurt we all live with. Joey can rock the house with the best of them, but even when he does, his music cries. It cries for anyone, and out to everyone, who has felt broken and down.

When, back as a kid, Joey became committed to the music of Hank, he reinforced his status as an outsider. Joey remains the outsider. Yet he's not fifty years too late; he's what country music needs now if it is to achieve a diversity and richness apart from Nashville pop. Joey got here, as the Miccosukee Indian "queen" says, when he was meant to.

> *I spend my days out on the highways,*
> *At night I sing these songs....*
> *There's no telling where I'll be*
> *When you start back to wanting me.*
> "When You Start Back to Wanting Me"
> From *Nothing Left To Prove*

CODA

When I was writing this profile, Joey asked me to mention that one of the greatest moments of his life was when he got to play on stage with the legendary steel guitarist Don Helms. So here's the mention . . . not to be gratuitous, but to emphasize that to Joey, roots country is where he's meant to be. That honky tonk hell. It's home.

Joey Allcorn, Miccosukee Indian Reservation, FL (2011)

Wayne Mills, Howlin' Wolf, New Orleans, LA (2012)

CHAPTER 17

WAYNE MILLS

One of These Days

Terry Adams rode the same bus as me,
We mapped out our lives on Bluebird Three.
He was going to be a football star
In spite of his family.
He was only nineteen years old when he died
In a head-on down at Shoal Creek....
My friends lost their lives,
But I remember their dreams.
"ONE OF THESE DAYS"
FROM THE LAST HONKY TONK

Every November near Thanksgiving, the Five Flags Speedway in the Florida panhandle hosts a three-day event called the SnoBall Derby. The night before the competition, dozens of race cars sit out on display with their front hoods propped open, as if, like in a Disney movie, they might be getting ready to speak. Instead, they show off their engines. The night I arrived, about a thousand people had descended on the speedway to commune with the race cars, talk to the drivers and mechanics, and swap stories about other tracks they had been to. They had also come to see a couple of bands play on an outdoor stage and to look over Miss SnoBall. It was a celebration of Southern culture, of what some outsiders, in fact, might mockingly call redneck high culture.

I had gone to the Five Flags Speedway in Pensacola to interview Outlaw artist Wayne Mills. While there, I wandered among the race cars, bathed myself in the local ambience, and looked for the stage where Wayne would be performing. It was an unusually cold night, and by the time I located the site, my feet and hands were feeling the weather. I am not a Southerner by birth, but I have lived below the Mason-Dixon Line long enough for me to become, in terms of climate, a thin-blooded Southern boy.

I found the small stage sitting atop a trailer. Within a short time, Wayne and his band arrived in a van and began setting up. I introduced myself to him, and he suggested that we wait until after the show for the interview, which could then be done in a friend's RV.

Tall, large-boned, powerfully built, with a long goatee and a firm, don't-give-no-quarter face, Wayne looks every bit the former tight end that he is. Rather than delivering crushing blows, however, he prefers to give bear hugs as he greets friends and even acquaintances warmly and openly.

Before he began his set, Wayne met the attractively blond, petite SnoBall queen. They posed for photographers, and at one point he jokingly swapped his cowboy hat for her crown and put it on his head.

As Wayne and his band kicked into their first song, I perched myself on the stage and started taking pictures. Everyone in Wayne's group was bundled up against the cold. Standing next to me was Big Steve, one of Wayne's friends, who, on occasion, helps out as his roadie. Big Steve was wearing a black leather biker jacket and a black woolen ski cap to complement his black beard. The jacket bulked up his already bulky frame and added an exclamation point to the phrase "Don't mess with me!"

As the cold penetrated everyone deeper, Big Steve left the stage and a few minutes later returned with a Mason jar brimming with moonshine. Wayne, his band, and Big Steve began drinking, and for them the cold soon became less bothersome and the night more enjoyable.

Wayne played for about ninety minutes and then told the crowd that he was having so much fun he would continue "until they unplug my guitar." The show went on for another half hour, by which time it became clear to me that the Mason-Dixon Line had become a World War II-era Maginot Line to the invading northern cold front and I would never again be able to feel my fingers or my toes.

When Wayne finished playing, I waited as his fans came up to him and he signed more autographs and again posed for pictures. Finally, he turned to Big Steve and asked if he wouldn't mind driving us over to the far side of the race complex, where the RV was located. Big Steve agreed to the request and said he would take us in his car.

Wayne sat in the front. I sat in the back, feeling a bit awkward since I was still carrying my satchel and my camera and looking every bit the academic nerd in the company of two country cats.

> *Just the good ol' boys,*
> *Never meanin' no harm.*
>
> Theme from *The Dukes of Hazzard*
> Written by Waylon Jennings

As Big Steve pulled out from the dirt parking lot, Wayne glanced at the racetrack. "Let's do a lap," he said as his eyes gleamed wide and imploringly. "Do a lap?" Big Steve replied. "Yeah," said Wayne. "Let's do a lap, and then we can exit from there to the RV."

Big Steve took the car onto the track, gunned it, and before long we were part of the SnoBall Derby. I tried to fit in, but my knuckles turned white as the car sped up, and I recalled the moonshine that had been consumed by the guys in the front.

We didn't last long. About halfway around, as we entered a curve, Big Steve miscalculated and the car slammed into a barrier of orange-and-white water-filled barrels. The liquid sprayed upward like Old Faithful exploding for Yellowstone tourists and drenched the car and racetrack alike. Wayne laughed, and as I caught my breath, I had the feeling that the open-hooded race cars were laughing too. "Man, that was fun!" Wayne said. "But let's get the hell out of here before security comes."

When we got to the RV, Big Steve checked his car, ran his hand over his face and through his hair, and bemoaned the damage; his Alabama Crimson Tide plate had been destroyed. As we entered the RV and as its heater defrosted us, I looked back on the adventure and realized how much it meant to me: a once-in-a-lifetime experience filled with a take-life-as-it-comes, fuck-the-chances element.

My conversation with Wayne in the RV began awkwardly. It seemed like he had been rehearsing what he would say to me, and, usually, rehearsing for a book interview doesn't work well; combining it with a residue of moonshine works even less well. I would later learn, however, that the awkwardness of the start had more to do with something other than these two influences, and the first steps toward that revelation occurred quickly.

Before I could ask Wayne anything, he sat down in a chair—his hulking frame taking over the small room—and boomed forth a pronouncement: "The torment of playing Outlaw country music and playing shit that's against the grain is you want the attitude that you don't give a rat's ass about what they think."

Yet Wayne quickly admitted that he wished he had more fans, that his music had more of an appeal. "I want everybody to like me," he said in a quieter tone. "I can't stand it, I can't stand for somebody not to like me, but at the same time I don't understand why the hell people like certain music they like."

That he's a rebel who nevertheless wants others to like him seemed a bit baffling to me and was the beginning of the revelation. Wayne likes to please people, and maybe this is true for other musicians who need to appeal to their audiences. But with Wayne there's more: his people pleasing comes from the core of who he is, namely a compassionate man.

Fun and friendly, Wayne also has a big, big heart. He's so *selfless* that he probably doesn't know what *selfishness* means. He's also talented and versatile—musically and otherwise. Indeed, there are so many things he *could* do that he gets confused about what he *should* do. His most powerful inner conflict, however, arises whenever his desire to please others and treat them with caring clashes with his desire to do what feels right to him.

What does this mean for Wayne as an Outlaw artist? He isn't going to go rumbling down Music Row on a Harley, attitude blazing and boots stomping, and declare to the record companies (as one Outlaw artist from the 1970s, David Allan Coe, purportedly did) this is my music, so sign me, record me, or I'll kick your ass. That would hurt too many feelings and too many people. That he will instead play what he *feels,* at any given time—that is the genuine Wayne Mills as he continues to learn, continues to search, continues to discover himself as an artist and a person.

His music will likely grow (as it still must) to reveal Wayne Mills gradually, akin to peeling the layers from an onion—the good-times Wayne Mills, the angry Wayne Mills, the compassionate Wayne Mills, but always the true-to-himself Wayne Mills, listening to his own beat, wherever it might take him. Exactly where that might be, well, with Wayne that's hard to predict, as he could roam the country range all the way from honky-tonks to Music Row and have his feet planted in both places at once.

Sometimes in articulating his essence, he finds it less stressful and easiest to sum up in a single modest statement: "I'm just an old redneck out there singing country music with a jam band, which is cool to me." Anything beyond that would be presumptuous, confusing, and potentially confining.

Question: What's wrong with country music today?

Wayne: Everything's a gimmick. Everything's about making money—how can we make money fast? It's about what song is going to appeal to a fifteen-year-old because those are the people that are downloading to buy music. But I really believe it's gotten to a point now, it's gotten so saturated, so crossed over, that the genres of music have all blended to a point that there is no genre of music anymore. How do you say what kind of music do you play? I don't know what kind of music I play.

Wayne then reconsidered his opening statement and became reluctant to call himself Outlaw. It was as if the word had a meaning to it, or an implication, that made him uncomfortable. "I never ever called myself an Outlaw, ever," he insisted. "I always refused to call myself a rebel, but I obviously got labeled that because I play…. That's the kind of music I like. But I think it's because it tells real life stories." Because of his contradictory statements, I pursued the term Outlaw some more and was able to get a bit deeper into what makes up Wayne Mills.

Question: I looked at your new website—

Wayne: I know where you're going with this…

Question: Well, because it says "Outlaw" on it.

Wayne: I know, but it's all corporate bullshit. It's about branding. These corporate dudes all want to brand you.

❧⚜❧

It was becoming clear that Wayne didn't like being labeled ("I don't know what kind of music I play"), and he certainly didn't want a label applied to him as a gimmick thought up by a businessman simply to promote records. (Such behavior was, in fact, one of the reasons he eventually broke with his publicist.) He doesn't want to be *that kind* of branded man. He wants to keep his versatility as *he* defines it and as *he* feels about it on any given day. Indeed, the very use of the term Outlaw can be anti-Outlaw if it encourages people to ignore the individuality that makes Outlaw musicians different from the Nashville pop assembly line, where the performers are interchangeable.

As Wayne wavered over the descriptive "Outlaw," he began thinking about his friend Jamey Johnson who made enough money writing songs for the Nashville music grinder that he can now do the music he wants to do. Some music critics have labeled Jamey's music Outlaw.

"Jamey's a good buddy of mine," Wayne says, "and last year when he came out with 'In Color' and a new record *[That Lonesome Song]*, he broke out of a shell that I was so happily, pleasantly surprised that he broke out of and did wonders for music in general. And now I think maybe it's time to say, 'Hell, yes, I'm an Outlaw.'"

So Wayne embraces Jamey for being genuine, the essence of Outlaw, even if it meant that at some point in his career he had to grease the production wheels of Music Row to get his own palms greased and build the bankroll for his music. When the grease was washed from his hands, there appeared a few blisters, but the sincerity of his talent remained to bring his guitar to life.

After nearly twenty years of playing country music, Wayne still agrees with a friend of his who told him: "You haven't recorded the definitive Wayne Mills album."

Wayne told me: "I just pick up my guitar and play." In effect, wherever the music lands, it lands. Given the many musical influences on him, and given this independent mentality, Wayne's music can often be seen as inconsistent—not so much in quality as in genre. This makes it much more difficult to produce a definitive album.

Wayne grew up in Arab (pronounced with a long A and then "rab"), a small town in northeastern Alabama ("nestled on top of Brindlee Mountain," says one of his press releases), not far from Scottsboro, where in 1931, amid a mob atmosphere and using unreliable evidence, an all-white jury convicted eight black youths of raping two white women. Arab got its name when the US post office mistakenly misspelled the first name of Arad Thompson, the son of the town's founder and the person for whom the town was supposed to take its designation.

For Wayne growing up in Arab involved doing what most any boy would do in a rural setting: wandering lazily across the fields, fishing along the riverbanks, and venturing along off-road trails. His dad owned a small plot of land on which the family raised vegetables and a few horses. Wayne remembers picking peas and "getting my ass whipped if I didn't feed the horses."

Wayne's dad worked for NASA at the Redstone Arsenal in Huntsville. He was a technician who analyzed rocket propulsion and helped design the first moon buggy. But he got hurt on the job when Wayne was in his early teens and from then on received workmen's compensation and worked as a general contractor.

The older Mills was also athletic, and it ran through the family. "Pa-paw coached women's softball for twenty-two years," Wayne adds. His dad helped build the softball park down the street from where Wayne lived. "He won seven state championships," Wayne says, "and was just super-competitive. My older three sisters all played ball." Wayne himself was athletic—"I grew up with a ball in my hand"—and played baseball, basketball, and football in high school. (He later played baseball on scholarship at a community college.)

Wayne says he was "very, very close" to his mom, although they were not much for conversations. She played some piano and loved to sing. In fact, everyone in the family liked music. Wayne remembers singing at the Baptist church and how, on many Sundays, there would be a big cookout at his house, followed by his dad, mom, sisters, and himself gathering in the kitchen to clean and put dishes away, and, as they did so, also sing their cares away. They would even frequently kick into five-part harmony.

In 2011, while his mom was dying from cancer, Wayne had her join him in recording a song. Her voice was weak but sweet. It was, he says, as if she were already singing for the angels.

Wayne was "a little redneck" in high school. He liked to drive around in his "good ol' Z24" and listen to music as it blared from two fifteen-inch speakers tucked behind his front seats. He delved into all kinds of songs and would crank up the sounds to anything that to him sounded cool.

When he was in college, he never skipped a class, and at the University of Alabama, he made the president's list with a 4.0 average. "I usually hide how smart I am," he told me. Wayne says that he entered college with no idea of what he wanted to become and that this typifies the way he thought back then and how he still thinks today: his mind focuses on the present and doesn't get much into the future.

He changed majors three times "because I wanted to do something that made money at first, but then I hated it. So I ended up back in education because I wanted to be a coach." It was for Alabama that he played football as a tight end, and he did so as a walk-on. He had gotten scholarship offers from other colleges, but not from the Crimson Tide, the team he wanted most to play for. ("I finally got in a game," he told me, "when we were beating Tulane by about forty points.")

Although Wayne had learned some piano while he was a teenager and took up the guitar when he was sixteen, he was more concerned with athletics until his senior year at Alabama, when he formed his first band. "I was just doing it to get laid," he says. It was a jam band that played covers. He liked to play music that he grew up on, so the band got into Springsteen, Dylan, the Rolling Stones, Counting Crowes. "God, I can't even remember all the songs that I did back then," he says. "I used to do a ton of [them]." The band played a lot of country too, so much so that Wayne estimates about half their music was of that kind.

> *When the band starts playing all them songs,*
> *From Lynyrd Skynyrd to ol' George Jones,*
> *The girls and the boys are making some noise*
> *Down in the heart of Dixie.*
> > "Heart of Dixie"
> > From *Under the Influence of Outlaws and Mama*

Wayne's band was successful as a regional group, to the point that "the very second I got my degree, and I was out from under my mama's and daddy's wings, I was hell bent for leather." The money was rolling in, primarily from playing college bars, and the partying was going full tilt. At that point, Wayne admits, he got "stupid." He says: "I was making about a hundred, a hundred twenty grand a year for about five, six, seven years and ain't got a dime to show for it. I mean I had a house in Tuscaloosa that had parties in it every single night. I would burn my clothes in my fireplace because I was too lazy or too hung over to go cut wood. And so, I would just go to my dresser and pull out a drawer full of blue jeans, and throw them in my fireplace, and that would be our fire for the night. Then I'd go out the next day and buy me some new clothes. That's the God's-honest truth.

"I've got a problem. Money is just not my thing. But I've got to realize I've got a kid now, and I got a wife who wants a house, and I've got to do that. The biggest thing to me is I just like going out and playing music and having fun."

Shortly after forming his college band, Wayne met his future wife, Carol. He first saw her at a college bar in Tuscaloosa, and immediately fell in love. He even went to his mom and dad, who were sitting at the bar, and told them "she's the one." Carol, however, didn't take to Wayne at first, and so it was about a year before they started dating. ("I remember that after a show," Wayne says with laughter, "we would sit in her car and listen to her Donnie and Marie [Osmond] songs. I just loved it because I was so in love with her.")

Wayne has a six-year-old son, Jack, who, like his father, loves sports. And he's also getting into music, and has a little drum set, which he enjoys playing. Jack means all the world to Wayne; the child has stabilized Wayne's life, and the relationship that Wayne has with him makes Wayne appreciate his time at home more.

Although Wayne was a rocker—and remains passionate about rock 'n' roll—he gravitated toward country music. In part, he says, that was because his dad listened only to country, and so the music was a big influence in the Mills household. Also, he adds, when it came to writing songs, he felt more comfortable with country.

Wayne sings one tune in which he claims to be the "wildest branch on the family tree." He certainly was a hell-raiser in his early years, especially as he drank heavily. He says: "Everybody's got this interpretation, that if you play Outlaw country music, you're supposed to be an out-of-control idiot. Early on, I kind of thought that was what I was supposed to be."

Wayne's music reflects the cross currents of rock and country that have influenced him over the years. He counts AC/DC as his favorite rock group, but adds to that the distinctly Southern sounds of Lynyrd Skynyrd, the Allman Brothers, and 38 Special. He says that in the future he wants to include more Southern rock in his music. "I've got a lot of heavy guitar in my blood," he adds.

Question: The country influences on your music, how far back do you go? Do you go back to Hank Williams, do you go back earlier?

Wayne: I would say Hank was an influence, but not real big. I think my first biggest influence was Alabama. John Prine. Merle Haggard was *huge* to me. I've learned a lot from him about phrasing and how to deal with life experiences. [Then there's] Willie [and] Waylon, which is kind of weird because I didn't get into Waylon until ten years after I started playing music.

Wayne feels so connected to Merle Haggard that he wanted nothing more than to open a show for him. In August 2012 he did so, and in none other than Tuscaloosa, the site of Wayne's college days. Wayne recalls that his dad listened to many Merle Haggard songs, and to open for The Hag was for Wayne one of the highlights of his career. He even brought his wife , Carol, and his son, Jack, to meet Merle. The Hag signed two guitars Wayne carried, his and Jack's. Committed to playing with Merle Haggard? Wayne went onstage feeling terribly sick and suffering from what he later learned was a collapsed lung.

Wayne considers Johnny Paycheck to be "the most under celebrated honky-tonker of all time." He adds: "He's a man who don't give a shit about nothing but playing music and partying." Wayne enjoys many of the songs written by David Allan Coe and how Coe pulls no punches with his lyrics. "When you think he's just a hell-raiser, he comes out with 'Would You Lay with Me in a Field of Stone.' With songs like that, it really hits you that it's not about partying and raising hell, it's about playing what you feel and not worrying about what people think."

Wayne praises Kris Kristofferson, who influenced an entire generation of music lovers with his intricate and impressive wordcraft. "Kris Kristofferson, oh my God!" Wayne says. "Let's talk about Kris Kristofferson. Oh my God! I love songs that have a story and a meaning behind them. It's got to mean something."

Yet Kristofferson's music doesn't rock, and Wayne gets into music that rocks. "I'm an underground Widespread Panic fan," he says. "I love groove music. I love music with just really, really good jams." He adds: "If you can't put your foot to the floor while you're shaking your ass, then you're not having a good time."

For Wayne, combining storytelling and ass-shaking in his own songwriting has been a challenge. He says, "I really want to get to the point where I could do a show to where I have people coming to see me play [and they're] thrashing their freaking brains out in the front row, banging their heads, like literally banging their heads, going nuts.

Then I want a set in my show where people are really kind of like laid-back in their chair, going 'Oh my God!' It just melts them.

"I love a good beat," he continues. "I love a good groove, but it's got to have lyrical content, and it's got to have a good footstone to it." He wants to write and sing songs that express his deepest feelings. But as he seeks to blend storytelling and tenderness with rocking and grooving, he also seeks to blend sincerity with appeal, and it has been a struggle too.

"Every time I write a song, every time I do a record," he says, "I really want to write a record that I think people will enjoy but at the same time that I know I enjoy. But there's a balance in between there too. Because if I just play the shit that I want to hear, then I've limited myself as to my audience. So you have to stretch it out a little bit. At the same time, you don't want to sell out, neither. Otherwise, you become one of them." Them: The Nashville Monster That Ate Country Music.

> *I've always fallen somewhere in between...*
> *I never knew where I would go,*
> *I never knew what I would be.*
> *I just kept moving,*
> *I have never known what's to become of me...*
> *I am the dark horse in the gate.*
> "Dark Horse"
> From *The Last Honky Tonk*

Question: If you had one thing to say to the Nashville music establishment, what would it be?

Wayne: Listen and pay attention to what's going on and quit being assholes. Basically it's become like a mafia; they just think they know everything, and they want to force-feed everything to the masses. I've got mixed feelings. The crossover into pop with Garth Brooks, well, I love his first record, and Tim McGraw came along, and it snowballed. They reached people who would have never [cared] about country music. Now I want to reeducate them because I'm not playing all that pop bullshit. There's nothing wrong with it, I just wish they'd come up with a different name for it because *it's not country.* The music I play is very similar to the music of the '70s Outlaw music, but Outlaw wasn't like Hank Williams. The music has to evolve.

Wayne sees hope for some commercial Nashville performers, such as Blake Shelton and Jason Aldean, to develop into true artists. He isn't about to dump on them. Blake is a good friend, and Jason "is one of the nicest people I've met in my life. I would definitely invite him to Thanksgiving dinner."

Question: But what do you think of his music?

Wayne: I think he's young. I think he got pushed in directions he might not necessarily have wanted to get pushed in, but it was smart because now all of a sudden he's freakin' huge, and I think the older he gets, his music is going to develop into music that is more of his style.

In January 2012 Wayne played at the Howlin' Wolf, a nightspot in New Orleans. The Alabama and Louisiana State University football teams were in the city to compete for the national title as part of the college Bowl Championship Series. A large number of Alabama fans turned out to see Wayne, and they whooped and hollered as he unabashedly shouted "Roll, Tide!" between numbers, although with apologies to any LSU fan who might have gotten caught in the crowd.

(And Alabama did roll, 21–0.) Wayne was thankful for the Alabama faithful who came to see him, especially since there was little publicity for his show. In fact, if there was a Wayne Mills poster outside the Howlin' Wolf, it must have gotten eaten by some wild night creature.

While I was there, I spoke with Wayne about touring. Like most Outlaws, he loves it. Doing a show pumps life into him. "I don't wanna ever stop," he said. "No, I will never get tired of the road, ever. I can't be still. It drives me nuts. Can't you tell?" He waved his arms, paused, and then added for emphasis: "This is what I do. It's what I'm gonna do until the day I die. Oh God. Oh God, help us all!"

Wayne admits that it's tough for an Outlaw band that wants to play its own songs rather than cover songs to get a large turnout. Too many people want to hear oldies or something from the mainstream charts.

Wayne maintains a good friendship with Outlaw artist Dallas Moore. They first met years ago, and because their encounter involved the type of hijinks young bands sometimes find themselves in as the road makes its demands and the pressure builds, it would make for a hilarious, short, silent-movie-style skit.

Location: A popular bar, the Flora-Bama, located on the Florida/Alabama border east of Gulf Shores and west of Pensacola.

Characters: Dallas Moore, Outlaw musician and leader of the band Dallas Moore and the Snatch Wranglers.

Wayne Mills, another Outlaw musician and leader of his own band.

Band members.

Setting: A beach house built on stilts, surrounded by sand, a waterway behind it, with wooden stairs leading up to the main entrance. Inside, a kitchen, a small dining room, a cramped living room, and several bedrooms, all decorated in beachfront dishevel.

Background Music Played on Theater Piano: Swell into "Down Yonder" (from the Willie Nelson album *Red Headed Stranger*); play accelerando to prestissimo to freneticmo.

Format: Black-and-white, grainy film; fast motion, as with old silent movies when run through modern projectors.

Action: In rides Dallas Moore. He pulls up to the paint-peeling beach house on a Road King motorcycle. He has long hair to the middle of his back, is wearing biker clothes, looks tired and soaked—has just ridden through a downpour. The rest of his band pulls up in a van, unloads their gear, and climbs the stairs.

Inside they break open Kentucky bourbon, roll some joints, and set themselves to drinking and smoking. They tell animated stories before getting tired as night deepens; they go to sleep.

Cut To: In comes Wayne Mills and his band. They arrive in a van. They get out; their muscles are sore from the cramped ride. They stretch, walk up the stairs, and talk about how they are looking forward to a few drinks and some dope and then going to bed. They have no idea they are supposed to share the beach house with Dallas Moore.

Wayne and his band try to open the bedroom doors; they are locked. They start pounding their fists on them, shouting, and seem to be using the f-word as their lips move frantically. Several close-ups of their angry-looking faces, eyes squished and nostrils flaring.

The bedroom doors all open at once. Out come Dallas Moore and his Snatch Wranglers; no snatch, they're set to wrangle. Commotion. All hell breaks loose—pushing and shoving, then Dallas and his guys wave guns. Wayne and his guys flee for their lives; they run out of the beach house and down the stairs, skipping steps, falling into each other at the bottom. Close-up of Dallas twirling the tip of his mustache, sinister style. Dallas and his guys glare down at Wayne. The two groups point and shout at each other; they shake their fists.

They soon realize the mix-up and start laughing, then guffawing. Dallas motions to Wayne to come back up. The two bands shake hands, then they hug. They enter the beach house as friends.

Close-up of Dallas and Wayne drinking together and smiling.

CUT

END SILENT FILM

The director's cut to such a movie might include another brief scene where, after the two bands become friends, they try to hot-wire the Flora-Bama bus and take it on a trip, only they fail to get it started. (Keystone Cops style—only in this case, Keystone Outlaws.)

Wayne says that he and Dallas quickly hit it off because "they loved that I came in there raising hell, and I loved that they came out with guns." He says that "after I played that night, I brought them to Tuscaloosa with me to do a show and everybody fell in love with them. I love Dallas Moore."

Dallas says that "Wayne was shocked to find out I had rode all the way from Myrtle Beach in the rain [for ten hours] and that we were packin' about fifteen firearms and a truckload of whiskey and smoke. To this day, the old timers at the Flora-Bama who remember this story refer to us as the Bureau of Alcohol, Tobacco and Firearms!"

> *I learned all the rules to the games they played,*
> *But no matter how I tried, it's just not my way....*
> *It's been a tough living, but I'm getting by.*
> *But I won't complain, no,*
> *It's just not my style.*
>
> "It's Just Not My Style'
> From *The Last Honky Tonk*

By Wayne's own assessment, his 2010 CD *The Last Honky Tonk*, with songs written by himself and others, comes closest to showing the definitive Wayne Mills. (Although a case could be made for the earlier *Under the Influence of Outlaws and Mamas* for its more consistent adherence to the Southern rock influences that make up so much of Wayne's music.)

The Last Honky Tonk shows Wayne's versatility. If Wayne wants people to be contemplative, he's got it. In his cover of "Old Willie Nelson Song," for example, his acoustic guitar work shifts the listener from *thinking about* Willie's music to *communing with* Willie's music. I could see Wayne onstage, playing this song with intensity, embracing the lyrics—"All I want to do is fly away on the stardust to the moon"—his head bowing over his guitar—particularly during the instrumental part—his ears taking in every acoustic note, string by beautiful string. Wayne owns this song, and his performance makes a person melt.

If he wants people to be able to shake their asses while stomping their feet, he's got that too. ("Don't Bring It Around Anymore" gets it done as he sings, boogie style, "I've been down to the bottom/ I'm trying to get back up.") And if he wants to take us back to an earlier George Jones era, we can "go to a shrink," as the song "The Truce" says (which he sings as a duet with Presley Tucker), and get ourselves "shrunk."

Then there's the title track, "The Last Honky Tonk" (written by John Phillips, Jill Kensey, and Keaton Allen). It's a roots-infused song with a heavy, relentless beat tolling the end of the honky-tonk era, and it allows Wayne to declare his allegiance to the music he loves most. "I'll be there when they burn the last honky-tonk down," he sings.

The video to the song was directed, edited, and filmed by Outlaw musician Josh Newcom. It was nominated for several awards, and the song itself made nearly every Top Ten country list—*in Europe*, where country fans listen to Nashville pop but also have a strong attraction to roots and Outlaw. Wayne has never toured Europe but will likely do so soon. "They love hardcore country over there," he says. "As far as my style of country, they want roots country."

But the most definitive *song* in this nearly definitive CD is a real-life story, "One of These Days." . Wayne wrote it about two friends of his who died back in high school. He was particularly close to Jay Cobb, who was "like a brother" to him and appears in the song as a fellow athlete. The close relationship developed because Wayne was good friends with Jay's younger brother, Mike, and would often stay over at Mike's house for a week or two. "Mike's siblings," Wayne emphasizes, "became my siblings."

In telling the story of the tragic death of Jay and another friend, Terry Adams, Wayne reveals much about himself as his lyrics peel away at the onion. First, the melody emerges firmly planted in roots country, with a touch of Southern rock.

Second, the song comes across as truthful and soul-searching. When he says, for example, "I know I don't think enough of them/I'm just trying to get through," he admits a personal fault. The same can be said for the more puzzling lyric "Sometimes I feel I'm looking down on me/And I guess maybe it makes me feel a little bit guilty." And he says, "I wonder if I'll ever change my ways/ Well, I'm sure I will."

Indeed a third characteristic of the song appears in its clever structure, as the lyrics sometimes hit the listener with double meaning. For example, when Wayne expresses his own desires, he also connects back to those of his friends: "One of these days I'll fly to the moon/ One of these days I'll have nothing to prove."

Fourth, and most importantly, the song conveys Wayne's compassionate nature: "But I remember *their* dreams." They—his friends *and* their dreams—still live with him.

"Yeah, yeah, the story's all true," Wayne says. "It's all true." He encapsulates their short lives (and his own feelings) in a song about three and a half minutes long, a song short in comparison to the minutes in a day but long in the emotion it evokes.

"One of These Days" makes the listener wonder what a thematic CD about Wayne's own life would be like. Such a project holds the promise of being a captivating, powerful piece of art, should it ever be made. For now, however, the words of Wayne's friend echo in this profile: Wayne has yet to record the definitive Wayne.

"I believe in good country music," Wayne says. "I believe there's a place for it. And I believe there's an audience for it. But unless people are putting me up there in front of folks who are paying to come see my shows, then I'm screwed. I can't get on radio with it; radio won't play it."

For sure, the Outlaws of the 1970s had a definite advantage over those of today, and it gnaws at this later generation. In the previous era, Outlaw music developed a widespread appeal, and as more fans flocked to Willie and Waylon, the big record labels latched onto the trend. There was gold in them thar Texas hills, and RCA, Columbia, and others were ready to mine it for all it was worth, and the artists were ready and anxious to reap the financial fruits of their musical labor. Roots-based Outlaw country had merged with popular demand, and while pop country remained vibrant, there was a large audience that wanted something else and was willing to pay for it.

Whenever that last honky-tonk that Wayne sings about has become nothing more than charred wood and embers—either because there are no fans left to support it or because musicians have deserted it, or both—Wayne will be standing there, pulling the "devil from the rubble."

Flames be damned, Wayne will be playing whatever moves him at the moment—artistically and otherwise—and in that sense he may well have an intimate connection to those earlier Outlaws. Given his indecisiveness, his greatest challenge appears clear: to keep his commercial instincts from overwhelming him to the point that he shapes his music primarily for the sake of selling records to the mainstream.

Question: When you say, "I'll be there when they burn the last honky-tonk down," what are you committing yourself to?

Wayne: I mean that literally. I wish that I could be there. I think that the honky-tonk band era is dying, because over the past fifteen or twenty years that I've been playing, I've seen all these really, really cool live music venues, where people come out and watch good music, turn into a more urban kind of thing with the be-bop, the boom-boom scene, the dance scene.

He observed: "Nobody listens to lyrics no more; there's not enough *listeners*.... It's just not real music anymore." Then he added with laughter: "They just want to take their drugs, take their clothes off –which I've got no problem with that, but I'd rather they do it to our music than the boom-boom music."

Everyone I talked to describes Wayne as someone quick to help others without considering the repercussions. If there's a dispute with a promoter or club owner over money, he makes sure his band gets paid, even if he gets nothing. If a friend needs money, he's quick to lend it. If he learns of a great venue, he gladly tells other musicians about it, rather than keep it secret, as usually happens in the cutthroat world of band competition. In fact, he loves to see other musicians succeed.

Wayne knows that he often acts against his own best financial interests, and he kicks himself for it. At the same time, in a comment he made to me he expressed a curious outlook about what makes for a life of challenge and accomplishment. "My compassion gets me into a lot of trouble," he said. "That's the reason I'm forty-two years old and I'm broke. [But] I don't feel like I'm doing something if I ain't struggling."

In one of the most telling parts of my interview with Wayne, I asked him to make three wishes for *himself.* Silence. I waited a minute, two, three.... He hemmed and he hawed. Finally he said, "Would wanting to build a house for my wife count as one?" Wayne couldn't think of a single wish for himself. Not a one. *He was so completely into thinking about others, he couldn't do it.*

> *My friends lost their lives,*
> *But I remember their dreams.*

"It's hard for you, isn't it Wayne?" I said to him. "Damn, it is," he replied. "Hey, I've got one: I wish the driver's side door to my van would open and shut as it ought to." With that comment, we both laughed.

Question: To you, what would be the most perfect day?

Wayne: I would go fishing with my son, come home, and hang out with my wife and my son for a little while. Then I would go and bring my family to see me play at the *Grand Ole Opry.*

At the Howlin' Wolf, Wayne and I were sitting at a table across from each other, drinks in hand. It was getting close to his show time, and recorded music was blaring from the speakers. I leaned closer to him so we could hear each other better and asked: "What do you want people to remember about you as a person? As a musician?"

"That I never gave up," he replied. "I've made it because I busted my ass to have a living making music, and I've earned every inch I've gotten. I just want people to know that I've worked hard and that I appreciate that they listen to my music. I love my fans and my family, and I've tried to find a balance between the road and my family."

He stood up and looked at the crowd that had gathered. With his hands, he brushed his jacket, first one sleeve and then the other, as if to remove some road dust.

> *One of these days*
> *I'll have nothing to prove.*

"As for my music," he said, "that's still a work in progress, except to say that I know I've touched people deeper than I realize. I don't expect anything. I just hope my music helps people move on and deal with life."

> *One of these days*
> *I'll fly to the moon.*

With that, he walked toward the stage, all the time greeting his fans with a big smile and embracing many of them with his bear hug. He was in his element: the music, the crowd, the moonshine at the Snowball Derby, the water bursting over the racetrack, Dallas Moore at the Flora-Bama waving a gun at him.

It might not be the life he mapped out in high school, aboard Bluebird Three with his friend Terry Adams in Arab, Alabama. But it is the life he has chosen for himself as he faces each day.

Wayne took the stage, strapped on his guitar, and from beneath his cowboy hat peered out beyond the stage lights. Maybe he was thinking about his first song or the house he wanted to build for his wife or how the crowd might react. Or maybe he just wanted to have a good time.

Perhaps, though, he was looking down the road at that darkened honky-tonk, similar to the one on the cover of his *Last Honky Tonk* CD, where a weathered and tired structure stands next to two forlorn-looking trees and harbors the end of its life. It stands there like an old Outlaw musician wanting one more chance, one more day, one last moment to reach for his guitar and dance with his soul.

One of these days, perhaps, but not now. Wayne was far from his last honky-tonk, and Outlaw music remains a creative force. Wayne still has to find out more about himself; he still has to write about his life, his soul, and his dreams. Songs that he is bound to write, *required to write because of who he is*—an Outlaw of talent and compassion and heart, and one who still has to find *his* road.

Unlike the outdoor show in Pensacola, there was no starry sky over Wayne's concert. But the colors of the stage lights and the way they were angled made it look as if Wayne was basking in stardust that could take him to the moon. It was time for him to move on, so he gave a signal to his drummer and began to play.

> *It's been a long time since I lost my friends,*
> *And I know I don't think enough of them.*
> *I'm just trying to get through,*
> *Living like I've got nothing to lose....*
> > "One of These Days"
> > From *The Last Honky Tonk*

Wayne Mills, Pensacola Speedway, Pensacola FL (2011)

Dale Watson, Blanco's, Houston, TX (2012)

CHAPTER 18

DALE WATSON

Legends—What If

Each time one slips away,
We say, man, they were great,
Wish I'd went to see them their last show.
Radio may have buried them,
While they're here let's cherish them,
Before all our legends are gone.
"LEGENDS—WHAT IF"
FROM LIVE IN LONDON

"If anybody can take anything away from the whole catalog of stuff that I wrote, some twenty albums," Dale Watson said to me as we sat on his tour bus in Houston, Texas, "they'll be able to see some of the things I've seen and meet some of the people I've met, because I write about people a lot. I write about real people and real places. If they ever took a road map and went to all the places I sing about, they'd have a helluva time."

Real people and real places—not the contrived nonsense that passes for mainstream country. Sincerity runs through Dale's music as strongly as a Texas twister whipping across the brown-hued terrain, swirling together his experiences and the stories of those he has met, touched, and loved into a colorful, artistic house of songs that sits heavily, and tellingly, on the wicked witch of Nashville pop.

What if Dale were an *insincere* man? What if...?

It's sometimes fun to play with "what if" questions: What if such and such was the case, what would our world be like? Historians know the difficulty of doing this, because the past cannot be reconstructed with the alternative in place. Nevertheless, Dale offers up this approach in his song "Legends—What If?" in such a way that it leaves the listener despairing over the fate of country music should Nashville pop be all that we have. Had we not had the country legends in our world, we would be much worse off, and once they pass, well, the holes will be huge and gaping.

For Dale, real country means real roots. Real country remains intimate with Hank Williams, Johnny Cash, Bob Wills, Elvis Presley, Loretta Lynn, Ray Price, Tammy Wynette, and those who founded the 1970s Outlaw movement. Real country lives on not as mere nostalgia but as a vibrant, creative force.

Each of these people in turn knew *his or her* country roots and, above all else, knew how to sing from the heart. For Dale, singing from the heart has been joyful, fulfilling, and, in one instance, one soul-wrenching period, painful and nearly beyond endurance.

Dale was born in 1962 in Birmingham, Alabama, and he and his three older brothers grew up in a family he describes as "a couple of rungs below middle class." His early childhood was spent in

Wilmington, North Carolina, where he lived in a trailer along a dirt road. His parents divorced, and his mom remarried when he was seven years old. For a time Dale's dad lived in Chicago, where he had a country band. Dale would go up there in the summers and listen to what was called "countrypolitan" music. This was music that merged Nashville country with Texas swing as pioneered by Bob Wills.

When Dale's dad moved to Jackson, Tennessee, Dale spent time there in a rural environment, where, as was the case when he lived in Wilmington, he did typical country boy activities, such as catching crawdads, frogs, and fireflies. But he also loved to listen to his dad play country music.

"My dad was a really good singer," Dale says. "He sounded like a cross between Charlie Pride [an African American country singer popular in the 1970s] and Roy Drusky [known as the "Perry Como of country music" and popular in the 1950s and 1960s]. I grew up listening to my dad's music; he would do covers [with his band]. And I loved it.... It was Merle Haggard, George Jones, and Hank Williams."

Dale lived in a world barely touched by the rock music of his youth. "I guess rock had to be an influence on me at some point," he says nonchalantly. "My [two oldest] brothers had a rock band, but when they played with me, the name of the band was Classic Country because that's all that I did." Dale never considered joining his brothers' group. He was too much into the music his dad was listening to; he was too country for rock. Dale did listen to the songs of Carl Perkins, Jerry Lee Lewis, and Elvis Presley from the 1950s, but he never considered their rockabilly music to be rock 'n' roll. To him it was country.

Dale's Classic Country band was named after a TV show on PBS that was dedicated to roots music. Dale played in the honky-tonks in and near Houston. He had moved to the area in the mid-1970s, at age fourteen, and went to school in the day while doing his gigs at night. He was so into his music and spent so much time working that the adult world hit him straight on, and he had little time for typical teen-age activities. Although he graduated from Southeastern High School in 1977, he had no buddies there (a situation that further insulated him from the rock scene). Instead he hung out with people at the honky-tonks. He says that he preferred socializing with those who were quite a bit older than him.

Dale made his first record when he was only sixteen, about the time the 1970s Outlaw movement was in full stride. At first Willie Nelson and Waylon Jennings were just musicians he could sing along with while learning chords on the guitar. "I was mainly writing my own songs about the girl next door," he says. "But then in 1978, 1979, they really did come into play. The first concert I ever snuck into was Willie Nelson at Gilley's in Pasadena [Texas] in 1979."

Question: I read one comment online about your music that there is something of a Waylon influence in there. Would you say so?

Dale: Yeah, Waylon is a very huge influence. His early stuff was more of an influence on me because while most people think of Waylon as a [*he imitates the Waylon four-on-the-floor beat with his arm and his voice*], I thought he was a great crooner as well. When you hear his version of "Crying" [a Roy Orbison song] and "The Chokin' Kind" [written by Harlan Howard], you know he was a singer's singer.

Dale would also include in that category of huge influences an earlier artist, Ray Price. Dale claims that if he were stranded on a desert is-land with one album, the one he would want to have would be Price's *Nightlife.* He calls Price "the country guy's Sinatra." He adds: "Even now at eighty-five or eighty-six years old, the guy sings circles around these people out there who call themselves singers."

In 1988 Dale moved to Los Angeles and experienced another musical change when he delved much more heavily into rockabilly. "When I got to Los Angeles and started playing, there was a lot of rock while I was there, and rockabilly," he says. "I really wasn't into rockabilly, but I got hired for a rockabilly band at the Palomino Club [a Hollywood venue for alternative country] because of the way that I wore my hair. I wore my hair like my dad wore his [in a pompadour]. That's just kind of the way it was. So that rockabilly influence [then] came more heavily." He started listening to more of the 1950s rockabilly artists, such as Eddie Cochran and Gene Vincent.

In his modesty Dale would never describe himself, as he does Waylon, as a "singer's singer." But he is. His smooth baritone voice and phrasing that makes love to most every word leave an indelible imprint. But they are perhaps the most striking features of an artist who has other talents as well to make up a whole package: Artistic songwriting that takes Texas swing, rockabilly, classic country, and '70s Outlaw influences and combines and reshapes them. An adept hand with the guitar. A genial and even humorous stage presence. And to top it off, movie-screen, leading-man good looks. The main obstacle to Dale making it big in Nashville has been his unyielding attachment to country roots and his strong desire to keep it alive.

He is, as he has been told more than once, too country for country, meaning Nashville country. "In 1990," he says, "I had a Curb Record deal, and they put out two 45s to test the waters, and it was way too traditional for back then. I don't think anybody in their right mind would say to a rock 'n' roll band, 'That's too rock for rock 'n' roll.' But you can get away with saying that something's too country for country."

Question: Did you ever go to Nashville to try to write songs for the mainstream labels, the bigger labels, that type of thing?

Dale: I went to Nashville [in the early 1990s] to be a staff writer for Gary Morris Music. I only lasted ten months; it was miserable. I hated the whole thing. They would make you an appointment with one or two other guys, and you would sit in a room, and they would give you a pitch sheet.... We sat in the room, and we were supposed to write that song to pitch to [a singer]. And I just sat there thinking I can't believe that I'm even going to sit through this.

Dale moved to Austin, Texas, and then released his first widely acclaimed CD, *Cheatin' Heart Attack,* in 1995 on Hightone Records. With it he distanced himself from his already tenuous Nashville links. All fourteen songs on the CD reflect *roots country.* A Merle Haggard influence is most pronounced in the title track; the influence of Texas swing, in the style of the swing master Bob Wills, appears in "Texas Boogie"; there are numerous traces of rockabilly and Waylon Jennings-infused crooning. And in using guitarist Dave Biller, pedal steel player Jimmy Day, and fiddler Gene Elders, Dale reaches into the Austin music scene to display its vitality in contrast to Nashville.

Dale pulls no punches in a full-fledged assault on Nashville pop when he includes on the CD his song "Nashville Rash." If, as he sees it, the shaking of the money machine on Music Row has resulted in a complete break with country as country should be, then it needs to be declared. "Too country for country?" Well, Nashville is "too *commercial* for country."

I shoulda known it when they closed the Opry down,
Things are bound to change in that town.
You can't grow if you rip your roots out of the ground,
Looks like that Nashville rash is gettin' around.
"Nashville Rash"
From *Cheatin' Heart Attack*

Question: Why wouldn't Nashville appreciate your writing for what your writing is?

Dale: I think I shot myself in the foot a lot, especially with "Nashville Rash." When you call out people by name, that makes them accountable. It makes me accountable too. There are people absolutely to blame for the shit we're hearing now, but everybody just wants to say, "Corporation, corporates." That's such an easy out. But if you put a fucking name on somebody—you know, it's this singer, it's that producer, it's this record label—things will change.

It reminds me of just recently, I went to Australia [in 2011], and this airline [Tiger Airways] charged me five hundred euros to buy this little box for CDs that was going to make them transportable. They lost it. They said, "We can't do anything about it, sorry." I wrote a song about it, and I did a video on YouTube of it, and it went viral. It wound up going to Fox TV in New York; they flew me up there, and it was huge, all over talk radio in Australia. Once the airline heard it, or seen the lyrics, they said, "Wait a minute, we're going to give you your money back. Don't release nothing." I did anyway because in the song I named the two people that I was talking to and [who] told me to forget it, you're not going to get your money back, you're screwed and we don't care....

So it made somebody accountable for this shit that was happening. So if you can do that, if you can actually point a finger at somebody and say, "You are killing fucking country music, you're the one doing it, *you,*" I think it would make a difference, everywhere.

Yet while Dale has this opinion of Nashville, he thinks that he has said so much about it that other voices need to be heard. "At this point," he says, "I'm looking like the angry old bitter man if I do it. It's gonna take the younger generation to point the finger and name the names."

Maybe, Dale. But I have a feeling that you're not going to be quiet. Exhibit one: Dale writes a new song, and in early 2013 a performance of it by him is posted on YouTube. The title: "A Song for Blake Shelton" or "I'd Rather Be an Old Fart than a Modern Country Turd." Dale wrote the song in response to a controversial statement made by Blake, a country pop singer, who said, "Country music has to evolve in order to survive. Nobody wants to listen to their grandpa's music. And I don't care how many of these old farts around Nashville [are] going, 'My God, that ain't country!' Well that's because you don't buy records anymore, jackass. The kids do, and they don't want to buy the music you were buying."

It's been a long road for Dale. He's been on the alternative scene for many years. With *Cheatin' Heart Attack,* Dale was part of the first wave in an assault on Nashville pop. This cutting-edge movement appeared in the 1990s and sometimes bore the cumbersome label No Depression music or, more pleasing to the ear, Americana. Like the Outlaw movement of today, it too was diverse and ranged from the heavily rock-influenced group Blue Rodeo to the traditionalist Texas swing artist Wayne "The Train" Hancock. This was all happening while Nashville country phenom Garth Brooks was attaching himself to cables and being hoisted into the air so he could fly above stadium stages.

Real places and real people populate Dale's CD *Blessed or Damned,* released in 1996 as a follow-up to *Cheatin' Heart Attack.* The rockabilly-tinged "Truck Stop in La Grange," puts Dale along Highway 71 in Texas with "a damned good cup of coffee." (Dale had actually gone to truck driving school a few years earlier.) In "The Honkiest Tonkiest Beer Joint in Town," Dale paints a vivid picture about a local hangout where the owner, Rosie, sells pickled eggs "by the pound."

But as in *Cheatin' Heart Attack,* with its "Nashville Rash," Dale bemoans the sad state of country music. In "Real Country Song," he longs for some Loretta Lynn, Conway Twitty, and George Jones, and he implores the deejay to have a "conscience" and some guts to "speak up and say what's wrong."

In the CD's title song, "Blessed or Damned," Dale fills a tender ballad with the picture of a lone country artist singing in a honky-tonk amid empty beer cans, playing only to himself, as if he were part of a riddle: What if a song fell to the floor in an empty building and there was no one around to hear it—would it still make a sound? Would it still have meaning?

Clearly, early in his career Dale knew what it was like to sing to only a handful of people. And he knew what it was like, as he says in "Blessed or Damned," to look around and see other singers, less genuine, get commercial acclaim and take home "all the rewards."

It's easy, he sings, "to figure out who's blessed or damned." But consider the song more closely, and it really isn't so easy. Sympathy and even admiration resides with the solitary artist in the beer joint, ignored but real, wanting more than anything to have another day with his music. Maybe the commercial performer and the country pop sound are what are damned.

God blessed some folks with music,
What a holy art.
Then the devil seen us envious souls,
And damned the songs in our hearts.

"Blessed or Damned"
From *Blessed or Damned*

As more roots country fans encountered Dale and appreciated the "realness" of his music, his tours became more extensive. At the same time, he showed no retreat when he reiterated his disdain for developments in Nashville on his CD *Live in London.* He even sharpens the point to "Nashville Rash" when he changes the word *hits* in the original version to *shit* and so sings: "Rock 'n' roll back in the '70s passes for the Nashville *shit* today." Moreover, to the delight of his fans, he doesn't hesitate to name names. "It breaks my heart to have to listen to *Shania Twain*," he says, while he laments the passing of so many country heroes, the true country artists.

The CD contains yet another salvo: "Country My Ass." As Dale embraces the lyrics, the London crowd provides its own cheers for him and jeers for the characters he sings about before joining with him for a raucous chorus.

That's country my ass,
Who do they think we am?
Force-feed us that shit,
Ain't you real tired of it?
Tell them stick it up high,
Where the sun don't shine....

"Country My Ass"
From *Live in London*

Despite such criticism of Music Row, Dale has made numerous appearances at the *Grand Ole Opry*. "I play it two or three times a year," he says. "But you got to remember, that's not the Top 40 radio people who are buying tickets to the *Grand Ole Opry*. That's why people like Jim Ed Brown and Charlie Pride will get a standing ovation. [Whereas] Montgomery Gentry will go in there, and you hear a few screaming girls" and some polite applause and that's it.

Dale found the love of his life when, at a friend's birthday party, he met Terri Herbert, an attractive, cheerful blond and an attorney in the Texas state attorney general's office. Terri and Dale began living together and soon talked about getting married. In the mornings they would hold each other, not wanting to leave the bed where their love had gone beyond the physical to where they were now sharing their dreams, their fears, and their passions. "Write me a song, Dale," she said to him. And he promised that he would. But he cautioned her: "It's just gotta come."

Then while Dale was playing at a honky-tonk on the outskirts of Austin, they got into an argument at the bar. Dale had said he was going to drive on to his next show in Houston, but it turned out that he was too tired, and so he changed his mind and went back to his apartment. Terri tried several times to reach him, but he had left his cell phone in his van.

At that point, perhaps because she was frustrated at not being able to reach Dale and believed that he had already left Austin, she decided to drive to Houston. She left the honky-tonk, and a few minutes later, where the road curved, she lost control of her car. Because Terri was not wearing her seatbelt, she was thrown out of the vehicle and killed. The police believe Terri may have fallen asleep at the wheel or dropped her cell phone on the floor and tried to reach for it. But no one can say for sure exactly what she was doing at the time of the crash.

When Dale heard about the accident, he became distraught and uncontrollable. He waved a gun at the police who had shown up at his apartment with the news. He threatened to kill himself, and he even fired a shot into the air. Dale blamed himself for Terri's death. What if he had told her of the change in his plans? Then she might not have tried to drive away on her own. What if he had had his phone with him? Then he might have been able to apologize to her. On top of that, she left this life upset with him. What if...?

Dale grew so depressed that he checked into a hotel room in Austin, away from his friends, and tried to kill himself by mixing sleeping pills with vodka. Fortunately, his road manager found him in time and took him to a hospital. He later received psychiatric counseling and found some relief through therapy.

Dale needed to return to the recording studio. Looking back at that time, he said to me: "What kept going through my head is she asked me to write a song for her. 'It doesn't matter what you say in it, would you mind writing a song?'" she'd asked. The song had finally come to him. "I wrote her 'Blue Eyes.' She only got to hear it once, and only in part because it wasn't finished. I was just making it up on the stage at the time...." He said that when Terri died, he decided "to write not only one song [but] write the whole album for her." Thus came about the CD *Every Song I Write Is for You.* He added: "It was therapeutic, but it was also the toughest album I've ever recorded. It's also my favorite album."

The album might have been therapeutic, but it failed to solve Dale's bout with grief and depression. The song lyrics indicate over and over again that he was still struggling, even though he might have thought he had moved on.

What if...? He sings: "If I knew then what I know now,...I'd have loved you more and you'd still be around." Wow. What a burden to put on himself.

> *You liked to sway to the music,*
> *You liked the feel of a tune,*
> *A woman of words, you liked what you heard,*
> *And you wanted a song just for you....*
> *Every time I write the word "love" down on paper,*
> *It's like scratching your name into my heart.*
> "Every Song I Write Is for You"
> From *Every Song I Write Is for You*

One song in particular winds up foretelling Dale's future, "I'd Deal with the Devil." In it Dale sings: "I've prayed every day since she went away/But something in my prayers they must lack/I talked to the man above/But he ain't listening up/So I'd deal with the devil to get her back.... He can throw my soul into a fiery hole to burn for all eternity."

Dale indeed tumbled into a dark pit. "I went a little nuts," he says. "I went through a real weird thing in 2002 and came out the other side in 2003."

So weird, in fact, that his experience became the subject of a documentary, *Crazy Again* (2009), directed by Zalman King. "When you actually go crazy from losing somebody, you try extreme things," Dale says in the film. "I tried everything from psychics to the Ouija board. That was the bad thing."

Dale kept touring and playing music, but on a European trip some three years after Terri died everything unraveled. "I wasn't boozing, and I wasn't taking pills," he assured me before he told me his story.

Before leaving for Europe, he had used the Ouija board to contact Terri, his deceased dad, and even Jesus. He says that a voice he heard seemed to come from God, and it began telling him what to do in order to be saved and to take salvation to others. In London he began preaching on the streets. He heard the voice many more times and saw strange images.

His story stirred in me memories of William Blake's work. An English mystic, Blake wrote and painted in the late 1700s and early 1800s. He's perhaps best known for his poem "The Tiger." ("Tiger, tiger, burning bright/In the forests of the night/What immortal hand or eye/Dare frame thy fearful symmetry?") Blake claimed to have experienced visions throughout his life, to have conversed with his departed brother's spirit, and to have had a deep love for and connection to Jesus and God. Blake's paintings convey surrealistic images filled with searing colors, bright one moment, dark the next. That sort of imagery—reflective of the comradeship that artists share with their emotions, inner feelings, and the irrational—became a real part of Dale Watson's mind.

The voice that Dale heard, which he thought to be the voice of God, told him to write a book, and Dale did so. He wrote automatically, without thinking, with his pen moving rapidly across the page.

"Some things I know because I know them; some things I know because I am told them. Things that I am told are up to question. But the things that I know are not," the voice told him. Dale was writing in a way he had never written before, using thoughts he knew he could never possibly have had on his own.

The voice then told him to write two new commandments and take them to the pope. Dale wandered outside the doors of the Vatican, thinking one of the pope's aides would see him and call him in, but as the days went by and that failed to happen, Dale began to doubt the voice.

Suddenly, the voice sounded mean and evil and told Dale that he hadn't really been talking to Jesus: "You were really talking to me, Satan." There followed three days of Dale being tossed around in a hotel room, suffering mental torment from the voice in his head, being battered and bruised, and becoming so worn down that he was in a state of total collapse. He later likened the scene to "a bad B movie." He felt he had gone crazy, and as his body trembled and he sweated and cried and screamed in anguish, he asked for God's help. Dale promised that once the horror had ended, once the darkness had given way to light, he would record a gospel album.

When Dale returned home to Texas, he checked himself into a mental hospital. He was given tests and prescribed pills, but he still heard voices. Then he decided to see a chaplain, who reminded Dale that, out in the wilderness, Jesus himself had been challenged by Satan. ("The devil showed...him all the kingdoms of the world and their glory. And he said to him: 'All these things I will give you if you will fall down and worship me. Then Jesus said to him: 'Away with you, Satan. For it is written: "You shall worship the Lord your God, and him only shall you serve."''" [Matt. 4: 8–10]) The chaplain advised Dale that only faith could pull him through.

William Blake had seen God and heard voices nearly throughout his life, and some people have called him mad. Had Dale, for a much briefer period, gone mad? Had he suffered a nervous breakdown? Had something otherworldly been at work? He would be the first to admit that he wasn't born-again. But he did become more spiritual. What really gave him comfort, he says, were passages he read in the Bible.

Dale says that once he felt better, he knew he had to record the gospel album. Titled *Help Your Lord,* it was released in 2008. In "Hey There Sinner," Dale speaks directly to his encounter with the devil. He sings: "Go see a fortune-teller/Get your fortune read/And you're telling God/That he don't exist/God's told your fortune/It's in the Bible to read/Trust no other/So your fortune you'll see." Then he adds: "Everywhere you look/There are psychics around/Can't put yourself there/And be heaven-bound/They'll talk of love and life and God and Jesus to you/That's the only way you'll listen/and *Satan knows that too.*"

Back in Austin, Dale stayed at a cabin once owned by Johnny Cash and recorded a new CD there, *From the Cradle to the Grave.* The album cover shows him in a cemetery, standing with his legs wide apart and his hands grabbing the lapels of his black coat. It's a pose of strength and determination. Behind him a tombstone displays the words COUNTRY MUSIC RIP, in reference to the Nashville scene.

As evident in the CD, he was still under the influence of the recent tragic events in his life. In the title track, a song with a heavy beat that pounds away, he sings: "I knew a man that took his life/He couldn't take losing his wife/It'll cross your mind somewhere along the way/At least one time from the cradle to the grave."

Question: Do you feel that there's a strong spiritual side to you?

Dale: Whiskey or God. [*Laughter.*] Yeah, there's a spiritual side to me. I'm at odds with it often, but yeah.

> *Whiskey or God,*
> *Gonna bring me relief.*
> *Believin' or not,*
> *Bending my elbow or my knees.*
> *I'm gonna drink until my conscience bleeds,*
> *Before I fall asleep I'm gonna say a prayer for a brighter day.*
> *Whiskey or God,*
> *Bring salvation to me.*
> > "Whiskey or God"
> > From *Whiskey or God*

Among the meccas for Outlaw artists, none stands holier than the Sun Records studio in Memphis, Tennessee. It's a musical temple that has housed some of the great craftsmen of country and rock 'n' roll. A widely circulated photograph from 1956, which was originally printed in the *Memphis Press-Scimitar,* shows Johnny Cash, Carl Perkins, Elvis Presley, and Jerry Lee Lewis at a piano in the Sun studio. Presley is seated at the keys while the other three artists stand behind him, apparently looking down at some sheet music. (Lewis was actually fixated on an attractive, provocatively clad dancer who was perched on top of the piano but was cropped out of the picture before it was printed.)

A wall of acoustic tiles appears behind the quartet. Enter the Sun studio today and you will see those same tiles. All the walls, the ceiling, and the floor are unchanged from nearly sixty years ago. The layout of the small recording room is exactly the same. (This preservation comes from the studio having been vacant from 1960 to1985.) Only the technology has changed. Except for an eight-track machine, the reel-to-reel tape recorders are silent, and the acetate tapes that could handle one track in the early '50s, and three a bit later, have been supplanted by computers that produce multi-track digitized recordings.

Dale made a pilgrimage to the Sun studio to record *The Sun Sessions,* which was released in 2011. He begins the CD in an unabashed Johnny Cash style. As he sings his own song, "Down Down Down Down Down" the sound of his voice and the guitar beat conjure up the legendary Man in Black. Moreover, the lyrics could have been written by Johnny himself: "Well, I had my first taste of whiskey/I had my first taste of love/Both got me high and twisted up inside/Only one way to go after up, oh yeah/Down, down, down, down, down."

Question: You could have conceivably recorded the *Sun Sessions* CD somewhere else...

Dale: Nope. Nope. Nope.

Question: Why not?

Dale: The bottom line is that Sun Studio, the music that came out of there, does have a certain sound. Elvis went elsewhere to record, so did Johnny Cash and Jerry Lee, but nothing they ever recorded sounds like what they recorded at Sun. It's something about this room and doing roots music. If you go in there and do electronic, techno, or whatever, or any kind of music other than roots music, then, yeah, you can do that anywhere and you'll get the same sound. But when you're talking about doing real honest roots music with guitars and drums and bass and piano, the acoustics in that room are totally unique to the universe.

Dale made the CD without his usual band, the Lone Stars, and thus without his usual trademark honky-tonk sound of a steel guitar and fiddle. Instead, Chris Crepps plays standup bass and Mike Bernal plays the snare drum behind Dale's guitar. Dale named his backup duo the Texas Two.

With *Sun Sessions* Dale reconnects intimately with what he loves about music, particularly roots country. The bare-bones sound, created in an attempt to get back to what was made during those early Sun years, carries with it a topical diversity. Two songs show Dale's penchant for writing about real people. In one, "Jonny at the Door," he sings: "There's a fellow we all know at an Austin water hole/That's Jonny, Jonny at the door..../He's the kind of guy you'd swear that you met somewhere before/Oh Jonny, Jonny at the door..../Well, I heard him said he had himself Tennessee parole/Oh Jonny, Jonny at the door."

Dale goes back to his religious connection with "The Hand of Jesus," which condemns ungodly financial greed: "You think you got it made, boy..../Sittin' high on Wall Street, lookin' down at me/I have something better, boy, than all your beggar's gold/I've got the hand of Jesus restin' on my soul."

While Dale was eating a hamburger in his tour bus, I asked him how he went about writing songs. He told me that he used to do it mainly while driving. But the times have changed and so has the technology. Now, he said, he writes mainly while he's onstage.

I didn't understand how that could possibly work. How could he write while playing and singing? "That's how I [have written] a lot of songs of late," he reassured me, "such as 'Tequila, Whiskey, and Beer.'" Then he took out his iPhone and played part of a song he had written just the night before. He explained that he writes during instrumentals. He takes his guitar aside and plays what comes into his mind. How he could do that while surrounded by other music baffled me and still does. "I just find it easier to write onstage and then come back to it later and fine-tune it," he said.

When Dale appeared in England at the Borderline Club to record his *Live in London* CD, the announcer introduced him as "the man keeping country music alive." I wondered if he ever would be able to find a common ground with mainstream Nashville.

Question: So do you think that there's some compromise position you could move to without sacrificing your type of music but also reaching out to more people?

Dale: Sure, in these later years, I have been trying to do that, you know, trying not to be so judgmental. For me, the genre that I tell people that I am [is] Ameripolitan, just because it doesn't mean anything to anybody.... I picked that name because people automatically get a question mark on it: "What the hell are you talking about?" But once they hear my music they think that's Ameripolitan, it's kind of country, it's new, whatever they call it.... I don't tell people that I do old country music or classic country music.... I don't use the word country music at all because nowadays they think about modern country music, and if somebody likes that stuff and comes to listen to me, they're going to be disappointed. At the same time, I would do package shows with any of these guys to get my stuff out there and to get it heard, but I don't think that's going to happen.

Dale's CD *Preaching to the Choir* expresses the frustration he sometimes feels over trying to get those unfamiliar with roots country to listen to him. "This is definitely a niche genre," he says. "I break out of the genre a little bit with rockabilly influence, and even with a Frank Sinatra, Elvis-swing type of thing. But it's a niche, that's why I've tried not to go on that bandwagon and start preaching onstage anymore. But in the beginning it was a platform to spread the word." Now, he says, he's been around long enough where people come to his shows because they are dedicated fans and understand him.

For Dale there's room under the roots umbrella to include a wide number of musical styles. He has even recorded with punk-influenced Jackson Taylor, doing the song "Back on the Bottle" which appears on Jackson's CD *Aces 'N Eights*. Dale believes that Jackson's music works because Jackson keeps well connected to roots country.

Dale also believes that the modern media has helped him withstand the domination of country music by Nashville pop. SiriusXM Radio, for example, with its microprogramming makes roots country available through its Outlaw station. And YouTube gives people a feel for what his shows are like.

When I first met Dale, it was outside a small honky-tonk in Houston called Blanco's where he had performed many times before and was scheduled to play again that night. I was waiting for him on the side porch of the wooden building and staring across the gravel parking lot at his tour bus, which had emblazoned on its side in prominent gold-colored letters against an antique maroon background DALE WATSON.

While I was looking at the bus, a white-haired man stepped out from the driver's side wearing a tight T-shirt, jeans, and black motorcycle boots. He strode quickly across the lot and appeared distinguished in stature and determined at what he was doing. I was puzzled as to who it might be until I realized it was Dale. It turned out he was driving his own bus. We shook hands and he told me that following his sound check he would be ready for the interview we had scheduled.

Question: If there's a young musician out there who doesn't want to do the Nashville scene, who wants to do more of roots music, would you advise him or her against that, given the financial challenge and the nights on the road?

Dale: No, unless you just want to be financially successful and do that to the end. Obviously I dreamed about being on the bus, touring and doing this thing and having fame. But I'd rather have done this on my own terms. I sleep a lot better. But they've got to know it's a hard road. It's a lot harder than if you were mainstream.

Dale appeared onstage wearing a black dress coat in sharp contrast to the generally scruffy attire worn by many Outlaw artists. He was neat as a pin, and his clothes highlighted his gentlemanly appearance. He was friendly and gracious with everyone he met and posed patiently with his fans as they took photographs. During his show he spoke frequently to the packed house and encouraged people to make requests. He was often funny with his comments, such as when, between songs, he segued into pretend commercials for Lone Star Beer, the beer "with additives to keep your teeth white and all the vitamins you need to make for a healthy body." But it was more than his stage presence that was commanding: his *overall presence* took over the room.

Dale later told me how he was about to return to Sun Studio to put the finishing touches on a CD he had just recorded there, to be titled *Dalevis: Sun Sessions Two.* He said he was lucky to be at a point in his career where he could do what he felt like doing. "I don't worry about the marketing of it," he said, "or the reasoning to do it. With the first Sun session I felt like I represented the influence [on me] of Johnny Cash, Carl Perkins, and Jerry Lee. But I just don't think the Elvis stuff was represented very well, so that's why I wanted to go in and do it again." (Dale released *Dalevis* in January 2013.)

At Blanco's, Dale performed for nearly four hours. His road manager told me that he does that "a lot" and "barely gives the band enough time to go to the bathroom." Dale enjoyed every moment of his show as his fans danced to his music.

Part of the joy of Dale Watson is that he can make fun of himself. At one point he told the crowd he would show them how to dance the two-step even though he couldn't dance well. "One, two, one, two,... that's it," he intoned. As his fans brought him buckets packed with ice and beer bottles along with shot glasses filled with one of his favorite—some would say his ultimate—liquid enjoyment, tequila, I marveled at his capacity for alcohol and how he, like his band, wasn't two-stepping over to the urinal.

Dale told me: "I know how to keep my overhead down. As long as the shows are supported, I'll just keep touring and keep recording and keep putting out records. I'm doing some acting and stuff that's helped financially to keep me going too. I'll probably be branching out more into that and [I'll] keep touring."

Question: If you're looking back at what you've written, do you think that you are blessed or damned?

Dale: I guess at the beginning of the day I'm damned for doing what is natural to me. You can't get out of your own skin. That's just where I live. But the blessed part is that there's still an audience for the stuff that I do, and the stuff that I love.

That audience can range anywhere from the one at Blanco's to the *Grand Ole Opry* to Jennie's Little Longhorn, a small honky-tonk on the outskirts of Austin. Dale often plays there on "chicken-shit Sundays." The day gets its name from a game played at the honky-tonk whereby a chicken moves atop a table fenced in by mesh wiring and marked with numbered squares, and the customers bet on where the bird will deposit its poop.

Dale loves to be authentic and to play from his heart. Real rockabilly and real honky-tonk and real roots is where he's at. It's where he's always been; it's where he always will be. Like the other Outlaws, it's the choice he has made, and for him it still rings true, even at the sacrifice of Nashville stardom.

Nothing seems to slow him down. After all the CDs he's released over the years it would seem fathomable that he would by now have run out of original songs, or at least good original songs. But along comes his latest, *El Rancho Azul* (2013), and there he goes again. The upbeat Texas swing "I Lie When I Drink," the tender "Daughter's Wedding Song," the honky-tonk paean "Smokey Old Bar," and the captivatingly humorous "Thanks to Tequila," to name a few from a solid album. Keep writing those songs while performing, Dale, it's working full blast, and what a blast for all of us.

The last time I spoke with Dale for this book was during a stop he made in Minneapolis to appear at Lee's Liquor Lounge. "Check out my song about Lee's Liquor Lounge," he told me. "I recorded it a few years ago. It's what I mean about real people and real places."

> *That's Louie at Lee's Liquor Lounge.*
> *He bought it from a man name Lee,*
> *But he didn't change the sign,*
> *Because Louie thinks what really counts,*
> *Is what you've got inside.*
> "Lee's Liquor Lounge"
> From *Live in London*

What Dale has inside him is the legends of roots country. He's no mere replicator, nor does he make his point about Nashville pop simply by criticizing Music Row. He makes it primarily by taking the spirits of roots country and raising them to life, by wrapping his soul around them before he creates his music. The man who is the complete package may not have made it big in Nashville, but he has made it big in keeping roots country alive. For his commitment to what is real—real people, real places, real experiences applied to real songs—he's an Outlaw.

> *What if no more Branded Man,*
> *No more Man in Black.*
> *What if no more Possum,*
> *No more George Jones.*
> *Picture a world without Willie or Waylon around,*
> *When all of our legends are gone.*
> "Legends—What If"
> From *Live in London*

What if Dale had never recovered from his ordeal with the devil? What if he had never loved the roots country played by his dad? What if he had sold out to Nashville?

What if...?

Picture a world without Dale Watson. Country music would be suffering, honky-tonk nights would be emptier, and the legends would be crying.

Dale Watson, Blanco's, Houston, TX (2012)

INTERLUDE: LELA

By Neil Hamilton

If I saw a mountain with a locket of your hair,
I'd climb it as a man whose love never knew despair.
If I saw a river raging against the beauty of your eyes,
I'd tame it with my anger 'cause the truth can conquer a lie.

Guatemalan lady, let me bathe you in the flowers,
Resting by the lake you had studied for endless hours.
Monja Blanca, the beauty in your science,
Marimba song, your spirit in endless defiance.
La noche de los tiempos no sun could ever take,
A sultry, tender, eternal craft only we could ever make.

If I had a seashell wrapped around your time,
I would take your hand in bed and the shell be mine.
Nothing would change except the locket in your eyes,
Which would open and reveal our endless love arise.

Caitlin Rose, The Basement, Nashville, TN (2012)

CHAPTER 19

CAITLIN ROSE

Learning To Ride

Learning to ride, oh, learning to ride,
I get knocked down when I'm learning to ride....
Now all I need is a sinful steed,
Take me where I need,
Without putting up a fight.
"LEARNING TO RIDE"
FROM OWN SIDE NOW

The Basement, a club in Nashville, had the look and feel of a folk music hangout. With its intimate setting consisting of a small stage and posters plastered on the ceiling and on the brick walls, I half expected a young Bob Dylan to step forward, flash a peace sign, perch himself on a stool, and strum his acoustic guitar for an audience sitting in collective silence and clinging to his every word.

In fact, when I arrived at the venue early to see Caitlin Rose, a young Outlaw singer/songwriter, there was a musician onstage in much the same arrangement as my imaginary Dylan. This was, I assumed, going to be the night for a "listening room" experience.

But when Caitlin and her band entered, the atmosphere changed. It didn't exactly go from sedate to rowdy, but her fans brought with them their country music flair and their affection for her music. As a result, the crowd grew larger, the voices louder, the beer more plentiful, and the Basement changed from coffeehouse chic to roots-music hip.

Caitlin, who is in her mid-twenties, took the stage wearing a black blouse, a leather jacket, and a short leather skirt that accented her shapely legs, which she had covered in sheer black stockings. Her straight brown hair was parted in the middle and just touched her shoulders. Her roundish face, smooth and young, glowed beneath a battery of hideous blue lights. As she moved about, she projected a demure but let's-get-down-to-business air.

"I never thought I'd do anything; I'm just doing it," she told me after the show. "That's one of the biggest problems for me, that there might be boundaries in the future.... But I don't know how to fit into boxes, and I'm not saying that to be contrary. I'm not good at it. I'm not a good people person. So I try to do what I think people would like, but usually that's not the case. I'm pretty resigned to the idea of being a little strange.... I don't know what I want to do.... I just do what feels right."

Put the human lifetime up against geologic time and it amounts to nary a mite in nature's eye. About a billion years ago, a continent tore apart, and this cataclysm created an ancestral ocean where the Atlantic now exists. It didn't last long—some 250 million years later it began to close up as several landmasses came together. But then, about

200 million years ago, rifting began, and mountains and entire land-masses came unglued. From this, the Atlantic Ocean formed.

Today that ocean feeds our souls and has stirred this writer's imagination. For in my mind, I could see Caitlin standing on a beach, at the juncture where the ocean meets the land and where the periods, the epochs, and the ages collide with human life. There she sings along to the waves, her voice dancing atop whitewater crests as she happily creates her art in tune with the muses of country music, with the only boundaries being what she might discover in her own creativity.

We might be nary a mite, but we are here. And as we try to find our way in this planetary evolution, we make decisions and infiltrate each day with our lives. We embrace our talents, and in doing what we do, we shift the world a little bit, nudging it as microscopically, maybe as painstakingly, as does one landmass when it shifts in the course of a year. The shift, however slight, might, just might, be great enough to create a place where someone else can be happy and maybe, just maybe, find their own inspiration.

Caitlin brings an embryonic approach to roots country. Her catalog of songs is limited in number but sincere in form. One reviewer says, "What Caitlin Rose represents is nothing less than the fresh-faced, Outlaw-minded future of country music." Other reviewers compare her voice to Loretta Lynn and Patsy Cline. That's a lot of praise and, embodied in it, expectations that could potentially place a ton of pressure on Caitlin. But she has taken it all in stride and wants nothing more than what any genuine Outlaw artist would want: to play her own music and play it from her heart.

"I don't really consider myself Outlaw," Caitlin says, "but it's a great term. It makes people feel pretty rebellious. For me the only thing that makes people Outlaws is that they didn't ever care to be anything else. That's what Outlaw should signify; it's not going against the grain. It's just that it's there, and people notice it, and it's not what everything else is.... I think it's people who didn't really want to do anything else. [They start] doing their own thing and somehow that catches on."

Caitlin deplores the tendency to jam people into boxes. For musicians who have talent, it ruins them artistically. "I was watching VH1's *Behind the Music* about Jennifer Hudson," she recalls, "and I was floored. She has one of the most gorgeous voices of anybody around, and the producer was talking about [how] his challenge was to take that voice and put it in this little box. He literally made the shape of a little box, and he cups his hands around each other, and he says, 'I put it in this little box and it's pop music.'

"It was so upsetting to me to see somebody glorifying this beautiful thing and then saying, 'I know how to make it less than what it is.' That's what a lot of what music is now; it's people thinking listeners are stupid, or its people being scared that there will be too much competition. It's just upsetting to me."

No boxes for someone whose voice sings and dances atop the ocean's crests to its own rhythm. To plan and then be confined by a prescribed form would ruin everything.

Question: One label I have seen attached to your music is alternative. Do you agree with that?

Caitlin: I don't agree or disagree with any of it because people are going to say whatever it is that comes to their minds. I do the same thing with music, with other people's music, but it's not really that important to me. I guess I'm alternative; I'm not doing what anybody else tells me to do. Whatever everyone else is doing that they're told to do is either working for them or not, but what I do seems to work for me. It's a weird thing—you can want or aspire to be in the pop world or to be in the mainstream world, or you can aspire to be in the underground world or the Americana world, but I don't strive to be in anything. I just don't want to end up not being able to do something that I enjoy doing because I'm in a certain category.

Caitlin's musical influences come less from the 1970s Outlaws than from other artists. When I asked her what she thought about Waylon Jennings and Willie Nelson, she said, "I love Willie for his song-writing. I'm ashamed to admit I don't know much about Waylon Jennings." Then she added: "The [1970s] Outlaw country might be a little smoky for me." It was a peculiar statement given that she likes the individualism of the original Outlaws and given that although she hasn't played many honky-tonks, she would like to play more of them. Caitlin can throw back whiskey with the best of them, burn multiple cigarettes down to their butts, and retort to any alcohol-inspired barb with a caustic comeback.

> *One night at the bar didn't get me very far,*
> *I didn't find the answer I was looking for.*
> *Drink one, drink two, I'm a drinking just for you,*
> *The only answer I have found is to drink more....*
> *There's an answer in one of these bottles, I know,*
> *So I'm a gonna drink until I forget the question.*
> "Answer in One of These Bottles"
> From *Dead Flowers*

Question: Have you listened to Hank Williams quite a bit? Is his presence there in your musical background?

Caitlin: I'm a big Hank Williams fan. For me it's always been about songs [and] with Hank Williams, some of the songs, they're inescapable, so everyone grows up around it. You walk around downtown Nashville, and they've got music playing [aimed from the clubs into the streets], and it's not even something you can avoid. But country music in general is something I got really heavily into, to the point where [in my car] I would never change my radio from 650 AM.

I got heavy into it, and I was dating a guy about six years ago, and the second year of us dating, I got so into country music that he couldn't even take it anymore. One day I started listening to some Linda Ronstadt, and he was like: "You really aren't being ironic. You actually enjoy that?" I was kind of floored; I had known this guy for years, and he thought I was kind of joking about it. I don't joke about country music. I really love it.

Caitlin owns every Linda Ronstadt record ever released and more, for she also owns a demo tape with songs on it that Ronstadt never included on her records. Caitlin likes her because she came at her music from an intellectual stance, and with her covers of songs done by Irving Berlin and Nat King Cole, Ronstadt took on the role of being a music historian, communicating their work to a whole new generation of listeners while giving it her own feel and style. Moreover, Caitlin claims that Ronstadt "happens to have one of the most brilliant voices I've ever heard."

Gram Parsons has also been a big part of Caitlin's musical development. Caitlin particularly likes the way he brought together the rock generation of the late 1960s and 1970s with the tradition of country music. "There was a year," she says, "when all I could listen to was Gram Parsons." She tried to figure out his musical background, what influenced him when he was growing up, and even what he listened to. "It's a definite love affair I have with his music," she says. "Underneath that sparkling Nudie suit [that he wore], he had this earthy quality that made everything he did seem so pure and without motive."

Add to this a contemporary of Parsons: Townes Van Zandt. Her attraction to him became evident when I asked her about "Dead Flowers."

Question: "Dead Flowers" is a Rolling Stones song. Why did you cover that?

Caitlin: It's a good song. I was a big Stones fan. I was a big Townes Van Zandt fan. Before I was a Stones fan, other than *Beggars Banquet,* I was a big Townes fan. So I heard his version of "Dead Flowers" before I even heard theirs. Yeah, I was a really big-time Townes Van Zandt fan, and he was the reason for me recording that song.

For Caitlin, country music has been like a natural set of footprints left in some alluvial soil deposited by previous generations. Not only was she raised in Nashville, where she still lives, but her parents are also prominent names on Music Row. Her mom, Liz Rose, won a Grammy as a songwriter for Taylor Swift, the country pop star whose appeal to teenage girls has resulted in millions of sales for the Nashville record machine. Caitlin says that her mom didn't begin writing songs until she reached forty and that "it's been encouraging to me to see her no-fuss, no-hang-up attitude." Moreover, Caitlin says that her mom "knows a hell of a lot of songs and has a sort of sixth sense when it comes to word placement."

Caitlin says that her father, Johnny B. Rose, has a wall-to-wall CD library "and a vast amount of knowledge to back it up." He has been writing music since he was a kid and traveling and performing as well. He also has spent a lifetime in the distribution and marketing of records for several different labels. "Sometimes I'd be in the bars with him," Caitlin says, "and I'd be drinking Shirley Temples and listening to him play his song 'Last Nicotonian' [a country/blues song] or Willis Alan Ramsey's '[The] Ballad of Spider John.' That stuff sticks with you forever, no matter how young you are. My father's voice has been breaking my heart since I knew I had one to break, and surely that helped guide the instincts that led to my own singing style."

Even though her parents divorced when she was ten, Caitlin says that she has remained close to both her mother and her father and that music has played a big role in both relationships. "We were just a music-loving family," she says. Then she adds: "When I grew up around country music I grew up around *all* country music, and that includes '90s country, which I still have a particular affinity for."

As a teenager Caitlin remembers "guzzling watered-down coffee and chain smoking Camel lights in a Waffle House" while "debating the existence of God with a bunch of video gamers until it became all too boring a topic to bear." And she admits to an era of rebellion during that time, when she rejected the music her parents liked until she "stopped being irrational" and gained some maturity.

Question: Do you feel that you have learned more about songwriting from other artists? Or has it been more of a vocal and instrumental thing?

Caitlin: It's more of a rabbit trail. I like to follow rabbit trails. If I fall into one thing, two hours later I'll be on a completely different level. It's something I just *do.* I don't think it's something I *try* to do. I know a little bit about a lot of stuff, and that works for me. But country music I feel I know enough about to claim that I do. Country music was easier for me because when I stumbled upon that, I figured out what it was that I liked about it, and that was the songwriting.

While still in her teens, Caitlin got into Japanese and Indian pop, among other types of music. She says that she tried to absorb everything she could and that anything she stumbled across and liked she consumed voraciously. She got heavily into punk and alternative rock: Bikini Kill, the Ramones, and the Donnas.

I wanted to explore Caitlin's earlier experiences playing with a band. I knew that she had put together a group called Save McCaulay, so thinking it was her first band, I asked her about it. In doing so I used the word "serious," which led her to correct me and clarify the nature of the group.

Question: Was that your first serious band?

Caitlin: It was probably the furthest from serious you could possibly get. Save McCaulay was less of a band and more of a friendly review show where I got as many male friends as I possibly could to sing a funny duet. I had full band shows with it, for sure, but...

As she steered me away from the word serious, she began thinking about the impetus for her singing career. She hesitated for a moment, shifted gears, and then said: "Did I tell you earlier that this all started out as a joke? [My singing career] started out as a joke, and Save McCaulay is the punch line." Caitlin recalled that she began writing and singing songs as a lark and wanted to find a way to have fun with them. "Save McCaulay was something that got me out of my house," she said. "It got me onto stages and got me into the local scene where I could meet all these fabulous musicians that I still know today. Save McCaulay wasn't so much of a band as it was a conduit for my own growth as an artist."

It was also a way for her to get closer to the punk scene. "I used to open up for my friends' punk bands. I didn't want to play coffee shops,

I wanted to play punk clubs. It's like the Mountain Goats [another band], all these singer/songwriters who don't want to call themselves singer/songwriters and love the punk ethics and rock bands and everything, but you don't want to take yourself too seriously. I still try not to, and that's an easy way to do it—to have this mysterious nom de plume where people go 'Who's this?'...[or] 'What is this band?' So [Save McCaulay] did what it was supposed to do."

I thought that Save McCaulay might have been strictly punk, but she told me by that time she had regained her affection for country and that the band played those songs too. "One of the reasons I fell back into country music," she says, "was because the Mountain Goats' John Darnielle covered a song by Merle Haggard called 'I Think I'll Just Stay Here and Drink.' As soon as I heard that song and figured out that it was a cover, I went out and bought Merle's *Greatest Hits*. That was one of the first country records that I ever went out and purchased and felt an affinity for and that was because of how well the song was written."

Question: And a lot of your friends were thinking, *Man, how crazy is she, she's into this country stuff?*

Caitlin: You know they were confused about it for a long time, but I swayed them. I found out [that] Gram Parsons, [when he was] in LA going around trying to play George Jones records, people were not having it. And then once he got them to start having it, it bridged that gap between these rockers and country music.

I'm not going to say that he was the only one who really did that, but he brought a hip quality to it and was really shoving it in peoples' faces with the [Western suits he wore] and the accent and George Jones songs in general. I idolized him in that respect. I wanted to do something like that. And I loved country songs, so I started writing them.

❧⳹❧

When Caitlin released her EP *Dead Flowers* in 2009, it received favorable reviews in England. In London *The Guardian* said: "Just wait till you hear her songs about teenage pregnancy, ruined love, or female braggadocio." The *Daily Mirror* added: "Her voice is as sweet as Saturday night whiskey and as clear as a Sunday church bell."

With that reaction, and with the realization that country roots music was gaining popularity in Europe, Caitlin decided to tour there, with a focus on England. She traveled the country for two years and was singing many of the songs from her later CD *Own Side Now.*

Question: Why do you think they liked you so much?

Caitlin: My wonderful sense of humor. [*Laughter.*] It was a big surprise to have such a great response over there. I never expected it, and I don't know how that happened. I can only be thankful for it and hope that they like the next record too.

It's interesting that they listen to lyrics a lot. It's quiet, and coming from Nashville, I'm used to some drunk guy yelling at me from the back of a bar. When I was over there, I remember being terrified for the first few months because I was playing places and there wouldn't be anybody talking, and I didn't know how to deal with it. Now, in Nashville, where everybody's talking, I usually get pissed off about that. A lot of England and some of Europe has this thing about listening to what you're saying so they can pick you to pieces later. [*Laughter.*]

❧❦❧

Most of her shows were in pubs, where dark wood, dartboards, and warm beer enveloped her music. In London she played at the Old Queen's Head, in the northern part of the city. Many a world-class band has performed there, and it's a hip hangout for underground groups. Caitlin calls it "one of the most decorative, beautiful places

I've ever seen. It almost felt like something out of a period piece." And well it should have. According to legend, the pub was once owned by Sir Walter Raleigh back in the 1500s, and it has a seventeenth-century stone fireplace with master-crafted engravings, a Victorian living room, a main bar with thickly cushioned leather benches, and chandeliers that hang above the concert room and sway to the musical beat. Often packed to the rafters with young people, the club can host punk rockers one night and disco bands or banjo pickers the next.

At the Basement in Nashville, Caitlin was four or five songs into her set when she paused to tune her guitar and speak to the crowd. They were into her music, but the beer was still flowing and the noise level still elevating, and for a moment Caitlin lapsed into the expectations she had developed in England and offered an observation that was part reprimand: "I know you are loud. That's just the way you are. I've come to expect that."

When Caitlin first returned to the states from Europe, *Own Side Now* was rereleased and she toured for another year and a half. She told me that she enjoyed the experience, but that "for the most part, it's six people and a van driving way too far."

Because Caitlin's mom wrote music with Nashville pop sensation Taylor Swift, it seemed peculiar to me that Caitlin had not herself become a *pop* performer. When Swift started out in Nashville as a teenage singer around 2004, she impressed Music Row record execs who came to see her shows. She moved quickly up the star ladder as a performer and songwriter; some say her talent moved her along, others say it was more a case of her family fortune (connected to the Swift trucking business) opening doors for her.

Whatever the case she has sold millions of records and won a cartload of awards. In 2009 she became the first country music artist to win an MTV Video Music Award. Her work has received many favorable reviews, although some, such as prominent critic Bob Lefsetz, have predicted that her career will be short-lived and little remembered. Swift is anathema to Outlaw artists because her success has fueled the Nashville drive to debase country music in pursuit of the highest dollar and because Swift herself views country music as part of the pop world. So why couldn't Caitlin be another Taylor Swift and quit being stuffed into a van with six other people?

Question: Your style is quite a bit different from Taylor Swift's. I'm trying to figure out why.

Caitlin: Well, we're two completely different people with many different influences. The other thing is this isn't something I started doing to accomplish anything. I started doing it because I enjoyed it. I'm not saying that Taylor doesn't enjoy it. What I mean, though, is that I never had plans. I never had plans of any kind. That's why I didn't end up in college. It's something that I started doing for fun and that I still do for the most part for fun. If I'm not having fun, I wait until I am.

Question: But people would say, in terms of what mainstream Nashville is producing right now, that your music is not very commercial or is not commercial enough. So why don't you become more commercial?

Caitlin: What I do does have a commercial aspect. The way I structure a song is very traditional. I don't go out of my way to be interesting; I don't go out of my way to be controversial. If I'm stepping outside of any lines, it's just because I never knew that they were there. I don't think that I do anything that wild. I have a very pop mind in the fact that I love pop music, and I love pop songs going all the way back to the '20s and '30s.

Many of Caitlin's comments reveal how much she likes to write songs and measures an artist by the standard of songwriting. Most of her songs reflect her personal experiences, from her teenage years through her current young adulthood.

Question: Is your writing an emotional outlet for you?

Caitlin: It can be. I think it's more of an exploitation of my own emotions. I'm not a very fast writer, as a whole. I'm a little slow with it. But once it starts, it doesn't stop for a minute. So until I have a big push of some kind, it's harder to put things down.

Question: Do you have to work hard at it? Does a song come to you at most any time?

Caitlin: Like I said, I'm not a very fast writer. I'm not a very prolific writer. I don't have that big of a catalog yet. At this point I'm still trying to figure out what the process is and what really turns it. When you're writing personal songs, you have to work off of what is going on in your own life.

Question: Where does something like "Sinful Wishing Well" come from?

Caitlin: A breakup. It's the same thing as teenage girl bullshit. But I tie into it in a different way.

※～※

If the song reflects teenage bullshit (and Caitlin exaggerates that point), the music itself is nevertheless complex, penetrating, and sophisticated. Caitlin's voice, sadly sweet and emotional and in its own way as beautiful as Linda Ronstadt's, conveys heartache so powerfully that the spirit of Hank Williams himself must have found its way into Caitlin's soul. Creating an intriguing metaphor, she artfully links her emotional well to a physical one and sings that no matter how much she hurts, her lost lover will never hear her calling for him;

that that desire, if it is one, will be kept inside. Why it is a *sinful* wishing well, Caitlin told me, is because it's full of *mean-spirited* wishes. That adds yet another dimension to the song and speaks even more strongly to Caitlin's creativity.

> *Every poison penny as it falls*
> *Carves your poison name upon the wall.*
> *And they're piling up so fast, I can't make my wishes last,*
> *I don't think they're doing any good at all.*
> *Because I've been thinking hurricanes and bullets falling down like rain,*
> *I think of you and that's just when it starts.*
> *In the dark, you know I've seen it,*
> *But you know that I don't mean it, from the bottom of my angry, broken heart.*
> "Sinful Wishing Well"
> From *Own Side Now*

Complicated and broken relationships connect the songs on her CD *Own Side Now* (2011). "Fall back into my desperate arms/ Fall back into this old disaster," Catlin sings in the sultry "For the Rabbits." In "Own Side" she plaintively asks: "Who's going to want me now/And who's going to take me home?" The standup bass and brushes on the drums give it a swishy sound reminiscent of a boozy-smelling nightclub filled with the taut faces of desperation; the touch of steel guitar provides a country flavor. "Things Change" contains a mesmerizing instrumental undercurrent of pain that threatens to pull Caitlin and the listener into an ocean of woes; "some things have got to change," she sings, but with an air of doubt, as her lover has left her. Toward the end of the song, Caitlin's voice crescendos into a waterfall of heartbreak as she "holds back the tears" because she "knows that love never dies." Despite her youth the pain must run strong for her to be so expressive, sound so sincere, and reach so deeply into such a dark space.

Caitlin goes bluesy and even a bit jazzy with "Coming Up," a song about stamina and bouncing back in the face of a boyfriend who "keeps coming up with new ways to say good-bye." It features a mean, wicked guitar, harmonica, and piano and ends exhaustingly balls-to-the- wall. It's a big fuck-you to excuses that hurt: "I'm going to darken your days by putting the grays in your skies" and "I'll be the echo that you can never find." And, yes, as in "Sinful Wishing Well," Caitlin displays her knack for getting back at someone through her weaponry of mean thoughts.

In "Shanghai Cigarettes" she combines her love for cigarettes with a broken love affair and brings together a traditional country twang, most evident at the beginning, with a strident modern beat: "Remember the day that the whole thing started/And the little gold box in the glove compartment/And I think I told you so it was always waiting/To be opened at the first sign of breaking." That last line offers a tremendous double entendre.

Caitlin says that the stripped-down sound in her recordings comes about because "that's the kind of sound that I know how to do." She points out that one of her favorite songwriters, Cindy Walker, "didn't even play guitar that much. But she wrote that she got her mother to accompany her on piano, and I always thought that was the coolest thing. I mean, Harlan Howard [one of the greatest of Nashville song-writers] said she was the best country music songwriter of all times, and she didn't even really play guitar."

(Cindy Walker died in 2006 at the age of eighty-seven. Among the many songs she wrote was "You Don't Know Me," which was a hit for Eddy Arnold. Walker's songs made the Top 40 country or pop charts more than four hundred times. Walker was known to use a guitar when she composed music, but she was not a prolific player, and she worked closely with her mom in developing melodies.)

Caitlin adds: "I think [not becoming a well-versed guitar player] helped Cindy create these melodies without feeling like she had to catch up.... Your brain works this way, and you want it to do this thing, and you're really good at this one thing, but if you try to start something else into it, you might end up screwing yourself over because your simplified knowledge of this subject might hinder your creative side with that one."

As might be expected, with her stripped-down sound she abstains from any extensive layering of her work in the studio. "I like to track all the sounds of the band and then maybe overdub the more adaptable parts, like pedal steel," she says. "I haven't done that much recording, though.... That's what's so funny about talking about methods or musical habits; I haven't really formed mine yet. I'm trying to figure this all out."

The artistic success of *Own Side Now* stems in part from her more relaxed approach to the album. "I have a really bad habit of being nitpicky," she says, "but with this record I was not so nitpicky, and I think people really enjoyed that." Then she laughingly adds: "So I don't understand why I'm still that way."

Caitlin has decided to switch gears with her most recent songs. "Lately I've been doing co-writing," she says, "but it's co-writing with people I know pretty well.... I'm at a loss with my own emotional material, so I've been having a lot of fun just writing about more imaginary people.

"Own Side Now was a personal record; this one is personal in a more reserved way. Spending three years of my life reciting an old diary every night started to wear on me, and I began to feel stifled by all those songs that were essentially battle cries to a war that was long

over. So it was refreshing, breathing life and emotion into the songs' protagonists instead of simply pouring out my own. Far from a new concept, but definitely a concept I've had little experience with."

She adds that "story-writing was something I started out doing naturally at sixteen, with songs like 'Shotgun Wedding' and 'For the Rabbits.' I was more of an observer and rather rudely straightforward in recounting other people's situations, but back then it was all about telling stories, not creating them. That may be the biggest difference in this album and the most fun thing about making it."

Creating stories. She has titled the new album *The Stand-In.* Black dominates its cover, with a dark-clad sensual looking Caitlin giving a backward stare over her left shoulder. It's a melancholic work in attitude both in its presentation of personal relationships and its portrayal of the current music scene. "So long ago my radio heart got broken," she sings in "No One to Call," before adding: "Now the songs I wanna hear, they never play." The song has a catchy rock beat mixed with steel guitar and a pronounced country twang.

Time goes so fast when staring out windows, she sings in "Pink Champagne," a clever tune that appears to be celebratory of a recent wedding but portrays the newly married couple as more weary than happy. Caitlin's beautiful voice comes through most powerfully in "Dallas," a song about loneliness on the road.

Caitlin has once again done what she wants to do. She may be looking back over her shoulder at us, but not at any critics or purveyors of categories as she continues to follow those rabbit trails.

At the Basement Caitlin launched into "Answer in One of These Bottles." In the context of mainstream Nashville, the song was jolting. You just don't hear it anymore: lyrics about a woman drinking herself into a stupor. She wrote the song right after graduating from high school, at a time when she was "barring it up."

Caitlin neither sees herself as a crusader for women in a male-dominated music world nor as a visionary with some grand master plan about what she would like to do artistically. She simply wants to create. She doesn't want to be compared to anyone, let alone Loretta Lynn or Patsy Cline, or at least she doesn't want to know about such comparisons. She says: "If somebody compares me to something, you're either going to try to be less like that or be more like that. You're going to forget that you have to do what you do because you're so worried about people thinking you're doing something in another way. It will mess with anybody, especially the way the press works now, where everything is literally copied and pasted. You'll hear the same thing from ten different interviewers, and you'll have people always talking about it. You're left with not being able to explain it."

Copied and pasted: the bane of originality, like a string of Nashville pop songs. Or like a world filled only with *predictability*, such as the relentless movement of landmasses whose every incremental shift unfolds as we have theorized it would.

Geologists lay out their science in an attempt to understand the natural world, but unanimous views seldom exist and contrary developments can always surprise. In 1959 two geologists set up camp in southwestern Montana at a ranch near the Gallatin Mountains and close to a fault line that was thought to be dormant. Nearly all of their colleagues had taken the view that the region would be devoid of any significant seismic activity for many years to come. One dissented, however: David Love, who worked for the United States Geological Survey in Laramie, Wyoming. A great shock, he said, could devastate the landscape most anytime.

Then it happened. First, birds began flying away, and most of the bears lumbered off into the distance. Both provided a warning sign to anyone versed in the natural world that there was soon to be an earthquake. Suddenly, around midnight, it hit, and according to the encamped geologists the solid earth became "like a glop of jelly." The shock was felt some 350 miles away as huge trees toppled and half a mountain tore apart and clogged a river to form Earthquake Lake. By one account for some thirty seconds as the shock wave reverberated across the land the earth's soil "moved like ocean waves."

The unexpected had reshaped the land, and for a moment the natural world resembled human society, where unforeseen developments have sometimes tumbled entire governments, plundered economic systems, and shattered musical genres.

And here Caitlin stands at the juncture where the ocean meets the land, where she sings her music and does so with sincerity. It's possible, just possible, that with her artistry she will help create a seismic change in country music, one that will return to Nashville a creativity based foremost on roots, heart, and guts. She certainly has no plans—let alone any expectation—to propel such an event, but she could well help bring it about by just doing "what feels right."

The great country artist Buck Owens did what he felt was right for him. He invented the sparse style called the Bakersfield sound. At the time, mainstream country had turned to smooth, pop-style songs, infused with strings. Owens went back to country's roots, and with heart and guts he challenged the studio moguls on Music Row. He finally hit the country charts with his song "Second Fiddle" and set off a shock wave that shifted the landmass of country music, enough to create a fault line beneath the surface of Nashville pop that led to the original Outlaw movement.

The year was 1959, the year of the unexpected earthquake.

When I asked Caitlin about why she liked Gram Parsons's music, I was curious as to whether Parsons had influenced the structure of her own songwriting. But in her response, she made me realize that there was something deeper at work, something that makes up the essence of Caitlin's artistry. Something to assure that what she does will exceed the fleeting human moment—ever so fast compared to geologic time—and provide another lasting layer to country's musical heritage. She so loves her music, she told me, that she wants to be dedicated to turning it "into something universal."

The artist, her love, and the *drive to make it universal*—the mite writ large. That's what makes her feel at the center of existence and propels her to push beneath the tectonic plates of life all the commercialism that panders to an empty amusement as she continues to learn what it takes to be a roots country artist.

> *Learning to ride, oh, learning to ride,*
> *I get knocked down when I'm learning to ride.*
> *A few broken bones for a place to hide,*
> *I get knocked down when I'm learning to ride.*
> "Learning to Ride"
> From *Own Side Now*

Caitlin Rose, The Basement, Nashville, TN (2012)

Whitey Morgan, Wichita Ballroom, Wichita, KS (2012)

CHAPTER 20

WHITEY MORGAN

Hard Scratch Pride

Twenty years have passed now
Since I hit the road.
I can hear the whippoorwill,
Hell, the dogwood they calling me home....
And I can hear old Hank,
He gonna moan me that lonesome whistle song.
"HARD SCRATCH PRIDE"
FROM WHITEY MORGAN AND THE 78S

The sound from the radio comes across scratchy as someone moves the dial from one station to the next. At first we hear a man strumming a guitar and singing in a hillbilly twang: "I live my life in sorrow since mother and daddy are dead." Then someone moves the dial again, and we hear an evangelical preacher praising the Lord—yes, praise the Lord!

These are the sounds of a rural, distant America, and they lead into Whitey Morgan singing his tune "Hard Scratch Pride," the lyrics of which tell about his granddad, whose influence on Whitey has been far-reaching (so much so that the voice singing in that hillbilly twang is indeed Whitey's granddad). In fact, that influence remains embedded in Whitey's music as strongly as the limestone and sandstone formations found among the hollows in the family's home state of Kentucky. When his granddad moved from there to Michigan, where Whitey would be born, he brought with him the country music that walked hand in hand with a hard-scratch life.

Today Whitey follows in that tradition, both musically and materialistically. From a working-class background, he continues to fight and claw and scramble, trying to gain the traction that his artistic honesty deserves. He follows his own Wilderness Road—steep and rough and blazed by the pioneer Outlaws from the 1970s, only to become overgrown—as he cuts through the thicket of commercial pop with soulful music that echoes through America's honky-tonks.

When I first met Whitey, he was feeling the pressure. He was at the start of another year of 240 shows, of mile after mile of lonely highways, of beer-soaked crowds that could range anywhere from a few hundred or so to a couple of dozen. It was the typical grime-infused, sleep-deprived Outlaw life.

I was sitting with Whitey in his van behind a cavernous concert site, a former warehouse (the same place where I had met up with Jackson Taylor) in Wichita, Kansas, on a cold January night. The fans from the heater were blowing hard and circulating air that carried with it the sweet, pungent aroma of bygone ganja.

Whitey had just finished playing his set. He's a tall man with long hair and a long beard, and when he's on an elevated stage, as he was in Wichita, he towers commandingly over his audience. Through his voice, his picking, and his intense focus on his craft, he makes it clear that his music means serious business. As he plays, he furrows his brow and his eyes become steely. With his mannerisms, he declares: "Leave me alone, music means my life." But he otherwise exudes such little emotion that it's hard to determine what else might be going on inside of him.

"I tell you what," Whitey said to me, "this new management we've got, it's pushing me toward Nashville. I'm going to get ready to go through the same stuff that those guys [the 1970s Outlaws] went through: wanting me to record a certain way and record with certain pickers instead of my guys." Whether or not this ever comes about, his debate and deliberation over the move at the time I met him serves as a revealing backdrop to the trials and anguish faced by today's Outlaw artists.

Whitey is quite a musician. He's an impeccable guitarist, and an original, creative songwriter. He reminds me of Billy Joe Shaver—an artist who can turn a heartfelt phrase and with a few words leave a marked impression in a listener's head. Whitey does this and at the same time keeps both feet firmly planted on those honky-tonk floors. Without a doubt, if Whitey were recording back in the 1970s, when the original Outlaws were attracting big audiences, his popularity would be on the level of Waylon Jennings, Willie Nelson, and Johnny Paycheck. That he doesn't have a larger audience today comes close to being an unforgivable sin.

To see Whitey contemplate making an appeal to the Nashville mainstream also comes close to being an unforgivable sin. But as with the other Outlaw artists, his predicament raises the question of whether some compromises could be reached that would widen the audience for Outlaw while still keeping the music outlaw. Being a purist has its place but can, at the extreme, degenerate into a self-damaging obstinacy by restricting an artist's audience to a small knot of fans. Where to draw the line becomes at heart an issue *of the heart* as much as of the head and becomes tremendously difficult to confront, let alone try to resolve.

Question: How are you going to react to the Nashville scene?

Whitey: I won't know until it happens. Trying to be an optimist about it, I feel like I can meet them halfway. I feel like there's a sound that I could record and that I could put out there that could be mainstream, even though to me, and everybody that likes this old school stuff, it doesn't feel like it's that mainstream. Nashville's all about the right tempo that you're playing at and the right feel and all that.

I could, if they would just let me have my own way, I could record a song that almost sounded like an old Waylon Jennings or David Allan Coe or Johnny Paycheck song but would still cross over to this mainstream audience. [With the way conditions are today in Nashville], I feel like they're just going for the easy out. They're just going for the, well, we're gonna use this picker and we're gonna record another song in the key of G, for Christ's sake, with some good-looking girl and the same damn band that's recorded for the last, you know, how many Nashville records. They're not taking any chances, and it's the same shit that was going on in the '70s, with Waylon and all those guys.

I asked Whitey if he were going to try to "fix Nashville." He said there was no fixing it. This led to some more observations by him of the current Nashville scene and some revelations about his own approach to country music. "I just get sick of hearing these guys that we tour with from Nashville," he says. "This is a quote that I've heard from almost every band that I've ever played with that's basically, that has crossed over, that's just doing the mainstream stuff. And we opened for them, and we get done, and they say to me, 'Oh, I wish I could do what you're doing.'"

Whitey says that he tells them they can, that it requires nothing magical and nothing more special than writing from the heart. Instead the Nashville guys write from a programmed position, and they especially write for a young female audience, the group that buys most of what Nashville produces.

He adds: "I write songs for people that enjoy real stripped-down, good old writing and guitar playing and all that. To me it's less about the studio than it is about the live show. I want my band to sound like [the old Outlaws], to have that energy, where every song is a little hotter than the studio version."

This gets to another point about Nashville pop. The Music Row assembly-line approach carries over to the stage. "These guys in Nashville when they go on the road," Whitey says, "the fucking drummer is listening to a click track that's the exact same tempo as the studio record so that they don't misrepresent the song to these people that only are interested in hearing it sound the same way it sounded [on the radio].

"In the old days, your band was a completely other animal live. Now they strive to sound exactly like the CD. Well, that's boring as shit, as far as I'm concerned. I want you to come to a live show and have a whole 'nother experience than when you're listening to that record. It's one-sided to try to make it sound exactly like the CD."

Most people seek to find and capture a central essence in their work or elsewhere in their life, whether it be found in art or science or business or in the everyday need to survive. A historian might seek *the* force behind past developments; a physicist might seek to find *the* theory behind energy; a pilgrim might forge rivers, trek through valleys, and climb mountains to find a guru who will reveal *the* meaning of the universe. For Whitey, the Outlaw artist must seek and discover *the* soul in country.

Question: You sing about having soul. What does that mean to you, and in what way do you think you have it?

Whitey: First of all, it's writing a lot of your own songs. A lot of these guys in Nashville don't write [even] one of their own songs, or... maybe they do, but they don't get these put on the record because the record company is in control. These guys would never last a week in my van. You know, you gotta love it. I feel like they don't, that there's just no way in hell that before the show they're sitting in their van listening to Johnny Paycheck, and that's their preshow ritual. That's what I do; I've done it for I don't know how many years. It's just one of those things I do; it gets me in the zone."

Sure, soul. But what happens if an Outlaw artist takes his soul to Music Row? Does he sell it to the devil? Country singer/songwriter Jamey Johnson came back from the Nashville Hades, where he wrote songs for mainstream artists, to produce the CDs he wanted to make, filled with real, honest music. But would Whitey be irretrievably lost to the mainstream, or would he be able to retrieve his artistry as it existed before?

Question: Would you lose your soul in Nashville?

Whitey: No, no, no. Never, never. That doesn't have a lot to do with it. I'm always going to be the same person. It's hard to say until it happens, but you can't ever lose it if you've got it or you've been there,... played at some of the shows that I've played. I mean, it's just now getting better, and it's been bad for a lot of years. On the road, playing to ten, twenty people every night, you've just got to keep fighting on, and you pick up whatever fans you can.

Among the country artists who have influenced Whitey, the 1970s Outlaw Waylon Jennings holds a special spot in Whitey's musical upbringing. "When I fell in love with Waylon Jennings was when that double live came out on CD," Whitey says. "I think it was the year 2000, and when I heard that, it's flawless. Every song flows; it's an experience in itself. It's not contrived. You can tell that's just how comfortable he was with his band and with the energy that he put out there onstage every night. He didn't talk a bunch in between songs. He wasn't trying to be the entertainer that got up there and hyped up the crowd."

Above all else Whitey likes that Waylon just went out onstage and performed *his* way. Whitey says that the band may not have had the technical expertise to fit into the Nashville scene, but when they were playing their kind of music, they couldn't be topped. They knew how to "get their point across and just be solid every night. And they had that energy that nobody else could touch." This observation gets Whitey back to another criticism of current country. "Today," he says, "I feel like a lot of these guys, they just go out there and they over-pick, they over-sing. They over-entertain. It's so contrived and it's so phony."

Question: Have those Outlaws from the 1970s influenced your music structurally?

Whitey: I wouldn't say structurally. My sound, it's obvious I strip it down to the bare bones like Waylon did. Those guys, they created a sound and stuck with it. I always compare it to when people tell me that AC/DC keeps recording the same record; I'm like, well, yeah, they invented that sound, though. That's exactly what they should be doing. I don't want to hear AC/DC do a song that doesn't style like every other one of their songs. They invented that sound. Waylon invented that sound; why would he do anything else?

And I just love the simplicity of it. I tell you what, you get that kick drum and that bass guitar going, and I don't care where you're at, who you're playing in front of, they love it. I've seen it happen many, many times. For me that's the sound.

Whitey's band has that Waylon-style tightness and the kick-drum, kick-ass bass-guitar beat with its four-on-the-floor rhythm. The band's name, the 78s, was thought up by Whitey and Jeremy, his bass player at the time I saw them in Wichita, during a drinking bout, and the number has a double meaning for Whitey. On the one hand, it refers to the vinyl records on which many early country songs were record- ed, far back, back to the Jimmie Rodgers era. On the other hand, it refers to what Whitey calls the last great year for country music, and even rock 'n' roll. "Everything started getting slicked up after that," he says. "That's when George Strait came along; and don't get me wrong, the early George Strait records are fucking great. But every- thing started to get slicked up, and that's kind of the end of this thing we do, you know, that style." The stripped-down, Waylon-flavored, '70s Outlaw style.

When Whitey mentioned rock music, he brought up Bruce Springsteen, one of the artistic heroes of working-class America. That night in Wichita, he covered a Springsteen song, "I'm on Fire." (It appears on his CD, *Honky Tonks and Cheap Motels,* released in 2008.) The opening chords immediately evoke the Outlaws of yore. But Whitey does it his own way by adding a haunting sound to it; no replication of Waylon, no carbon copy of Bruce. And that marks him as a true artist, one who can use previous influences without merely repeating them, one who can so craft his own art that it merges with the past smoothly.

Question: How much do you like Bruce Springsteen?

Whitey: I am a huge Bruce Springsteen fan. I've got every one of his records on vinyl. I mean, he's a big influence on me as far as a songwriter, but I don't, I can't write his style. He's a little too dark; he's different. But that particular song is easy to turn into a country song, and a lot of his songs are that way. Those three-chord songs he does. Yes, I'm a big Springsteen fan. I've got a Springsteen tattoo.

Whitey admires Merle Haggard for having it all: he's an incredible songwriter, guitar player, and singer. Whitey also likes David Allan Coe because he's been such a prolific and spirited songwriter, one with the talent to shift from a hard-driving in-your-face melody to a sweet one and never lose a beat. Moreover, Coe has the guts to let his feelings loose, and if that sometimes means a song of his flops, it more often means that a song hits the bull's-eye, both in its musical structure and lyrical sincerity.

But Whitey saves his strongest praise for 1970s Outlaw artist Johnny Paycheck. Without hesitation, Whitey calls Paycheck "the greatest country singer that ever lived and nobody knows it." Moreover, Whitey identifies with Paycheck on a personal level because he was the little guy having to fight his way forward.

"He never could get his shit together long enough to be on top," Whitey says. "He'd have a hit, and then the drinking and the drugs would take him over, and he'd be back down on the bottom. To me, I just love that he was the underdog. I mean, when he died he was broke and George Jones had to pay for his funeral. Can you imagine that? George Jones had to pay for his funeral."

Question: What makes his music so great?

Whitey: His voice and his melody structure [are] leaps and bounds above everybody else's. He was so much more creative, and he had control of his voice like nobody else. The fact that he would do that, you know, night after night just out of his mind on drugs and whatever else, you know, it just blows my mind.

His version of Buck Owens's "A-11" [a song written by Hank Cochran] is ten times better than Buck Owens's version of it. I've seen the YouTubes of him singing a couple of years before he died, and he never lost it. He'd go up there and would just out sing everybody, even when he was not in the best health. I've got a spot in my heart for that guy. I just hate the fact that nobody knows how great he was. People just go, yeah, Johnny Paycheck, "Take This Job and Shove It" [written by David Allan Coe], a great song.

But what they don't realize is that he and George Jones learned to sing together in [their] van. That's why George Jones and Johnny Paycheck sound so similar, is that they were touring together, just like this, in a van in the late '50s, early '60s.

❧～❧

The little guys: Johnny Paycheck and Whitey Morgan. Brothers in arms against the hard knocks. "[I was] born in Flint, Michigan, one of the most important cities in the history of this country," Whitey says. "We invented the little thing called the automobile, for Christ's sake," he says, "but now my town, Flint, is on the list as one of the worst off economically. I feel like I've always been that underdog my whole life."

Well, I've got them ol' Buick City blues,...
Hell, I've got to leave this town.
Lord, when you're flat broke and busted,
It can get you down.

"Buick City"
From *Whitey Morgan and the 78s*

Whitey can feel the sting of the road on the soles of his shoes—the hot asphalt, the cold crust of grimy snow, the grease from oil slicks and leaky transmissions. He can feel particularly the pain of that ladder rung pressing against the bottom of his feet as he struggles to climb higher, often just to reach the step he had been pushed away from the day before.

Whitey says that whenever Paycheck got ahead, "he'd get beat back down." He adds: "When he had that 'Take This Job and Shove It,' that was the highlight of his career, and people don't realize he had [many] albums before that."

Perhaps Whitey thinks of himself when he says about Paycheck: "I wonder what would have happened if maybe [he] would have picked a hit song early.... It's crazy to think that that's all it took back in those days, because there were some great songwriters in Nashville, man, Harlan Howard and all those guys. All it would take was that right song, picking that right song, and his whole life could have been different. He might not have had to work so hard and..."

The thought remains incomplete. Maybe Paycheck would not have had to work so hard in the trenches, would have made it to the top well before "Take This Job and Shove It," and would have stayed there longer. Whitey repeats: "Of course there was the pills and the booze and...."

Paycheck, Jones, Jennings. But above all else, Whitey owes his own entry into country music to his grandfather, who loved to sing and play his guitar around the house. At that time Whitey didn't really know who had written the country songs his granddad liked, or who had originally recorded them. Whitey just knew that he liked them too.

Whitey developed a close relationship with his grandfather, partly because his parents had a rocky marriage. By way of him, he learned about his family's roots that stretched back to those hollows of southern Kentucky, where his granddad came from. It's a reason why Whitey describes him as a "wild-ass hillbilly." Whitey's granddad moved to Michigan in the 1940s, settling first in Ann Arbor and then, for a much longer period, in Flint, where he got a job at the Chevrolet plant.

> *I was born down south Kentucky,*
> *A hard-scratch holler I called my home.*
> *Well, my mama begged me, boy, don't you ramble....*
> *When I left that holler, I was just a boy,*
> *Flat broke and busted and helping to make it on my own.*
> "Hard Scratch Pride"
> From *Whitey Morgan and the 78s*

Whitey's granddad taught Whitey how to play guitar on a 1969 Gibson acoustic when Whitey was ten years old. He remembers that he and his grandfather would often sit at home, in the basement, and pick together. "And I learned to sing harmonies to Jimmie Rodgers and bluegrass gospel songs that he would sing in church," Whitey says. In "If It Ain't Broke," from the CD *Honky Tonks and Cheap Motels,* Whitey sings that his "grandpappy" set him down one day and told him that if you want to play country music, "you gotta have a lot of soul."

Whitey's grandpa played music in the bars around Flint "until he couldn't take it anymore." He was good enough—he had that soul—that he could have been a musician full-time if he only had had a bigger following.

Music held Whitey together; it kept him from going off the deep end. He describes himself as a "fuck up" when he was a teenager. He was angry all the time and skipped school a lot. His mom and dad divorced when he was thirteen, and he bounced from his dad's house to his mom's house in working-class neighborhoods. As he rode his skateboard, he listened to punk and other rock music, but country made the most sense to him and had the most appeal.

Whitey says that at age sixteen, he was hit hard by the death of his granddad. Yet he still had something physical that he could hold onto: he inherited his grandfather's old wooden cabinet, and as he rummaged around its drawers, he found his granddad's guitar straps. He clenched them tightly in his hands, as tightly as his mind clenched his granddad's music, and determined that he wanted to make his own soulful sound. But what sound, exactly? His granddad had already pointed him in the direction.

When Whitey opened the top doors to the cabinet, he found his granddad's vinyl record collection. It was then that he began to realize who had originally sung the songs that his granddad had sung. He began to learn which was a Jimmie Rodgers song, which a Waylon Jennings, and which a Johnny Paycheck.

As Whitey played his grandpa's records, he became obsessed with them and would sit in his room much of the day listening to them. He saw more and more the sound he wanted to make, and when he picked up the old Gibson guitar, which he had also inherited, and began strumming along to the songs, his feel for the music intensified. Some of his friends began to like the records as well, and with Whitey they decided to form a band. From this the first version of the 78s appeared early in 2001, playing covers and a few originals.

If there is anyone that Whitey has tried to style himself after in terms of voice, it's his grandpa, who even bought a tape recorder for Whitey and had him sing into it. "That's really where the singing thing started," Whitey says. "I've got tapes [of me] that he recorded and they're awful. They're just terrible. "

But Whitey listened intently as well to other country artists as he dove deeper into his granddad's record collection and soon became attracted to Merle Haggard's style. "The first guy I ever tried to sound like besides my grandpa was Merle Haggard," he says. "I just wanted to sound like Merle Haggard because, you know, he's the king. The honky-tonk sound he gets; he's just such a professional and in such control of his voice. If it wasn't for me doing that, I don't know where the hell I would be. I sang 'Swinging Doors' over and over for I don't know how many times just trying to understand what it is to be a country singer."

Just trying to understand what it is to be a country singer. "It's not much but I feel welcome here inside," Merle sings in "Swinging Doors" and then describes a jukebox and a bar stool and a flashing neon sign and a room engulfed by cigarette smoke—his "new home." And it certainly describes one of Whitey's homes, where Whitey feels comfortable singing and likes to mingle with the people whose backgrounds resemble his. Another of his homes: the house of integrity. That's where it all starts, Whitey insists. It all gets back, again, to having *that soul*.

"I'm obsessed with music," he says while emphasizing that means all kinds of music. The artist, however, must sing from the heart; he must be genuine. "You know, you hear somebody sing something that you like, you hear a certain phrasing that they do, and I'll sing it that way. But sometimes, [and this gets back to] Waylon Jennings, he says that sometimes you get sick and tired of singing it the way the original songwriter sang it, and you wind up singing it different, and that's when you start doing things your own way."

The "your own way" of Whitey Morgan stands out like a piece of handmade silverwork in a junkyard filled with the throwaway lyrics and melodies from the world of Nashville pop. It's an amalgam of those early influences forged by others, reshaped by him, and combined with his own experiences, and in every song, every tune, his grandpa has something to say.

There's nothing slick about his music. Listening to a Whitey Morgan song entails picking up that silverwork and feeling the pitted texture of authenticity, hewn by a hardscrabble life, while marveling at the beauty of the entire piece.

Question: How do you create a song? How do you write a song?

Whitey: For me, I always think of the hook first, the chorus. You know, we'll be driving down the road, or somebody will say something, and I'll say, "That's good, that's good. That's a good hook." For me, though, I can't write on the road worth a shit. I have to be at home; I have to have my guitar there and just be able to get away from everybody else. I come up with a lot of ideas on the road, but I never write songs on the road.

Question: So it would be not until you get home....

Whitey: Yeah, I'd get home and I'd start maybe writing a little bit of a verse here and there. I never write anything down. I don't actually write stuff down because my theory is if it's not that good, then I probably won't remember it. I think that every song on the first two records I never wrote down. I just sit there and sing them over and over again, trying to think of that next line. That's pretty much it.

While many people find mowing the lawn to be a tedious task, Whitey puts the chore to his songwriting advantage. As he sits on his tractor, he creates his music. He says it's because "when I'm out there, there's nothing else but what's going on in my head for two hours. My wife works, and I've got dogs and stuff, and I've got stuff to take care of at the house, and the only time I can focus on something,...I'll sit out there and just sing a song, a verse part or a chorus part that I thought of on the road probably, over and over again. And then I'll just start adding to it, building it. Here's the idea, the basic idea of the song; let's get a verse and let's start building it." When he finishes with the lawn, he wraps up his songwriting. "I'll go inside, sit down with the guitar, play it, and that's it," he says. He could compile a book of lyrics, *Blades of Grass*—in which he sings the song of America—and be true to the title.

Like other Outlaw artists, Whitey hates to be labeled. What makes for Outlaw can be confusing, he says. Moreover, Whitey doesn't even like to be called country, and that underscores a regrettable situation. To those into country roots, Nashville pop has hijacked country and distorted and ruined it so much that they don't want to be associated with it. To those into Nashville pop, what they hear from Whitey Morgan and other Outlaws, either from today or the 1970s, doesn't fit what they think of as country or what they want to hear as country. So country as a word denoting a musical genre has become quite muddled and, especially to a few Outlaws, pejorative.

Ultimately, Whitey says, the real Outlaws were Willie Nelson, Waylon Jennings, Johnny Paycheck, and so on from the 1970s because they were the true path-breakers and pioneers, the true masters of the cutting edge. "Their bands in those days were long-haired guys that didn't give a shit about what Nashville wanted," Whitey says. "They just wanted to play their own music."

He criticizes those who just throw around the word Outlaw for promotional or shock effect. He says: "Now I grant that there [are] a lot of people out there who will say that's what we're doing. But are you turning down money so you don't play with people you don't want to associate yourself with? Are you really bucking any kind of system? Most of them aren't. I'll be honest with you, there isn't an Outlaw out there, not one, I don't believe. It sure as hell ain't me. I wouldn't say that I am."

Yet Whitey has refrained from looking over his shoulder at Nashville and has written and performed music that fits him first and foremost. He wants to make money, he wants a larger audience, but he has rejected the commercial allure of pop country. It's almost as if his grandpa is looking over his shoulder and keeping him focused on the music *they both love.*

Question: Why wouldn't you say that you are Outlaw? You're doing your own thing….

Whitey: Because, I don't wanna….

Question: You just don't want to be labeled?

Whitey: That's some of it, but I…. You know, everybody's got their own opinion of what it is, but I feel like that time period has passed. I mean, those guys really changed the goddamn country world back then, and I don't think anybody's going to change it right now because it's too about money. I mean, we'll go out there, we'll do these shows every night. I'll probably do them until the day I die; I'll be playing a show for two hundred people out in the middle of nowhere. But it will never be like it was then, as important as what they did.

That last sentence undervalues today's Outlaws. None of them may ever be as *prominent* as Willie Nelson or Waylon Jennings (on a national level). But *importance?* How about keeping alive country's roots? Creating an original art? Touching people?

Whitey and I had originally set up our interview to begin before he was to take the stage in Wichita. I waited and waited for him inside the building, but no Whitey. I tried to reach him on the phone, but no Whitey. He eventually showed up but only a few minutes before he was to begin playing. "Oh, man, I'm sorry," he said to me. "I still want to do the interview. It's just that I had such a rough night yesterday. I'm still recovering, man."

He had performed at a honky-tonk the night before. The alcohol consumption must have been quite a bit to fell a man the size of Whitey. But he was ready to play his set.

"I go into a show like I'm a fan," Whitley told me. "You don't go up there and act like a fucking idiot and disrespect the fans because they're the reason why you're there."

He added: "I want people to feel like every time we went and seen Whitey, we were a part of the show with him. All of us were in it together. The same way I feel about these guys that I tour with: we're all in it together, and I just don't want anybody to think I thought I was better than anybody else, you know, or look down on anybody else."

He tries to tour with a four- or five-piece band. When I questioned whether this was expensive, he responded: "It is, but, again, these aren't Nashville guys. There's nobody in there that's just in there for a paycheck, I can tell you that. They love doing it."

About the typical Music Row musician, he says that "*those* guys" don't care about which band they're in. They have no commitment to the band as a fraternal unit. "They're in it for the money and maybe some ladies on the road." The bigger stars, he says, talk about a gig "the way the guy who works at the drive-through at McDonald's talks about his job." The 78s *must* be different; Whitey couldn't stand for it to be otherwise. It would be completely contradictory to and destructive of the sincerity that makes for Outlaw. "We've got to be a unit," he says, "[in] everything we do, from the drive to the music we're listening to, everything. If you're not into the same shit I'm listening to, I don't need you around because that doesn't help."

He adds that the difficulties of life on the road cause friction in the band and a turnover in personnel. "You love somebody one day, and you want to kill them the next," Whitey says. "But you've got to find those guys that all know how to turn it on and off. I always say you got to go into the zone and get the job done. Don't let all the bullshit get you worked up. If the sound is shady or the promoter is fucking up or the money ain't coming through, well, that's the business. You can't worry about that every night. You'll drive yourself crazy."

> *This old life I've been living,*
> *It ain't the life for everyone,*
> *But it's the life for me....*
> *When the morning comes,*
> *I'm leaving again,*
> *Like a tumbleweed I'm gone with the wind.*
> "Sinner"
> From *Whitey Morgan and the 78s*

Whitey says that for his studio work, "my arrangements are usually pretty solid." The band will lay down bass, drums, and guitar and a scratch vocal. "You've [then] got the foundation of the song," Whitey says, "and a lot of times then we'll come up with the hook guitar lick over the intro or the guitar solo that's double-upped. But it always starts with bass, drums, my guitar, and a scratch vocal, and we build it after that—unless it's a song we've been playing a lot live, where we've already worked out some guitar lines and stuff."

Bloodshot Records, the label for Whitey's *Honky Tonks and Cheap Motels,* describes that CD as one that reflects Outlaw music and the workingman's world (given Whitey's upbringing in the blue-collar city of Flint.) A combination of covers and originals, the CD shows Whitey's vocal and instrumental indebtedness to the 1970s Outlaws. "Back to Back," a song about a deteriorating relationship ("We lay back-to-back acting like strangers," Whitey sings, because "nothing lasts forever"), displays that Waylon Jennings beat and Jennings-like inflections within a distinctly different and alluring voice. The cheating and torn-love theme dominates the CD. Whitey shows himself to be sure of his music and confident of his talent; he's an artist with legitimate honky-tonk credentials.

> *One more dime for the jukebox,*
> *And one more waltz across the floor.*
> *You can play me the Rose of San Antone,*
> *For I won't be seen here anymore....*
> *Well, now, play me some Waylon on the jukebox,*
> *Hell, get drunk and drink every drink the whole night through.*
> *Well, my honky-tonk angel is leaving tonight.*
> *Well, hell, she's got a man down in Baton Rouge.*
>
> "Honky Tonk Angel"
> From *Honky Tonks and Cheap Motels*

The CD *Whitey Morgan and the 78s* (2010) continues in a similar vein. Whitey's cover of "Bad News" warns the listener that he once had to change his name, that wherever he goes he gets into trouble. "The Meanest Jukebox in Town" has him, Johnny Paycheck-style, losing a little bit of his life with each coin he puts into the jukebox and faces, or tries to forget, a catastrophe of crumbled dreams. "I Ain't Drunk" has Whitey humorously proclaiming to a bartender and a cop, when one cuts him off and the other pulls him over, "I ain't drunk, I've just been drinking."

Rousing honky-tonk songs that penetrate the core of the common person's life—the white man's blues performed at their soulful best—the CD stands admirably next to anything Waylon Jennings did. Whitey has come along too late to play with Waylon's band, to be on stage with those guys who "knew how to play together and get their point across and just be solid every night." But if we could use a way-back machine or a Star Trek transporter to take him to Waylon's era he would crystallize in the middle of those pickers he admires so much and never miss a beat.

And fortunately for Outlaw country, Whitey is planning to stick close to the genre's roots in 2013. It promises to be a busy year for him with three new CDs in the works: a live one, an acoustic one, and a studio one.

When I finished interviewing Whitey, I went back into the venue to catch Jackson Taylor's show. Jackson followed his gig with an unscheduled acoustic set. Soon after he got into it, Whitey sauntered onstage to join him with some vocals. It was laid-back, it was fun, and it was raucous. Whitey had been drinking before his impromptu appearance, and when he took up the guitar and then the drums— Jackson's drummer lay sprawled on the floor, waving a glass of whiskey in the air—his playing was erratic. Yet he contributed to the party atmosphere as the fans cheered and clapped and raised their own drinks in the spirit of good times among good neighbors.

At least for the moment, Whitey pushed aside the exhaustion and frustration he was feeling over going out on the road time and again with big expectations only to wind up playing to small crowds. But no doubt he would again feel the pressure to head for Nashville to see if he could wage the fight to make more money while holding onto to his musical integrity—while holding on to the soul he declared, and he knows to be, central to his artistry as an Outlaw musician.

Whitey had years earlier chosen to play the music he was performing this night in Wichita—ever since he learned to pick on his granddad's guitar. He plays the songs he does because he feels an aptitude for it, he feels drawn to it, and he's in love with it. But in doing so, he has placed himself outside the Music Row establishment. He now has to make more decisions, ones that could mine *his essence as a man and as a country artist.*

Should Whitey ever go to Nashville, maybe the record execs won't want him, or maybe he will turn his back on their advances. It's hard to say how the story will unfold, and it may take a long time to do so. A burden or a blessing or a little of both, Whitey carries the original Outlaws with him as he pushes onward through the thicket. And he carries those Outlaws by way of his grandpa, who taught him more than just how to play. He taught Whitey how to create honest music of the kind that echoes from the hollows of Kentucky, among the hills and dogwoods, all the way through the vinyl records of Johnny Paycheck and into the songs of Whitey Morgan and the 78s.

> *And I'm heading up to Detroit on a freight train, mama,*
> *I'm a finally be a man....*
> *But don't worry, mama,*
> *I ain't lost my hard-scratch pride.*
> > "Hard Scratch Pride"
> > From *Whitey Morgan and the 78s*

CODA

The year 2013 has been good to Whitey Morgan. Even though his travels have yet to take him to Nashville his fan base has increased substantially. Whitey has benefitted from a tour with the 1970s rocker Bob Seeger, and from his manager astutely using social networking, and because of this he has become more upbeat, even buoyant about his prospects. Most importantly he continues to turn out the music that would make his granddad proud.

Whitey Morgan, Wichita Ballroom, Wichita, KS (2012)

Lydia Loveless, Secret Stages Festival, Birmingham, AL (2012)

CHAPTER 21

LYDIA LOVELESS

Can't Change Me

Well, I had a lot to say last night.
I'm sorry, did I say that to you?
Well, I talk so much shit,
I'm forgettin' who I'm talking to....
Well, I say I'm not as bad as I seem,
But I used to be better, honey, can't you see?
You of all people should know this ain't really me.
"CAN'T CHANGE ME"
FROM INDESTRUCTIBLE MACHINE

If ever there was a poster boy for alienation, it was Richard Hell. Punk rocker. And a poet who wrote: "The nurse adjusted her garters as I breathed my first/The doctor grabbed my throat and yelled, 'God's consolation prize!'" Also a hitchhiking teenager, circa 1966. Writes "Chinese Rocks" with Dee Dee Ramone. Sees problem with chronology when history is warped by time: "Every intervening moment between then and now creates a separate and different meaning for any event that came before it." Nice, for, unknown to him, with that statement he was hitting at the problem of trying to write about Outlaw country, past and present.

Into the picture steps Lydia Loveless, in one of those moments between then and now. All of twenty-one years old, Lydia has been a fan of Richard Hell since she was in her early teens. I met Lydia at a bar in Birmingham, Alabama, where she was playing during a festival called Secret Stages. (For this event, bands of different musical genres appeared at downtown locales through much of the night.)

The bar was crowded with maybe a hundred people. It was more narrow than wide, just like its small stage jammed near several barstools. The atmosphere was low amber-light boozy, with dark walls and lots of wood, and the crowd was drinking, talking loudly, and paying little attention to the small table Lydia had set up to display her T-shirts and CDs. I was left to wonder how a woman so small in size (five feet tall) could possibly rock the house, even one as cramped as this, as she was known to do with her particular type of Outlaw country: roots ramped up to punkish rhythms and lyrics.

Behind Lydia was her drummer, to her left was her lead guitarist, to her right was her standup bass player. The strikingly diminutive Lydia seemed physically overpowered by her acoustic guitar as she tuned it.

At Lydia's feet, on the wooden floor scuffed by many a performer whose work and expectations may or may not have led them to larger venues, were two bottles of beer, opened but yet to be consumed. Lydia reached down, took a swig from one of them, briefly and quietly introduced herself, took another swig, and then launched into her set.

My shoulder-length hair pretty much blew back, and my eyes widened and facial skin distorted from the pressure of the impact as she began "Bad Way to Go." Fast guitar. Hyperventilating snares. Faster, fastest. Foggy Mountain Breakdown-style with banjo on the record, but here more like Eddie Shaver on guitar speed. Faster, fastest.

> *So turn my heart to paper, but seal it with a kiss,*
> *So you can write me a love letter in the gravel with your piss....*
> *Seem like such a pussy, babe,*
> *Because I know how to take you home with me and put you*
> *   back in place.*
>
> "Bad Way to Go"
> From *Indestructible Machine*

The self-punishment in Lydia's lyrics seemed as durable, and certainly could be as brutal, as any indestructible machine. Lydia has a voice powerful and gorgeous, stunningly clear and right on the mark with each note. Add the drums, bass, and guitars, and the music becomes a room-altering experience, like workers feverishly pounding away at the masonry while at the same time carefully engraving the woodwork with filigree.

> *Just as we were talking to Lou Reed [of the rock group the Velvet Underground], the Ramones [legendary punk rockers] hit the stage.... Then they counted off a song—"One, two, three, four!" —and we were hit with this blast of noise; you physically recoiled from the shock of it, like this huge wind....*
> —Legs McNeil, writer for *Punk* magazine*

---

* The italicized quotations about punk music in this chapter come from Legs McNeil and Gillian McCain, *Please Kill Me: The Uncensored Oral History of Punk* (Grove, 1996).

In the chronology of her life, Lydia developed an attachment to punk before delving heavily into country. Yet the punk in her music, with its pulsating simplicity, complements rather than overpowers her country elements.

Lydia counts Loretta Lynn and Dolly Parton among the roots artists she most admires. Lydia says that when she was growing up she watched *Coal Miner's Daughter*—the movie about Lynn—"a billion times a day." Lydia admires Lynn's feistiness and the way she sang about topics that were "edgy." It was, Lydia says, a characteristic that "would be totally lost on today's average country music singer," meaning that Music Row wouldn't know edginess even if it were grasping a knife positioned at it blade-first. She likes Dolly Parton "because she's been playing music since she was a little girl, and that to me is really inspiring. I've pretty much wanted to play music my whole life."

The original Outlaw movement of the 1970s became an influence too. For that she gives some credit to an ex-boyfriend. "He introduced me to David Allan Coe," she says. "I remember he was the first [artist] he played for me, and I remember him trying to impress me with all the music he used to like. One of the [musicians he played] was Hank Williams. I went out and bought a bunch of Hank Williams records, and I really liked it a lot."

She says that she became "obsessed" with the legendary Hank. "It was easy for me at the time to learn his songs," she recounts. "I was just starting out with guitar, so it was easy for me to sit there and play some Hank Williams just to get my bearings."

Question: So was Hank Williams mainly someone to learn the guitar by, or had he more of an influence than that on you?

Lydia: It was both. I loved the way he seemed to be able to write a song about anything, which is sort of a well-known fact about him, that he could basically sit down, work from a song title, and write a song about it. I found that pretty inspiring.

Inspiring enough to begin writing her own songs. In an online article, Lydia says that she wanted to capture his feeling: "Three chords and no bullshit lyrics—just say what you're talking about.... I like the way his music was so heartfelt and honest."

If Lydia's boyfriend provided an Outlaw influence, so too did her parents. "My dad had a lot of Outlaw records," she told me. "He had a collection of all the original Outlaws that we would listen to around the house. So I wouldn't necessarily give all the credit to my boyfriend, but he was somebody who made it seem cool to me; it wasn't something that my parents were shoving in my face.... It was something that was different."

Question: So how were these country artists—the Outlaws and the traditionalists—how were they influencing you?

Lydia: When I was a teenager, I had just left the countryside for Columbus, Ohio, and I felt really sad, and I didn't feel that I had any connection to society after that. I felt alienated, and listening to good country music made me feel like I had a place in the world. When I was growing up, my friends were listening to the redneck woman crap or whatever they were listening to, and it always just disgusted me, and as I got older I started realizing that there actually was something that was for country rednecks that wasn't awful and embarrassing to listen to. I guess the simplicity of country music for me, and the way people would say what they mean and there's no flowery style...it's just this is how I feel and I need to get this off my chest—that really spoke to me, much the same way that punk rock does.

While Lydia sees her move to Columbus as causing her alienation, she also felt that way previously, and punk rock addressed her outsider status while she was growing up in rural Ohio, in that countryside. She was completely homeschooled, and although she socialized with the nearby kids, she had little contact with their in-school cliques. Irrespective of that Lydia just felt different. "I took dance lessons and hung out with people," she says. "And I had a circle of friends that I would have had even had I gone to school, but I felt like I did not understand those people anyway. A lot of it had to do with growing up in a small, backwards town, more so than being homeschooled." She adds: "I was kind of a weird kid. I remember some of the things I used to wear. I would get all kinds of shit for it because I had no interest in trying to grow up the way everyone else did."

Lydia took the future to heart more so than did many of her friends. When she began dancing, for example, she approached it seriously, with the thought that she might make it her career, while the other kids were often just going through the motions. Music, however, reached out to her more strongly. She liked it better, and when her teacher scolded her for missing an important dance rehearsal so she could play with her band, she made the decision to drop dancing altogether.

Lydia describes her childhood relationship with her mom and dad as having been close, but one that was more like they were her peers than her parents. Her dad was a musician, and before Lydia was born he played the drums in a band. (He still plays drums and often appears with Lydia onstage.) For about a two-year period, when Lydia was around nine years old, he owned a bar. "Bluesy-type" bands played there, she says, although "there was even a metal one." All in all, she says, "It was just a lot of rural Ohio-types."

If her parents exposed her to Outlaw country of the 1970s, they also exposed her to punk and so handed down to her the rebelliousness of *their* youth. "My parents were actually big fans of punk," she says. "When I was a kid, it was around the house. Not to the extent that they had Black Flag records or anything, but my mom was a huge Velvet Underground fan, and the Clash she always loved, so I sort of grew up with access to it. I didn't really get that into it until I was about fourteen, when there was the big pop-punk breakout and all of these horrible bands that were calling themselves punk appeared, and I really enjoyed it."

> *But I hated most rock 'n' roll, because it was about lame hippie stuff, and there really wasn't anyone describing our lives— which was McDonald's, beer, and TV reruns. Then [we] found the Dictators [a punk rock band], and we all got excited something was happening. The word "punk" seemed to sum up the thread that connected everything we liked—drunk, obnoxious, smart but not pretentious, absurd, funny, ironic, and things that appealed to the darker side.*
>
> —Legs McNeil, writer for *Punk* magazine

"After a while I started reading about actual punk bands," Lydia says, "and started doing my research. It was weird. I grew up in a rural area, and I didn't really have a lot of access to records or anything like that. So I started out reading books, like *Please Kill Me,* which is an oral history of punk with lots of interviews from various punk rockers, and the one that stood out to me was Richard Hell, as a poet mostly, when I was younger.

"And then when I moved to the 'big city,' there was a record shop that I used to go to where I picked out random punk records and listened to them. And there was a bar where I would play shows.

"My parents have always been supportive of me. But I did have a crappy punk band that made my dad a little angry when I was a teenager. He was like, 'What are you doing with your talent?'"

I mean I could deal with the same matters that I'd be sweating over alone in my room, to put out little mimeograph magazines [of poetry] that five people would ever see. And we definitely thought we were as cool as the next people, so why not go out there and sell it?

—Richard Hell, punk musician

Question: What were some of these punk bands that you were into?

Lydia: The Stooges, Black Flag, and some raunchier stuff. GG Allin I was really into.... And GG Allin actually has a lot of country influence in his music.... The Mullens. Catholic Girls was not really a punk band, but they sort of had that punk edge.

ॐ∧ॐ

GG Allin was, to say the least, outrageous. Onstage he engaged in self-mutilation, and before performances he ate laxatives so he could defecate as part of his act. He was addicted to heroin and alcohol and abused other drugs. His music was usually poorly recorded and produced, and his small fan base attracted mainly a cult following. Interestingly, he idolized country music legend Hank Williams. He saw him as an outsider like himself, one who overmedicated, disdained possessions, toured ceaselessly, and burned, burned, burned with a passion.

GG Allin's last show was in June 1993 at a small club in Manhattan. As he performed he covered himself in his own blood and feces. When the power went out onstage, he strode naked into the street before putting on shorts and walking through the neighborhood with his fans tagging along. Later that night, at a party, he overdosed on heroin and died.

Question: How did you get into GG Allin?

Lydia: When I met my first boyfriend, he was playing an open mike, and he and his cousin were playing GG Allin covers on acoustic guitars. I had never heard anything like that before; it was so vulgar and so terrible, and my life up until then had been Catholic church, homeschool, and nice gal. It was just the complete opposite from everything I had ever liked, and when you're a teenager you just want to be really gross and awful sometimes. I just wanted to piss everybody off.

So, yeah, I started listening to that as a mixture of [wanting to score points with] my boyfriend and also [feeling] that I had something that was mine. Certainly, my parents wouldn't appreciate it. I listen to GG Allin now and I can't even stomach it. I have to turn it off. It's just interesting to think of myself as a teenager thinking I was so badass.

The Dictators lived in the Bronx and hardly hung out. And it seemed like everyone but me and Joey [Ramone] was a junkie. So punk, the entire movement, seemed like our own little in-joke and destined to stay that way.

—Legs McNeil, writer for *Punk* magazine

But "punk"—I loved it, because it meant to me a derisory word for a young, no count piece of shit. And then from [William S.] Burroughs's [novel] Junky—*you know, there's that great scene where William and Roy, the sailor, are rolling the lushes in the subway and there's two young punks. They cross over and they give Roy a lot of shit, and Roy says, "Fucking punks think it's a joke...."*

—James Grauerholz, former manager of novelist William Burroughs

While Lydia was moving through her GG Allin phase, and also diversifying her musical tastes by getting into other genres, she began performing in bars. She wasn't even eighteen at that point, but her dad helped her by playing drums and using his contacts to book gigs. "Just tell everybody you're eighteen," he said to her.

Lydia looks so young even today, I can't imagine anyone falling for the story about her false age, and she agrees. "I don't think they believed me," she says. "But they let me in anyway.... It was probably a lot of pervy men who wanted to think I was eighteen," she says with a laugh.

Question: You wrote a song, "Always Lose," and it's about how you always lose with men, which obviously isn't true today since you're married. You are writing about how the lover you are with tonight came from the corner store. You were seventeen when you wrote that song.... I'm trying to find out, where does that come from at such a young age?

Lydia: The starting point for the music is I was meeting a different kind of guy for that age than most people. Some lyrics are for rhyme. But all of my songs were very autobiographical, probably even more so when I was younger. I was in love with this rock 'n' roll guy that blew me off for many years, so that was my heartbroken song—much like many of those songs on that album [*The Only Man*].

> *Your man sure does look good in those cowboy boots,*
> *And the way he does his hair is just turning me on.*
> *Well, I saw him staring at me, but don't worry none....*
> *So I guess I could try to take him from you,*
> *But don't bother watching your back because I always lose.*
>
> "Always Lose"
> From *The Only Man*

Question: What do you think of the current Nashville music scene?

Lydia: Obviously it's a mixed bag. There are people in Nashville who are doing great things and making music with some integrity. But for me, anytime I've been there, it's generally been hard for me to connect with the scene. The Nashville sound nowadays is something like you would see on *American Idol,* sort of the Carrie Underwood type. When I was making my first album, the producers were trying to get the Nashville sound very polished and neat and clean and not really what I would think of as rootsy or raw or anything like that.

That CD, *The Only Man* (2010), does by and large project a polished style. Still, it veers from anything coming out of Music Row and shows glimmers of Lydia's more punk-infused second album. There's plenty of fiddle and banjo, to the extent that I asked her if she had been influenced by bluegrass music. "I don't have much knowledge of it," she told me. "I enjoy some of it, but it's never been a huge goal for me. A lot of that was the production. But a lot of times when I do play acoustically, people say, 'Well, that's not country, that's bluegrass.'"

She says "fuck" several times on the CD and includes the track "Girls Suck," in which she sings about blow jobs. Perhaps meant to be sensational, or at least risqué, the tune seems to reflect Lydia's adolescent desire to be "gross at times," maybe even a bit GG Allin lyrically, and it doesn't come off well. In fact, although "Always Lose" displays solid songwriting, the other tracks lack what Lydia really needed: not a contrived Nashville polish, but the polish that comes from experience and discernment.

Lydia's music career got a big boost when she signed with a prominent independent label, Bloodshot Records. The opportunity developed when her manager forwarded a recording of her work to the company. "The owner sent me an e-mail the next day," she says.

"I thought it was just a Bloodshot mailing list, so I was really shocked when I opened it and it was actually about my music." She literally jumped up for joy.

A couple of months later, in March 2010, she went to play at South by Southwest, a huge music festival (with bands from around the world) held annually in Austin, Texas. Executives from Bloodshot came to see her and liked her show. "We kept in touch for about a year or so before we started negotiating a contract," she says. That deal was completed in January 2011.

So far she enjoys her relationship with Bloodshot. "My last album [*Indestructible Machine,* released in 2011] was pretty much all me," she says, "with some help from the engineer." The record company had a few suggestions, such as "we don't like this song, or this song sounds too much like this other song so it needs to be cut."

Yet, thankfully, Bloodshot has allowed her the freedom to do with her music as she wants, and this distances her from the constraints imposed on artists who are a part of the Nashville money machine. Moreover, it allows her to be honest with her songwriting and with her performances.

Question: Has this thought ever crossed your mind: Maybe I can temper my music or change it in some way that would make it more accessible to today's wider audience? Or is that something that you would not want to do?

Lydia: Yeah, I don't think that's something I ever *could do*. It's hard for me to write anything but what I was already going to write. It's whatever comes out of me, so the only way I can think of to sell out in that regard would be to team up with some big-shot songwriters and producers, and that just doesn't seem satisfying to me at all.

When Lydia says, "It's hard for me to write anything but what I was already going to write," she is referring to what flows from *her* heart and *her* emotions, and the world be damned. They are usually intertwined in her work and are inseparable. Both of her CDs, *The Only Man* and *Indestructible Machine,* resonate in that way.

> *How many women does a man need?*
> *How many does it take to make him happy?...*
> *Every man seems to walk out on his woman.*
> > "How Many Women"
> > From *Indestructible Machine*

> *Each time somebody told me I had more than enough*
> *I just said, "Fuck it" and poured myself one more glass.*
> > "Back on the Bottle"
> > From *The Only Man*

> *I might be really pure,*
> *Or I might just be a whore.*
> *Lover, please let me leave.*
> > "Let Me Leave"
> > From *The Only Man*

> *Though you might go to church, bow your head and pray,*
> *That ain't always good enough to get you through the day....*
> *And if they look down on you, don't you know it's true,*
> *Jesus was a wino too....*
> > "Jesus Was a Wino"
> > From *Indestructible Machine*

Her song "Do Right," on *Indestructible Machine,* delves into her upbringing when she sings: "'Cause my daddy was a preacher, but he was a junkie too/I grew up on whiskey and God, so I'm a little bit confused/I didn't know it was so easy to let this world get its hooks in you."

That's a harsh assessment, both of her dad and of her life, as she mixes the profane—whiskey—with the religious—God. I at first thought that this stark depiction of her father was an exaggeration, but it wasn't. And I should have known better, for Lydia works within the Outlaw characteristic of shooting straight from the hip. So I asked her about the story behind the lyrics, and she told me that in the years before she was born, back in the 1970s and 1980s, her dad was indeed a junkie, or as she put it, "a straight-up junkie." When she was little, he was a preacher in the Presbyterian church, and she was prohibited from listening to rock music or trick or treating for Halloween. That didn't last long, however, because a conflict within the church caused him to leave it.

Her honesty comes through again in her song "Learn to Say No," from the same CD. "I wrote it when I was going through a bizarre time," she says. "I felt alienated from everybody because I had just moved in with my boyfriend [now husband], but he was working... and I was the unemployed loser girlfriend sitting around the house all day in this crappy neighborhood, and I never wanted to go anywhere because it was scary and there was a gang. So I didn't ever want to leave the house,... and I was examining my life and thinking about what the hell I was doing. Everybody thought that I was being an asshole because I didn't have a job.

"In particular it's about a social anxiety I had my entire life and [about my] drinking to become more social and outgoing, and [then] pushing it too far."

Question: Do you think you have retreated from that some?

Lydia: To some extent, but I still rely on alcohol to carry me through, especially shows, the whole social aspect of playing a show.

Not stage fright, I don't have a problem with that, but talking to fans and things like that.

> *Like an animal, I cannot seem to leave*
> *My house without shitting myself instantly.*
> *I can't go anywhere without being three sheets,*
> *I guess I'll always be this goddamn unhappy.*
> *Someday I'll learn what it's like to say no.*
>
> "Learn to Say No"
> From *Indestructible Machine*

Question: Is your music in any way cathartic for you?

Lydia: I write things in a state of emotional turmoil. I write as quickly as possible so all the original emotions are still there. I definitely use as much of my anger and pain as possible.

Question: The song "Crazy" that you do, which is a relationship song that involves heavy drinking,... was that a big part of your life at the time you were writing that song?

Lydia: That was a song about having a crush on somebody and being unable to keep it secret, and the way I tend to throw myself at people and scare them away. That's what that song was about and one person in particular I flung myself at in a moment of drunkenness. It's very romantic. [*Laughter.*] And I was shot down, so I wrote that song about it.

Another track on *Indestructible Machine,* "Steve Earle," tells of an amusing event in Lydia's career that involves the name and fame of that alternative country artist. It began when a guy in Columbus read about Lydia in a local newspaper and concluded that she was cool and talented. As a result he began showing up at her shows. Eventually he cornered her and said: "We need to write songs together. I'm the Steve Earle of Columbus, and you could be my songwriting partner."

One night, when Lydia and her band mates were laughing about the incident, they started calling the fan Steve Earle, and Lydia joked with them that "Steve Earle was really stalking me." She then went home, sat down, and the song "popped into my head."

> *He read an article that said I like to do cocaine,*
> *And now he comes to all my shows and says if I need some*
>   *he'll pay.*
> *He won't stop coming, and I'm not sure how to blow him off.*
> *He stands outside my window until I have to call the cops....*
> *Steve Earle won't stop calling me,*
> *Steve Earle.*
> *He says he isn't hitting on me; he just wants to write some*
>   *songs....*
>
> "Steve Earle"
> From Indestructible Machine

Question: This Outlaw country is male-dominant. What do you think a woman artist can add to it in terms of a perspective that these guys perhaps are not doing?

Lydia: Women have a different set of problems and a different set of feistiness. They can introduce different emotions to people. But country is written from a down-and-out, everyday workingman's/-woman's perspective, so it's hard to say if there's a huge difference. Definitely I think that women just have different troubles.... Maybe women can just give men more of an idea of what assholes they [men] can be. [*Laughter.*]

The infatuated, Lydia-imbibing "Steve Earle" has moved on to places unknown. Despite the departure, and the loss of a potentially drunk and strange songwriter, Lydia says that she thinks her career is moving in the right direction. "I want to reach a wider audience," she admits, "and be able to pay some bills." But she has no desire to become a supplicant at the gilded door of some Music Row studio. "I want to stay at this independent level," she says, "where I have all of this creative control. But I would definitely like to be a little more of a household name, if I can manage it."

It all must begin somewhere. Richard Hell once recounted in an interview how he and his punk band got their start: he decided to find a bar in New York City where there was nothing happening. He would get permission to charge a door price but allow the bar owner to let in for free any of the regular customers. This way, he concluded, the owner would have nothing to lose and, really, everything to gain since the music would likely draw at least a few additional people who would spend money on drinks. (Apparently Hell never considered that his music might actually drive some people away.)

The place they found: CBGB. Located in the Bowery and shoe-horned into a row of stores, the bar was owned by Hilly Kristal. When Hell asked him what the letters stood for, Kristal said: "Country, blue-grass, and blues." Hell responded by saying: "'Oh yeah, we play a little of that, a little rock, a little country, a little blues, a little bluegrass.'" In time CBGB became one of the premier spots for punk bands, and before it closed in 2006, it earned a legendary place in the annals of punk history.

And so the fans came. Punk didn't *change to suit them*; instead *they found punk*. Three chords and two-minute songs. Fast, faster, and fastest. Loud, louder, and loudest. When the seekers find Lydia, they will discover punk chords, punk power, and country roots.

Her *Indestructible Machine* absolutely sizzles with all of this, like an egg cracked open on the burner of punk, sautéed in the oils of country, and served hot side up.

Let whiskey and her music kick your ass. Get you right. Give it all. All she's got.

Get soaked. With the way she sings. Brings pop to its knees. Snares. Guitar on speed. Fast, faster. Fastest.

What a *good* way to go. What a *good* way to go.

The seekers will find an edginess, as in the era of Loretta Lynn; a commitment, as in the era of Dolly Parton; and, above all, an honesty, as in the new era of Lydia Loveless.

> *If you really want to raise your voice to me,*
> *That's going to change how I feel about you, buddy,*
> *But it won't change me.*
>
> "Can't Change Me"
> From *Indestructible Machine*

Lydia Loveless, Secret Stages Festival, Birmingham, AL (2012)

INTERLUDE: BLUES AND YELLOWS

By Neil Hamilton

If you ever left me, I'd be torn and shorn and thrown into someplace
Where I'd toss away the cross and tell my Jesus to take me home
    in disgrace.

Nothing could remove the blues but the yellows,
Painted not by numbers but by desire.
Nothing could hurt the yellows but the blues,
And then all hope would expire.

If you ever left me, I'd be torn and shorn and thrown into some pit,
Where the pendulum would cut my body and bleed me, no spear
    at the rib.

J. B. Beverley, Drunken Horse Pub, Fayetteville, NC (2013)

CHAPTER 22

J. B. BEVERLEY

Dark Bar and a Jukebox

I don't need me no Opry,
I don't need Music Row.
Just six strings and some heartache,
And I'll be good to go.
"DARK BAR AND A JUKEBOX"
FROM DARK BAR AND A JUKEBOX

ound dog and a pig. I had just pulled up to the Rebel Roots Studio outside of Fayetteville, North Carolina, where I was to meet Outlaw artist J.B. Beverley. My back was aching a bit and my eyes were bloodshot—not from the pleasant metabolic effect of alcohol pumping through my bloodstream, or the insouciant presence of ganja enveloping my brain, but from a twelve-hour drive in a Honda Civic with my vision restricted by the seemingly endless line of asphalt— doing the white line, highway style.

There behind a modest house, which was behind several other modest houses, stood the studio, and as I got out from my car and wandered towards the building I was greeted warmly by Susan Thrailkill, the wife of Buck Thrailkill, who is a roots country musician and, with J.B. Beverley, owns Rebel Roots. (Susan and Buck run something of a hostel for musicians, a way to get them over the hump to the next town, the next destination in life, the next stirrup on the half-ridden dream.)That's when I saw the hound dog and the pig, both of whom were wandering near the building—which had a woodsy rustic appearance—possessing my mind, and taking me back to the days of the Buck Owens-led TV show *Hee Haw.*

My immersion into the past was reinforced by the presence of several artists who were standing outside with guitars, banjos, and a standup bass, getting ready to begin a good ol' down country jam. It was with this group that I met J.B. He and I had talked at length on the phone before, but never face to face. He's a big guy, with long hair tied back into a ponytail, a forceful voice punctuated by laughter . . . and he's a talker. Quite a talker. It takes little prodding to get J.B. to converse, and he projects a comfortable atmosphere, yet one akin to the old saying "trust but verify."

Although the weather was cold, with patches of snow here and there on the ground, the sun was shining. There was nothing of the brooding atmosphere provided by the title of and the imagery behind J.B.'s CD *Dark Bar and a Jukebox* (2006). I had never gone out drinking with J.B.—although I would do so later that night—but when, months earlier, I had first pictured him in my mind it was in a situation similar to what we see on the CD cover: a forlorn figure sitting tucked away in the corner of a honky tonk, his back towards a jukebox, the lights turned low, a cigarette in hand, and a half-empty mug of beer in front of him as he listens pensively and melancholically to the music.

Fearless in his commitment to roots country as the "real country," J.B. declares at his web site: "All good music comes down to two things—three chords and the truth." He also states that Nashville pop has come to dominate country under the leadership of "the image-consumed, money-making monster of the corporate music industry." That last comment presents a populist critique that many an Outlaw would cringe at when applied to the economy as a whole (given their conservatism) but embraces when applied to Music Row.

J. B. represents the "little guy"—the Outlaw artist—against the corporate monolith as he's a self-sufficient music man who records, produces, and markets what he does without relying on an outside label. As he does so, he reaches out to the "little guy" in the honky tonk: the common Joe searching for music that touches his soul more than it does his wallet. And that happens because J.B. has connected himself to country's roots and to his inner heart. I asked J.B. if his musical home was indeed in that dark bar and by a jukebox. He replied: "I certainly wanted that record . . . to evoke or speak to those sitting in such a place."

And by "such a place," he means not just the physical location but also the mental one. I know what he's saying: I have been there, feeling so lonely and so low that I thought I would never again see the light of day. Clearly, anyone who has been in that situation, or who can empathize with somebody who has been there, can relate to J. B.'s music.

Although only in his mid-thirties, J. B. has been playing honky-tonk for many years. He says that he didn't grow up in a privileged family, and as a kid he wasn't the best student. In fact, he says, "I was a bit of a fuck up." He spent less time around books and more around card tables and pool halls. "I spent a lot of time getting in fights," he recalls. "I was never a bully, but trouble always found me, and I often had to fight my way out of it."

J. B.'s first exposure to country occurred in his childhood when he would go over to his Uncle Bill's house and listen to the songs of Hanks Williams and Patsy Cline. But he also got into Elvis Presley, Chuck Berry, and Jerry Lee Lewis, and into bluegrass and jazz. Ultimately Hank, along with Jimmie Rodgers and Johnny Cash, became the biggest influences on his music.

J. B.'s dad played string instruments as a hobby, especially the flat top guitar, and his mom sang professionally in a five-piece pop-music band that toured Virginia. J. B. himself started playing the drums in his early teens and at age 15 learned a few power chords on the way to becoming the picker that he is today. He went into a punk rock teen rebellion stage, but then re-discovered those early artists he had listened to, including the ones he had heard at his Uncle Bill's.

He turned eighteen with little money, no job, no girlfriend, and a limited social life. "All I really had was whatever means I had to rustle up an income for myself," he says, "be it at a restaurant or as a bike messenger, nights at the card table or billiards hall or whatever, selling fucking pot, all that kind of stuff."

But he also had his guitar and fortunately it provided more than a musical outlet: it was a friendly companion in a world where he often felt estranged. Moreover, his ancestral and musical roots intertwined to form a rich background for his songwriting. His dad's family came from Wise County, Virginia, home of several early country artists, including the Carter family. J. B. says: "I'm actually related to the Carters. I didn't know it until a couple of years ago. My dad started pulling down family tree records, and there's a direct line of descendants."

J. B. likens his teenage musical desire to that of the Carters and the father of country music, Jimmie Rodgers. "I wouldn't want to compare myself to them [in terms of musical ability]," he says, "but as far as what took them to Bristol, Tennessee, [as recording pioneers in 1927] with that little fire inside that said, 'I'm going to do this because that's all I can do,' in that sense, yes, I'm no different. There's two kinds of people in country music: there's people who find it, and there's people who it finds. I'm one of the people that it found." Almost mournfully he adds: "I didn't really have any choice. This is all I've ever had. I've never been married, I don't have any children."

> *The wind is whipping through the trees*
> *Like a train through this old town.*
> *And now that everybody's gone,*
> *That heartache's come around.*
> *Now the moon just will not shine,*
> *And I can't see the stars,*
> *I got nothing to think about except this broken heart.*
> "Wayward Drifter"
> From *Dark Bar and a Jukebox*

When J. B. went into his teen punk rebellion he took to listening to the Misfits, Motorhead, and Black Flag, and to spiking his hair, wearing leather jackets, and dangling cigarettes from his mouth. J.B. named his first band the Bad Habits, and in the mid-1990s, they built a credible following in the Washington, D.C. area. But when their bass player overdosed on drugs and died, the tragedy so shook up the band members that they called it quits.

J. B. then became the front man for another punk band, the Murder Junkies, before returning to a more intimate connection with his country roots in 1999 by forming the Wayward Drifters. While J.B. split his time between the two bands, he also worked at odd jobs and, primarily between 1999 and 2001, took to traveling the country as a vagabond exploring life's complexities. "I always wanted to see the world and had to find a way to do it," he says.

> *I've been sitting here all night long*
> *Singing these old sad songs,*
> *Wondering how I wound up on this road.*
> "Lonesome, Loaded and Cold"
> From *Dark Bar and a Jukebox*

Like Jimmie Rodgers, J. B. became acquainted with the rails. He didn't work on them as had the father of country music many years before; instead, he lived the hobo life. As he traveled he hopped on and off freight trains, learning how to survive in the countryside and where to go in the city in order to get by. (J. B.'s song "Gonna' Ride a Train" tells about how he met an old hobo who spun yarns that attracted J. B. to the wandering scene.)

J. B. wrote the first songs for the Wayward Drifters while on those trains. "I love Bob Wills [the master of Texas swing]," J.B. says, who adds that it's important for music to move and not just sit like a flat tire stuck on a rutted road. "You can still have rootsy music and a pretty traditional sound and not necessarily swing," he says. "Especially as country music evolved and progressed, or got more progressive, that element got lost. Country became much more rock influenced and blues influenced in a way, and it lost that element [of swing]."

Swing has been one of the underpinnings of the Wayward Drifters, for which J. B. uses no drummer, but employs a guitar, a standup bass, and an additional string instrument, usually a banjo or a fiddle. He performs in the mold of another alternative country artist, Wayne Hancock, and the two men have become friends. J. B. recalls, "It was meeting Wayne that showed me you could still make this kind of music, and you don't have to be some throwback, affected retro vaudevillian-type act. You can be current and still have that kind of tradition."

Question: Where did you meet him?

J. B. I met Wayne outside of a hotel, right outside Washington, D.C., when I was 19 years old. It was 1996. That chance encounter changed my life. As a matter of fact, I tell the story in great detail in a book I'm writing and I would be happy to let you basically copy and paste [it]…

Here's how J. B. recounts it in his work *Chase Down these Blues*:

After settling back in at home, I found myself working odd jobs, and pretty much hating life. I got myself a long-term room at some dive motel that used to sit on route 355 in Maryland. The motel is no longer there, but it was a spooky old unkempt building that I never felt comfortable in. Their weekly rates were something like $175, and I was easily able to survive there on my odd-job money and whatever else I could hustle up.…

On a particularly sunny fall day, I left my room to go get a pack of cigarettes down the street . . . . As I stepped outside, I walked past the lobby and noticed a young man standing by the door as though he was waiting for someone. He had his hair in an almost pompadour-like arrangement, with a bowling shirt and some nice boots on. At a glance, I could tell he was a musician. I walked over to him and looked him up and down. The stranger smiled at me and said hello.

"Something tells me that you are a musician?" I asked with a smile. The stranger turned to me and smiled.

"Sure am, brother!" he said with a confident grin

"What kind of music do you play, Rockabilly?" I asked, noting in my mind his hair and bowling shirt. The stranger smiled again and scanned the parking lot as he spoke.

"Some folks call it rockabilly," he began. "But it's more a mixture of honky-tonk, blues, western swing, and other traditional American music," he said with a nod. Was he serious? Honky-tonk? Western Swing? Traditional American Music? I raised my brow and leaned in toward the stranger.

"Who plays *that* kind of music *today*?" I asked with a grin. The stranger looked up at me with serious eyes.

"I sure do!" the stranger proclaimed with pride. I leaned in even closer and extended my hand.

"I'm J.B.," I said, taking his hand.

"Pleased to meet you, J.B.," the stranger said. "I'm Wayne Hancock," he said as we finished our handshake. Upon releasing my hand, Wayne reached into his bag and pulled out a little 7" 45 record. The Ridgetop Westernaires was the name of Wayne's band, and the songs listed on the back were "Lookin' for Better Days" b/w "Johnson City."...

Wayne left me knowing very little about him after that first encounter. All that I knew was that he played traditional music, and that he was from Texas. I sure didn't know it that day, but meeting Wayne Hancock proved to be one of the most important things that ever happened to me.

From:

Chase Down These Blues: Ten Years of Hardcore Honky-Tonkin' with The Wayward Drifters. Copyright © 2011 by J.B. Beverley.

When J. B. refers to chasing down the blues, he means it in two ways: the blues in his life and the blues in country music. He incorporates a lot of the blues genre in what he writes and sings, and it comes across particularly strong in his song "Walk across Texas." J. B. told me: "I love old Mississippi Delta blues. Skip James was a huge hero and influence of mine. And the Piedmont blues and old time music . . . Warner Williams was like my mentor. I used to pick with Warner, an old blues man. I picked with Warner every weekend for years when I was cutting my teeth up in Maryland. And guys like Doc Watson. I love people who tow that line; I love the artists who prove that there's really no separation between blues music and country music, or what I'm calling hillbilly music. Hillbilly music ain't shit but white people singing the blues, man. That's all it is."

That observation has been made before by other artists, but J.B. drove it home with a reference to the great African American bluesman Ray Charles. "[He] said it best when he duetted with Willie Nelson," J. B. observed. "He caught some flak for 'Why are you playing all this country shit?' Ray Charles was like, 'Look, I'm fucking blind. I don't see color. I only hear inference. To me, country music is poor white folks singing the blues.' God bless Ray Charles's observation, but it's true."

J. B. went on to say: "Listen to Hank Williams and you hear blues; listen to Skip James, and you hear hillbilly music. Listen to 'Drunken Spree,' by Skip James. It's on his original 1931 recordings; anything he may have recut in the Sixties doesn't count. Listen to that earliest recording of 'Drunken Spree' from the thirties, and then tell me if you don't hear that banjo roll on that damn guitar." J. B. then proceeded to find a copy of the recording and play it for me.

"People don't realize that back in the turn of the century, and in the 20's and 30's, and even up through the 50's, poor white folks and poor black folks, that's one thing they always shared was music and musical folklore. There's so much overlap there, it's not even funny. I don't denote a difference. To me it's the same."

Black blues and white country "the same." Maybe a bit overdrawn for the point, but it contains considerable truth. He's right about Hank Williams, and the blues can also be found in the music of Jimmie Rodgers and the Carter family. While Appalachia has its own historical white culture, it was no isolated island in the Piedmont and Tidewater of the South. As the mountain rivers flowed towards the Atlantic and the Gulf, the musical waters flowed, too, *but also uphill*, from the slave plantations and the black shanties found in the flatlands, and only a person blind to Southern cultural development would fail to see this.

Question: Which leads me to the question of the influence on you of Elvis Presley, especially given the influence on him of black musicians.

J. B. I know I'm going to catch shit for this, but Elvis's influence was minimal. I remember hearing Elvis as a kid, I liked him as a child, but people don't realize that outside of his earliest recordings for Sun, he was very manufactured. Elvis went from being the first rock star to the first pop star inside of five years. I respect Elvis. I think he had a great voice. I respect him, but I would not say that he had a very dramatic influence on me as a musician. Now Gene Vincent, on the other hand, I could talk to you about for hours.

Gene Vincent had none of Presley's good looks. Nor did he have Presley's stage presence—partly because his left leg had been so maimed in a motorcycle accident that he had to bind it together in a steel sheath. But in 1956 he had a hit rockabilly record, "Be-Bop-A-Lula." Three years later he was projecting a tough-guy image by wearing a black leather jacket and gloves. In 1960 he was involved in a high-speed traffic accident in England in which he broke his ribs and collarbone (and lost his best friend and fellow rock 'n' roll trailblazer Eddie Cochran). Vincent's musical contributions treated him better, however, by earning him membership in both the Rock and Roll Hall of Fame and the Rockabilly Hall of Fame.

"I'll put it to you like this, man," J. B. says. "You know that whole argument about the Beatles and the Stones? Even though this wasn't true, the Beatles looked kind of staged and prep-schoolish compared to the Stones, who looked like the kind of guys loitering outside the pool hall, getting ready to abduct your daughter. That's the difference. For as foreboding as [Presley] was initially to middle America, [he] became the first pop star. Presley was on the cover of *Teen Magazine*, whereas Gene Vincent was gnarly looking, man. Gene Vincent was a scrapper. Gene Vincent had a bum leg; he was part crippled. You talk about an intimidating, imposing man, I think up until Lyle Lovett came around, Gene Vincent was the ugliest motherfucker who ever played music. [*Laughter.*]

But again, raw and real. That's what I always respect. I like the guys who do it from the fucking gut, from the heart."

J. B. likes Johnny Cash for having the same sensibility and for having that intense love for music. "Johnny Cash is much like Hank Williams, he's sacred ground to me," J. B. says. "[He's] a huge influence on both my musical and lyrical structure. I learned how to play fun-loving bass-line picking by listening to Johnny Cash. The whole way that I play flat top guitar, I probably owe to Johnny Cash. He was one of the first artists that I heard that I really felt—again much like Hank—that he was really baring his spirit and that there was no affectation. To me that's the highest standard of quality."

Question: How about Willie Nelson?

J. B. I'll tell you where Willie inspired me the most. When I was a little boy I heard his version of the "City of New Orleans".... Willie has one of the most distinct voices you could ever hear in a singer. You hear Willie and there is no doubt who it is, and nobody sounded like him.

Question: And Waylon Jennings?

J. B. Waylon's been a huge influence on me. He's just an all-around class act, man, and all-around real-deal musician. Versatile, tender yet tough. Waylon was the real-deal good ol' boy, and that's part of the reason he had to go against the grain. He was too country for Nashville too, and he proved it repeatedly. Also Waylon's the one that reinvented the fucking wheel as far as country's concerned. He's the one that put some boogie-woogie and some balls into something that was becoming really stale.... When you hear all of that orchestral accompaniment and all of a sudden there's Waylon and his band,... it was an unbelievable musical force.

In addition to the Wayward Drifters, J. B. recently has returned to punk with his band the Little White Pills (formed in 2002). That might seem to go against his shift to roots country. But it really doesn't for two reasons. First, as a punk musician J. B. never lost sight of the originality, the creativity, and the daring found in Hank Williams and the 1970s Outlaws. Second, his punk showed the same alienation and sense of disgust with the corporate music kingpins who were engaging in prostate exams gone wild against real art.

In 2003 the Little White Pills issued their self-produced CD *Live at the Velvet Lounge.* They drew some large crowds in and near Baltimore but split up in 2006. The band has since reformed twice, and in its latest reincarnation has gone to work on a double CD.

In J. B.'s world punk and country are cross thatched, and while the sound of the Little White Pills and the Wayward Drifters stand apart from each other, the attitude merges. J. B. makes this point when he says: "A song like 'Don't Need No One,' on my last record, that's a song that my punk rock band's been doing. I wrote it years ago for that band, and I just turned it into a bluegrass version of a punk song."

There's quite a bit of populist sentiment in J. B.'s music, be it punk or country. There's that standing up for the little guy against the big guy, although, politically, in a nebulous way.

J. B. says: "I'm not lyrically saying, 'Society sucks, the government sucks,' and let's start a war. But I am standing up, and I'm acknowledging and embracing what I like, and I'm calling out that which I don't like. I'm crying a foul on certain social injustices. Over the years I've gotten a little bit more political on a couple of songs.

"For example, I wrote 'Blowing Down the Mountain' from the perspective of the big coal companies and their mountaintop removal stuff. [It's] about how I feel they look at hillbilly folk in Appalachia. I wrote it from the perspective of the company. The opening line is 'Over them hills we got our drills/We're blowing down the mountain/ We got the dynamite all set up right/We're blowing down the mountain/There's coal down there/Let's strip it bare/We're blowing down the mountain/Contract's signed, let's start on time/We're blowing down the mountain.' Then the next line is 'You sure look silly, you dumb hillbillies/While the money we're counting....

"I'm not political from the standpoint that I was in my first band, Bad Habits, you know, where I kind of stood up and was like 'Fuck the world, fuck the government, and let's raise hell.' It's more refined now; I'm older, I've been through more. I don't feel the need to stand up and point out things that obviously are fucked up. Anyone with a nickel's worth of common sense knows what's fucked up."

And what's fucked up to J. B. is that the little guy keeps getting the shaft, whether it be from the industrial companies in West Virginia or from the record studios in Nashville. You can serve corporate America as it demands, but it means giving up your soul, and it's sad that so many people are willing to pay that price.

He told me that he was angered by how economic monoliths hurt those beneath them. Coming from the Appalachians, the site of that extensive coal mining where the companies belittle and trample the hillbillies, he talked to me about the plight of families hurt by toxic runoff—how they had to endure, for example, the tragedy of women giving birth to stillborn babies.

J. B. *is the little guy*. He's the little guy worked over by bankers.

Question: You have a song, "Before They Get Those Cuffs on Me." How much is that autobiographical?

J. B. It was inspired by a trip to the credit union. I went into the credit union to inquire about a loan, and the guy told me, "Mr. Beverley, you don't own property, you don't have enough for collateral, your credit has been questionable in the past," etc. And I instantly made a joke. I looked at him, and I said, "If I had collateral and equity and money, would I be asking you guys to make me a loan?" He didn't see the humor in it, and he took a very judgmental and hostile disposition toward me, and I remember going back to my house and pacing the driveway, chain-smoking cigarettes, and being pissed off that I'd been disrespected like that and I should have knocked that guy out.

And J. B. *is the little guy* ignored by record companies and deciding to strike out on his own.

Question: Do you identify with the punk approach of we'll press our own records, we'll make our own T-shirts?

J. B. Absolutely. I do all my own artwork. I do all my own merchandise. I design my own shirts and my own album covers. I record myself, I mix myself, master myself, produce myself. I've run my own record label for eight years. I'm a self-contained fucking machine, man. I don't depend on any leg of the industry to do a fucking thing for me, and I'm proud of it.

That approach comes from J. B.'s Outlaw status. There's no room at the Music Row inn for J. B., and so he has even gone so far as to build his own recording studio. "I wanted a true home to record in," he writes at his website. "I got tired of being in commercial spaces, looking at the clock every few hours and thinking to myself, *We're going to owe this guy another few hundred bucks at the turn of the hour.*"

The country pop sound being poured from the big studios makes J. B. see bull-crazy red. "The crap I hear," he says, "makes Toby Keith look like fucking Willie Nelson. It's only gotten worse. That's the sad thing, when I hear Montgomery Gentry or Kenny Chesney or some of these new people that are half rapping. I'll give you a funny one. I pulled my fucking truck over to the side of the road when I first heard that International Harvester song. I got so pissed off and offended that

I couldn't believe my ears, man. I'm sitting there going, 'Who the fuck wrote this piece of shit?'"

Well, the answer, J. B., is that it took three guys to write an incredibly bad song: Jeffrey Steele, Shane Minor, and Danny Myrick. "International Harvester" was recorded by Craig Morgan. Released on the Broken Bow record label—home to country pop performer Jason Aldean—it was able to crack the *Billboard* Country Songs Top Ten. "International Harvester" represents country pop at its worst. Reprehensible for its insincerity and trite lyrics, I would say that it's to country what the song "Sugar, Sugar" by the Archies in the 1970s was to rock, but that would disparage "Sugar, Sugar" a bit too much.

"I'll sum up the problem with pop country for you in a heartbeat," J. B. says. "It's the same problem that you see with movies today. It ain't limited to country music, it's the music industry and it's the entertainment industry as a whole. Here's the problem: they try to make, as possible products, [those with] the most commercial appeal that caters to the widest demographic.

"But you lose art in there. You lose the value of substance. It becomes style over substance. It becomes fodder. It's no longer real at that point." Then he adds: "I'm not a stupid man; I realize they don't call it 'music art,' it's the 'music *business.*' You have to sell records. But the difference is, and what these idiots don't realize, is that there are people that want the real deal."

Question: In your song "Dark Bar and a Jukebox," you say that Toby Keith just don't cut it. Why doesn't he cut it for you?

J. B. Where Toby let me down, and where a lot of the pop country lets me down,... I mean, Toby Keith has a good voice, the guy can write a good song. I think he's a very dynamic entertainer. I mean, I've never seen him in concert, but I've seen footage of him live. He's got stage presence. The problem I have is when you step into a studio in Nashville by way of a major label, they tell you, "We're going to market you like this, so you have to stand like this and direct such and such like this, and we want you to lose that steel guitar in this song so we can bring in one of our session guitar players and an organist." They'll take a song you've written and they pretty much tell you how to play it.

And so when I heard that Toby Keith had gotten out of his contract, I forget the record company he was with, but when I heard that he was starting his own label to defy Nashville, I thought to myself, man, maybe this man might just play some real country. I knew he was capable of it. The problem is, what he did was start his own label and keep churning out this pop-type bubblegum bullshit with some of the same producer types in the industry that had pushed him into the corner to begin with.

That guy's certainly capable of being a real-deal country singer. I'll give you a perfect example: that song he wrote, "I Love This Bar".... When I hear the song, when I'm in a bar or something and it comes on the jukebox or on the sound system, I mean it's sad, not because it's an invalid song, but because it could be a great song, and it sounds like every other piece of shit in Nashville. That's why Toby doesn't cut it.

> *Give me a dark bar and a jukebox*
> *Over that radio.*
> *Yeah, Toby just don't cut it,*
> *Give me Haggard, give me Coe.*
> "Dark Bar and a Jukebox"
> From *Dark Bar and a Jukebox*

For all his railing against Nashville, J. B. knows his niche. He knows that while his fans care about him and what he has to say, Music Row doesn't give a shit. "As far as *Billboard* magazine is concerned, nobody knows who the fuck I am," he says. "So if I give Nashville the finger, outside [of] the devotees I've got in the underground, it doesn't make a difference."

If only more people could see that man sitting in the dark bar by the jukebox, they would see the neglected Outlaw. But Nashville keeps the lights dimmed low and the expectations even lower. "You ask why the pop thing has taken over and there's no real Outlaw order like there used to be," J. B. tells me, "well, my answer is the true Outlaws today are the people that the masses don't even know [are around]." He adds: "You know what the most common thing is that I have heard over the years of touring? The most common thing that I've heard over the years on the road has been people saying, 'Gee, I didn't know this kind of music still existed.'"

But that kind of music exists on J. B.'s two CDs with the Wayward Drifters. *Dark Bar and a Jukebox* reflects Texas swing with "Memories of You." Then there's the upbeat, rockabilly-style "Shoulda' Thought About It" that has J. B. hitting the road, or in this case the rails, that he has taken to in the past: "Now I'm gettin' on the train/Heading out of town/And don't come looking for me, baby/I won't be around." It's all "man punishing the woman by leaving (although ultimately biting off his nose to spite his face)" when J. B. adds to the lyrics: "You should've thought about it, mama, before you went and done me wrong." The song also displays guitars and banjo ablaze with fever-ish picking, and there's J. B. going into some Jimmie Rodgers-style yodeling at the end.

J. B.'s songs percolate with the themes of leaving, and drifting, and just going. J. B. embraces the age-old American penchant for physical mobility as a way to start over again, which once was one of the attractions of the Old West: that with each turn of the wagon wheel a person could leave behind personal grief and economic hardships and become, if not reborn, then restored. Of course, it's never a completely sweet deal. Moving means leaving friends behind and inviting loneliness; and constant leaving produces a broken, weary spirit.

J. B. begins *Watch America Roll By* (2009) with "Interstate Blues" and sets the tone for the album as one in which he rambles through the country by car, foot, and train. He cements this theme with the next song, "Watch America Roll By": "Well the sun is shining/And so am I/As we click off another mile.... Break out the stash/Put on some Johnny Cash/Let's watch America roll by." He turns more somber—spooky, even—with "End of the Road": "So when you hear that whistle blow/Said you'll hear why I have got to go/And I'll find you in the end, don't you know/I said I'll find you at the end of the road." Then J. B. gets on the "Drug Train": "Yeah, I'm on the drug train, mama, yes, indeed/I'm on the drug train, mama, trying to plant some seeds/Everything he knows he learned in them streets/How to do a little toke and to do a little line/Trying to find that homemade wine/All he knows it's just a matter of time."

J.B. says that sometimes he writes songs by picking up his guitar and finding out that "there is just something there." More often though a melody comes and sticks with him for weeks or even months. The melody for "Favorite Waste of Time" actually played over and over again in his mind for a year before he formalized it into a song. Once he finds a melody he waits for life experiences to give him the lyrics. Whether a song is any good, he says, is measured by the response he gets, most especially if it inspires someone else or gives them hope.

Three chords and the truth. If J. B. were punching those buttons on the jukebox, what would he likely play? His friend Wayne Hancock, of course. There would also be Bob Wills, Willie Nelson, Waylon Jennings, Johnny Cash, and David Allan Coe. It would be hard to fathom the jukebox containing records with Appalachian sounds or going all the way back to Jimmie Rodgers, but if they were there, J. B. would certainly play them.

Sadly, though, if J. B. were sitting in a modern bar and even able to find a jukebox, he wouldn't discover any of the names mentioned here. Instead there would be Taylor Swift, Lady Antebellum, and, yes, Toby Keith. The Outlaw, the honky-tonk, the roots country would be nowhere.

Thankfully for roots country fans, however, J. B. resides at Rebel Roots Studio, where we can find him in a business—if that is the correct word—so dedicated to music as an art that at any moment he and Buck Thrailkill might stop talking about recording schedules, grab their instruments, and just start picking—even if their only audience is themselves, the dog, and the pig.

This situation was reinforced for me when I first drove up to Rebel Roots and saw J. B., Buck, and the other musicians jamming, and again that night when they all got up on stage at a local bar and played their hearts out: J.B. on his acoustic guitar; Buck on his banjo; Adam Jones on upright bass; and Robert Norman on fiddle. Before the night was over they were joined by Shooter Jennings, Jake Cox, and Billy Don Burns (one of the original 1970s Outlaw heroes). J.B. had arranged the evening gig, but much of the music came forth spontaneously, and all of it came from what they felt inside themselves, from the musical spirit that moved them.

Because J.B. has as his comfort zone *Rebel Roots, and not Music Row*, he can draw deeply from his life on the rails, from his family roots, and from the genuine country music that has influenced him so much, and find a musical audience who appreciates his undaunted commitment. That, in the end, makes up the essence of Outlaw country: the sincerity that we all need and often find difficult to discover or pursue in a world where the marketplace demands our wallets and our souls. "If you're writing from the heart," J.B. told me, "you can't put a price tag on it."

I've seen the absurd,
Wrote some hits you've never heard,
'Cause I get no love from Nashville, Tennessee....
I can't afford to settle down and wed,
I've got to roam this ol' highway till I paint it red.
I could help Momma retire . . . If I ate some lead,
'Cause they'll only play my music when I'm dead.

"They'll Only Play My Music When I'm Dead"
From *Watch America Roll By*

J. B. Beverley, Drunken Horse Pub, Fayetteville, NC (2013)

Leroy Virgil, The Speakeasy, West Palm Beach, FL (2012)

CHAPTER 23

HELLBOUND GLORY

Lost Cause

There must be something wrong with you,
To want a man like me . . .
I'll just lead you astray,
'Cause that's just the life I lead. . .
I'm just a damaged good ol' boy,
With a self-destructive streak.
"LOST CAUSE"
FROM DAMAGED GOODS

It had been a long hard year of travel—some 18,000 miles—before
I arrived in West Palm Beach, Florida, for my Outlaw interview
with Leroy Virgil of the band Hellbound Glory. I found myself standing outside a small, grey brick building at a place called the Speak
Easy Bar, waiting for the band to show up while I was sweating under
the tropical sun.

When I learned that the band was running behind schedule, I decided to retreat to a nearby Italian restaurant to cool off and get something to eat. Through the front window I watched several surfer dudes ride by on their bicycles. The young men looked fit and tanned, and had long blonde hair that flowed across their chiseled shoulders. A few minutes later Hellbound Glory showed up. They arrived in a dirty brown, heavily dented van. As they exited from the side doors, they looked tired and as beat up as the vehicle itself. I had come to expect Outlaws to look this way from traveling mile after mile in cramped conditions, but Hellbound Glory sported a new version of rough: rough that had been roughed up.

I introduced myself to Leroy, and we agreed to go inside the bar for the interview. All of a sudden, I found myself in a maze—not the building itself, but a maze built by Leroy. He was a damaged man ("damaged goods," as he titles one of the band's CDs), and such men often erect walls and hope you get lost within them and never reach the center where truth resides, let alone discover the truth as to who they are. Leroy was hunkered behind such walls, and in front of the walls, he had built a moat, and in the moat he had placed sharks, and if you wanted to find any kind of bridge to let you into his maze and entitle you to search for his center, it would have to come through hard work or an unintended dropping of his guard.

Leroy, me, and a couple of his band mates sat on sofas in a cave-like room as seedy as some of the derelict buildings that can be found in their hometown of Reno, Nevada. As we passed around a joint, Leroy looked at me with suspicion and showed he was clearly uncomfortable with the whole interview scene.

In listening to the band's music, I was impressed by their creativity, but taken aback by the brooding, frequently drug-laden content of their lyrics. Outlaws sing about drugs, of course, but Hellbound

Glory sings about them *a lot*. While country pop bathes in streams of love, pickup trucks, dirt roads, and sentimental death throes meant to provoke crocodile tears, Hellbound Glory bathes in pot, coke, oxycodone, meth, heroin, various pain pills, and speed. That's just in three albums.

If their songs were autobiographical, I thought, this band has been living in a William S. Burroughs-type hell: a Naked Lunch stripped down to the bare essence of life lived as excess.

Question: How much of yourself do you put into your songs in terms of the lyrics?

Leroy: It happens, with the exception of the song "Hellbound Glory," but even that really happened. Some of it happened to people close to me and not me, though.

I started to ask him about the drugs. "You know you have quite a theme of drugs in there, and in most of those songs it seems as if the drug user is . . . their life is basically ruined." That caused Leroy's band mates to start wisecracking: "Maybe we should sing about the good side of drugs." "Maybe we can have Walt Disney . . ."

"Fuck, yeah," Leroy kicked in. "I should make songs about people dying and shit sound fun *and* sad. 'Knocked off the Horse,' [one of the band's songs] what a sick tale; what a fucking sad way to think about your friends. As that song was being recorded on the album, we got a call, 15 minutes later, that our buddy, he overdosed on heroin. [Leroy starts singing from a song made famous by Queen: "Another one bites the dust."] You know what I mean?" It is "sick," and the way Leroy was talking showed that he had some remorse for what he had written, but also that he couldn't help himself in writing it.

He paused and stared at me for a moment. Then he continued: "I grew up around junkies, dude. I grew up around drug addicts. I've been around drug addicts since the fucking day, the fucking day I was born; I've been around drug addicts. I've been a drug addict. I'm around drug addicts now."

> *Just out of rehab he'd been 28 days clean,*
> *A genuine certified recovered dope fiend.*
> *Just when we thought he'd put that drug all in his past,*
> *He walked on down to Broadway and that boy done relapsed.*
>> "Knocked Off the Horse"
>> From *Damaged Goods*

Leroy, who was raised mainly in Aberdeen, Washington, also sings that he was born "a bastard child." He says, however, that he knows and loves both his mom and his dad. I asked him for some details about what had happened.

Question: What were the circumstances?

Leroy: Dad liked young girls. Mom liked money. He had a couple of thousand pounds of marijuana. He came out to California to sell it. Here I am.

Leroy and his band like to call themselves "scumbags" and their music "scumbag country." They revel in the names and repeat them until they become a mantra and perhaps a self-fulfilling prophecy. To me, the word "scumbag," has nowhere near the panache as "Outlaw." I could see Time-Life books issuing a series on "famous American Outlaws"; I could not see such a series on "famous American scumbags." But maybe that's the point. Who needs Time-Life books?

"Why do you use the word "scumbag" in referring to yourselves?" I asked Leroy. He answered: "You take a name that someone calls you, and you adopt it for yourself, and of course, what worse thing can they call you?" He doesn't hesitate a second to add: "I'm a fucking proud scumbag. That's just part of Reno; that's what everyone calls each other. Fucking scumbag. 'Hey, scumbag? What's up scumbag?'

"Some people call us sleazebags, depending on the part of the country you're from," he added, while another band member chimed in, "scumbag is scummy as scum does." You name it, they say, and they've done it. But when I tried to pry into this Leroy said: "Let's leave it up to everyone's imagination. Scumbag fucking sounds cool, dude. Scumbag country."

When I kidded Leroy about how "scumbag" might start a whole new name for a kind of country music, he said: "That's why we have scumbag.com." And their first CD, *Scumbag Country,* released in 2008. It's a spirited, impressive entry that reveals the wealth of Leroy's musical likes and the influences on him by way of other artists. Rockabilly with a Junior Walker edge shines in "Hawaii Five-0" and "Get Your Shit and Go." In "I'll Be Your Rock," Leroy sings a sad drinking song—with the scumbag-style twist of willing to get drunk to be where he needs to be when his girlfriend gets drunk: "I'll be your rock at rock bottom/So you won't hit rock bottom alone," he sings and thus folds the lyric in on itself as traditional country songs often do.

He gets to the drug theme several times: in "Livin' This Way," he sings that the needle will do him in, that "I'm killing myself to be alive"; in "Chico's Train" he sings about Chico bringing in cocaine from Mexico (it's a faced-paced tune, tied to a train-like beat, or maybe it's like the fast pumping of blood through veins); in "Mickey Meth"—well, the title makes the song's contents self-evident; and in

"The Ballad of Scumbag Country," he tells about snorting coke in a bathroom stall.

That song, as does the entire CD, obviously flashes the band's scumbag credentials and makes it clear that Nashville would not want to deal with Hellbound Glory. In the lyrics, he also equates "scumbag" with "Outlaw," and says that making a lot of money would only attract him to excess and destroy him.

> *This song goes out to the scumbags,*
> *Just like every song I sing.*
> *It's just a song about this hard life we lead,*
> *Lord, Outlaws and scumbags like me.*
> *I'd never make it down to Nashville, Tennessee,*
> *'Cause they don't like my SCUMBAG songs.*
> "Ballad of Scumbag Country"
> From *Scumbag Country*

Carried along by a steel guitar, the song has an element of soulfulness to it more than boastful pride. The devil, after all, came to Leroy with a contract in hand—at least that's how he puts it in "Hellbound Glory."

Question: What pulled you to doing country music?

Leroy: It's just the type of songs I write. It's what comes natural. I wasn't taught to write country songs. It just happens.

Question: Were you ever in a rock band?

Leroy: I had rock bands, punk rock bands. Hard rock, punk, with a lot of country mixed up into that. When I was in a punk band, it was fucking big trouble, dude. We were a real punk rock band [meaning they were living the life of the songs]. I grew up around country music. I've liked Hank Williams Senior since I was eight years old.

My grandpa gave me his tape. I always liked him. [Hank's music] was also in a movie called *The Radio Flyer* . . . that [also] might have something to do with why I started liking Hank.

⁂

As I asked Leroy how long Hellbound Glory has been together, one of the band members said, "We're not so much a band as we're a fucking gang. There have been various characters who have come and gone, right Leroy?" To which Leroy smiled and replied, "I started Hellbound Glory about eight years ago. . . . You know like they say, the cream rises to the top, and I guess the scum does also."

Scumbag. Nashville beware. But wait. There's more to what Leroy thinks about Music Row, and while on the surface it sounds contradictory, ultimately it makes a lot of sense.

Question: How do you feel about what's going on with country music in Nashville today?

Leroy: We love it.

Question: Come on . . .

Leroy: "Honky Tonk Ba Donky Donk" [a song written by Jamey Johnson] I think is brilliant. It's like Roger Miller. [*Laughter*] It's like fucking Roger Miller. [Leroy starts singing the song, mockingly]. I'm completely fucking serious. We're going to cover that song . . . . We'll change it up and do it our own fucking way.

Question: You love Jason Aldean, then?

Leroy: No. I hate Jason Aldean. I can't stand him. That just sucks.

Question: Why does someone like Taylor Swift sell millions of records?

Leroy: She's a fucking talented girl . . . She's a talented girl writing her own songs, fucking doing her thing. I don't hold it against her. . .

Country music is so far removed from what is even my sphere, as far as what they call country music on the radio.

So Nashville is doing just what Nashville does. Taylor Swift is talented in doing what she does, which is to meet the demands of the pop song grinder. *But it doesn't fall within the realm of country.*

"What about alt country?" I asked him. "We're too alt for alt country," he says. "Excuse me," he says, and then goes and gets his guitar. I was beginning to understand a bit better how he wanted to communicate—music over the spoken word.

"Should I keep the recorder on?" I ask as he gets ready to play. "I don't give a shit," he says. "Post it on the Internet, do whatever you want with it."

He begins singing: "I'm just a cliché country singer, another mother fucker SCUMBAG hum dinger, flipping the world my middle finger, just like Johnny Cash." He continues: "Though it's all cliché, what the hell else could I say? Other than if you don't like me, you can kiss my ass . . . . If you're going to sing it proud, you've got to live it first."

Still singing he says, "As for Nashville, I don't need them. They can keep their trash, and I'll keep my freedom. To be a cliché country singer, another mother fucker SCUMBAG hum dinger, flipping the world my little finger and I'm trying to be like Johnny Cash."

So Nashville as country: *forget it.* The song came across with the tone that Leroy more often speaks with: somewhere between anger and petulance. He also snaps his responses and pushes his views with an insistent posture.

Question: How do these songs come to you? How do you do it?

Leroy: I just do it, I just get it done.

Question: Are you sitting with the band when they come to you? Are you sitting on the toilet?

Leroy: I'm sitting wherever . . . I woke up with some good shit today.

When I asked Leroy if he had played the song for many people, he answered defensively. "Of course," he said, "I've been playing it for everyone that would listen to it, since the day that I fucking wrote it."

Leroy counts Charley Pride, Lefty Frizzell, and Merle Haggard as the artists he has learned from. He likes them for their voices and their lyrics, and on the group's CD *Damaged Goods* (2011), he includes a Haggard song, "Livin' with the Shades Pulled Down." Leroy considers Hank Williams to have been "a great songwriter," and reaches into rockabilly with Buddy Holly and Elvis Presley—Hellbound Glory closes their CD *Old High and New Lows* [2010] with "I'm Leaving Now," a humorous rockabilly salute to Presley—and into rock with the Beatles, the Rolling Stones, and AC/DC; into punk with GG Allin; and into rap with Snoop Dog.

"You've got to learn from [all forms of music]," Leroy says. "How else are you going to have music that people want to listen to unless you listen a little bit to the music that everyone else likes?"

Question: You have recommended to me that I talk to Dale Watson. Why him when your music is so different from his?

Leroy: Dale Watson's music and our music is obviously different, but someone's got to preserve the roots of all this fucking music. Someone's got to piss on the roots, or else shit won't grow.

Question: You don't feel like you're pissing on Hank Williams, do you?

Leroy: No. Okay, let me rephrase that.

Question: You don't feel that you're pissing on Elvis Presley? Johnny Cash?

Leroy: No. I'm just doing whatever it takes to make them grow, to make it grow. Don't take it that way. I would never piss on any of those guys. Those guys are my fucking heroes. But when anyone calls certain bands "Outlaw," and they don't seem Outlaw to me, all of a sudden I don't want to be called a fucking Outlaw. I've painted myself into a corner, here . . .

Being misinterpreted might be something that Leroy worries about with interviews. His initial comment displays his tendency to shoot from the hip and his intent to project himself as a scumbag, but, as he clarified himself, he made it clear that he didn't mean any disrespect— he just wants to make Outlaw country, or roots country, get a bigger audience.

When I asked Leroy what would seem Outlaw to him, he gave me a quick, one-word answer: "me." When I didn't react, he thought some more about it, and continued, "Outlaw is a term that's been coopted by people who are not Outlaws. So I don't want to be associated with that shit." But he backtracks when I ask him how he feels about a radio station calling itself Outlaw. "I love it," he says. "I think it's great. Thank you for playing our music; please keep playing our music; Outlaw SiriusXM country; we love you; we think you're awesome. Mojo Nixon . . . fucking Elizabeth Cook; Shooter Jennings; you guys fucking rule."

Then he clarifies himself, and in doing so sounds like the other Outlaw artists that I interviewed when he says: "Let's not get too hung up on what we call this shit. I don't recall hearing them play Justin Moore . . . or who else they call fucking Outlaw these days. . . . Eric

Church, I don't hear them playing that much. It's a term that doesn't mean that much to me. We're scumbag country."

He was also sounding and acting more and more like David Allan Coe: throw comments out there, and see how they hit the wall and whether they stick to it. But whether you agree with *what* he has to say, or *how* he says it, he speaks with conviction. With that in mind, towards Coe he feels like a brother in arms.

Question: You guys go back to the Outlaws of the 1970s?

Leroy: They all had different personality types . . . Waylon was just a bunch of badass. . . . Willie is like the godfather of what I consider scumbag country. David Allan Coe is more punk rock than most of the punk rock you'll hear. He's just as punk rock as the fucking Sex Pistols. He's just as punk rock as Black Flag. David Allan Coe: scumbag. The godfather of scumbag country. Not even the Outlaws wanted to associate with David Allan Coe; consider us like him.

Consider us like him. Leroy pushes the point hard. No one wants to hang out with them. You should stay away from the scumbags for what they might do to you. You should fear them, and that's an interesting point that comes back around to Leroy's own fears.

It's on *Damaged Goods* that Leroy leads off with the song "Bastard Child" to set the tone for the entire CD, much as his titled status has set the tone for his life. "I'm proud of who I am," he sings, "and proud of who I ain't."

Most of the tracks on the album deal with people who are more than down on their luck: they are hurt and hurting bad; they have low self-esteem; often, they are beyond damaged, and when they look in the mirror they can only see the eviscerated remains of what had once been their childhood beauty.

These are songs from the decayed alleyways of American society, where lead paint in derelict buildings peels in grey slabs from the walls of cheap rooms, and where drugs and desperation walk hand-in-hand, and the pitter-patter of tiny feet comes from rats, not little kids.

"Till the Lights Go Out" has Leroy vowing that even though his run-in with a bouncer has left him bleeding, it's happened to him in the past, and he ain't going down so easy. With "Lost Cause," Leroy brings together a captivating melody, reminiscent in parts of an Old West theme song, with lyrics about being a "lost cause" on a "lost highway"—a woman who sticks with him . . . well, forget it, she's bound to get hurt. And, if he has issues centering around his being self-destructive, hell, she has issues, too: she comes from *a good family.*

"Gonna Be a Goner," has Leroy singing about being an alcoholic, and not being able to stand it when his woman tells him that she no longer wants to be an enabler. And when he says that he has no other choice than to make a living in a country band, she says that she can't stay with someone who's always on the road—and presumably often drunk in some honky tonk. "You'll take my life if you walk out the door," he pleads.

It's also on this CD that Leroy covers the Haggard song, "Living with Your Shades Pulled Down." He says: "[The song] reminds me of a time in my life . . . that's how I was living—with the shades pulled down, doing dope with my old lady, watching *Sopranos,* and having nasty sex . . . Yeah, I love that song."

Despite the quality of *Damaged Goods* Hellbound Glory could stand to diversify their topics and their mood. The band's considerable talent seems to call for it, and Leroy's songwriting ability could clearly move the group in that direction. Presumably and hopefully, though, it would not be anything like a Disney theme.

When I went to interview Leroy, I was surprised to see him so far south in Florida (much as I had been when I went to see Outlaw Joey Allcorn in Miami). He, on the other hand, found it quite in keeping with the appeal Hellbound Glory has to a diversity of fans. "Everyone likes us," he says. "If you had a shitload of Hispanic people here we could get up and play, and they would like us. There's not one ethnic group, not one type of person, who doesn't like us, for the most part."

Question: You are playing mainly the honky-tonks; anywhere else?

Leroy: We'll play anywhere they'll pay us. We'll play basements. Punk rock bars. I have no fucking clue what this place is like. . . Our shows are all underground. . . We ain't doing this for fame. I just now started doing this for money. I have a fucking wife and kids to support. Fame and fortune have never been my aspirations in playing music, or in life.

Question: You would like your fan base to get bigger?

Leroy: I suppose, yeah. . . . But being famous does not sound fun.

Question: Do you think that to get a bigger fan base you will have to change your music?

Leroy: No, dude. The more I just be myself, the more people will love me.

Leroy must be a tough person to love. He has a hard outer shell, and what's inside seems to be tightly wound. He's complex, however, and even though he might be proud of being a "bastard son," his feelings remain unsettled. In my discussion with him about musical influences, he mentioned country star Don Williams, who charted 56 records and attracted fans worldwide with his baritone voice—smooth in contrast to Leroy's gruff sound—and his reputation as the "Gentle

Giant"—laidback in contrast to Leroy's aggressive nature. So what was it about Don Williams that attracted Leroy Virgil? "His singing and his words," he told me, "make me want to be a better man. *They make me want to be less of a scumbag.*"

With that comment, the room became silent, and I wondered where to proceed with the questions. I decided to explore how comfortable Leroy is in his own skin. I asked him: "Doing the music that you're doing, how do you feel about yourself?" He responded: "I scare the shit out of myself on a daily basis." There it was again: fear. He scares himself and fears who he is.

Question: Why? What do you mean?

Leroy: I mean . . . I listen to my lyrics with a little bit of hindsight . . . and a little bit of distance, and I think, fuck, this is a pretty sick way to think. "Another Bender Might Break Me" [a song of his] is pretty much about not giving a shit; like fuck it; that fucking feeling, because, you know, I don't care whether I live or die. Party hard. That's pretty fucked up. You know, that's a pretty fucked up thing to make sound funny . . . the lyric of "Are we chasing a rush, will we take too much/ You'll find me face down in the bed." That's about a person taking too many Xanax, too many painkillers, too much whiskey . . . and not waking up. Finding you dead; your wife finding you dead. Your best friend finding you dead.

It's like, fuck, dude, what sort of crass person am I to be writing about death like this? It's scary shit. But the day I stop scaring myself, is maybe the day I stop writing good songs.

Only about 20 people showed up at the Speak Easy. The crowd was middle-aged, middle income—no surfers in sight—but nearly every-one knew the band's music. Leroy smiled, bantered with his fans, and played with as much passion as if he were performing for a crowd of several hundred or thousand. He was with his music . . . where he was meant to be and meant to excel, and his tiredness, his roughness, faded. He connected well with his fans.

But I also thought of the dissonance between them and him. The fans had arrived in the comfort of their plushy cushioned cars after a leisurely drive. Leroy had been on a soldier's march—all guts and determination—an infantryman plodding though miles of dirt and grime to reach this point where his music could ignite his artistry and his feelings and reveal life as he was experiencing and seeing it.

Hellbound Glory may soon attract much larger audiences than the one that had gathered at the Speak Easy. Later in 2012, the band appeared on the pilot episode of a show being hosted by Shooter Jennings for Country Music Television. Also, they were beginning the year 2013 as one of two opening acts for a Kid Rock tour that through its larger venues and extensive publicity promised greater exposure.

But as I left the Speak Easy in the summer of 2012, what kept playing over and over in my mind, as I felt the ocean breeze brush against my face, and bathed in the pleasing sunlight I felt relieved to be in while also realizing how precarious it is, was an exchange I had with Leroy Virgil towards the end of our interview.

Question: Do you feel good about where you're at, personally?

Leroy: I don't know how to feel.

That from a man who says that he often scares himself. It could be that he doesn't want to feel, or at least he doesn't want to feel beyond the scariness and the fear attached to it that has found a home within him, that might well be coming from the feeling there is nowhere he could possibly run—a fear that keeps him from wandering beyond the alleys of derelicts and destitution; that somehow holds him back from walking alongside Don Williams and becoming "less of a scumbag."

In the end, of course, he will never be able to out run himself. But down the road, he need not be the same man that he is today, and if that happens, we will see his change through his music. He's an artist whose demons, *once wrestled to the ground and in the process of being wrestled to the ground*, promise to make him more, not less, creative.

> *So let me build this burning bridge,*
> *Before we get too deep.*
> *And let me dig my ditch,*
> *Along a one-way dead-end street.*
> *It ain't that I don't want ya',*
> *I'm just the last thing that you need.*
> "Lost Cause"
> From *Damaged Goods*

So many names. So many faces. So many songs from so many guitars. So many other Outlaw artists who could have been profiled in this book. But then there's only *so much time and so much space,* and rather than churn out an encyclopedia, I wanted to write a story about the music, the personalities, and the sacrifices of those artists whose work has meant so much to me as I have come to explore their music.

Any work on current Outlaw music, however, must recognize the contribution of **Jamey Johnson** to the genre. While in Nashville years ago, Jamey wrote for mainstream performers and turned out some bad songs and some good ones. His songwriting enabled him to make enough money to begin writing and singing the music *he* wanted to in the way that *he* wanted to. His CD *The Lonesome Song* (2008) was a milestone in showing that a highly gifted and creative artist can still get a wide audience even though he thinks outside the box. The melancholic album, largely centering on Jamey's tribulations following his divorce, includes the captivating track "In Color," a tremendous reach-across-the-generations tune, enriched all the more by Jamey's superb voice.

Hank Williams III, the grandson of Hank Williams, is a puzzlement. As a child he began playing onstage with his father, Hank Williams Jr. Then, in his late teens, he turned to punk rock before coming back around to country. He did much to generate an alternative movement among young fans dissatisfied with Music Row. The three albums he made for Curb Records between 1999 and 2006 include numerous honky-tonk songs. Hank III fits the bill for being experimental too as he continues to record rock music. Lately his performances have smacked of self-indulgence. During the first half of his show he typically plays country; during the second half he plays experimental rock and jumps around the stage wearing a mask or some other strange headgear. The Outlaws I spoke with hardly mentioned Hank III and when they did it was to criticize him for causing rifts within the Outlaw movement. Apparently he has angered fellow musicians with charges that they have copied him or has said they are not as talented as him. That, at least, is the general assessment.

Like Dale Watson—the famed Texas Troubadour—**Wayne Hancock** hails from Austin and has been recording roots country music for many years. He closely identifies with Texas swing but also likes rockabilly and the blues and incorporates those sounds into his music. His 2003 CD *Swing Time* has more honky-tonk on it. Wayne performs without a drummer; he has a three-piece band, with two guitars and a standup bass. A tremendous talent, Wayne has been consistent in presenting high-quality roots music as a contrast to the latest era of Nashville pop.

Rachel Brooke has been called the Queen of Underground Country. In her CD *A Killer's Dream* (2012), she rolls out the blues, jazz, and rockabilly influences. She recorded the album on analog tape without many overdubs, thus staying honest to the core.

Then there's **HalleyAnna**, a young Texas artist who keeps good company by counting as her musical favorites Kasey Chambers, Caitlin Rose and Elizabeth Cook. HalleyAnna combines a lighthearted approach to her songwriting with a heavier introspective one. She owes the lighthearted side to the storytelling influences of Hayes Carll and John Prine. The mix of influences can be found most especially on her CD *The Country* that ranges from the upbeat, jazzy "Tonight!" to the darker "Back in Your Arms." (The album title rightfully proclaims her musical legs as being firmly planted in roots country with instrumentation heavily guitars, fiddles, and pedal steel.)

Her songs are primarily autobiographical, which she sees as important to the honesty of her music. She sees little of worth coming from mainstream Nashville, although the underground or east Nashville scene in that city, she says, has much to offer with the work of Caitlin and Bobby Bare, Jr., for example. "In Nashville," she says, "you'll record whatever is needed to get a record deal." Bet on HallyAnna *not* recording whatever is needed but instead recording what touches her heart in an indie scene she believes offers a vibrant alternative to Music Row.

Blues, folk, country, and punk swirl together in the music of **Scott H. Biram**, propelled by a strong, relentless voice that uses singing, growling, yodeling, and whatever other sound he can muster. "I kind of pride myself on being able to release my emotions freely and not hold back at all," he says. "So many people these days have timid little weak voices, like they're scared to belt it out." Scott employs the one-man-band technique: he plays several instruments simultaneously, such as the harmonica, guitar, and percussion. Of him the *Houston Press* observes: "His raucous blend of physicality, blues, country, metal and rock suggests an inner starvation for true expression and honesty that, frankly, should lead you to question the conviction of everyone you've ever seen set foot on a stage."

Such music icons as John Prine and Kris Kristofferson praise the work of **Todd Snider**. Outlaw artists laud the poetry of his lyrics and the complexity of the influences behind his music. *Rolling Stone* calls him "America's sharpest musical storyteller." In terms of recordings, he has been fulfilling that descriptive ever since his debut album in 1994.

Beginning in 2011, **Pure Grain** began getting the recognition due them. They take Southern rock and country roots and bring it together into an energy-filled jam session. When their "Truckin' Song" video was released on YouTube, it became so popular that the band began touring with, or opening for, bigger national acts, such as the Zac Brown Band. Pure Grain is a joy to hear live. And when Brian DeBruler starts wailing on those congas—yes, cool congas—you know there's going to be some foot stomping and ass wiggling unleashed.

If you want old school take a listen to **WC Edgar**. His CD *Old School Survivor* (2011) reaches deep into roots country as he displays the influences of Hank Williams and such 1970s Outlaws as David Allan Coe. And he backs it all up with a superlative voice reminiscent of George Jones and Johnny Paycheck.

Heather Myles, from California, performs honky-tonk that keeps alive the Bakersfield sound pioneered by country great Buck Owens. She has opened shows for Waylon Jennings, Charlie Daniels, and

Merle Haggard, and on her CD *Sweet Talk & Good Lies* (2002), she holds back nothing in accusing Nashville of having "gone Hollywood."

So many names. So many faces. So many songs from so many guitars. The list could be expanded tenfold, at least. But this book, this venue, is meant only to be an introduction to the current Outlaws, who in those honky-tonks are keeping roots country alive and, in doing *what they want and choose to do,* are making Outlaw, phoenix-like, rise again.

Hellbound Glory opening on the road for Kid Rock (2013)

CHAPTER 24

REMEMBER ME

I remember reading many years ago *Zen and the Art of Motorcycle Maintenance* (William Morrow, 1974) by Robert M. Pirsig. Near the beginning of his book, Pirsig makes several observations about the nature of our modern, technology-driven society and how it affects the feelings we have about ourselves and others. Recently I went back and reread his work and discovered in it a number of observations pertinent to today's Outlaw country scene.

Pirsig's story revolves around a motorcycle trip that he and his young son and two friends took through parts of the West. For the journey they bypassed the main highways and rolled along the back roads. Those roads had been there all along, he says, ready to offer fresh revelations. He then adds: "We were trained not to see it. Conned, perhaps, into thinking that the real action was metropolitan, and all this was just boring hinterland."

What he applies to the landscape can be applied to much else, including country music. The main highway runs through Music Row, and Nashville pop has conditioned us into thinking that *it is the real country* where *the real action is*, and that anything beyond is just a boring hinterland or in some other way unworthy of our attention. According to this view, country music coming out of Nashville must be superior in quality to that coming out of, say, Bright, Indiana, (home of the Sol indie label) or some other place along some back road of musical production.

In some ways Nashville has become our music GPS: it shows us not only our destination but also how we should get there. And how we should get there may well be the quickest route *without any consideration for the majesty of the countryside,* unless we program the device on our own.

If we want to break monotony and bring a little surprise into the music we listen to, we have to venture beyond the interstate and open ourselves up to obscure markers and our own instincts. We must deprogram ourselves. That doesn't mean that what we discover will always be enjoyable, but it does assure a more varied experience. In that way—and here I will again borrow from Pirsig—we can create our own Chautauqua, the name for the early nineteenth-century traveling tent shows, where people would hear speakers whose topics—diverse and imaginative—would bring to a wider audience the edification and entertainment otherwise missed.

Nashville pop has flowed so strongly along the channel of country music that it has drowned out alternative sounds, spilled over the banks, and become a more widely dispersed, blander product. To use Pirsig's observation, we need to "dig deeper" into old channels of consciousness "that have become silted in with the debris of thoughts grown stale." We need to be less concerned with responding to the question "What's best?" with the answer "That which makes money" and more concerned with responding with the answer "That which is of better quality." It's possible the two may correspond, of course, but when making money *sacrifices* creating quality, then artistry suffers and the human mind becomes cheapened.

To find Outlaw country requires breaking with the Nashville instruction manual and proceeding slowly and thoughtfully outside the rush to latch on to whatever is popular. As Pirsig points out, you can approach the Rocky Mountains aboard a plane, and that's not bad. It's not wrong. It has its own worthwhile values. It's quick, it's convenient, it's how most people do it. To approach it from a back road, through the curves and switches and forests and plains and small towns, however, opens an entirely new dimension.

To break with the Nashville prescription might cause withdrawal pains, but the reward in enjoying the fruits of Outlaw artistry, with its originality and attachment to roots country—where the artists say, "Remember me for playing from the heart"—will far exceed any discomfort or dissonance that might occur from taking the less-traveled back road.

SECTION VI

PROMOTING THE OUTLAWS

Chapter 25

A CERTAIN TRUTH

Most people if they want success, they're willing to tuck in their tail
and suck a little dick to get what they want.... That is the defining
moment. Your Outlaw is going to say,
"My way or no way."
—Joe Swank of Bloodshot Records

Money and power. The two go hand in hand in Nashville and keep that country pop machine humming. If you're an Outlaw without power or money, or without the type of music that power and money wants to hear in order to keep power and money growing, you're screwed. The major labels won't open the door, pick up the phone, or even answer the e-mail. Stooping to the use of snail mail won't get you an audience, either.

For many Outlaw artists, getting exposure and putting bread on the table means turning to an indie label for recording, and even for help in touring. There are many indie companies in the hinterlands, and many unstable ones. Two of those that have shown durability and a keen sense of the art Outlaws want to make are Sol Records and Bloodshot Records.

At Sol, Brian DeBruler, the owner and producer (and accomplished musician in his own right with the band Pure Grain), explained to me that he first started toying with the idea of starting an indie label in the mid-1990s, when the technology began changing. By that time it was possible to buy a multi-track recorder for about $4,000 that could produce the same quality as one that formerly cost $125,000. Then in 1997, at age twenty-two, he recorded a CD for Outlaw artist Dallas Moore, *My Heroes Have Always Been Cowboys,* and began talking to friends and other bands about pooling their resources to put together a recording company. Dallas Moore and the group Pure Grain were the first to be produced by Sol, as Brian located the firm in the teeming metropolis of Bright, Indiana, population five thousand.

"We're meaner, leaner, and greener," he says in comparing Sol to the major studios in Nashville. With those qualities he believes that Sol has an edge over the record giants in an age when downloads via computer have largely destroyed CD sales. "We know how to utilize the social media and the Internet through nonconventional means of marketing," he says. He takes pride in marketing Sol releases based on what he calls the "lifestyle" of fans, rather than their age or gender. For example, given the type of music Dallas Moore makes, Brian puts on his business hat and thinks about the type of activities a person who likes Dallas would engage in, and that happens to be partying at honky-tonks and riding motorcycles. (My own penchant for cross-stitching is ignored, but, hey, everything has a glitch.)

Brian says: "People aren't looking toward artists for somebody that they want to be when they grow up. Where people really get vested in artists they like is where they feel they can relate to them."

Sol artists interact more with their fans than artists have in the past. They go beyond signing autographs and shaking hands at a show. They participate in contests for CDs, downloads, and T-shirts. They also frequent Facebook and blog and tweet.

Brian says that YouTube has "helped dramatically" in marketing the Outlaws because "it has the capacity to generate tremendous awareness at no expense." It certainly helped Dallas Moore's videos "Crazy Again" and "Blessed are the Bad Ones" recently go straight to the top of the alternative country charts, with "Crazy Again" staying in the number one slot for more than fifty weeks.

Brian believes it's important for the artist to control what goes on in the studio. He says that as a producer and engineer he seeks to capture the essence of "what makes Dallas Moore, Dallas Moore," for example. He says: "I really try to have them embrace what they do depending on where they're at. Some artists are further along musically, while others are just trying to find themselves." Whatever might be the case, Sol takes seriously its commitment to what defines Outlaw: being honest and real. The music might have a niche appeal, but it's a niche appeal that gravitates toward the artist, *his* talent, and *his* desires.

Sol functions much like a community, where each of the artists helps out fellow artists. An artist might appear on a colleague's CD or onstage at the other artist's show. That way everyone benefits from "the hype." Brian says that this "keeps a constant state of action and of fresh content [going], and I think it's key to keep people interested, given the attention-deficit-challenged world we live in."

Brian would love Sol to get together with other regional labels as a way to fight some of the splintered nature of the Outlaw movement. And he expresses confidence that if country pop fans were exposed to more alternative music, they would like it. "I really think that the people who are into Jason Aldean records or that sort of stuff, I definitely think they would identify with Sol artists if they somehow got more aware of our artists." Moreover, the coming to Sol would not undermine his label. "Sol artists would remain true to themselves. *We are ourselves.* So I really don't see that being something that could be influenced or changed by any outside force."

As with Sol and its approach, Bloodshot Records emphasizes the importance of respecting the artist in the studio. "What we do is put out records that are created by the artists," says Joe Swank, the person in charge of radio promotions and tour press. (As a musician he has, at various times, been the leader of several cowpunk bands.) He adds: "Whereas Nashville is more of several people getting together and deciding what a record needs to sound like, at Bloodshot we have a lot more leeway, and I think that's going to be the case at almost all indie labels."

Most any deal with a major label comes at the price of freedom. "They're going to have ways that they want you to sound, and they're going to want to put you into a round hole," Joe says. "If your music isn't quite round, they'll keep chopping the corners until they've got the round peg they need. Whereas on the indie, it's 'We've got a bunch of square pegs here, let's treat them like a bunch of square pegs.'"

Joe doesn't think it possible that an artist at Bloodshot would ever catch on with a major Nashville studio. "We're not set up to deal with that crowd," he says about the Music Row head honchos. "There's still a lot of red tape you have to go through to even deal with those people. On this end it's not bad until you start getting someone whose popular, and then you start running into people who still have their payola in place. For the most part, we are dealing with [radio] stations who like to play the music because they like to play the music. And that helps a lot."

Technology has been a blessing and a curse. On the one hand, recent developments have allowed Bloodshot and other indies to be able to record at a level close to those studios along Music Row. On the other hand, he says, "There are fifty thousand voices where there used to be a thousand. I talked to a guy at a radio station who said that in 2005 he used to get an average of a CD or two a day [to review]. Now he gets ten a day."

One Nashville artist can still sell hundreds of thousands of records, maybe millions, because the major studios have so much influence over the radio stations. Joe explains that the studios will tell a consultant what they want to have played, and that it will get played by everybody the person consults for, which could be all of the Clear Channel stations or all of the stations under some other conglomerate. "What they play," he says, "has nothing to do with what they like or what the people call in to request."

Because of that, and because the big studios have the money needed to position CDs in the store and online, an indie label "can only take somebody so far until the next step is spending hundreds of thousands of dollars to promote them." Joe adds: "The catch to that is only the top echelon get paid in scenarios [where big studios have to spend large sums of money], because there's always posters to write off and radio mailings to write off. It's the way the whole business does it, but when you're at a label like Warner Brothers or Capitol, you don't think anything about sending out a box of thirty CDs to a station. So they put a lot of money behind the artists, and they have a lot of power in places that aren't seen by folks like you and me."

He adds: "They have the journalists in their pocket when they tell them: 'Hey, we'll give you a ticket to the CMA Awards this year if you give this guy a good review.' Or 'Pump up this new kind of trash by Rascal Flatts, and we'll make all kinds of nice things happen for you.'" Joe says that all Bloodshot can afford to do is say to a writer: "Come to town and we'll buy you a beer."

But much as Brian sees a future for Sol, Joe sees one for Bloodshot. While a number of the Outlaws have taken to avoiding labels altogether, Joe cautions that producing and marketing your own work can be an extremely tiring and labor-intensive chore. "It's a full-time job," he says. "So if you're not already successful enough to have an income coming in where you can afford *not* to have a job, if you really want to make a push, you have to get distribution, you have to hire a radio person, a press person, [and even] a digital person who deals not only with iTunes but also makes sure that the MySpace and Facebook pages are kept up to date. Also e-mail lists are important, so you can let people know that you are coming back into town. You have to do a Facebook-marketed target ad. That's all stuff that we spend all day in the office trying to do for our handful of active artists."

In addition to the indie labels, there are agents and publicists who represent Outlaws and other country artists outside the mainstream. One of these groups is Thirty Tigers, located in Nashville. The owner, David Macias, who founded the company some twelve years ago, says that he represents those artists who typically sell 10,000–15,000 units. His goal is to enable them to earn a living without having to compromise their work.

Thirty Tigers casts a wide net and has signed everyone from bluegrass musicians to Aaron Watson, who is in the George Strait mold of country, to Elizabeth Cook, profiled in this book as part of the Outlaw movement. David says that Thirty Tigers got to represent Elizabeth and help her career when the record label she had been with, Warner Brothers, was unable to find the right fit for her. She's attractive and personable and talented and *looks like* she should fit into the mainstream, but she doesn't. Apparently, Warner Brothers just couldn't find a way to shave enough of the square peg to make it as round as the company executives wanted.

As with the indies, David sees technology as a mixed bag. There's so much noise out there—so many artists, so many promoters, so many advertisers—that it's hard to get "enough ears" to focus on any one artist. But the technology also provides more outlets for the non-mainstream musicians, represented by firms such as Thirty Tigers and recording for companies such as Sol and Bloodshot.

But what about honky-tonk radio? Most prominently there's SiriusXM. In 2004 SiriusXM inaugurated its Outlaw Country channel (channel 60) after Little Steven Van Zandt (of Bruce Springsteen E Street Band fame) advanced the idea. Consequently the channel morphed from an existing one, titled the Border, into what it is today.

Van Zandt was working as a programmer for SiriusXM and was concerned about all the country that mainstream radio was ignoring. "There were too many cool things falling between the cracks," he says. "All the things that got squeezed out happened to be all the best stuff. I thought: 'How can you have a country format and not include Johnny Cash, Waylon Jennings, and George Jones?'"

And of course there are the contemporary Outlaw bands. The Outlaw Channel plays Texas swing, rockabilly, country rock, alternative country, Americana, and straight-out shit-kicking honky-tonk Outlaw.

SiriusXM likens the Outlaw channel to a massive jukebox found in a honky-tonk. Much of what goes on the air fits what would be chosen by a patron in one of those bars. SiriusXM sees the unifying feature to the channel as the artists, all of whom have a deep love for country music and a desire to make it *their* way, without having to do anything more than please the honky-tonk crowd.

The Outlaw channel has played such an essential role in creating bigger audiences for Bert David Newton, Jackson Taylor, Dallas

Moore, Whitey Morgan, and the other artists profiled in this book that they all communicated to me their thanks to SiriusXM for providing them a prominent outlet at a time when commercial radio has chosen to ignore them.

Shortly after the Outlaw channel began, SiriusXM hired Shooter Jennings and Elizabeth Cook to host their own shows. I asked the station programmer, Jeremy Tepper, about this, and he told me that he was the one who brought the two artists aboard. Shooter was showcasing at CBGB in New York about eight years ago when Jeremy asked him to host a weekly show. Jeremy met Elizabeth through her husband, Tim Carroll, who had played in the Blue Chieftains, a band that recorded for Tepper's Diesel Only label. Elizabeth made such an impression with her downhome charm and professionalism that she was a natural fit for the channel

Jeremy also hired Mojo Nixon to host a show. At the time Mojo was a deejay for a classic rock radio station and was burned out on his job. For Mojo coming to SiriusXM was like being issued a deejay's emancipation proclamation.

I asked Jeremy what qualifies an artist to be on the Outlaw channel, and he said that he has to get out his "bullshit protector" to make sure that the station stays away from performers who try to position themselves as Outlaw through crafty promotion but who wind up making hokey overproduced records.

He also pointed out that although his title is "program director," the deejays enjoy considerable freedom in choosing what songs they will air. The suffocating playlists found at most radio stations don't exist at SiriusXM, and that allows a deejay such as Hillbilly Jim or Cowboy Jack Clement to display his considerable musical acumen without having his choices handcuffed.

This atmosphere of freedom gets even more oxygen from the Outlaw channel having little concern with ratings. Jeremy insists that SiriusXM has never tried to tell the Outlaw channel what to program based on audience numbers—in fact, the parent company has never collected such numbers and has never talked to him in such terms. He says that for the folks at channel 60, Outlaw really means Outlaw—no fences and no borders; no badges and no orders.

To have the Outlaw channel run in this way clearly complements what the artists are doing. "There's a spirit and honesty to this music," Little Steven says about Outlaw. "It communicates a certain truth."

SECTION VII

GRAND FINALE:

A Red-Blooded Outlaw and the Poetic Truth

ELEMENTS

By the time I got to see Jason Boland, the last Outlaw on my interview list, I had earned quite a few stripes in the honky-tonks. Consequently, I could more clearly identify the similarities and the differences among the various artists.

That in turn gave me the desire to bookend this work with Jackson Taylor, the more punkish Outlaw, and Jason, the more mellow one. Even though they come at their art from different directions and use different elements, they both convey the ultimate nature of Outlaw music: its heart-felt honesty.

Jason Boland, Gladewater, TX (2012)

JASON BOLAND

Every Moment I'm Gone

The waters are sailed,
The feast shall be made.
There's always a tailwind
Once the pirates are paid.
We'll cling to the old ways
That we finally have learned,
Find a place next to Nero,
And then we'll watch it all burn.
"EVERY MOMENT I'M GONE"
FROM RANCHO ALTO

Gladewater, Texas—population 6,078—straddles US Highway 80 in the far northeastern reaches of the state, not far from the Louisiana border. The town grew fast in the 1930s, when iron rocking horses appeared and started extracting oil from beneath the ground.

But the boom ended just a decade later, and as Gladewater shrank in size, it's residents receded into the pursuits of making furniture and paper products, and of raising crops and cattle.

The Gladewater Round-Up Rodeo each spring includes a trail ride, a cook-off, and a Party in the Dirt. It was in the dirt that I met Outlaw artist Jason Boland as he and his band were pulling up in their tour bus behind the rodeo grounds. A stage had been set up inside the arena for the party, which featured Charlie Robison, David Allan Coe, and Jason. No attempt had been made to temper the potent cow shit that dotted the terrain on which the crowd stood, and on which some of them had placed their folding chairs. The sun and the heat combined to ensure that a barnyard smell penetrated everyone's nostrils and left an odiferous imprint to be carried home with the physical one.

Jason ain't a Texas boy, but he spends much time there and on occasion has lived there (as he does now) so that the state has become a second home for him. He's from Oklahoma and was born in Harrah, located about twenty-five miles east of Oklahoma City. He looks so boyish that when I first saw him, I was unsure of who he was. I thought maybe he was one of the many young men milling around the tour bus, waiting to help unload the equipment. Moreover, he appears not so much as to walk onto a scene as to glide onto it, so it takes some time to discern his presence. He would make a good spirit, if one were needed.

Jason, who is in his thirties, and is thin, tall, handsome, and articulate, was dressed in jeans, plaid shirt, cowboy hat, and boots. As we shook hands and walked over to his bus, we made small talk, and I asked him what he thought about Gladewater. He smiled the type of smile that must have melted, and probably still melts, many a woman. "This is a rodeo in the middle of America with David Allan Coe playing," he said. "This is as real as it gets." And there they were: the Stars and Stripes flying from a nearby flagpole and the oversized Ford and Chevy pickup trucks jammed onto the grass parking lot.

What first attracted me to Jason's music was his CD *Bourbon Legend*, released in 2006. On it a track titled "Last Country Song" refers to more than the tune itself; it also refers to social conditions. The song becomes Woody Guthrie-like when it creates common ground with those Americans restricted by the fences and signs that say not "This is your land, and this is my land" but rather "This is my land, and it's not your land." And it speaks to the Gladewaters that in the flood of conformist modernism struggle to maintain a unique identity, or even to survive. (He sings: "Another burned out summer/ Into a fruitless fall/I hope everyone is having fun/When the world's a shopping mall.")

As Jason and I stepped inside his tour bus, the air conditioning cooled us down. So did the bottled water we started to gulp, which removed some of the bite from the Texas dust and the acidity from the cow dung.

A number of observers have labeled Jason a Red Dirt musician. After all, his birth state of Oklahoma claims to be the home of the Red Dirt movement. The difficulty in determining Jason's genre stems from Red Dirt having as nebulous a definition as Outlaw. Elements of folk, rock, country, bluegrass, the blues, Western swing, and honky-tonk (the lifeblood of Outlaw) can be found in Red Dirt. Cody Canada, of the group Cross Canadian Ragweed, calls Red Dirt "country, folksy, bluesy, and rock" and says: "It's just blue-collar music. It's a lot about the lyrics. It's a lot about the feeling of it.... It's everything from a Merle Haggard influence to full-blown Rolling Stones."

Marc Ringwood, who has analyzed the Texas and Oklahoma country music scene for a number of years, says, "I don't think there is a true way to define it.... A lot of artists carry the same influences going back to the days of Bob Wills (the king of Western swing) and Woody Guthrie. And then you have new guys who have followed in stride with their peers by feeding off their influences. Red Dirt also has more of a spiritual quality.... It's honest and true." With those elements, and because it disdains clichés, it has more in common with Outlaw than with Nashville pop.

Jason owes much to Red Dirt, and even typically covers songs by Bob Childers—including "Outlaw Band." Childers was the singer/ songwriter who defined Oklahoma Red Dirt and who, five years before his death in 2008, was inducted into the Oklahoma Music Awards Red Dirt Hall of Fame. Moreover, Jason once played in the bars of Stillwater, the geographic center for Red Dirt. (He also went to college for three years at Oklahoma State University, located in that town.) But Jason also has those honky-tonk lights burning in his soul, and they burn brightly through much of what he sings about.

I asked Jason if he considered his band, the Stragglers, to be Outlaw. He said yes, in the sense of being attached to Outlaw individuality, meaning "do what you want to, and do the best you can."

Question: You're on the bill tonight with David Allan Coe, and if you go back to Coe's early years the image he projected was this hard-driving, Outlaw motorcycle guy, basically, fuck you, fuck everybody, I'm David Allan Coe. And I think some people interpreted that as saying that type of behavior is what it means to be Outlaw. How do you feel about it?

Jason: I guess whenever you deviate from whatever social norm at any given moment...it's gonna place you as Outlaw. Yeah, that's weird to think that it really just comes down to which one of those taboos you're breaking, whether it be swearing onstage or whether it be *not* signing with a label. And it's weird that we call [music]

Outlaw, because it's not really [about breaking the law]; it's anti-pop-machine, really.

༼ ༽

With regionalism a big part of the Outlaw movement, I asked Jason what was distinctive about the Oklahoma and Texas music scene. "It's the enthusiasm of the fans. They might just be more hooked up into local music," he told me as we sat in the back of his tour bus. "If there is a strength behind it, it's the opportunity people have to see the artists they like" because there are so many bands. He says that Stillwater was a great place for the alternative music scene. Many bar owners "would pay you to come in and sit down with an acoustic guitar and just entertain their folks."

Jason says about his upbringing in Harrah that it was "straight as middle class, middle of the road as you can be from a pretty small town, but not too small. I grew up where I-35 and I-40 meet. Both parents worked. I played a little music, I played some sports. Got in some trouble, stayed out of some. Just as average a middle-class small-town raising as you can try to find." Then he comes to the sheltered part of his youth: "[We grew] up knowing all was right with who we were and where we were from."

"A lot of my extremes in life," he says, "have been going to touch a stove I knew was hot. Going from a place that had no stoves to having to go touch a couple of them."

Jason's dad had a stack of vinyl that he listened to: Johnny Cash, Charlie Rich, Hoyt Axton, and some Limeliters. Although Jason's parents were not inclined to play musical instruments, they always supported Jason with his interests and willingly agreed to pay for any music lessons he wanted.

The guitar fascinated Jason, and the 1986 movie *Crossroads* sealed the deal for him in wanting to become a musician. The movie takes a familiar theme of good versus evil and presents it in the form of a kid guitarist, Eugene Martone—performed by Ralph Macchio—engaged in a challenge with the devil's guitar player, Jack Butler—performed by Steve Vai—to save another man's soul. At the end a tremendous guitar duel erupts in which Eugene vanquishes Jack, in effect using the power of music as a moral weapon to expose the devil's evil ways.

Vai's pulverizing and intricate guitar work shows the reason why Vai has won three Grammy Awards. When the movie ended, Jason left the theater with his ears ringing, his spirit surging, and his voice saying to his dad that he wanted to learn the guitar. His dad responded that he had an old one in the attic that Jason could use, sans the devil.

Question: Were you playing with a band in high school or not until later?

Jason: Just some buddy garage stuff. Nothing serious.

Question: And in college or was it after?

Jason: It was the transition out of, and then I already quit college by the time I got together with these guys.

By "these guys" he means the Stragglers. Jason says he left college with doubts as to whether he was making the right move but that he felt he was being trained in school rather than encouraged to think for himself anyway, and so with that, and with his love for music, it ultimately made sense to do what he did. He met his band mates among the "hippies" and other dropouts in Stillwater, a number of whom hung out at the Farm, an old two-story, five-bedroom house from which much Red Dirt music emerged. The house was truly communal: all of the musicians who lived there contributed to its upkeep. They took the money they made playing gigs and threw it into a community jar. (The Farm burned down several years ago.)

Jason already knew Brad Rice (drummer). He then met Roger Ray (lead and steel guitar player), who knew Grant Tracy (bass player). Together they decided to play the local clubs and parties. Jason says: "Then it was organic from there out." Organic to the point that, joined by Nick Worley on the fiddle and mandolin, they have become a beautifully symmetrical band.

Jason got a boost in confidence when, as a neophyte, he met Bob Childers. Jason was looking at an "unattainable mountain of how to play music" when Childers gave him the advice he needed: Don't try to be anything. Instead, he said, "Be who you are and write your songs."

Other artists he met soon gave him similar advice. "They all pointed to the spirit of Woody Guthrie," Jason says. "In Oklahoma you heard Woody's songs all the time." It was as if Woody was embedded in the soil on which Oklahomans walked. Jason has since recorded a Childrers song, "Woody's Road," which includes the lyrics: "He was a ramblin' friend of man/Just reaching out his hand," and so that's why he went down Woody's road.

Jason has always wanted his music to be transformative, even if the transformation was only "a really, really good feeling." He says: "I don't want the music to be about me but about us,... about this existence together."

As with any Outlaw artist, for Jason "being true to yourself" doesn't mean that he writes and sings without using and channeling the music he has heard and absorbed over the years. Quite the contrary; those musical influences reside deep within him and burn intensely, much like oil feeding an eternal light.

From the country genre, Bob Childers would certainly be one musician whose work Jason counts as a profound influence. Add to Childers the music of Waylon Jennings, Willie Nelson, Johnny Cash, and Hank Williams Sr. and Hank Williams Jr. Jason says that he doesn't imitate anyone else's style nor does he seek to "take this from here or that from here." Rather, he says, "It's in my background, and it's the sounds and chord progressions that still ring and resonate in my ears."

Jason credits Steve Earle for showing him that "country could rock and not be hokey about it." He adds: "And that's a weird line to walk, between rock 'n' roll and country. It can get hokey really quick." An artist, he says, must be careful to make sure his music stays true to itself. He must avoid being tempted by the demons in the commercial wilderness for the sake of making money or, from the other side, he must avoid becoming too experimental, either one of which can result in that hokeyness.

"Country fans don't realize," Jason says, "that they were taken over by show tunes a long time ago. Even some of the stuff that I listened to when I was a kid: Ronnie Milsap and Alabama. I love Alabama too, but when you listen to Merle Haggard, Buck Owens, you say, 'That's country music.' When you listen to Alabama, you find more of a pop and rock style, influential in its own way, but different."

Question: So why does a teenager from Stillwater gravitate toward country and performing country?

Jason: I guess the easiest answer is that it just came naturally. Maybe I couldn't sing high enough to be in a rock band. [*Laughter.*]

❧❧

Jason comes closest to playing rock in the song "Ball and Chain," which he recorded with fellow Outlaw artist and friend Jackson

Taylor. The song was written by punk rocker Mike Ness, who has been a big influence on Jackson. It was Jackson's idea to record "Ball and Chain" as a cross between punk and country and to ask Jason to be on the record. Along with the punk element, Jason sees a lot of rockabilly in the song—indeed, Jackson loves early Elvis Presley—and this, combined with the country roots, keeps it from that hokey level in an experimental sense. "I thought I fit in with that track," he says, "the way he was going for it."

Question: What do you think about using punk in country?

Jason: I love it, I love it. I think it is part of what will save [country] as a valid musical form. You're always going to have traditional music with its barriers, that this is bluegrass and this is not bluegrass, for example. That's great [in order to keep alive that] snapshot of Americana. But as far as saving country, I think the Outlaw movement, or the honky-tonk movement, should have a good relationship with punk music.

Question: If your music, and the music of Jackson Taylor and Dallas Moore and a number of other Outlaw musicians, is heartfelt and sincere, why are we so inundated by Nashville pop? Why are millions of records being sold out of that?

Jason: It's about money. That's the oldest answer in the book, and it's still true; it's just about money. People with the most decide to make even more of it. Therefore they take control, from the barriers of entry to the production end to the distribution. And in this world, people go buy what they know, if it's visible to them, accessible.

They'll say, "Well, I don't want to go spend my $15.99 on this album I've never even heard of, and it looks like somebody put their art and their life into it…. I'm going to go ahead and buy the one that I heard jamming at every car at Sonic, because I'm going to be with everybody else. It's not worth it to me to spend my $15.99 to try something new, to try it out and take a shot." So that's what you're dealing with, and the businesspeople with the most money will make sure that their records are out there being marketed the most.

Nevertheless, Jason believes that sometimes people do start buying CDs when they know little about a band because "it might be somebody's honest take on the world or honest take at stringing three chords together and playing it with their friends." If that trend gets big enough, he says, "Then the people with all the money say, 'Wait we're losing them, we need to shoot somewhere in the middle and get back some of those that country music got too bubblegum for.'" Clearly, should Outlaw country take hold with a larger number of people, Music Row will then embrace some of it—much as it did in the 1970s—and compromise other parts of it.

Question: Do you want to change, or would you be willing to change, your music so that you could attract a bigger audience?

Jason: No, I really don't. I really want to play it the way we see it, stick to what we do. I think we are successful. There'll be different levels of success, I'm sure: higher, lower. Who cares, though? That's not the reason we're out here.

Question: Did you ever go to Nashville and try to write music for any of the labels?

Jason: We've worked with publicists from there, and our booking agent still lives there. A lot of the infrastructure for the business we are in is based there. But I've never gone [to Nashville] and hunted a deal down. I have gone and met with a couple of publishers there, but we still do our own thing.

Because Jason does few covers, he relies heavily on the music he writes. His songs come to him in different ways—sometimes by playing with chord progressions, sometimes by coming up with a word hook, and sometimes by just getting an idea or even a feeling. He says that he never knows how a song will materialize. "Every once in a while I think I can get out an emotion," he says. "A lot of times I can get a chord and a melody and a lyric to cross right with an emotion." At that point he knows that he has struck the creative mother lode.

He calls songwriting "a strange process" that involves going through dry spells. Five songs in a month "would be a bunch for me," and even the ones he writes in just five minutes take a long time to iron out. "I have to get the nuances and vocal lick [perfected] and make the melody a little bit more interesting and not so much a shave and a haircut." Jason believes that most songwriters have to search for "the sweet spot" that makes a tune "take off." When it happens for him, he thinks, *Did I do that?* It's as if he were given five artistic talents and made them into ten, or given two and made them into four.

Jason says it makes him feel good whenever somebody requests that something he wrote be played. "[My band and I] were talking about how weird it is that you can take many things for granted out here [on the road].And one of them is just the fact that somebody wants to hear a piece of music that you and your buddies made up."

The process resembles scattering seeds on the ground and then having them sprout and grow without knowing how it happens. "It's proof that the folk-networking still works," Jason says. "Just the fact that that piece of Americana is still alive, that regional songs go around and people say, 'Ah, I know this one, do you know this one?'"

Jason told me that he wants to record a CD where the engineers and producers don't get hold of it and make it into something other than what he was expecting. To him the best CD will be close to being a live one, with little if any overdubbing or layering of sounds. Studios have become so technologically advanced, he says, that most anything can be altered. That works well when the musician uses the technology in an artistic way, but not when it's used to "slick something up."

As for how he and the Stragglers work in the studio, he says: "We get in there and capture something pretty live and try to keep it as analog as possible. I wouldn't say we'd scrap a song just 'cause one little thing [turns out wrong]. So maybe we'd drop a note in or something. But we've been working back to front, really, because the CD *Pearl Snaps* was cut live [in the studio], and then we overdubbed vocals and lead instruments. Pretty standard, but it was recorded to tape. Everything's gotten really compartmentalized as a studio process, but I also see a lot of people fighting back to get into capturing a live sound and recording multiple people playing together. It sounds crazy that it's gotten away from that."

Pearl Snaps contains songs that rank among the most requested from Jason's catalog. When Jason goes on tour, many in the audience sing along to the lyrics from the CD's tracks. For Jason and his fans, the record has indeed turned out to be the proverbial pearl of great reward.

Question: When you do a live album outside of the studio—and I'm thinking of your *Billy Bob's Live,* for example—do you do much overdubbing then?

Jason: *Billy Bob's* had some. We all,... everybody went out to Nashville, and you go and you fix problems. For *High in the Rockies,* we recorded four shows, and we gave it to the engineers and said pick the version you think is best, and they were ninety percent what we would have picked. We kept that one very live. There's not one over-dub on that record.

Much of Jason's music reflects a spiritual presence (and a certain amount of peacefulness or at least harmony with that spirituality), and in doing that *it goes to the heart of Jason Boland.* Some of that comes from his attachment to the people in those small towns whose own spirituality derives from their community and who seem askew when-ever they digress from that attachment, or whenever a barrier to that attachment appears, or perhaps whenever modern America becomes too overwhelming for them. But much of it comes from a sense of God at work in the world in the ways that make him a mystery to all of us.

Question: I could point to several of your songs where there seems to be almost a religious or spiritual element to them. Where does that come from?

Jason: That comes from growing up thirty miles east of Oklahoma City, you know? Really, it's so ubiquitous to people from all over this area, growing up under the evangelical message, and— for better, for worse—it has its positives, and it definitely has its things that I've had to liberate my mind from. I have had to define who I am on a spiritual path rather than [simply adhere to] some of the dogma I grew up with.

> *And I have been baptized in water,*
> *I have been baptized in fire.*
> *Oh, I've knelt with both hands on the altar,*
> *I've even sang in the choir.*

There've been forks in the road when I've had to choose,
I pray he'll forgive me for singin' the backslider blues.
"Backslider Blues"
From *Pearl Snaps*

Question: But you do feel that your spiritual quest is an important part of you as a person?

Jason: Yeah, I feel at least that the search for meaning should be a point of everybody's life. Really, if there is no meaning, there's nothing to have faith in.

The instrumentation in "Backslider Blues," a song from *Pearl Snaps*, comes across as simple and direct, with nothing standing between Jason and the listener, or between Jason and God. It mixes temptation with redemption, and as much as Jason might criticize evangelical excess, the religious imprint from his youth remains and works to generate some guilt, and also to help shape his moral compass.

From the stained glass light of the chapel
To the neon haze of the bars,
From the wine of the Holy Communion
To the liquor that left me the scars,
From the Bible that sits on my dresser
To her clothes strung all across the floor,
From the prayers from my friends when they need me
To the times that I've ran out the door,
I've been taken by surprise by some women in rouge,
I pray He'll forgive me for singing the backslider blues.
"Backslider Blues"
From *Pearl Snaps*

Jason confides that his parents weren't particularly religious. He attended church with them, but they went irregularly. What really shook him up spiritually was while he was in high school, when the first Gulf War broke out in 1991. "I remember thinking," he says, "that it sounds biblical." So he went to church and started searching for answers to who he was, to what life meant, to how he fit into the grander scheme of the world. He rejects a religion where somebody says, "Here's the rules." He observes: "Well, if those are the rules, there's a lot of people out there who are screwed. I had to make peace with that, that maybe everything I knew about God isn't the only thing there is to know about God."

Still, Jason felt lost for a long time, and when he formed the Stragglers, he felt as if he had nothing figured out. "I don't know what started to wake me up," he says, "but it might have been the music."

He battled mightily with demons that were summoned by the traveling, the parties, and the honky-tonks. His dance with the devil was done with booze, and in 2005 he spent nearly a month in the Sierra rehabilitation center in Tucson, Arizona.

Three years later he released his CD, *Comal County Blue*, which includes "Bottle by My Bed." He begins the song with: "My life was as empty/As the bottle by my bed."

I think the lyrics are intense, and I said so to Jason. He said they had to be, that he had to write them that way because of all that had happened to him. He called it a "rebirth" song to reflect his having come to terms with his alcoholism and his having moved further along with his spiritual quest.

I couldn't imagine him playing the song in a honky-tonk. But he said he does get requests for it. "People are honest with themselves," he said. "They don't ever get to hear anybody talk to them that way. I'll take the risk on turning somebody off. I think that goes back to the Outlaw movement of just putting out the message."

The conversation about "Bottle by My Bed" led to Jason talking some more about his own experience with alcohol. He said: "For some reason I didn't know when to shut it off, or couldn't. I just kept on and on and on, and then it got to be where I was just physically addicted to it, and I would get sick every time I'd try to quit. Then it was time to get back out on the road, and it was just a constant race. I never knew you could have a seizure just by quitting drinking. I did not know that if you become addicted to alcohol and just quit, you could seize up and die. And I got a little shaky one night, trying to white-knuckle it and not drink. I made it about day two or three and I had to pull over, and then I woke up and the ambulance was there." Shortly after that, he wound up at the rehab center.

He adds: "I'm fine as long as I don't flip the switch on. That's not to say that people that don't have a problem with [alcohol] shouldn't be allowed to drink and cut loose and have fun. I still cut loose and have fun myself—I just can't do it at the bar."

Jason's insightful lyrics are among the most erudite yet readily accessible lyrics that can be found among any of the Outlaws. Indeed they are sheer poetry: so beautiful and so captivating they can place you in a musical trance. Sometimes they are confessional, as in "Bottle by My Bed."

> *Jesus came and found me there*
> *That day those demons bled.*
> *When my life was as empty*
> *As the bottle by my bed.*
>
> *My first taste of the spirit,*
> *It brought me to my knees.*
> *I knew that I was helpless,*
> *I prayed, Lord, help me please....*

Oh, I found it hard
To practice what I preached.
Now I'm going back home,
It's down this path I'm led.
And I'm no longer empty
Like the bottle by my bed.
"Bottle by My Bed"
From *Comal County Blue*

If those lyrics don't convey emptiness, desperation, rebirth, and the revelation of the true Spirit in a song filled with simple yet strong, powerful, and determined instrumentation, I don't know what does. "And now I'm going back home/It's down this path I'm led." How can it be doubted as to whose yoke he has taken? How can it be doubted as to whom he has turned in order to find rest for his soul?

Jason's *Comal County Blue* takes its title from the county that sits on the Edwards Plateau in south central Texas, near San Antonio. The county's hills sport vegetation that ranges from scrub brush to mesquite to live oak trees, and the Guadalupe River cuts through the land to wear away at rock strata and form a pebbly beach by the sparkling water whose color at sunset often turns to red. Tourism has become a big part of the county's economy, and the region has attracted many Anglo retirees. About a quarter of the residents claim Hispanic heritage, so a cultural mix has been created.

With the title song on the CD, Jason presents the county as a place to get away from. His brother has moved to Houston, most of his friends are gone, and although "I have a harmless habit/Of being fine wherever I am," the discontent, the depression, has been rising, and he needs "to get above the dam." So Jason undertakes an exodus down the flooded double-striped highway that appears on the CD cover and forges ahead, moving beyond his problems.

Jason's spiritual quest comes through in several of the CD's tracks, not the least of which is "Bottle by My Bed," but also "God Is Mad at Me." As church-like organ sounds emerge in the background, he sings: "I feel like God is mad at me/Because he thinks I worship you." But he leaves the "you" ambiguous (a woman? mammon? pride?) and reinforces its universal application with reference to Exodus 20:3: "You shall have no other gods before me."

> *I'm here waiting for all the stars to fall,*
> *Lord, I'm hating what I've become.*
> *Now I can't breathe,*
> *There's no one I can call.*
> *So if you'd kindly let me up,*
> *I believe I'm done.*
>
> "God Is Mad at Me"
> From *Comal County Blue*

Back in Gladewater, as late afternoon was blending into night, I met up with my wife, Lesli, and her sister, Lorie, both of whom had come with me on this trip, and we descended on a long table of food that had been placed behind the rodeo grounds for the artists and their guests. As we peeled the foil back from the inviting trays, however, we found that most of the victuals had been eaten by ravenous musicians who seemed to have no respect for freeloaders. So we decided to head into town for a bite. We figured there was likely to be at least one restaurant open.

And there was—exactly one. As we approached its front door, several locals were milling around. We greeted them and they smiled back. Once inside, however, the atmosphere became less friendly. The faces got pinched and the eyes turned steely as the diners looked at us with suspicion, as outsiders who had to be measured by their standards, and we obviously weren't measuring up to them. The scene reminded me a bit of the movie *Easy Rider*, when Jack Nicholson, Peter Fonda, and Dennis Hopper walk into a diner located somewhere in rural Louisiana and are greeted with stares, a few sneers, and some wise remarks. Unlike them we weren't "Yankee queers," but we had been tagged for some harsh assessment.

Among the regional options we encountered was the K2 Burger. Because it was listed on the menu without any description, we puzzled over what it might be. At first, we thought that the name referred to some computer problem, like the one that was supposed to imperil the nation's financial system as the twentieth century morphed into the twenty-first.

Before long we put our speculation aside and asked the waitress to describe the item. The K2 turned out to be a fried hamburger placed between two Krispy Kreme donuts. It seemed to be the perfect example of backcountry gastrointestinal excess and yet another contribution to America's obesity problem.

I was going to order the K2 just to see what it looked like and to take a picture of it. But the sisters agreed that would be a bad idea because the locals were still looking at us suspiciously. So we ditched the K2 order and opted for something more familiar. As we were getting ready to leave, however, Lorie couldn't resist the desire to experience Americana at its best and thus ordered a slice of key lime pie. She asked the waitress if the pie was homemade. "Of course," the waitress replied, "and it's the best pie that you'll find anywhere around here."

It nearly superseded the nutritional content of the K2 burger. The pie was a glob of lime filling from a Jell-O box topped by pseudo-cream from a tub of hydrogenated oils. It appeared ready to slide from its plate, crawl along the restaurant floor, and devour the nearby townspeople, and us, in an orgy of overkill that would make the Blob, from the movie of the same name, seem like a friendly creature. As creative as she was, it took Lori nearly ten minutes to grapple with the slice of pie and hide it away. I was afraid that she might let it slither into her purse, and leave a suspicious trail of dripping fluorescent green along the floor, but instead she hid it among the dirty plates on our table, and we were able to escape the restaurant without further looks from the locals.

From there, we drove back to the rodeo grounds. We were ready for Jason Boland to take us back to *his* America.

Jason's 2011 CD *Rancho Alto* weaves together the experiences of the people who live in the fictional town of that name. One reviewer describes it as telling about their "struggles" and how they "react to their travails." That's true, but it really goes beyond that, for Jason's continuing spiritual quest makes another pronounced appearance. And that quest opens him up to the struggles faced by those who live and work in America's Gladewaters and whose tribulations often parallel those of people elsewhere.

The first track makes that clear. On one level "Down Here in the Hole" can be read as being about a miner in Rancho Alto trapped beneath the ground. But on another level, it stands as a metaphor for anyone trapped at any time—maybe Jason himself—in the gloom of life that can envelop us.

> *I'm finding out a thing or two about being below,*
> *The sun never shines down here in the hole.*
> *When I'm free from this place,*
> *I'm gonna find myself a different set of wheels,*
> *Move out past the end of the road, meditate what's real....*
> *But I'm praying now for daylight,*
> *The bright shining into this one eternal night.*

I'm finding out a thing or two about being below,
The sun never shines down here in the hole.
"Down Here in the Hole"
From *Rancho Alto*

The song has a distinct gospel rhythm, most pronounced during the chorus when Jason moves into the refrain: "But I'm praying now for daylight/Bright shining into this one eternal night." At that point his voice also takes on a decided gospel melody and chant; it feels as if a white-robed choir could step onto the scene behind him and fit right in.

"It would make sense," Jason said to me when I told him of my observation. "Of course, it raises the question of who are you trying to affect... And in some ways, it speaks to what you hear in the music too. But I definitely have spiritual tones in my music. I grew up knowing everything, just like the people who taught me about religion. I was completely sure of all of it, and then I got older and found out they were full of it.... It's too complex. But I definitely see music's kinship with spirituality because it moves people."

Question: The first two lines, you are doing a G chord, G7, C, G, C, D, and G. Then you go to the third line and use an E minor. Then I'm dropping down to your verse two, which begins with the word "darkness." And you are at an E minor again.

Jason: I don't think those are intentional.... Why do they play a minor chord when the bad guy walks in? There are vibrations that don't jive or have different harmonics. For [human beings] it's the way we interpret things with our ears, that separation, that uncomfortable vibration from minor chords; it's something deep [within us].

Question: The song has an upbeat feel, and then you go to the minor chord on the word "darkness." That's what I'm getting at.

Jason: It does ruffle feathers because it creates irony with the subject matter. Those qualities create a rough surface area, an abrasiveness or whatever, at least in a good deal of my tunes.

"I'm fascinated by the Bible," Jason says. "Compared to people [hundreds of] years ago, we're scientifically savvy. We have a few more changes in our perspective than those people had. Some people today still insist on 'Two animals, two of every animal in a big 'ol boat.' People put that on their kids, so the first thing they see as a child is this giant lie. It goes to controlling people."

For Jason the beauty of the Bible can be found not in any literal structure but in its contradictions and puzzling allusions. Revelation comes through investigation, not through indoctrination; through contemplation, not proselytization. He said to me: "When you mix music with spirituality, it can be a powerful tool."

The song "Between 11 and 2" moves back and forth between a lonely man and a lonely woman at a dance hall, each looking for a companion—someone to help them through the night, or maybe through a lifetime. The dance between the lyrics complements the dance among the individuals and sways smoothly, like a Bob Wills tune with a steel guitar and fiddle rustling the imagination and stirring the leaves of thought. These lyrics go well beyond clever: the creativity behind them displays genius. The song ends with: "Twin souls tripping through space and time/The exclamation when they finally find/God, it's you, here between eleven and..../They'll take whatever road they find/And ride it somewhere outside the lines for a few/Out there between eleven and two."

In "Mary Ellen's Greenhouse," Jason sings about a band working to get its muse behind them at a place in Rancho Alto where they gather to rehearse. The band was actually Jason and his friends back when Jason was a teenager in Oklahoma. (The mother of one of the boys let them use her greenhouse.) The lyrics come across filled with double meaning about human existence at an age when everything was bathed in wonder. The band goes "chasing ghosts down the road and across the yard" and finds that "sometimes it's hard to find your song." And Jason calls our attention to something nearly everyone realizes in this life of fleeting experiences: "Feelings for the moment/ And we only hope they stay, along with old friends/I've been blessed beyond belief with folks I know."

> *Something's growing in the greenhouse,*
> *Lighter than a church bell,*
> *Higher than you'd care to sing along,*
> *There's a lot of love in Mary Ellen's greenhouse,*
> *Won't you look at all we've grown.*

The love comes from the camaraderie and the music and it all merges together in one sensate surge: on the one hand, melancholy for the past, and on the other, gratitude for what has resulted, along with hope for the future.

> *Looking back from time to time, mostly forward now,*
> *The present day is a gift and if we lift it up somehow,*
> *I know we are healed.*
> *Let the music take your prayers towards the sky.*
> *Let 'em fly*
> *Toward something real.*

"Chasing ghosts," "healed," "prayers"—again Jason reaches into the spiritual. Indeed, whenever he lowers his bucket into the river of life, he invariably comes up brimming with the ethereal presence that flows through our world and shapes our earthly moments.

Question: What do you think has changed the most in your music from when you first started out to today?

Jason: If you ask somebody, I'll give you what I think [they] would say: that it's not about drinking anymore. The early stuff, if you go back and listen to it, it was never, "Hey, this is a lot of fun, and it's going really well for me, join in." There wasn't a bunch of that. If you listen even to a song with a title like "Drinking Song," it's actually a pretty negative look at it. But the writers I was around—and this is as you're starting to write, you're starting to write about your life and what you see—they said, "Be honest and write about what you know." Well, as the party escalated, that's what we did.

Moving away from that era, developing different music, has become a challenge. Any artist can become trapped in the past, either because he fails to grow and his creativity dries up or because his fans expect him to stay the same.

"I guess sometimes we get a little, not confused with it,... it's just they end up [among] the most popular songs," Jason says in reference to his earlier alcohol-referenced works. "They end up hitting home the most with everybody. They end up being so popular that you have to do them forever, and then you look up one day and you've got a set list of songs that you don't think really reflects who you see yourself as, either as a writer or as an entertainer."

Yet Jason realizes that he has a "musical contract" with his fans. "Everybody walks the line of what they'll do to sell tickets," he says. "That's a big deal, you know, what you can do to sell more tickets. What if we were gonna go out there and the only thing we played was off the new album—the new stuff that nobody has even heard? Some of our fans would think we broke the contract with them, and maybe we did. They expect to hear some of the old, some of the new."

He adds: "We try to stay true to ourselves and do the best we can in every moment. But I guarantee you, six months later we'll think, 'Oh, fuck it,' and we start over again. It means that we're growing and that we're moving forward." It is, Jason admitted, one of the painful experiences of being an artist.

Jason's fans have become enamored with his doing "the best we can in every moment," because the "best" means a musical structure that few artists can equal, let alone surpass. But the hijacking of country by pop, which has confined Jason's fan base as it has those of the other Outlaw artists, means that millions of people are missing out on music that's creative and fun, original and bold, sincere and heartfelt.

As I was leaving Gladewater and smiling at the adventure—the interview with Jason, the party in the dirt, the K2 burger—I popped his *Rancho Alto* CD into my car's system and began playing it through.

It was then that I realized how much the CD was in the tradition of Woody Guthrie. Much like Guthrie, Jason connects to the common people, and he does so with empathy. It was as if the Oklahoma dirt had collected on the soles of Jason's boots; it was as if Guthrie's land was also Jason's land—from California to the New York island. His inclusion of "Woody's Road" only reinforces the picture. On the CD Jason follows Woody's path and his inspiration.

When I got to the track "Fences" on *Rancho Alto,* I saw in Jason's lyrics a parallel between what was happening in America's Gladewaters and what was happening in Nashville— actually, what was happening to America as a whole. I decided to toy with the words, not because I thought I could write them any better but because I wanted to shape them to what I was feeling at the moment. I wanted to take his Guthrie-like sense and sentiments and apply them to the obstacles and hardships faced by the Outlaw artists. (I think this is exactly what Jason would want, to see his music have this kind of an impact.)

All I see now are fences.
The cards turn a profit,
But the people are gone.
These old holes in the highway
Are so brutal on bones.
If you don't dance with who
  brought you,
It's a lonesome walk home.
Can I catch a ride, sir,
If you're going this way?
I forgot, what would all
  the Protestants say?
She was there for the takin',
There were promises made,
The smallpox and whiskey
Were a mighty bad trade.

All I see now are fences.
Nashville turns a profit,
But the real country's gone.
These posers and controllers
Are so brutal on souls.
You can dance with the devil if he
  brought you,
It's a lonesome walk home.
Can I catch a ride, sir,
If you're going my way,
Before I forget Hank had some-
  thing to say?
It's there if we seek it,
Lots of work and little pay.
The fame and that glitter
Were a mighty bad trade.

—Jason Boland

Both at Gladewater and at the Bourbon Street Bar in Auburn, Alabama, where I interviewed Jason a second time, I was impressed by the several times that emotions surged as Jason established a holy musical communion with his followers. If he was, in fact, taking five artistic talents and converting them to ten, or taking two and converting them to four, he was as he did so connecting with a heavenly dynamo that brings together the artist with his followers to create an intuitive common ground. The music was Jason's mustard seed, growing stronger from its roots and shooting out large branches under whose shade weary souls might rest.

Jason was my last interview for the profiles I planned to write for this book. Intended to be a saga of roots country music from the 1970s to the present, it has become more than that. With all due modesty, I can say it stands as one big saga of the heart—the musicians and me linked together, looking out on some vast sea, sometimes of despair and sometimes of hope.

In Auburn, Jason revealed to me that when I interviewed him the first time in Gladewater, he was keeping tight-lipped about his plan to get married the following week. The marriage, he told me, has made him a better person, and he greatly appreciates that his wife, Mandy, understands the grueling demands of recording and touring. Several of the lyrics I quote in this profile, he says, refer to his love for her, although in doing so he's also reaching out to others.

Jason has such a gifted ability to connect that when I heard him play "Every Moment I'm Gone" in Auburn, I too found my place under the shade from his mustard-seed tree and felt transformed as I touched the rhythm of the world.

> *So keep your eyes on the horizon*
> *And your hand on your heart,*
> *A prayer on your precious lips*
> *For those wandering in the dark.*
> *And now when I am lonely,*
> *I'm never alone,*
> *'Cause I carry you with me now*
> *Every moment I'm gone.*
>
> "Every Moment I'm Gone"
> From *Rancho Alto*

CODA

When I stood back and looked at Jason's work as a whole, its romantic qualities became even more evident, to the point that they nearly overwhelmed me. I don't mean romantic in the sense of some schlocky Nashville pop ambiance. I mean romantic in the sense of intuitive, inspirational, and beautiful.

I have said in this book several times that these artists are much like each of us in having to make choices every day (within a context of sometimes imponderable external forces). As we make those choices, we do so amid chatter and clatter—an assault on our senses from what we see, smell, and hear—and our minds become cluttered. To make sense of what we have been exposed to requires us to take selected portions of our experience and make them into a whole.

Yet to inquire about the whole—to analyze, for example, *why* something happened (and better understand it)—means we must cut up the whole, a procedure that of course destroys it. To break the whole into its component parts, if you will, and then analyze one of those parts to death, if you wish, is like using a knife to cut through a canvas. No matter how fine the lines of the incision, the parts can never again make up the whole. If the whole were not a work of art, this might not carry as much weight. But to cut through an Albert Bierstadt, a Thomas Cole, or a Thomas Moran—all great painters of the American wilderness—would threaten a terrible loss.

And for us Jason has painted some Morans. They come out of the landscape of American culture, and fortunately therein lies the answer to being able to appreciate his work, even if we must cut it up to analyze it. The whole remains because for Jason the whole is tied to the romantic view of what is real in our society. Amazingly, *and this is true because of the nature of Jason's music,* the intuitive, the inspirational, and the beautiful as reflected in what Americans do pulsates, thrives, and lives on whether analyzed in parts or as one. It's the quality of his work that allows this to happen. Such cannot be said for what comes from Music Row.

Jason Boland, Gladewater, TX (2012)

CLOSURE

Several decades ago the Lone Ranger and his sidekick, Tonto, were the mythical heroes of the Old West. Their adventures, broadcast first on radio and then television, were fraught with peril as they struggled to save someone at the last minute from an evil that could cost them their lives. In one episode a giant landslide begun by bandits fills a canyon trail with debris and causes a stagecoach to overturn. The driver scrambles from the wreckage and then finds himself in a fight for survival as the bad guys descend on him.

When I began this book, I was stuck in my own rock-strewn canyon—an emotional one. As I searched desperately for a way out, a way to fend off the malevolent forces, a way to right my stagecoach and move on, I realized that my terrain had changed forever and that to survive I needed to reinvent myself. While I did so I found solace in Outlaw music, past and present.

In the artist profiles contained herein, I often mention the *choices* made by each of the Outlaws and how, much like you and me, the Outlaw makes a conscious decision every day about his or her professional and personal life. Jackson Taylor *chooses* to live on the road, away from two of his sons. Elizabeth Cook *chooses* to create music that will express what is in her heart rather than what will sell on Music Row. Jason Boland *chooses* to write his own poetic songs, even though he could work inside a music factory. And, importantly, every Outlaw, whether of today or the 1970s, has *chosen* to resist the pressures exerted by the Nashville pop machine.

But in the artist profiles, I also refer to the complex, sometimes indecipherable forces that swirl around the Outlaws, as they do around all of us. Shooter Jennings can hardly escape the influences of his father and mother, whose talents have been passed on to him. Charlie Starr of Blackberry Smoke recognizes in one of his songs how important it was to him that his grandmother sent him along the Jericho Road. Whitey Morgan feels so strongly the pull from his late granddad that he lives with his ancestor's spirit onstage for every performance. And most tellingly, every Outlaw, whether of today or the 1970s, has realized how greatly his or her music has been shaped by the roots country artists who have preceded them.

The debate between free will and determinism I will leave to the philosophers. Most assuredly we choose and we don't choose; we are forced and we are not forced. The degree to which each becomes the case varies so much that it makes up one of the great complexities of life.

I liked Outlaw music even before I began this book. I like it even more now (of course, not all of it equally as well), and my journey has given me a much greater appreciation and respect for the Outlaw artists, those I have interviewed and those I have yet to meet.

A relative of mine who used to work in the Nashville industry said to me during my work on this project, "Give Nashville a break. They are only providing what sells and what the audience wants." I agree, and I disagree. They certainly are providing what sells—no doubt about that. And they are providing what the audience wants. But what the audience wants has been conditioned by the makers of the product, by Music Row itself. Good salesmanship involves creating the "want." The Nashville labels certainly have been good at selling—very good at it.

It is, in fact, hard to find a true work of anything in a world that has been so pulverized by commercialism. When the mind has been so conditioned to accept the money changers in the temple, the temple itself becomes a place of shallow worship where materialism etches the art, and the artist is left behind in the sinner's wake.

Much as I will let the philosophers debate free will versus determinism, I will let the marketing companies and consultants debate creating demand versus meeting it. I will point out, however, that it's difficult for an audience to want that which it never knows. It's kind of like people living in a dictatorship because they never know about democracy. In some way the people have to desire a change because of the oppression they feel, but democracy has also to be made known and promoted by those who want it or they will never realize what form the desired change could take.

Outlaw music will advance as people feel more discontent under the reign of Nashville pop. But the Outlaws also have to continue to push, to make their art known. They have to continue to promote themselves, either on their own or, preferably, in league with others, such as the indie labels—Sol, Bloodshot, and so on—the hip promoters—Thirty Tigers comes to mind—and the flexible broadcasters—SiriusXM Radio, for example.

In short, the blame for the sad state of Nashville country today—its overproduced, overhyped phoniness—can be levied on more than Nashville. After all, it takes more than one person to line dance. The audience must want a change, and the Outlaws must push yet harder. But, yeah, Nashville, given its money, its influence, its insistence that *it* is country, the *real* country—yeah, Nashville should shoulder most of the blame.

Maybe someone can find in the commercialized Nashville pap—eh, I mean, pop—some music that will help save them or transform them. That would be all to the good. For me, I found it where creativity and honesty lurks, on the Outlaw side.

But I must place the emphasis on the word "help." There will be no Lone Ranger to sweep away problems in some magical way, and, in fact, in the episode with the overturned stagecoach, the driver survived by fending off those bandits by himself. The help of the Lone Ranger came only later to fight other banditry, and he would never have been able to save the day at any time if others had failed to take the initiative to save the day with him.

My own rock-strewn canyon, my emotional landslide, came from my mom's death, and part of reinventing myself was the realization that I would have to be the one to bite the bullet and move on. The early twentieth-century American novelist Thomas Wolfe was right when he said that you can't go home again: "You can't go back home to your family, back home to your childhood,... back home to a young man's dreams of glory and of fame,... back home to the old forms and systems of things which once seemed everlasting but which are changing all the time—back home to the escapes of Time and Memory."

I can't go home again. Not to the home and hearth that existed in the past. The realization hurts, and it hurts bad. It's a difficult one to live and struggle with. Every day remains a challenge, every *day* a fight to give my life some purpose for *today*.

But this book, the Outlaw music, and the Outlaw spirit have *helped.* So too has something extraordinarily special in my life. To reveal this I must again turn to the Outlaws and, in particular, to Elizabeth Cook.

As I discuss in my profile of her, when I interviewed Elizabeth she told me about how her mom, who passed away a few years ago, speaks to her. Elizabeth has spoken to her mom. Elizabeth has heard her even in the middle of a show.

I have never heard my mom's voice like that, but *I have felt her presence*. My continued contact with my mom, however, has come about as a result of my conscious decision to open myself to her and to God by engaging in prayer and reflection, which has turned out to be a challenge given my rational and material makeup.

At one point I was confused about whether I was really feeling the presence of my mom or of God or of Jesus. But an Episcopal priest friend of mine, Don Smith, said don't worry about it. Ultimately, he told me, there's no difference among the three since the Lord might come to me through my mom, and in time the contact might shift from one to the other anyway.

Every step in the journey behind this book has been along a path walked with God and my mom. At the Jason Boland concert in Gladewater, Texas, the one I went to with my wife, Lesli, and her sister, Lorie, I had the opportunity to interview David Allan Coe.

I was standing behind the stage, speaking with Coe's son, Tyler, when the Outlaw legend from the 1970s pulled up in his limousine. I asked Tyler if he thought I could speak with his dad. Tyler said he was sure that I could. As I stared at the limo, I saw Coe begin to exit from the rear door. I didn't see his face, only his left leg as he stretched it out the door and planted his booted foot on the dusty ground. I had done so much with Coe over the years.

I had rolled a smoke with him.

I had done coke with him.

I had stolen a car with him.

I had been in reform school with him.

I had dropped acid with him.

I had spent my nighttime in mourning with him.

I had been under a woman's wings with him.

I had painted a picture full of girls with him.

I had been on the highway with him.

I had been driven to drinking with him.

I had spent a lifetime looking for the answers with him.

And I had burned bridges with him.

It was in Gladewater, as that foot came out of the limo, that I made yet another choice, one which came as much from feeling as from any rational calculation: I turned away from Coe and walked over to the front of the stage. There would be no interview. Too much had changed. I had experienced enough of the past, and something was telling me to look forward, to cherish what had been, for sure, but to embrace more closely what awaited.

So now I can say from where the ultimate motivation, guidance, and direction for this book was derived: it came from my mom. Her spirit lives within it, *as it still lives within me*. I have no doubt about it, and I thank God for it. I have made many choices, no doubt, but I find it amazing how a spiritual presence helped bring me together with the Outlaws, many of whom, if my mom were still alive, she would disapprove of for their drinking or swearing or whatever. In the end, though, the earthly pales in significance to the heavenly, and I believe that will always be so.

I have looked into my mother's eyes. I have looked into the eyes of the Outlaws. To both I can say that I found myself in you. Let me repeat: *I found myself in you*. And I love and cherish that I did.

My hunt for Outlaws now comes to an end. For those who stayed with me through all or nearly all of this book—and God bless you—it should be apparent that my search for roots country was also a search for meaning. That's an eternal search for everyone. Right now, I feel that I need a song to help me move on, one that will modify what Thomas Wolfe said (as I quoted above).

While it's true that you can't go home again, you can find new homes of comfort and of meaning and of love. So it's an old Willie Nelson song I turn to, "Hands on the Wheel." At a time when so much seems to be spinning within and around me, sometimes out of control, Willie strums his guitar, and his sweet, gentle voice enters my soul and helps me to realize what I have become—what has become real to me—to realize *that which has made me a home.*

I have no doubt the prayers of my mother
Take me a ways down the line.
Jason Boland
"Backslider Blues"
From *High in the Rockies*

Wayne Mills, the Snoball Queen, and "Big Steve" McKinley, Pensacola, FL (2011)

Fans at the Gladewater Rodeo Grounds, Gladewater, TX (2012)

The names on Bert David Newton's guitar

Dale Watson signing autographs, Blanco's, Houston, TX (2012)

Rebel Roots Studio near Fayetteville, NC (2013)

Shooter Jennings, Buck Thrailkill (on banjo), Robert Norman (on fiddle), and Adam Jones (on standup bass) at Rebel Roots Studio (2013)

The Outlaw Backline. All of the current artists profiled in this book connect to the entire backline. This sketch, however, is meant to highlight the most important influences on each.
(Sketch by Efren Flores)

BE SURE TO BUY

OUTLAWS STILL AT LARGE!
THE MUSIC

AND ENJOY MANY OF THE SONGS DISCUSSED IN THIS BOOK

AVAILABLE AS A DOWNLOAD AT AMAZON.COM

Also at Itunes and other sites, and as a CD at Outlaw venues

23246890R00323

Printed in Great Britain
by Amazon